Viet-Nam Crisis

A DOCUMENTARY HISTORY

VOLUME I:

1940-1956

Viet-Nam Crisis

A DOCUMENTARY HISTORY
VOLUME I: 1940-1956

Edited, with commentary and annotation, by

ALLAN W. CAMERON

Cornell University Press / ITHACA AND LONDON

International Standard Book Number 0-8014-0582-3
Library of Congress Catalog Card Number 72-127600

PRINTED IN THE UNITED STATES OF AMERICA
BY VAIL-BALLOU PRESS, INC.

Contents

PART TWO

FRANCO-VIETNAMESE WAR AND FORMATION OF A RIVAL VIET-NAM
JANUARY 1946–DECEMBER 1949

III. *Franco-Vietnamese Negotiations and the Outbreak of
     Hostilities: January 1946–January 1947*   71

IV. *The Formation of a Rival Viet-Nam: February 1947–
     December 1949*   100

PART THREE

THE INTERNATIONALIZATION OF THE WAR IN VIET-NAM
JANUARY 1950–OCTOBER 1953

PART FOUR

INTERNATIONAL CRISIS AND THE GENEVA CONFERENCE

NOVEMBER 1953–JULY 1954

PART FIVE

EMERGENCE OF THE TWO VIET-NAMS

JULY 1954–NOVEMBER 1955

Preface

After 1961 the United States became involved in what was to be the longest, second-largest, and most unpopular foreign war in American history—the conflict in Viet-Nam. The new American role was only the latest stage of a crisis that had continued since the end of World War II. Throughout this period the level of military activity at any given time largely determined the amount of public attention Viet-Nam received. But the forces that constantly threatened not only the peoples of Indo-china but also world peace were found in the diplomatic activities of the many nations involved in Viet-Nam. It is with the international diplomacy of the Viet-Nam crisis since World War II, and especially the development of American policy, that this collection of documents is primarily concerned.

The collection is intended to help both the serious scholar and the concerned citizen to analyze and understand the complex Vietnamese situation. It will serve, hopefully, to bring order and meaning to the mass of material on the conflict by clarifying the sequence and nature of the events that marked the crisis. It also attempts to give the reader a historical tool for evaluating the many differing arguments and conclusions about Viet-Nam.

The documents have not been selected in support of, or in opposition to, any particular point of view. Since some basic principles are needed for selecting from the thousands of available documents, for editing those too long to include in full, and for presenting the background necessary to make them meaningful, it is only fair to describe the considerations that shaped the editor's choice of documents and influenced his commentary.

The primary focus of the collection is on the development of the

Viet-Nam crisis as an international issue. As such, the crisis is unique, for not only has it endured at a high level of intensity but also it has involved all the world's great powers almost continually. The editor sees two issues as important causes of the crisis. The first is the conflict between Communism and anti-Communism, both among the Vietnamese themselves and among the foreign states that became involved in Vietnamese affairs. The second is the unification of the country, which involves the questions of nationalism and anticolonialism. In the editor's view the second issue is the crucial one, for the crisis endures because Viet-Nam is not unified, not because of "Communist expansionism." So long as there are two Vietnamese governments, in explicit or implicit conflict with one another, the crisis will continue. The issue of unification was crucial in the Paris negotiations begun in 1968, at the Geneva Conference in 1954, in the implementation of the Geneva Agreements, and in the outbreak of the initial conflict between France and the Democratic Republic of Viet-Nam in 1945 and 1946. The issue of Communism versus anti-Communism which has divided the Vietnamese people as well as their various foreign supporters has been reflected in the continued political division of Viet-Nam, so that these two issues have reinforced and exacerbated each other.

This volume covers the period from the beginning of World War II to the summer of 1956, when the elections called for in the Final Declaration of the 1954 Geneva Conference were to have been held. This period corresponds to the phase of French involvement as the primary Western power concerned with Viet-Nam, beginning with the reassertion of French authority after World War II and ending with the replacement of France by the United States during the two years after the Geneva Conference. The summer of 1956 was therefore marked not only by the failure of the 1954 Geneva Agreements to end the Vietnamese crisis but also by the nearly complete elimination of France as a primary actor in it. A second volume, covering the period from the summer of 1956 through the beginning of major American military involvement in 1965, will be concerned with the dominant role of the United States and the continuing partition of Viet-Nam confirmed by the failure of the Geneva Agreements.

In the years covered by the first volume, the development of five questions is emphasized. The first is the policy of the Western allies, and particularly the United States, during World War II and the months immediately following the Japanese surrender. The second is the independence of Viet-Nam, whether Communist or non-Communist, from

France. The third is the growth of the (Communist) Democratic Republic of Viet-Nam and its relations with the Communist powers. The fourth is the Geneva Conference of 1954, the agreements it produced, and the failure of those agreements to resolve the crisis. The last is the emergence of the Republic of Viet-Nam under the leadership of Ngo Dinh Diem with the strong support of the United States.

Because all these questions, and their ramifications and interrelationships, could not be treated in equal depth without expanding the collection to an unacceptable length, the editor has chosen to emphasize the development of United States policy and to include the complete texts of a number of documents which mark the development of the Vietnamese Communist movement. Documents in the latter category frequently dwell at length upon domestic matters, but form an essential basis for understanding the development of later events, particularly policies endorsed by the National Liberation Front of South Viet-Nam after 1960.

The 190 selections included in this volume were chosen from more than three thousand documents available to the editor. Obviously all the important and interesting documents could not be included. Many crucial items remain classified by the governments concerned, and for many others no complete and reliable text could be found. Particular difficulties were encountered in locating documents which adequately illustrate Chinese and Soviet policy before the Geneva Conference in 1954. Many United States documents, notably for the period after 1945 but in some instances before that time, remain classified. Of the thousands available the editor has chosen those that mark essential events or that show succinctly the development of contending positions. Commentary has been kept to the minimum necessary to place the documents in a meaningful context. The selections are not analyzed in depth, nor is there detailed examination of the development and interaction of the various forces of which the documents are a product and reflection. In many cases the documents themselves provide information of this type. More complete interpretative treatments are to be found in the analytical works listed in the Selected Bibliography.

Whenever possible, reference has been made, in the introductions and annotation to the documents, to other pertinent items. The reader may find it useful to consult Ho Chi Minh's *Selected Works* (4 vols., Hanoi: Foreign Languages Publishing House, 1961–1962), since only a few of Ho's statements and writings are included. Many of the more important items from the *Selected Works* are available in *Ho Chi Minh on Revolu-*

tion: Selected Writings, 1920–1966, edited by Bernard B. Fall (New York: Frederick A. Praeger, 1967). Neither collection, however, is complete, and in some instances the *Selected Works* texts have been altered from their original form by the North Vietnamese.

The documents in this collection are presented in chronological order and are included in the form and wording of the source indicated, with only glaring typographical and grammatical errors in the original corrected where necessary for clarity. All documents for which a foreign-language source is cited were translated anew, although they may have appeared in English elsewhere. Where alternative texts were available, the editor has tried to select the most accurate and readable one; in many cases the alternative sources are indicated. The reader may have confidence in the authenticity of all the documents included, with due regard to questions of source, wording, or legitimacy indicated by the editor.

The extended research project of more than three years that has culminated in the publication of this work had its origin in an attempt to revise and update the valuable collection *Conflict in Indo-China and International Repercussions: A Documentary History, 1945–1955.* This work was assembled by Professor Allan B. Cole of the Fletcher School of Law and Diplomacy, Tufts University, and was published in 1956 by Cornell University Press under the auspices of the Fletcher School and Cornell's Southeast Asia Program.

It rapidly became apparent, however, that the revised collection would have to be so much larger than the original that it would constitute less a revision than an entirely fresh effort. In the first place, the period of time since the original collection appeared had produced many important events and much attendant documentation. Second, developments since 1955 have given the observer a new perspective on earlier events. As a result many documents omitted from the first collection have been added and others, less vital, have been dropped. Finally, a great amount of new material on events prior to 1955, particularly on American policy during 1944 and 1945, has become available.

The Cole collection presented documents covering events in all the countries of Indochina (Viet-Nam, Laos, and Cambodia). The present collection concentrates on Viet-Nam and includes documents pertaining to Laos and Cambodia only when they are directly relevant to Viet-Nam. Likewise, documents dealing with purely internal matters in Viet-Nam, such as land reform laws, have been omitted except when they are directly relevant to the international aspects of the crisis.

It was necessary to make a judgment on the usage of certain proper names. Vietnam, Viet Nam, and Viet-nam are variant spellings in current use, but Viet-Nam is the form most in accord with the Vietnamese language, so the editor has adopted it. Vietnamese names are presented according to common English usage, without hyphenation or diacritical marks and with all syllables capitalized ("Ho Chi Minh"), except in cases, mostly place names, where usage has made a variant form so common that to change would be confusing ("Danang" instead of "Da Nang," "Saigon" instead of "Sai Gon"). In all cases the spelling in the documents has been left as in the original, so the reader may expect to encounter substantial variation.

The editor is grateful to the staffs of the libraries where a number of the documents in this collection were located: the Edward Ginn Library of the Fletcher School of Law and Diplomacy, Tufts University; the Widener Library, the Library of the Harvard Law School, and the Library of the Russian Research Center, Harvard University; the Library of Congress (and particularly Mr. Cecil Hobbs and Mr. Abdul Rony of the South Asia Section, Orientalia Division); the Wason Collection of the Cornell University Library; the Library of the Hoover Institution on War, Revolution and Peace at Stanford University; the Western History Collections of the University of Oklahoma Library; and the New York Public Library. Dr. William M. Franklin and Dr. Arthur G. Kogan of the Historical Office of the Department of State helped locate a number of United States documents and provided much useful advice. The French Press and Information Service in New York helped to find several scarce French documents. Professor Allan B. Cole of the Fletcher School generously made available materials from his personal collection. Sincere thanks are also extended to Dr. Herbert L. Sawyer for the translation from the Russian of Document 77 and to Mr. Alexander A. L. G. Zampieron for translation from the Italian of Document 39. Dr. Truong Buu Lam of the State University of New York at Stony Brook graciously made numerous valuable suggestions about the historical content of the introductions as well as about the translations from the French. Dr. Phan Thien Chau of Rider College was most generous in making available the results of his own research along parallel lines.

A special word of thanks is due Professor Allan B. Cole, whose constant advice and cooperation have been invaluable and without whose stimulation and initial efforts this project would not have been undertaken. Cornell University Press has been unfailingly cooperative and patient. Much of the research on which this collection is based was made possible by a Kent Fellowship from the Danforth Foundation. Finally, a personal tribute is due the late Dr. Bernard B. Fall, who on several occasions took the time to talk and correspond with a young scholar interested in Viet-Nam.

A. W. C.

The Fletcher School of Law and Diplomacy, Tufts University

PART ONE

Developments from 1940 to December 1945

The War Years

January 1940-March 1945

Introduction

The first part of the collection deals with the development of Allied policy toward Indochina during World War II and the events of 1945. This period saw the successful Vietnamese "August Revolution," spearheaded by the Communist-led Viet Minh movement, and the beginnings of reimposition of French colonial control. At the end of the period, with both France and the new Democratic Republic of Viet-Nam (DRV) claiming authority in Viet-Nam, the stage was set for the pivotal negotiations of 1946 and the outbreak of war between France and the Viet Minh.

French dominion over Viet-Nam was established during the second half of the nineteenth century and had been in effect nearly 80 years by the outbreak of World War II. French rule extended to Cambodia and Laos as well, and the three nations were known collectively by the artificial term "Indochina" or "French Indochina." Indochina was ruled in five administrative divisions. Cambodia and Laos were protectorates, and there France ruled through the traditional monarchs. Viet-Nam had been divided into three parts. Cochin China in the south was a direct colony, while Annam, in the center, and Tonkin, in the north, were nominally protectorates ruled by the Vietnamese Emperor, Bao Dai, from his capital at Hué. In fact, however, French rule in Tonkin was nearly as direct as that in Cochin China, and even in Annam the Emperor was virtually powerless.

World War II, particularly Japanese expansion into Southeast Asia, undermined the hold of France on her most prized Asian colonies and made possible the eventual overthrow of French rule. After the fall of France in 1940, Japan put irresistible pressure on the Vichy government and the colonial administration in Hanoi for concessions in Indochina, with particular emphasis on intervention in Tonkin to seal off that Allied route of access to China. Japanese success was facilitated by a tacit agreement of British and American policy that the war should, if possible, be confined to Europe.

In the opening months of 1941 France found herself involved in a short war with Thailand (Siam), then allied with Japan. Before the conflict could be carried to a decisive conclusion, the Japanese intervened and imposed a settlement favorable to Thailand as well as a series of Franco-Japanese agreements giving Tokyo a privileged position in Indochina.[1] On July 28, 1941, Japanese troops landed in force in Cochin China, where the airfields and ports provided support for further expansion into Southeast Asia. Japan chose to leave nominal sovereignty in Indochina to the French in order to ensure stable administration and to relieve the strain on Japanese administrative personnel; the French colonial administration in turn had little choice but to collaborate with the Japanese.

The failure of the United States and Great Britain to pose active resistance to Japanese expansion in Indochina was an encouragement to Japanese designs elsewhere, but it was the seizure of Cochin China which touched off the chain of moves and countermoves which led shortly thereafter to general war in the Pacific.[2] Nonetheless, during the war the problem of Indochina occupied a subordinate position in the policy considerations of the Allies.

American policy toward Indochina was shaped by three contending forces: the ongoing planning for the postwar period carried on by the State, War, and Navy Departments; the requirement for cooperation with the Allies in order to ensure the defeat of the Axis powers; and President Roosevelt's anti-French attitude, which strongly influenced his feelings toward the French colonies and the Free French movement of

[1] Texts of the various agreements of 1940 and 1941 are in France, Direction des Informations, *Notes Documentaires et Etudes,* No. 78 (June 15, 1945).

[2] For the American position on Indochina at this time, and some indication of its importance to American policy, see United States, Congress, House of Representatives, *Message from the President of the United States Transmitting a Summary of the Past Policy of This Country in Relation to the Pacific Area and of the More Immediate Events Leading up to This Japanese Onslaught upon Our Forces and Territory,* 77th Congress, 1st Session, House Document No. 458 (Washington: Government Printing Office, 1941). See also United States, Department of State, *Foreign Relations of the United States, Japan, 1931–1941* (2 vols., Washington: Government Printing Office, 1943), *passim; Foreign Relations of the United States, 1940* (6 vols., Washington: Government Printing Office, 1959–1961), Vol. IV, pp. 1–250; and *Foreign Relations of the United States, 1941* (7 vols., Washington: Government Printing Office, 1958–1962), Vol. IV, pp. 1–729.

General Charles de Gaulle. During 1942 and 1943 the major issue was whether Chinese forces should be allowed to conduct military operations against the Japanese in Indochina, a course which was opposed by both Vichy and the Free French.³ But by early 1943, if not before, President Roosevelt was questioning whether Indochina should be returned to France after the war (Document 1), and he began to advocate that the colony be placed under an international trusteeship (Document 2).⁴ That idea was discussed with Generalissimo Chiang Kai-shek at the Cairo Conference in October 1943,⁵ and with Marshal Stalin at Tehran in November (Document 3).

The Free French government of General de Gaulle, however, had no intention of abandoning Indochina. The Free French declared war on Japan on December 8, 1941,⁶ and began to promote a resistance movement in Indochina; for that purpose the Algiers government established a military mission (Mission 5) in Kunming, China, in 1943. On December 8, 1943, the Free French issued a declaration on the prospective postwar status of Indochina (Document 4). French plans apparently received at least tacit support from the British, who were concerned with the status of their own possessions in Asia.

By the early part of 1944 President Roosevelt had become so committed to the idea of postwar trusteeship for Indochina that he was willing to oppose the British openly on the matter (Document 5). He had also decided that the French should be excluded from any role in the liberation of the colony.⁷ But Roosevelt's personal ideas had not been

³ For documentation on this question see *Foreign Relations of the United States, 1942, China* (Washington: Government Printing Office, 1956), pp. 749–760; *Foreign Relations of the United States, 1943, China* (Washington: Government Printing Office, 1957), pp. 882–892; and *Foreign Relations of the United States, 1945* (9 vols., Washington: Government Printing Office, 1967–1969), Vol. VII, pp. 43–44, 55–62.

⁴ The earliest mention the editor has found in an official document of American advocacy of an international trusteeship for some territories in Southeast Asia (but with no specific mention of Indochina), is in a draft of a letter from Owen Lattimore to Generalissimo Chiang Kai-shek, written in late 1942 and edited by President Roosevelt in December of that year; text in *Foreign Relations of the United States, 1942, China*, pp. 185–187.

⁵ See *Foreign Relations of the United States,* THE CONFERENCES AT CAIRO AND TEHRAN, 1943 (Washington: Government Printing Office, 1961), p. 325.

⁶ A summary of the Declaration is contained in a message from the United States Ambassador in London, John G. Winant, to the Secretary of State on December 8, 1941, in *Foreign Relations of the United States, 1941,* Vol. V, p. 380.

⁷ See the February 17, 1944, memorandum to the President from Under Secretary of State Edward R. Stettinius, Jr., proposing French participation in both liberation and administration of Indochina, in *Foreign Relations of the United*

elaborated into an official and operational policy and apparently ran counter to the desires and activities of other Allied powers. In addition, both in Washington and in the field American policy makers at lower echelons often concentrated on objectives and policies which were effectively, although not necessarily overtly, competitive with Roosevelt's ideas. In August 1944 the British proposed that a French military mission be attached to the South East Asia Command (SEAC) under Lord Louis Mountbatten, and that French forces be prepared for participation in military operations in the Far East. Despite lack of American concurrence, the British went ahead with the establishment of a French mission at SEAC headquarters.[8]

The substance of any discussions regarding Indochina with Prime Minister Churchill at the Quebec Conference in September 1944 is not yet available,[9] but subsequently the President appeared to moderate his anti-French position. In response to a suggestion that the Office of Strategic Services (OSS) cooperate with resistance groups in Indochina (Document 6), the President replied that the United States should "do nothing" at that time (Document 7). British and French activities, which apparently were conducted on the assumption that Indochina would remain French after the war, caused increasing concern in Washington (Document 8) and prompted a strong response from the President stressing American interest in the future of Southeast Asia (Document 9). Subsequently American personnel in the Far East were informed that American policy on Indochina could not be defined until after consultation with the other Allies (Document 10).

The British, at the end of November, renewed their proposals of the summer and stressed the importance of Indochina for operations in the South East Asia Command, which at that time did not include either

---

States, 1944 (6 vols., Washington: Government Printing Office, 1965–1967), Vol. III, p. 774. President Roosevelt responded verbally to the effect that "no French troops whatever should be used in operations in Indochina. He added that in his view the operation should be Anglo-American in character and should be followed by the establishment of an international trusteeship over the French colony"; as reported in the March 14, 1944, memorandum from the Director of the Office of European Affairs, James Clement Dunn, to Major General John H. Hilldring, Director of the Civil Affairs Division, War Department, in *ibid.*, Vol. V, pp. 1205–1206.

8 See the October 10, 1944, memorandum from Secretary of State Hull to President Roosevelt, in *Foreign Relations of the United States, 1944,* Vol. III, pp. 775–776.

9 Documentation on the Quebec Conference will be published in a forthcoming *Foreign Relations* volume.

Indochina or the bulk of the Indonesian archipelago.[10] President Roosevelt, however, again reaffirmed that the time was not right for action in Indochina (Document 11).

France, meanwhile, undertook more active planning for the liberation of Indochina after the installation of the Provisional Government in Paris in the fall of 1944. Paris publicly called for volunteers to participate in the liberation of the colony, began to assemble military forces for that purpose, and, at the beginning of 1945, established an interministerial committee for Indochina. On January 20 the French Embassy in Chungking delivered a note to the American Embassy outlining French policy for Indochina and the Far East (Document 12).

At Yalta, in February 1945, President Roosevelt again expressed his preference for a trusteeship over Indochina and, again, Marshal Stalin appeared to agree (Document 13).[11] Nonetheless, the necessity for Allied cooperation in the achievement of more important ends continued to force American policy to moderate in practice if not in theory.

Events in Indochina, and particularly in Viet-Nam, did not lend themselves easily to outside manipulation but went their own way independently of the desires of the Allied powers. Although Vietnamese opposition to French rule had never ceased, after World War I it began to take on new, modern forms under the impact of Western liberal ideology and the doctrines of Marxism. In the interwar period a number of nationalist movements were formed and on several occasions undertook armed uprisings against the French. By the beginning of World War II the best organized of these movements was the Indochinese Communist Party (ICP) under the leadership of the brilliant nationalist/Communist Ho Chi Minh. As early as 1941 Ho Chi Minh, living in exile in China under the name Nguyen Ai Quoc,[12] was calling for armed uprising against both Japanese and French. The ICP was successful in sponsoring the formation, in 1941, of the "Viet Nam Doc Lap Dong Minh Hoi" (Front of the Allies for the Independence of Viet-Nam), known more popularly as the "Viet Minh."

[10] The text of the British *aide-mémoire* of November 22 is in *Foreign Relations of the United States, 1944,* Vol. III, pp. 781–783.

[11] See also Roosevelt's statement at a press conference on board the U.S.S. *Quincy* on February 23, 1945, in *The Public Papers and Addresses of Franklin D. Roosevelt: Victory and the Threshold of Peace,* compiled by Samuel I. Rosenman (New York: Harper & Brothers, 1950), pp. 562–563.

[12] Meaning "Nguyen the Patriot." "Ho Chi Minh" is also a pseudonym ("Ho Who Is Enlightened"). Ho's real name is open to some dispute, although most scholars now accept "Nguyen Tat Thanh" as most likely.

The Viet Minh, operating from southern China and guerrilla bases in northern Tonkin, was often in conflict with Chinese leaders who desired a Vietnamese movement more amenable to their control and made several largely ineffectual efforts toward that end. But it rapidly proved itself the only indigenous force in Indochina capable of providing significant opposition to the Japanese and, moreover, of serving as a source of intelligence for the Allies. By early 1945 the Viet Minh was cooperating closely with the Allies (although not the French) through the American Office of Strategic Services (OSS) and the Chinese Nationalist forces. The Viet Minh and the ICP leadership were also directing their activities more and more toward military organization and planning for revolution. On December 27, 1944, Ho Chi Minh directed the establishment of the "Viet-Nam Propaganda Unit for National Liberation" which, under the leadership of the young Communist and former history teacher Vo Nguyen Giap, was the precursor of the later Viet-Nam People's Army (VPA or PAVN).[13]

1. *President Roosevelt: Remarks on French Possessions* [*Extract*] *
January 7, 1943

[President Roosevelt's remarks were made at a meeting of the Joint Chiefs of Staff at the White House, attended by Admiral W. D. Leahy, U.S.N., General G. C. Marshall, U.S.A., Admiral E. J. King, U.S.N., Lt. General H. H. Arnold, U.S.A., and Brig. General J. R. Deane, U.S.A. The extract of the official minutes of the meeting given here is that portion directly relevant to Indochina; earlier in the conversation the President had remarked that "the sovereignty of France ceased in June of 1940 when President LeBrun disappeared."]

THE PRESIDENT said that Mr. Murphy [1] had given certain written pledges to Giraud [2] to restore France and the colonial possessions of

* *Source:* United States, Department of State, *Foreign Relations of the United States,* THE CONFERENCES AT WASHINGTON, 1941–1942, AND CASABLANCA, 1943 (Washington: Government Printing Office, 1968), p. 514. For a record of prior American statements relevant to the status of French territory after the war, see Secretary of State Hull's January 14, 1944, memorandum to President Roosevelt, particularly Enclosure 1 thereto, in *Foreign Relations of the United States, 1944* (6 vols., Washington: Government Printing Office, 1965–1967), Vol. III, pp. 769–773.

[13] The text of Ho Chi Minh's instruction is in Ho Chi Minh, *Selected Works* (4 vols., Hanoi: 1960–1962), Vol. II, pp. 155–156.

[1] Robert D. Murphy, Consul-General in Algiers and U.S. Political Advisor in North Africa.

[2] General Henri Honoré Giraud, who succeeded Admiral Darlan as French High Commissioner in North Africa.

France after the war.[3] He said that in doing this Mr. Murphy had exceeded his authority and that he as President was not prepared to make any promises. There are some of the colonial possessions which he was certain would not be returned to France, and he had grave doubts as to whether Indo-China should be. He thought that the Chiefs of Staff in their discussions in North Africa should make this plain to both Mr. Murphy and to General Eisenhower.

2. *Secretary of State Hull: Memorandum of Conversation* [*Extract*] *   *March 27, 1943*

[The introductory paragraph, listing the participants in the White House conversations, is omitted. President Roosevelt and Anthony Eden, the British Foreign Secretary, were the principals. One paragraph on discussion of China is omitted.]

Another question had to do with our joint or respective post-war policies relating to Manchuria, Korea, Formosa and Indochina. The President suggested that a trusteeship be set up for Indochina; that Manchuria and Formosa should be returned to China and that Korea might be placed under an international trusteeship, with China, the United States and one or two other countries participating. As to the disposition of the Japanese mandated islands, the President remarked that they should be internationalized for the purpose of keeping the peace. Mr. Eden indicated that he was favorably impressed with this proposal.

[Discussion of general mechanisms of trusteeship, France, Germany, the United Nations, and international bases is omitted.]

C[ORDELL] H[ULL]

* *Source:* United States, Department of State, *Foreign Relations of the United States, 1943* (6 vols., Washington: Government Printing Office, 1963–1965), Vol. III, p. 37. Further information on this meeting is contained in a November 2, 1944, memorandum by H. Freeman Matthews, Deputy Director of European Affairs, Department of State, in *Foreign Relations of the United States, 1944* (6 vols., Washington: Government Printing Office, 1965–1967), Vol. III, pp. 777–778.

[3] Footnote in the original: "For texts of correspondence exchanged between Murphy and General Giraud in October and November 1942, see *Foreign Relations, 1942*, Vol. II, pp. 412–422." Among other things, Murphy told Giraud that "It is thoroughly understood that French sovereignty will be reestablished as soon as possible throughout all the territory, metropolitan and colonial, over which flew the French flag in 1939."

3. *The Tehran Conference: President Roosevelt and Marshal Stalin Exchange Views on France and Indochina [Extract]* *
November 28, 1943

[Roosevelt-Stalin meeting, November 28, 1943, 3 P.M., Roosevelt's Quarters, Soviet Embassy. Present for the United States were President Roosevelt and Mr. Bohlen; [4] present for the Soviet Union were Marshal Stalin and Mr. Pavlov. Discussion of general European matters, China, and the Free French movement is omitted.]

MARSHAL STALIN expatiated at length on the French ruling classes and he said, in his opinion, they should not be entitled to share in any of the benefits of the peace, in view of their past record of collaboration with Germany.

THE PRESIDENT said that Mr. Churchill was of the opinion that France would be very quickly reconstructed as a strong nation, but he did not personally share this view since he felt that many years of honest labor would be necessary before France would be re-established. He said the first necessity for the French, not only for the Government but the people as well, was to become honest citizens.

MARSHAL STALIN agreed and went on to say that he did not propose to have the Allies shed blood to restore Indochina, for example, to the old French colonial rule. He said that the recent events in the Lebanon made public service the first step toward the independence of people who had formerly been colonial subjects. He said that in the war against Japan, in his opinion, that in addition to military missions, it was necessary to fight the Japanese in the political sphere as well, particularly in view of the fact that the Japanese had granted the least nominal independence to certain colonial areas. He repeated that France should not get back Indochina and that the French must pay for their criminal collaboration with Germany.

THE PRESIDENT said he was 100% in agreement with Marshal Stalin and remarked that after 100 years of French rule in Indochina, the inhabitants were worse off than they had been before. He said that Chiang Kai-shek had told him China had no designs on Indochina but the peo-

* *Source:* United States, Department of State, *Foreign Relations of the United States,* THE CONFERENCES AT CAIRO AND TEHRAN, 1943 (Washington: Government Printing Office, 1961), p. 485.

[4] The minutes are as recorded by Charles E. Bohlen, the President's interpreter.

ple of Indochina were not yet ready for independence,[5] to which he had replied that when the United States acquired the Philippines, the inhabitants were not yet ready for independence which would be granted without qualification upon the end of the war against Japan. He added that he had discussed with Chiang Kai-shek the possibility of a system of trusteeship for Indochina which would have the task of preparing the people for independence within a definite period of time, perhaps 20 to 30 years.

MARSHAL STALIN completely agreed with this view.[6]

[Discussion of general mechanisms for trusteeship and of India is omitted.]

4. *Declaration of the French Committee of National Liberation* *
December 8, 1943

"free lands"

The venture of war and conquest undertaken by Japan in order to impose its domination on the free lands of the Far East and the Pacific fell, in 1940, on Indochina. Indochina was deprived of all external assistance, not having been able to receive the necessary aid from the great democracies, then still insufficiently united and organized, and was forced, after a heroic but vain resistance, to submit to the demands of the enemy. The stages of the Japanese invasion were marked by the cession to Siam, allied with Japan, of the provinces of Battambang, Siem Reap, and Sisophong and of the right bank of the Mekong in Laos; by the institution of Japanese control over Tonkin; and then by the pro-

What heroic resistance

---

* *Source:* France, Direction de la Documentation, *Notes Documentaires et Etudes,* No. 548 (February 15, 1947), p. 3. Translation by the editor. The declaration was made in the name of General de Gaulle.

[5] Presumably at the Cairo Conference; see United States, Department of State, *Foreign Relations of the United States,* THE CONFERENCES AT CAIRO AND TEHRAN, 1943 (Washington: Government Printing Office, 1961), p. 325.

[6] Footnote in the original: "On March 17, 1944, in a conversation with Stettinius, Roosevelt recounted what had been said at Tehran regarding Indochina. Stettinius's notes on the conversation, prepared that night, read as follows: 'Then at Teheran the President raised the question with Joseph Stalin, who said that Indo-China should be independent but was not yet ready for self-government. He said that the idea of a trusteeship was excellent. When Churchill objected, the President said, "Now, look here, Winston, you are outvoted three to one." ' Edward R. Stettinius, Jr., *Roosevelt and the Russians; The Yalta Conference* (Garden City: Doubleday and Co., 1949), p. 238. The number 'three' apparently refers to the concurrence not only of Roosevelt and Stalin, but also, at the First Cairo Conference, of Chiang Kai-shek; see *ante,* p. 325. See also *F. D. R., His Personal Letters, 1928–1945,* Vol. II, p. 1489."

gressive infiltration of Japanese troops into all the territory of Indochina.

Free France has never bowed before this action of force and conquest. On December 8, 1941, on the morrow of the Japanese aggression against Pearl Harbor, the French National Committee declared itself in a state of war with Japan.[7] France solemnly repudiates all the acts and cessions to which she had to consent at the cost of her rights and interests. Bound to the United Nations, she will continue the battle at their side until the aggressor is defeated and all the territories of the Indochinese Union are completely liberated.

Just as France remembers the nobility and the uprightness of the reigning sovereigns of Indochina, she will remember the proud and loyal attitude of the Indochinese peoples, the resistance which they have led at our side against Japan and Siam, and the fidelity of their attachment to the French Community. To these peoples, who have thus been able to affirm at the same time their national sentiment and their sense of political responsibility, France intends to give a new political status within the French community. There, within the framework of the federal organization, the liberties of the various countries of the Union will be extended and consecrated, the liberal character of the institutions will be strengthened without losing the stamp of Indochinese civilization and traditions, and, finally, the Indochinese will have access to all the posts and offices of the State.

Along with this reform of the political status of the Union, there will be a corresponding reform of its economic status which, on the basis of fiscal and tariff autonomy, will assure its prosperity and contribute to that of the countries which are its neighbors.

Friendly and neighborly relations with China and the development of our intellectual and economic relations with that great country will assure Indochina, in the role which it will have, a secure and fruitful future.

Thus France intends to carry on, in free and intimate association with the Indochinese peoples, the mission for which she has responsibility in the Pacific.

[7] A summary of the Declaration is contained in a message from the United States Ambassador in London, John G. Winant, to the Secretary of State on December 8, 1941, in United States, Department of State, *Foreign Relations of the United States, 1941* (7 vols., Washington: Government Printing Office, 1958–1962), Vol. V, p. 380.

5. *Memorandum from President Roosevelt to Secretary of State Hull* * 8
January 24, 1944

I saw Halifax [9] last week and told him quite frankly that it was perfectly true that I had, for over a year, expressed the opinion that Indo-China should not go back to France but that it should be administered by an international trusteeship. France has had the country—thirty million inhabitants for nearly one hundred years, and the people are worse off than they were at the beginning.

As a matter of interest, I am wholeheartedly supported in this view by Generalissimo Chiang Kai-shek [10] and by Marshal Stalin.[11] I see no reason to play in with the British Foreign Office in this matter. The only reason they seem to oppose it is that they fear the effect it would have on their own possessions and those of the Dutch. They have never liked the idea of trusteeship because it is, in some instances, aimed at future independence. This is true in the case of Indo-China.

Each case must, of course, stand on its own feet, but the case of Indo-China is perfectly clear. France has milked it for one hundred years. The people of Indo-China are entitled to something better than that.

F[RANKLIN] D. R[OOSEVELT]

* *Source:* United States, Department of State, *Foreign Relations of the United States, 1944* (6 vols., Washington: Government Printing Office, 1965–1967), Vol. III, p. 773. Another version of this memorandum appears in *Foreign Relations of the United States,* THE CONFERENCES AT CAIRO AND TEHRAN, 1943 (Washington: Government Printing Office, 1961), pp. 872–873; it differs from the version printed here in that the final paragraph is omitted. The memorandum was in response to a memorandum of January 14, 1944, from Secretary of State Hull, who indicated that British Ambassador Lord Halifax had expressed concern over President Roosevelt's views on Indochina as stated during his trip to Cairo and Tehran: text in *Foreign Relations of the United States, 1944,* Vol. III, pp. 769–773.

8 Footnote in the original: "Copy obtained from the Franklin D. Roosevelt Library, Hyde Park, N.Y."

9 Lord Halifax, the British Ambassador.

10 Footnote in the original: "President of the National Government of China and Supreme Allied Commander of the China Theater."

11 Footnote in the original: "Chairman of the Council of People's Commissars of the Soviet Union."

6. *Memorandum from Secretary of State Hull to President Roosevelt* *
   October 13, 1944

A letter has been received from General [William J.] Donovan, Director of the Office of Strategic Services, asking the views of the State Department on the following contemplated operations:

The staff of the Theater Commander for the CBI [12] theater has under consideration operational plans involving the furnishing of supplies and equipment to resistance groups. It is contemplated that these operations will be under American command although there will be collaboration with the French.

In amplification of the foregoing, it was explained orally that the proposed assistance would be to resistance groups within Indochina; that the proposed collaboration would be with the French Military Mission at Chungking; [13] that such collaboration would not prevent assistance to all resistance groups whether French or native, but that without such collaboration, it would not be possible effectively to assist resistance groups among the French military forces in Indochina, and that this would result in retarding resistance efforts.

Subject to your approval, the Department will reply to General Donovan that it has no objection to furnishing supplies and equipment to resistance groups, both French and native, actually within Indochina, nor to American collaboration with the French Military Mission at Chungking or other French officers or officials in furtherance of the contemplated operations or any other military operations in Indochina for the defeat of Japan.

C[ORDELL] H[ULL]

* *Source:* United States, Department of State, *Foreign Relations of the United States, 1944* (6 vols., Washington: Government Printing Office, 1965–1967), Vol. III, pp. 776–777. See also Secretary Hull's earlier memorandum, of October 10, 1944, on "French Participation in Liberation of Indochina," particularly the sending of a French military mission under General Roger Blaizot to work with the British at South East Asia Command: text in *ibid.,* pp. 775–776.

[12] Footnote in the original: "China, Burma, India."
[13] And, presumably, with "Mission 5" under Jean Sainteny at Kunming.

7. *Memorandum from President Roosevelt to Secretary of State Hull* *
October 16, 1944

In regard to this Indochina matter, it is my judgment on this date that we should do nothing in regard to resistance groups or in any other way in relation to Indochina. You might bring it up to me a little later when things are a little clearer.

F[RANKLIN] D. R[OOSEVELT]

8. *Memorandum from Under Secretary of State Stettinius to President Roosevelt* †
November 2, 1944

INDOCHINA

In order that you may be kept fully informed on developments in relation to Indochina, there has been prepared the memorandum attached hereto.

EDWARD R. STETTINIUS, JR.

[Annex, Washington,] November 2, 1944

RECENT DEVELOPMENTS IN RELATION TO INDOCHINA

The following are recent developments in relation to Indochina: Colombo [14] has reported that:

The British staff at headquarters of SEAC [15] has protested to the British Chiefs of Staff in London against the inclusion of Indochina in

---

* *Source:* United States, Department of State, *Foreign Relations of the United States, 1944* (6 vols., Washington: Government Printing Office, 1965–1967), Vol. III, p. 777.

† *Source:* United States, Department of State, *Foreign Relations of the United States, 1944* (6 vols., Washington: Government Printing Office, 1965–1967), Vol. III, pp. 778–779.

[14] Footnote in the original: "Seat of the American Consulate in Ceylon." The material on which Stettinius's information appears to have been based was prepared by Max W. Bishop, the American Consul. Two of Bishop's memoranda—one transmitted as Enclosure No. 3 to an October 6, 1944, dispatch from Consul Robert L. Buell; and the second transmitted as an Enclosure to an October 24, 1944, dispatch from Buell—are in the Patrick J. Hurley Collection, Western History Collections, University of Oklahoma. There were quite obviously memoranda in addition to those two.

[15] South East Asia Command.

the theatre under the new United States Army Commanding General in China,[16] urging that Indochina be included in the SEAC theatre.

The French Military Mission, which is large, has arrived in Ceylon and has received American approval and is now recognized openly and officially. Apparently, General Blaizot has not yet arrived. Baron de Langlade [17] who parachuted into Indochina some weeks ago with a letter of introduction from de Gaulle is also in Ceylon. He spent twenty-four hours with French Army officers in Indochina, and stated, upon his return that a basis for a French resistance movement exists there, but reportedly declined to say more until Blaizot's arrival. Blaizot, a Lieutenant General, was formerly Chief of Staff in Indochina. He is a "colonial" general.

Although SEAC was advised specifically that only military, and not political, questions might be discussed with the French Mission, political questions are in fact under discussion.

The British SOE [18] which is actively engaged in undercover operations in Indochina has recently received orders from the Foreign Office that they should have nothing to do with any Annamite or other native organizations in Indochina, but are to devote their efforts to the French.

The OWI [19] representative at New Delhi has received indication that the British wish OWI activities directed at the native populations in Thailand and Indochina be eliminated so as not to stir up native resistance to the Japanese and so incite the Japanese to send more troops into those areas. Colombo states that it is apparent SOE desires severely to restrict OSS [20] operations in the SEAC theatre and to give SOE preeminence or, failing that, to establish combined SOE-OSS operations.

British propaganda agencies are emphasizing the recent appeal by the French War Ministry for recruits to participate in the campaign for liberation of Indochina on the ground that news of any French military efforts to recover Indochina would encourage the French in Indochina.

---

[16] Lt. General Albert C. Wedemeyer. The reference is to the dissolution of the China-Burma-India Theater on October 24, 1944, and its replacement by the China Theater, under General Wedemeyer, and the Burma Theater, under General Sultan.

[17] Major de Langlade, Political Adviser to Lt. General Roger Blaizot. He first parachuted into Viet-Nam on June 6, 1944, and, apparently, returned several times thereafter to assist in organizing the resistance among French forces.

[18] Footnote in the original: "Secret Operations Executive." The British counterpart of the American Office of Strategic Services (OSS).

[19] Footnote in the original: "Office of War Information."

[20] Footnote in the original: "Office of Strategic Services."

OWI has so far refrained from mentioning the French appeal or other phases of French preparations for military participation fearing the adverse effect on the native populations in Indochina and elsewhere in the Far East on the restoration of the *status quo ante* which such preparations would appear to imply. OWI has specifically requested State Department guidance on United States policy in this regard, and have been advised to be silent on the subject despite the anticipated British broadcasts.

General Donovan has submitted to the Secretary of State a report from the OSS representative in SEAC reading in part:

> There can be little doubt that the British and Dutch have arrived at an agreement with regard to the future of Southeast Asia, and now it would appear that the French are being brought into the picture. . . .[21] It would appear that the strategy of the British, Dutch and French is to win back and control Southeast Asia, making the fullest use possible of American resources, but foreclosing the Americans from any voice in policy matters.

9. *Memorandum from President Roosevelt to Under Secretary of State Stettinius* *
November 3, 1944

I have yours of November second,[22] enclosing memorandum on recent developments in relation to Indo-China. I wish you would make it clear that:

1. We must not give American approval to any French military mission, as it appears we have done in the first sentence of the first [*sic*] paragraph.

2. Referring to the third paragraph, it must be made clear to all our people in the Far East that they can make no decisions on political questions with the French mission or anyone else.

3. We have made no final decisions on the future of Indo-China. This should be made clear.

4. In the final paragraph it is stated the British and Dutch have arrived at an agreement in regard to the future of Southeast Asia and are about to bring the French into the picture. It should be made clear to all our people that the United States expects to be consulted with

* *Source:* United States, Department of State, *Foreign Relations of the United States, 1944* (6 vols., Washington: Government Printing Office, 1965–1967), Vol. III, p. 780.
21 Footnote in the original: "Omission indicated in the original memorandum."
22 Document 8.

regard to any future of Southeast Asia. I have no objection to this being made clear to the British, the Dutch or the French.

F[RANKLIN] D. R[OOSEVELT]

10. *Telegram from President Roosevelt to Ambassador Patrick J. Hurley, Chungking* *
    November 16, 1944

Referring to Wedemeyer's CFB NR. 26367,[23] inform Wedemeyer that United States policy with regard to French Indo-China cannot be formulated until after consultation with allies at a forthcoming combined staff conference.

Please keep me informed of activities of British-Dutch-French missions in Southeastern Asia.

ROOSEVELT

11. *Memorandum from President Roosevelt to Secretary of State Stettinius* †
    January 1, 1945

I still do not want to get mixed up in any Indochina decision. It is a matter for post-war.

* *Source:* Telegram, White House No. 120, in the Patrick J. Hurley Collection, Western History Collections, University of Oklahoma. Used by permission of the University of Oklahoma Library. A similar message was sent to General Wedemeyer on November 21 by the Joint Chiefs of Staff, at the direction of the President. It included this statement: "This Government has made no final decisions on the future of Indo-China, and it expects to be consulted in advance with regard to any arrangements applicable to the future of southeast Asia." Quoted in undated [June 1945] Memorandum by G. M. Elsey, Assistant to the President's Naval Aide [Admiral William D. Leahy], subject "Indo-China," in *Foreign Relations of the United States,* THE CONFERENCE OF BERLIN (THE POTSDAM CONFERENCE), 1945 (2 vols., Washington: Government Printing Office, 1960), Vol. I, p. 916. A number of documents relative to Hurley's reporting of British-Dutch-French activities are in the Patrick J. Hurley Collection, Western History Collections, University of Oklahoma.

† *Source:* United States, Department of State, *Foreign Relations of the United States, 1945* (9 vols., Washington: Government Printing Office, 1967–1969), Vol. VI, p. 293. President Roosevelt's memorandum was in response to a December 27 memorandum from Secretary Stettinius, which called the attention of the President to the problems raised by a British *aide-mémoire* of November 22. The British note was in support of French participation in the activities of the South East Asia Command and in eventual liberation of Indochina. Texts of both the British *aide-mémoire* and Stettinius' memorandum are in *Foreign Relations of the United States, 1944,* Vol. III, pp. 781–784.

23 The message from Lt. General Albert C. Wedemeyer, Commanding General of U.S. Forces in China, dated November 15, indicated that British, French, and

By the same token, I do not want to get mixed up in any military effort toward the liberation of Indochina from the Japanese.

You can tell Halifax [24] that I made this very clear to Mr. Churchill.[25] From both the military and civil point of view, action at this time is premature.[26]

F[RANKLIN] D. R[OOSEVELT]

12. *Note from the Provisional French Government to the United States* *
January 20, 1945

The political position taken by the Provisional Government of the French Republic regarding Indochina is plain. A few sentences will be sufficient to make it clear.

First, France cannot admit any discussion about the principle of her establishment in Indochina. Her presence founded on agreements consistent with international law and based on the immense task carried out by her for the sake of the Indochinese population has never been disputed by any Power. The occupation of Indochina by the Japanese has not changed anything in that state of affairs. This occupation is nothing but a war incident similar to the invasion by the Japanese forces of Malaya, of the Netherlands East Indies and Burma. The activity of the underground movement, the formation of the

---

* *Source:* United States, Department of State, *Foreign Relations of the United States, 1945* (9 vols., Washington: Government Printing Office, 1967–1969), Vol. VI, pp. 295–296. Translation by the Department of State. The Note was handed to Counselor Atcheson of the American Embassy in Chungking by Mr. Achilles Clarac, Counselor of the French Embassy in Chungking, on January 26, 1945, in French and in English translation. The American Embassy made no comment to the French Embassy with regard to the contents of the Note, which was transmitted to the Secretary of State by Ambassador Hurley on January 31; Hurley's transmittal letter is in *ibid.,* p. 294. The French original as well as the English translation made by the French Embassy are in the Patrick J. Hurley Collection, Western History Collections, University of Oklahoma.
Dutch interests were making an intensive effort to ensure recovery of their prewar interests in Southeast Asia and that one indication of this was the establishment of General Roger Blaizot's mission at South East Asia Command. General Wedemeyer requested policy guidance regarding Indochina. See the undated Elsey Memorandum, cited in the Source Note to this document.

[24] Footnote in the original: "Viscount Halifax, British Ambassador in the United States."

[25] Footnote in the original: "Winston S. Churchill, British Prime Minister. Conversation on the subject took place at the Second Quebec Conference in September 1944. Documentation on that Conference is scheduled for publication in a subsequent volume of *Foreign Relations.*"

[26] Footnote in the original omitted.

expeditionary forces that we are ready to send to the Far East, reveal the energy with which France intends to take part in the liberation of those of her territories that have been momentarily torn away from her by the enemy.

This being clear, the French Government is prepared to consider with her allies all the measures that may be taken to insure security and peace for the future in the Pacific area; with respect to these measures she intends to play her part to which the importance of her interests in the Far East entitle her.

Furthermore, the French Government has already decided at the Brazzaville conference [27] the principles of the policy she means to follow in her overseas possessions. Accordingly she will determine together with the populations concerned the status of Indochina on a basis that will secure for the Union a satisfactory autonomy within the frame of the French Empire. Besides, Indochina will be granted an economic regime that will enable her to profit widely by the advantages of international competition. These decisions, having no international character, come solely within the competence of the French Government. Thoroughly aware of the importance of the principles at stake in the present war, France will not shrink from her responsibilities.

For the time being, however, France's concerns in the Far East are mainly military. As early as June 1943, the French Committee of National Liberation made it known to its allies that it considered that area as one where it would be extremely desirable for all the interested parties to establish thorough military collaboration. On the 4th of October 1943, it decided to form an expeditionary force that would take part in western Pacific operations and in the liberation of Indochina. At the same time the French Government established in Indochina a network of connections with the French and Indochinese underground. By this action, the efficacy of which has been proved by the role of the French Forces of the Interior in France, it will support the assault of the forces attacking from without and help them in their task in a way that can be decisive.

The French Government has informed Washington and London of all the measures it has taken in that respect. It has repeatedly asked that the expeditionary forces should be sent to the area and used to the

[27] Footnote in the original: "French African Conference held at Brazzaville, January 30-February 8, 1944, under chairmanship of René Pleven, Commissioner for the Colonies. It was attended by the Governors General of French West Africa, French Equatorial Africa, and Madagascar, and by 'observers' from Algeria, French Morocco, and Tunisia."

best advantage; but the answer was that the decision belonged to President Roosevelt and the Combined Chiefs of Staff. They have not yet responded. Nevertheless, the French Government is prepared to have its expeditionary forces used in the American as well as in the British theatre of operations. Considering therefore the part France is entitled to play and ready to assume in the military operations in the Pacific, it would be useful that she be admitted to the Pacific War Council and particularly to the Sub-Committee responsible for the operations involving French Indochina.

13. *The Yalta Conference: President Roosevelt and Marshal Stalin Exchange Views on Indochina* [Extract] *
   February 8, 1945

[Roosevelt-Stalin Meeting, February 8, 1945, 3:30 P.M. Livadia Palace. Present for the United States were President Roosevelt, Mr. Harriman,[28] and Mr. Bohlen;[29] present for the Soviet Union were Marshal Stalin, Foreign Commissar Molotov, and Mr. Pavlov. Discussion of strategy, sale of ships to the Soviet Union, Soviet desires in the Far East, and trusteeship for Korea is omitted.]

THE PRESIDENT then said he also had in mind a trusteeship for Indochina. He added that the British did not approve of this idea as they wished to give it back to the French since they feared the implications of a trusteeship as it might affect Burma.

MARSHAL STALIN remarked that the British had lost Burma once through reliance on Indochina, and it was not his opinion that Britain was a sure country to protect this area. He added that he thought Indochina was a very important area.

THE PRESIDENT said that the Indochinese were people of small stature, like the Javanese and Burmese, and were not warlike. He added that France had done nothing to improve the natives since she had the colony. He said that General de Gaulle had asked for ships to transport French forces to Indochina.

MARSHAL STALIN inquired where de Gaulle was going to get the troops.

* *Source:* United States, Department of State, *Foreign Relations of the United States,* THE CONFERENCES AT MALTA AND YALTA, 1945 (Washington: Government Printing Office, 1955), p. 770.

[28] W. Averell Harriman, Ambassador to the Soviet Union.

[29] The minutes are as recorded by Mr. Charles E. Bohlen, the President's interpreter.

THE PRESIDENT replied that de Gaulle said he was going to find the troops when the President could find the ships, but the President added that up to the present he had been unable to find the ships.

[Discussion of internal conditions in China is omitted.]

CHAPTER II

Revolution and the
Return of the French

March-December 1945

Introduction

The critical months of 1945 began with the Japanese overthrow of the French colonial administration on March 9 and culminated with the return of the French to Indochina during the fall. In the interim, World War II came to an end, and in Viet-Nam the "August Revolution" produced the infant Democratic Republic of Viet-Nam (DRV). North of the 16th parallel that new government existed in uneasy tension with Chinese occupation forces. South of the 16th parallel the DRV and the Viet Minh competed both politically and militarily first with the British occupation forces and then with the French. The DRV was unable to establish effective control over most of Cochin China but established itself solidly in southern Annam. The stage was set for the fateful Franco-Vietnamese negotiations of 1946.

On March 9, 1945, in order to preclude possible French action in cooperation with the Allies, the Japanese struck against the rump French regime in Indochina, disarming and interning French military forces and assuming all governing powers. The following day the Japanese ambassador informed Emperor Bao Dai that his country was now "independent," and that in return Viet-Nam was expected to cooperate in the "Greater East Asia Co-Prosperity Sphere"; Emperor Bao Dai proclaimed independence and cooperation with Japan on March 11 (Document 14).[1]

French resistance to the Japanese coup, lacking support from and

---

[1] Vietnamese "independence" did not include Cochin China, which the Japanese kept under their direct control until August 14. The Japanese also granted similar "independence" to Cambodia and Laos during March.

coordination with either external Allied forces or the indigenous Viet Minh guerrillas, was mostly ineffective. It did, however, attract considerable attention in France where General de Gaulle, on March 14, reaffirmed French determination to recover Indochina and criticized the Allies for their slowness in coming to the aid of French forces in the colony.[2] But Allied aid was hamstrung by American reluctance to give the French a role in Indochina as well as by dissension over the respective spheres of authority of the China Theater, under Generalissimo Chiang Kai-shek, and the South East Asia Command under Admiral Lord Louis Mountbatten.[3] By this time the question of American policy toward Indochina was intimately connected with the forthcoming San Francisco Conference which was to form the United Nations, particularly with regard to the question of trusteeship. President Roosevelt, in a March 15 conversation, reaffirmed his views on Indochina in terms which indicated that his position had softened somewhat and which also seemed to imply that his views were at variance with those held in the State Department (Document 15). Prospective French policy for Indochina was stated in a Declaration issued by the Provisional Government on March 24 (Document 16).

Within Viet-Nam, however, the situation appeared differently. Japan was weakening, France was discredited, Emperor Bao Dai had little popular support, and the position of all was complicated by a serious famine in the North. The force to be reckoned with was the Viet Minh and its most important component, the Indochinese Communist Party (ICP). The latter was quick to respond to the Japanese coup with a policy analysis which looked toward a successful revolution, but only after Allied invasion or the collapse of the Japanese.[4] The Viet Minh movement began to gather momentum, and by June the decision had been taken to found a "free zone"—a liberated area—in North Viet-Nam as a base for the "forthcoming insurrection."

[2] The text of de Gaulle's statement is in France, Ministère de l'Information, *Notes Documentaires et Etudes,* No. 115 (August 17, 1945), p. 3

[3] A number of documents on the question of Allied aid to the French forces in Indochina and on the related question of the use of French forces in the war in the Pacific are in United States, Department of State, *Foreign Relations of the United States, 1945* (9 vols., Washington: Government Printing Office, 1967–1969), Vol. VI, pp. 296–311, and Vol. VII, pp. 68, 70–71, 99–100.

[4] "Instructions of the Standing Bureau of the Central Committee of the Indochinese Communist Party Issued on March 12, 1945," in *Breaking Our Chains: Documents on the Vietnamese Revolution of August 1945* (Hanoi: Foreign Languages Publishing House, 1960), pp. 7–17. This publication contains a number of Viet Minh documents on events during 1945. The authenticity and accuracy of many of them cannot be confirmed from other sources.

The death of President Roosevelt on April 12 marked the end of efforts to remove Indochina from French control, a process which was further facilitated by developments on the proposed United Nations trusteeship mechanism. In early May Secretary of State Edward R. Stettinius, Jr., informed French Foreign Minister Georges Bidault that the United States did not question French sovereignty over Indochina (Document 17). There was, however, some delay in communicating this policy position to officials in the Far East. On May 28 the American Ambassador in Chungking, Patrick J. Hurley, inquired, sharply, whether United States policy had changed from opposition to support for reassertion of French control in Indochina.[5] The reply from the State Department on June 10 confirmed that the United States had abandoned any idea of completely excluding France from Indochina and would, rather, attempt to influence Paris toward a liberal policy (Document 18). This position was further elaborated in a policy paper prepared by the State Department during June (Document 19), which also pointed up the conflict between American desires for an end to colonial rule and the necessity for cooperation with the European allies. On the scene, agents of the Office of Strategic Services (OSS) continued to work with the Viet Minh and in July served as intermediary for transmittal of a Viet Minh *aide-mémoire* to the French Mission 5 in Kunming (Document 20). The French response reaffirmed the policy of the government in Paris.[6]

At the Potsdam Conference in July, Indochina figured in high-level policy discussions primarily as part of the question of "command and control"—which parts of the Allied command structure were to have responsibility for which areas. The ultimate decision was to divide Indochina at the 16th parallel for command purposes (Document 21) with the southern portion included in an expanded South East Asia Command.

[5] Ambassador Hurley read the text of his message during his testimony at the MacArthur Hearings in 1951: United States, Congress, Senate, Committee on Armed Services and Committee on Foreign Relations, *Hearings before the Committee on Armed Services and the Committee on Foreign Relations, Eighty-Second Congress, First Session, to Conduct an Inquiry into the Military Situation in the Far East and the Facts Surrounding the Relief of the General of the Army Douglas MacArthur from his Assignments in that Area* (five parts, Washington: Government Printing Office, 1951), Part IV, Session of June 21, 1951, pp. 2890–2892. An original text of the message is in the Patrick J. Hurley Collection, Western History Collections, University of Oklahoma.

[6] Text not available. See Jean Sainteny, *Histoire d'une Paix Manquée: Indochine 1945–1947* (Paris: Amiot-Dumont, 1953), pp. 57–58. American documentation on the activities of the OSS during this period remains classified by the United States, and much French documentation is also unavailable.

The Japanese war effort collapsed on August 10, when the cabinet made an offer of surrender. Allied policy for the surrender, as contained in General Order No. 1 issued to General MacArthur on August 15, provided that Japanese forces in Indochina north of the 16th parallel were to surrender to forces from the China Theater and those south of that line to South East Asia Command. France's desire to participate in the surrender of Japanese forces in Indochina was supported by the United States (Document 22). British policy was indicated by a statement contained in a memorandum delivered to the Chinese government on August 16:

His Majesty's Government trust that His Excellency the President [of the Republic of China] will agree with them that the common object of both Governments should now be to restore the French administration of Indo-China and to facilitate the return of French forces and administrative officers for this purpose, as soon as they are available.[7]

The Japanese surrender touched off the Viet Minh insurrection, which was conducted in accordance with policy being set by the ICP at its Congress held from August 13 to 15 in the village of Tan Trao, Tuyen Quang Province, in the "free zone" of North Viet-Nam. The Congress began by approving the establishment of an "Insurrection Committee" which issued the "Order of General Insurrection" on August 13. The Congress then adopted the policy later summarized by Truong Chinh, leading ICP theorist and Secretary General of the Party:

During the historic Congress, the Indochinese Communist Party advocated an extremely clear policy: to lead the masses in insurrection in order to disarm the Japanese before the arrival of the Allied forces in Indo-China; to wrest power from the Japanese and their puppet stooges and finally, as the

[7] Quoted in a memorandum of August 16, 1945, from the Chinese Acting Foreign Minister, K. C. Wu, to the British Embassy in Chungking, quoted in a telegram of August 16, 1945, to the Secretary of State from Ambassador Hurley, in *Foreign Relations of the United States, 1945,* Vol. VII, pp. 500–501. An original text of the Chinese memorandum is in the Patrick J. Hurley Collection, Western History Collections, University of Oklahoma. Adequate documentation on the Chinese position during this period, and particularly on the policies followed by the Chinese occupation forces in northern Indochina, is not available. The best secondary account of Chinese policy and activity, which maximizes use of available materials including interviews, is King C. Chen, *Vietnam and China, 1938–1954* (Princeton, N.J.: Princeton University Press, 1969), Chapter 3; see particularly Note 60 on p. 117.

people's power, to welcome the Allied forces coming to disarm the Japanese troops stationed in Indo-China.[8]

The ICP Congress was followed, on August 16 and 17, by a "People's Congress." The major decisions of that Congress (Document 23) were later interpreted by the official Communist Party history:

The People's Congress wholeheartedly approved of the policy of general insurrection advocated by the Indochinese Communist Party and the General Committee of the Viet Minh. Representing the Party at the Congress, Comrade Truong Chinh made it clear that *We must wrest power from the hands of the Japanese and their stooges before the arrival of the Allies in Indochina, and, as masters of the country, we shall receive the Allies who come to disarm the Japanese.*

The Congress adopted the ten-point Viet Minh policy and elected the Viet Nam National Liberation Committee, which was tantamount to the Provisional Government of the Democratic Republic of Viet Nam headed by Comrade Ho Chi Minh.[9]

During the following days the insurrection moved rapidly to success in North Viet-Nam with almost no opposition as the Japanese chose to stand aside. Although revolutionary activities had less success in Annam and Cochin China than in Tonkin, those parts of the country were not unaffected by the events in the North. There were revolutionary committees throughout Annam. The Japanese had, on August 14, allowed Bao Dai to proclaim the reunification of Cochin China with the rest of Viet-Nam, but shortly thereafter Saigon was seized by a revolutionary committee. This "Provisional Executive Committee of the South Viet-Nam Republic," under the leadership of the Communist Tran Van Giau, pleged its allegiance to the Viet Minh regime in Hanoi.

In Hué, after the resignation of the imperial government headed by Professor Tran Truong Kim, Bao Dai sent one of his ministers to Hanoi to invite the Viet Minh to form a new government, an invitation to which the Viet Minh did not respond. He also sent an appeal to General de Gaulle, urging him to recognize the independence of Viet-Nam (Document 24). De Gaulle, however, was on his way to Washington for consultations with American officials. One subject to be

[8] Truong Chinh, *The August Revolution* (Hanoi: Foreign Languages Publishing House, 1963), reprinted in Bernard B. Fall, ed., *Primer for Revolt* (New York: Frederick A. Praeger, 1963), p. 14.

[9] Central Committee of Propaganda of the Viet Nam Lao Dong Party and the Committee for the Study of the Party's History, *Thirty Years of Struggle of the Party, Book One* (Hanoi: Foreign Languages Publishing House, 1960), pp. 93–94. Emphasis in the original.

considered was Indochina. De Gaulle stated his position on that matter at a Washington press conference on August 24,[10] and he reportedly received assurances from President Truman that the United States would not oppose the reassertion of French sovereignty.[11] That policy was confirmed by the Department of State (Documents 26 and 27).

Meanwhile Bao Dai was beset by conflicting pressures and deserted by his advisors. Finally, after receiving a telegram from a mass meeting in Hanoi demanding his abdication, he decided he had no choice but to abandon the throne. The news was communicated to Hanoi by the Privy Council on August 24, and the following day a Viet Minh delegation arrived in Hué. On August 26 Bao Dai publicly read his abdication rescript (Document 25) and turned over the grand seal; he then became simply Mr. Nguyen Vinh Thuy and, temporarily, was "Supreme Councillor" of the DRV.

On September 2 Ho Chi Minh appeared before a mass meeting in Ba Dinh Square in Hanoi and read the Declaration of Independence of the Democratic Republic of Viet-Nam (Document 28). On the same

[10] The text of the de Gaulle press conference is in Charles de Gaulle, *Discours et Messages 1940–1946* (Paris: Editions Berger-Levrault, 1946), pp. 654–655.

[11] Documentation on conversations on Indochina during de Gaulle's visit to Washington does not appear in published volumes of the *Foreign Relations* series. According to de Gaulle (*The War Memoirs of Charles de Gaulle, Volume III, Salvation, 1944–1946*, Richard Howard, trans. [New York: Simon and Schuster, 1960], pp. 242–243), the following exchange took place: " 'In any case,' he [President Truman] said, 'my government offers no opposition to the return of the French Army and authority in Indochina.' I replied, 'Although France need ask no permission or approval in an affair which is hers alone, I note with satisfaction the intentions you express. The enemy recently seized Indochina. Thanks to the victory in which America has played an incomparable part, France is about to return there. She does so with the intention of establishing a regime in harmony with the will of the people. Nevertheless, in this area too, we find ourselves hampered by the arrangements our allies are making without consulting us first.' "
Neither this subject nor, indeed, the de Gaulle visit to Washington are mentioned in the Truman memoirs: *Memoirs by Harry S. Truman, Volume One, Year of Decisions* (Garden City, N.Y.: Doubleday, 1955). The subject did, however, come up in a conversation between the President and Madame Chiang Kai-shek on August 29, according to the Memorandum of Conversation prepared by Assistant Secretary of State James Clement Dunn (*Foreign Relations of the United States, 1945*, Vol. VII, pp. 540–542): "Madame Chiang then asked whether any decisions had been made with regard to the future of Indo China. The President replied that no decisions had been made with regard to Indo China, that in his discussions with General de Gaulle a few days ago he had received satisfactory response from the General when he gave us his opinion that Indo China should receive its independence and that steps should be taken immediately with a view to arriving at that state. Madame Chiang recalled that President Roosevelt had spoken of a trusteeship for Indo China, whereupon the President stated that there had been no discussion of a trusteeship for Indo China as far as he was concerned."

day the General Committee of the Viet Minh issued an appeal in which it took credit for the successful revolution but, at the same time, warned against the return of the French:

The French are on the lookout for the opportunity to come back to Indochina to enslave us once more. We must be ready to smash all their savage attempts at aggression. We must resolutely brush aside all their deceptive promises. We must extirpate the French colonialist regime.[12]

Vo Nguyen Giap, then serving as Minister of the Interior (i.e., Prime Minister) in the Provisional Government, also delievered a speech outlining government policy. He described the United States as a "good friend" but excoriated the policy of the de Gaulle government:

They [the French] are making preparations to land their forces in Indochina. In a word, and according to latest intelligence, France is preparing herself to reconquer our country. . . . The Vietnamese people will fight for independence, liberty and equality of status. If our negotiations be unsuccessful, we shall resort to arms.[13]

The new Vietnamese government on September 8 issued a decree on general elections for a national assembly.[14] Although that decree called for elections in November, they were delayed first until December and then until January 1946. The prime reason for the delay was the Chinese occupation of Viet-Nam north of the 16th parallel. As they descended on the north, the Chinese to some degree supported the Viet Minh regime but at the same time attempted to increase their own influence by forcing the Viet Minh to incorporate pro-Chinese nationalist elements into the government. That process reached its climax in December when the Viet Minh were forced to reach a compromise with opposition groups guaranteeing them representation in the new national assembly regardless of the outcome of the January elections.

[12] "Appeal by the General Committee of the Viet Nam Front on the Day of the Proclamation of Independence," in *Breaking Our Chains*, pp. 98–99.

[13] "Message of the Minister of Interior Mr. Vo-Nguyen-Giap to the Vietnamese People on Independence Day," in Democratic Republic of Viet-Nam, *Documents* (n.p., n.d.), pp. 10–24; extracts in Allan B. Cole, ed., *Conflict in Indo-China and International Repercussions: A Documentary History, 1945–1955* (Ithaca, N.Y.: Cornell University Press, 1956), pp. 22–27.

[14] A Russian text of this document, citing a Vietnamese text in *Organizational Bulletin of the Democratic Republic of Viet-Nam*, No. 1 (September 29, 1945), appears in O. A. Arturov, ed., *Demokraticheskaya Respublika Vietnam: Konstitutsia, Zakonodatelnia Akti, Dokumenti* (Moscow: Izdatelstvo Inostrannoi Literaturi, 1955), pp. 15–16. This valuable collection contains a number of documents, in Russian, dealing with DRV internal matters during the period before 1954.

In the south things went differently, for the revolution was not so popular in Cochin China as in Tonkin, and the revolutionary movement itself was badly split among a number of factions. British forces reached Saigon on September 13; their activities during the fall of 1945 were described in the report which Vice-Admiral Lord Louis Mountbatten, Supreme Allied Commander South East Asia, submitted to the Combined Chiefs of Staff in 1947 (Document 29). The British forces under the command of Major General Douglas D. Gracey viewed their role as the maintenance of law and order until such time as French forces could relieve them. General Gracey refused to deal with the Viet Minh, represented by the "Provisional Executive Committee of the South Viet-Nam Republic," as a governmental body and adopted rules which served not only to help maintain law and order but also to inhibit political activity on the part of the Vietnamese population.[15] His policy made it impossible for the Viet Minh to consolidate their power in the south and thus effectively limited their sphere of control to the Chinese-occupied areas north of the 16th parallel and to the rugged areas of southern Annam, particularly the provinces of Quang Ngai, Quang Nam, and Binh Dinh. The situation was much worsened when, in the early morning hours of September 23, French troops recently released from Japanese internment staged a coup against the Viet Minh and returned Saigon to French rule.[16] The DRV protested that action to the British Prime Minister (Document 30).

General Gracey's activities and those of the French brought about armed opposition from the Viet Minh, accompanied by fighting among Vietnamese groups themselves. In an effort to enforce his authority, General Gracey resorted not only to the use of French forces but, in several cases, to the use of Japanese forces as well. Meanwhile new French forces and officials began to arrive in Indochina and France began to take governing responsibility from the British. On October 9 an exchange of letters in London between British Foreign Secretary

15 Notable in this regard was General Gracey's proclamation of September 21; text in Great Britain, Parliament, Papers by Command, *Documents Relating to British Involvement in the Indo-China Conflict, 1945–1965* (London: Her Majesty's Stationery Office, Cmnd. 2834, 1965), pp. 52–53. A comprehensive summary of the proclamation is in Document 29, paragraph 25.

16 A communiqué on the incident issued by the delegate of the French High Commissioner in Saigon was broadcast by Radio Ceylon in English on September 26, 1945, 8:30 A.M., E.W.T. [Eastern War Time]: "The reinstatement of the French administration in Saigon began on the morning of September 23 and was completed within 24 hours. It has been effected without any unprovoked incident. The French troops suffered only slight casualties when action was taken to eject a group of subversive elements armed with Japanese automatic weapons. The town is calm and the French administration has commenced to function."

Bevin and French Ambassador René Massagli defined relations between the forces of the two countries in southern Indochina; although the text was not published, the terms of the agreement rapidly became known (Document 31). In a written answer to a question in the House of Commons on October 24, Bevin justified British policy as an interim measure pending reassertion of French authority (Document 33).

In an October 20 speech, John Carter Vincent, Director of the Office of Far Eastern Affairs in the Department of State, publicly defined American policy (Document 32). Reportedly this statement encouraged the DRV to hope for American assistance or mediation in attaining Vietnamese independence from the French.[17] In an effort to stabilize their own authority and to gather maximum domestic and foreign support for their opposition to the return of French rule, the leaders of the ICP determined that the Party should be dissolved as an overt organization. That decision was made official on November 11 (Document 34). As the situation in the south continued, from the Viet Minh point of view, to deteriorate with the consolidation of French authority, the Viet Minh came to view the struggle as a "resistance war" against the return of colonial rule. The French, by contrast, stressed their rights of sovereignty and emphasized the benefits their rule would bring to the Vietnamese.[18]

14. *Emperor Bao Dai: Imperial Proclamation of Vietnamese Independence* *
   March 11, 1945

In view of the world situation, and particularly that of Asia, the Government of Viet-Nam publicly proclaims that from today the

* *Source:* Philippe Devillers, *Histoire du Việt-Nam de 1940 à 1952* (Paris: Editions du Seuil, 1952, p. 125); copyright 1952, reprinted by permission of Editions du Seuil and The Bobbs-Merrill Company, Inc. Translation by the editor. The proclamation was broadcast by Tokyo, DOMEI, in English to the Pacific Zone, March 11, 1945, 11:00 A.M., E.W.T., with somewhat different wording.

17 On October 15 Radio Hanoi broadcast the text of a letter from Ho Chi Minh to President Truman, including a request for DRV representation on the Far Eastern Advisory Commission. Only fragments of this letter are available from radio monitoring sources. According to some authorities another letter was sent to President Truman after the Vincent statement; if so, the editor has been unable to locate a text.

18 For contrasting statements of position at this time, see Ho Chi Minh's "Speech Delivered in the First Days of the Resistance War in South Viet-Nam," in Ho Chi Minh, *Selected Works* (4 vols., Hanoi: 1960–1962), Vol. III, pp. 48–50; and High Commissioner d'Argenlieu's speech of December 9 in Saigon, in France, Ministère des Colonies, *Bulletin Hebdomadaire d'Information*, No. 55 (December 17, 1945), pp. 3–6.

protectorate treaty with France is abrogated and that the country reassumes its rights to independence.

Viet-Nam will endeavor to develop itself by its own means so as to deserve the status of an independent State, and, considering itself as a part of Greater East Asia, will follow the directives of the Joint Declaration of Greater East Asia so that its resources may contribute to the common prosperity. Therefore the Government of Viet-Nam puts its trust in the loyalty of Japan and is determined to collaborate with that country to attain the aforesaid objective.

It is so proclaimed.

BAO DAI

Hué, the 27th day of the 1st month of the 20th year of Bao Dai (March 11, 1945)

[Countersigned by the Council of Ministers]

Interior: PHAM QUYNH   Justice: BUI BANG DOAN
Finances: HO DAC KHAI   Education: TRAN THANH DAT
Rites: UNG HY   Economy: TRUONG NHU DINH

15. *Memorandum of Conversation with President Roosevelt by Charles Taussig, Adviser on Caribbean Affairs [Extract]* *
    March 15, 1945

[The conversation was on the subject of the United Nations Conference in San Francisco, particularly the matter of trusteeship. Only the three paragraphs directly relevant to Indochina are printed here.]

THE PEOPLES OF EAST ASIA

The President said he was concerned about the brown people in the East. He said that there are 1,100,000,000 brown people. In many Eastern countries, they are ruled by a handful of whites and they resent it. Our goal must be to help them achieve independence—1,100,-000,000 potential enemies are dangerous. He said he included the 450,000,000 Chinese in that. He then added, Churchill doesn't understand this.

* *Source:* United States, Department of State, *Foreign Relations of the United States, 1945* (9 vols., Washington: Government Printing Office, 1967–1969), Vol. I, p. 124.

INDO-CHINA AND NEW CALEDONIA

The President said he thought we might have some difficulties with France in the matter of colonies. I said that I thought that was quite probable and it was also probable the British would use France as a "stalking horse."

I asked the President if he had changed his ideas on French Indo-China as he had expressed them to us at the luncheon with Stanley.[1] He said no he had not changed his ideas; that French Indo-China and New Caledonia should be taken from France and put under a trustee-ship. The President hesitated a moment and then said—well if we can get the proper pledge from France to assume for herself the obligations of a trustee, then I would agree to France retaining these colonies with the proviso that independence was the ultimate goal. I asked the President if he would settle for self-government. He said no. I asked him if he would settle for dominion status. He said no—it must be independence. He said that is to be the policy and you can quote me in the State Department.

CHARLES TAUSSIG

16. *Declaration of the Provisional French Government Concerning Indochina* *
    March 24, 1945

The Government of the Republic has always considered that Indochina was destined to hold a special place in the organization of the French community and to enjoy there liberty appropriate to its degree of evolution and to its capabilities. The promise of this was made in the declaration of December 8, 1943.[2] Shortly afterwards the general principles set forth at Brazzaville clarified the intention of the Government.[3]

Today Indochina is fighting: the mixed French and Indochinese military units, the elites, and the peoples of Indochina—who cannot be deceived by the maneuvers of the enemy—are lavishing their courage and deploying their resistance for the triumph of the cause which

---

* *Source:* France, *Journal Officiel de la République Française, Ordonnances et Decréts,* March 25, 1945, pp. 1606–1607. Translation by the editor.
[1] Col. Oliver Stanley, British Secretary of State for the Colonies, who had lunched with the President and Mr. Taussig on January 16, 1945.
[2] Document 4.   [3] See Note 27, p. 20.

is that of the entire French community. Thus Indochina is acquiring additional rights to receive the place for which it is destined.

Confirmed by events in its earlier intentions, the Government considers that it should now define what the status of Indochina will be when it is freed from the invader.

The Indochinese Federation will form with France and the other parts of the Community a "French Union," whose interests outside the Union will be represented by France. Within that union Indochina will enjoy appropriate liberty.

The nationals of the Indochinese Federation will be Indochinese citizens and citizens of the French Union. On that basis, without discrimination by race, religion, or origin and with equality based on merit, they will have access to all the federal posts and positions in Indochina and in the Union.

The conditions according to which the Indochinese Federation will participate in the federal organs of the French Union as well as the status of citizen of the French Union will be determined by the Constituent Assembly.

Indochina will have its own federal government, presided over by the Governor General and composed of ministers, responsible to him, who will be chosen from among both the Indochinese and the French resident in Indochina. With the Governor General, a Council of State composed of the most respected personalities of the Federation will be charged with the preparation of federal laws and regulations. An Assembly elected according to the method of suffrage most appropriate to each of the countries of the Federation, and where French interests will be represented, will vote taxes of all kinds as well as the federal budget and will deliberate bills. Commercial and good-neighbor treaties concerning the Indochinese Federation will be submitted to its examination.

Freedom of the press, freedom of association, freedom of assembly, freedom of thought and of belief and democratic liberties in general will form the basis of Indochinese laws.

The five countries which compose the Indochinese Federation and which are distinguished from each other by civilization, race, and traditions, will keep their own character within the Federation.

In the interests of each the Governor General will be the arbiter of all. Local governments will be improved or reformed; the nationals of each country will have preference for the posts and positions in that country.

With the assistance of the Metropole and in the interest of the general system of defense of the French Union, the Indochinese Federation will organize land, sea, and air forces, in which the Indochinese will have access to all ranks equally according to ability with personnel coming from the Metropole or other parts of the French Union.

Social and cultural progress will be continued [*poursuivi*] and accelerated in the same direction as political and administrative progress.

The French Union will take the necessary measures to make primary education obligatory and effective, and to develop secondary and higher education. The study of local language and thought will be closely associated to French culture.

Through the implementation of an efficient and independent system of work inspection and through the development of trade unions, the well-being, the social education, and the emancipation of Indochinese workers will be continually carried on.

Within the French Union the Indochinese Federation will enjoy an economic autonomy permitting it to attain its full agricultural, industrial, and commercial development, and particularly to achieve the industrialization which will allow Indochina to cope with its demographic situation. Thanks to that autonomy and in the absence of any discriminatory regulations, Indochina will develop its commercial relations with all other countries and especially with China, with which Indochina and the entire French Union intend to have close and friendly relations.

The status of Indochina, as it has just been outlined, will be put into final form after consultations with the qualified organs of liberated Indochina.

Thus the Indochinese Federation, within the peaceful system of the French Union, will enjoy the liberty and the organization necessary to the development of all its resources. It will equally be able to fulfill the role which is returning to it in the Pacific and to make the most of the quality of its elites throughout the whole of the French Union.

17. *Telegram from Acting Secretary of State Joseph C. Grew to Ambassador Jefferson Caffery in Paris ** *May 9, 1945*

1949. Following telegram dated May 8 received from the Secretary [4] at San Francisco,[5] is repeated for your information.

"The subject of Indo-China came up in a recent conversation I had with Bidault [6] and Bonnet.[7] The latter remarked that although the French Government interprets Mr. Welles' statement of 1942 [8] concerning the restoration of French sovereignty over the French Empire as including Indo-China, the press continues to imply that a special status will be reserved for this colonial area. It was made quite clear to Bidault that the record is entirely innocent of any official statement of this government questioning, even by implication, French sovereignty over Indo-China. Certain elements of American public opinion, however, condemned French governmental policies and practices in Indo-China. Bidault seemed relieved and has no doubt cabled Paris that he received renewed assurances of our recognition of French sovereignty over that area."

GREW

* *Source:* United States, Department of State, *Foreign Relations of the United States, 1945* (9 vols., Washington: Government Printing Office, 1967–1969), Vol. VI, p. 307. Acting Secretary Grew informed Ambassador Hurley in China of the substance of Secretary Stettinius' telegram in a June 2, 1945, message; text in *ibid.*, p. 312.

4 Edward R. Stettinius, Jr.

5 Footnote in the original: "The United Nations Conference on International Organization met at San Francisco from April 25 to June 26, 1945."

6 Footnote in the original: "Georges Bidault, French Minister for Foreign Affairs."

7 Henri Bonnet, French Ambassador to the United States.

8 Footnote in the original: "For text of note dated April 13, 1942, from Acting Secretary of State Sumner Welles to Ambassador Gaston Henry-Haye, see *Foreign Relations,* 1942, Vol. II, p. 561, or Department of State *Bulletin,* April 18, 1942, p. 335." The note included the statement: "The Government of the United States recognizes the sovereign jurisdiction of the people of France over the territory of France and over French possessions overseas. The Government of the United States fervently hopes that it may see the reestablishment of the independence of France and of the integrity of French territory."

18. *Telegram from the Department of State to Ambassador Hurley, Chungking [Extract]* *
    June 7, 1945

The President thanks you (FOR THE AMBASSADOR FROM THE ACT-ING SECRETARY [9]) for your considered telegram [10] in regard to the problems presented by the reestablishment of French control in Indo-china and the British desire to reoccupy Hongkong and fully appreciates the difficulties in which you and General Wedemeyer may be placed on account of the lack of specific directions in respect to both of these problems which have been under careful study both here and in connection with the discussions at San Francisco.[11]

I have also received your message no. 1548 of June 6 [12] and regret that there has been delay in replying to your earlier one [13] owning [*sic*] to the study which has been required of these matters in connection with present developments at the Conference. The President has asked me to say that there has been no basic change in the policy in respect to these two questions and that the present policy is as follows:

The President assumes that you are familiar with the statement made by the Secretary of State on April 3, 1945 with the approval of President Roosevelt in which Mr. Stettinius declared that as a result of the Yalta discussions the "trusteeship structure, it was felt, should be defined to permit the placing under it of such of the territories taken from the enemy in this war, as might be agreed upon at a later date,

---

* *Source:* Message No. 873, of June 7, 1945, from Washington to the American Embassy, Chungking, as received in Chungking on June 10, in the Patrick J. Hurley Collection, Western History Collections, University of Oklahoma, pp. 1–3. Several typographical errors in the original have been corrected. Used by permission of the University of Oklahoma Library.

[9] Joseph C. Grew.   [10] Of May 28, 1945; for citation, see Note 5, p. 25.

[11] I.e., the United Nations Conference on International Organization.

[12] Copy in the Patrick J. Hurley Collection, Western History Collections, University of Oklahoma. The message contains the statement: "This morning I received definite information, through another source, that the State Department has advised the War Department of a change in policy in regard to Indochina." See also May 23, 1945, memorandum from H. Freeman Matthews, Director of the Office of European Affairs, Department of State, to the State-War-Navy Coordinating Committee, in *United States, Department of State, Foreign Relations of the United States, 1945* (9 vols., Washington: Government Printing Office, 1967–1969), Vol. VI, pp. 309–311.

[13] Probably Hurley's message No. 809 of June 1, cited in the June 6 message mentioned earlier in the same sentence.

and also such other territories as might voluntarily be placed under trusteeship." [14] The position thus publicly announced has been confirmed by the conversations which are now taking place in San Francisco in regard to trusteeships. Throughout these discussions the American delegation has insisted upon the necessity of providing for a progressive measure of self government for all dependent peoples looking toward their eventual independence or incorporation in some form of federation according to circumstances and the ability of the peoples to assume these responsibilities. Such decisions would preclude the establishment of a trusteeship in Indochina except with the consent of the French Govt. [*sic*] The latter seems unlikely. Nevertheless it is the President's intention at some appropriate time to ask that the French Govt. give some positive indication of its intentions in regard to the establishment of basic liberties and increasing measures of self government in Indochina before formulating further declarations of policy in this respect.

In the meantime the President has explained to the French Foreign Minister [15] that whereas we welcome French participation in the war against Japan the determination of the extent that it would be practiced [*sic*] and helpful to have French forces join with us in such operations must be left to the Commander-in-Chief, United States Army Forces, Pacific.[16] The Joint Chiefs of Staff are at present engaged in a study of the possibilities of French help along the lines of the following suggestions: [17]

(a). While avoiding so far as practicable unnecessary or long term commitments with regard to the amount or character of any assistance which the United States may give to French resistance forces in Indo-

[14] Text in United States, Department of State, *Bulletin,* XII (April 8, 1945), pp. 600–601.

[15] Georges Bidault. The conversation took place at the White House on May 19, and was prompted by a May 15 message from General de Gaulle to President Truman expressing "our extreme desire to have French forces participate at the side of American forces in the decisive campaign against Japan." Relevant documents, including the de Gaulle message, are in *Foreign Relations of the United States, 1945,* Vol. VI, pp. 307–311.

[16] General Douglas MacArthur.

[17] The following two paragraphs are a verbatim repetition of the policy recommended by Acting Secretary of State Grew to President Truman in a May 16, 1945, memorandum dealing with the United States response to General de Gaulle's May 15, 1945, request for French participation in the war against Japan. It was stated that this policy "is in harmony with the known views of the Joint Chiefs of Staff." Text of Grew's memorandum is in *Foreign Relations of the United States, 1945,* Vol. VI, pp. 307–308.

china, this Govt. should continue to afford such assistance as does not interfere with the requirements of other planned operations. Owing to the need for concentrating all our resources in the Pacific on operations already planned, large scale military operations aimed directly at the liberation of Indochina cannot, however, be contemplated at this time. American troops would not be used in Indochina except in American military operations against the Japanese.

(b). French offers of military and naval assistance in the Pacific should be considered on their military merits as bearing on the objective of defeating Japan as in the case of British and Dutch proposals. There would be no objection to furnishing of assistance to any French military or naval forces so approved, regardless of the theater of operations from which the assistance may be sent, provided such assistance does not involve a diversion of resources which the combined or joint Chiefs of Staff consider are needed elsewhere.

[The concluding three paragraphs, dealing with Hong Kong and unification of Chinese armed forces, are omitted.]

GREW (Acting)

19. *Policy Paper Prepared in the Department of State [Extracts]* *
June 22, 1945

AN ESTIMATE OF CONDITIONS IN ASIA AND THE PACIFIC AT THE CLOSE OF THE WAR IN THE FAR EAST AND THE OBJECTIVES AND POLICIES OF THE UNITED STATES

I. INTRODUCTION

[Four introductory paragraphs are omitted.]

Aside from the traditional American belief in the right of all peoples to independence, the largest possible measure of political freedom for the countries of Asia consistent with their ability to assume the

* *Source:* United States, Department of State, *Foreign Relations of the United States, 1945* (9 vols., Washington: Government Printing Office, 1967–1969), Vol. VI, pp. 557–558, 567–568. The complete text of the policy paper is in *ibid.,* pp. 556–580. The paper was prepared in response to a request by Secretary of War Henry L. Stimson, and was transmitted to him by Acting Secretary of State Joseph C. Grew on June 28. According to the Acting Secretary, "As it stands now, the paper is a policy paper representing the considered views of the Department of State as a whole" (*ibid.,* p. 556).

responsibility thereof is probably necessary in order to achieve the chief
objective of the United States in the Far East and the Pacific: continuing peace and security.

Another condition on which peace and security depend is co-
operation among the peace-minded states of the world. One of the fore-
most policies of the United States is to maintain the unity of purpose
and action of all the United Nations, especially of the leading powers.
Two of these leading powers are Great Britain and France, each of
which has dependencies in the Far East in which there is an insistent
demand for a greater measure of self-government than the parent states
have yet been willing to grant.

A problem for the United States is to harmonize, so far as possible,
its policies in regard to the two objectives: increased political freedom
for the Far East and the maintenance of the unity of the leading United
Nations in meeting this problem. The United States Government may
properly continue to state the political principle which it has frequently
announced, that dependent peoples should be given the opportunity, if
necessary after an adequate period of preparation, to achieve an increased measure of self-government, but it should avoid any course
of action which would seriously impair the unity of the major United
Nations.

The United States, also, may utilize either the force of its example
or its influence or both. Its treatment of the Philippines has earned a
rich reward for this country in the attitude and conduct of both the
Filipinos and the nationals of other Far Eastern states. The American
Government influenced the British Government to take parallel action
with it in the renunciation of extraterritoriality and other exceptional
rights in China.[18]

The solution which would best harmonize these two policies of the
United States would be a Far East progressively developing into a
group of self-governing states—independent or with Dominion status
—which would cooperate with each other and with the Western powers
on a basis of mutual self-respect and friendship. The interests of the
United States and of its European Allies require that the Far East be
removed as a source of colonial rivalry and conflict, not only between
the Great Powers, but between the Great Powers and the peoples of
Asia.

[18] Footnote in the original: "See treaties signed on January 11, 1943, Department of State Treaty Series No. 984, or 57 Stat. (pt. 2) 767, and *British and
Foreign State Papers,* Vol. CXLV, p. 129. With regard to negotiations leading
to the signing of the treaties, see *Foreign Relations,* 1942, China, pp. 268ff."

[Sections II through IV are omitted.]

V. French Indochina [19]

A. *Estimate of Conditions at the End of the War*

1. *Political*

At the end of the war, political conditions in Indochina, and especially in the north, will probably be particularly unstable. The Indochinese independence groups, which may have been working against the Japanese, will quite possibly oppose the restoration of French control. Independence sentiment in the area is believed to be increasingly strong. The Indochinese Independence League,[20] representing some ten different native political groups, is thought to carry substantial influence with between one-quarter and one-half million persons. The serious 1930 insurrection,[21] in which over 100,000 peasants actively participated, and similar insurrections which took place in the fall of 1940 indicate that the supporters of independence are neither apathetic nor supine and are willing to fight. It is believed that the French will encounter serious difficulty in overcoming this opposition and in reestablishing French control. What effect the Japanese declarations of independence for Annam,[22] Cambodia, and Luang Prabang [23] will have in the period immediately following the war cannot be estimated at this time, but clearly these declarations will make the French problem more difficult.

The French government recognizes that it will have very serious difficulties in reestablishing and maintaining its control in Indochina, and its several statements [24] regarding the future of that country show an increasing trend toward autonomy for the French administration. Even the latest statement,[25] however, shows little intention to give the Indochinese self-government. An increased measure of self-government would seem essential if the Indochinese are to be reconciled to continued French control.

---

[19] Cross-reference footnote in the original omitted.

[20] I.e., the Viet Minh.

[21] The so-called "Yen Bay Uprising" and subsequent disturbances.

[22] Viet-Nam; Document 14. "Annam" is derived from a Chinese term meaning "pacified south," and its use was generally considered offensive by the Vietnamese.

[23] Laos, more properly known historically as the "Kingdom of Luang Prabang."

[24] Notably Documents 4 and 16.   [25] Document 16.

2. *Economic*

Economically, Indochina has so far suffered least of all the countries involved in the war in the Far East. Bombing and fighting before the close of the war will probably, however, have resulted in the destruction of some of its railway system, key bridges, harbor installations, and the more important industrial and power plants. This will probably intensify already existing food shortages in the north and lack of consumer goods throughout the area.

Pre-war French policies involved economic exploitation of the colony for France. Indochina had to buy dear in the high, protected market of France and sell cheap in the unprotected markets of other nations. The French realize that this economic policy, which was very detrimental to Indochina, must be changed. They have pledged tariff autonomy and equality of tariff rates for other countries. There is no indication, however, that the French intend to pursue an open-door economic policy.

B. *International Relations*

French policy toward Indochina will be dominated by the desire to reestablish control in order to reassert her prestige in the world as a great power. This purpose will be augmented by the potent influence of the Banque de l'Indochine and other economic interests. Many French appear to recognize that it may be necessary for them to make further concessions to Indochinese self-government and autonomy primarily to assure native support but also to avoid unfriendly United States opinion. Chief French reliance, however, will continue to be placed upon the United Kingdom, which is almost as anxious as the French to see that no pre-war colonial power suffers diminution of power or prestige. Friction between France and China over Indochina will probably continue. The Chinese government, at least tacitly, is supporting the Independence League and is thought by the French, despite the Generalissimo's disclaimer of territorial ambitions,[26] to

[26] E.g., Chiang Kai-shek's statement to President Roosevelt at Cairo; see Document 3. According to General de Gaulle, Chiang Kai-shek received the French Ambassador in Chungking, General Pechkoff, in October 1944 and told him: "I promise you that we have no interest in Indochina. And if at any time we can help you restore French authority there, we shall do so gladly. Tell General de Gaulle that this is our policy. But let him also consider it as a personal commitment to him on my part." Again according to de Gaulle, Chinese Foreign Minister T. V. Soong made similar statements to him in Washington in August 1945; see *The War Memoirs of Charles de Gaulle, Volume III, Salvation: 1944–1946*, Richard Howard, trans. (New York: Simon and Schuster, 1960), p. 261.

desire to dominate, if not annex, northern Indochina. French economic policies interfered with all nations trading with China through its access to the sea at Haiphong. China particularly will look for a complete reversal of French policy in this respect.

The Thai consider the territory acquired from Indochina in 1941 as theirs by legal and historic right,[27] but they have indicated they will accept any border determined by an Anglo-American commission. The French consider the territory theirs and there will doubtless be border conflict unless a fair settlement is reached which eliminates causes for serious discontent.

C. *United States Policy*

The United States recognizes French sovereignty over Indochina. It is, however, the general policy of the United States to favor a policy which would allow colonial peoples an opportunity to prepare themselves for increased participation in their own government with eventual self-government as the goal.

[Sections VI through XI are omitted.]

20. *Viet Minh Aide-Mémoire Transmitted to the French Mission 5 in Kunming through an Agent of the Office of Strategic Services * July 1945*

We, the Viet Minh League, request that the following points be proclaimed by the French and observed in future policy in French Indochina.

1. A parliament will be elected by universal suffrage. It will legislate

---

* *Source:* Philippe Devillers, *Histoire du Viêt-Nam de 1940 à 1952* (Paris: Editions du Seuil, 1952), p. 134; copyright 1952, reprinted by permission of Editions du Seuil and The Bobbs-Merrill Company, Inc. Translation by the editor. The message was reportedly drafted in English. It also appears in Jean Sainteny, *Histoire d'une Paix Manquée: Indochine 1945–1947* (Paris: Amiot-Dumont, 1953), p. 57, in a slightly different French version. There appears to be no reason to doubt its authenticity, although whether it reflected the actual views and desires of Viet Minh leaders is open to question. The "independence" clause, No. 2, was referred to by the new French High Commissioner, Admiral d'Argenlieu, in an interview in Calcutta on September 19, so it would appear that French policy makers were aware of the message. See Agence France Presse in French Morse, September 19, 1945, 10:06 A.M., E.W.T.

27 This refers to the territories ceded by France to Thailand under Japanese pressure in 1941. They were returned after the war, and the border questions were settled by an agreement of November 16, 1946. The settlement was brought about in large part because of an implicit French threat to veto Thailand's application for admission to the United Nations.

for the country. A French governor will exercise the functions of president until independence is assured us. This president will choose a cabinet or a group of councillors accepted by the parliament. The precise powers of all these organs can be delineated in the future.

2. Independence will be given to this country in a minimum of five years and a maximum of ten.

3. The natural resources of this country will return to its inhabitants after equitable compensation to the present holders. France will benefit from economic privileges.

4. All the liberties proclaimed by the United Nations will be guaranteed to the Indochinese.

5. The sale of opium will be forbidden.

We hope that these terms will be judged acceptable by the French government.

21. *Telegram from President Truman for Generalissimo Chiang Kai-shek, Transmitted via Ambassador Hurley ** *
   August 1, 1945

Top secret from the President to Ambassador Hurley.

Please deliver the following message from me to Generalissimo Chiang Kai-shek.

"1. At the Potsdam Conference the Prime Minister of Great Britain and I, in consultation with the Combined Chiefs of Staff, have had under consideration future military operations in South-East Asia.

"2. On the advice of the Combined Chiefs of Staff we have reached the conclusion that for operational purposes it is desirable to include that portion of French Indo-China lying south of 16° north latitude in the Southeast Asia Command. This arrangement would leave in the China Theater that part of Indo-China which covers the flank of

* *Source:* United States, Department of State, *Foreign Relations of the United States,* THE CONFERENCE OF BERLIN (THE POTSDAM CONFERENCE), 1945 (2 vols., Washington: Government Printing Office, 1960), Vol. II, p. 1321. The text of the telegram also appears in *Foreign Relations of the United States, 1945* (9 vols., Washington: Government Printing Office, 1967–1969), Vol. VII, pp. 143–144. Chiang Kai-shek's affirmative reply, with reservations about a similar division in Thailand and mutual exchange of information on operations, appears in *ibid.,* pp. 149–150. It was transmitted through Ambassador Hurley on August 10. A note with the text printed here reads: "There is in the Truman Papers a typed draft of a telegram from Attlee to Chiang on which manuscript changes have been made to convert it into a message from Truman to Hurley which is substantially identical with the message here printed as received in Chungking."

projected Chinese operations in China and would at the same time enable Admiral Mountbatten to develop operations in the southern half of Indo-China.

"3. I greatly hope that the above conclusions will recommend themselves to Your Excellency and that, for the purpose of facilitating operations against the common enemy, Your Excellency will feel able to concur in the proposed arrangements.[28]

"4. I understand that the Prime Minister of Great Britain is addressing a communication to Your Excellency in a similar sense.

"Signed HARRY S. TRUMAN"

22. *Telegram from Secretary of State James Byrnes to Ambassador Caffery in Paris* *
    August 14, 1945

Secret for the Ambassador: Please inform Bidault [29] that under the plan which Japanese have been ordered to follow [30] they are to sur-

---

* *Source:* Message 1257 of August 14, 1945, from the Secretary of State to the American Ambassador in Chungking, in the Patrick J. Hurley Collection, Western History Collections, University of Oklahoma. Used by permission of the University of Oklahoma Library. A text of this telegram, omitting the last two sentences, appears in United States, Department of State, *Foreign Relations of the United States, 1945* (9 vols., Washington: Government Printing Office, 1967–1969), Vol. VII, pp. 499–500. For documentation on a subsequent French request to have Indo-China comprise a single surrender zone, the British zone, and Chinese reluctance to endorse this, see *ibid.*, pp. 513–514. The creation of a Chinese occupation zone in northern Indochina was the source of considerable ill-feeling on the part of the French. See Note 11, p. 28.

[28] Footnote in the original omitted.

[29] French Foreign Minister Georges Bidault.

[30] General Order No. 1. Text in Vice-Admiral The Earl Mountbatten of Burma, *Post Surrender Tasks: Section E of the Report to the Combined Chiefs of Staff by the Supreme Allied Commander South East Asia, 1943–1945* (London: Her Majesty's Stationery Office, 1969), Appendix H, pp. 313–315. The relevant sections are paragraphs 1.(A) and 1.(C): "(A) The senior Japanese Commander and all ground, sea, air and auxiliary forces within China (excluding Manchuria), Formosa and French Indo-China north of 16 degrees north latitude shall surrender to Generalissimo Chiang Kai-shek"; and "(C) The senior Japanese Commander and all ground, sea, air and auxiliary forces within the Andamans, the Nicobars, Burma, Thailand (Siam), French Indo-China south of 16 degrees north latitude, Malaya, Borneo, the Netherlands Indies, New Guinea, the Bismarcks and the Solomon Islands shall surrender to the Supreme Allied Commander, South-East Asia Command, or Commanding General, Australian Forces—the exact breakdown between Mountbatten and Australia to be arranged between them. Details of this paragraph will then be prepared by the Supreme Commander for the Allied Powers."

render in Northern part of Indo China to Chiang Kai-shek and in the Southern part to Mountbatten. You should emphasize that this division is a purely operational matter based on the available forces in the area and has no political significance whatever.

You should add that we are suggesting to the British and Chinese governments that they invite French representatives to be present on the occasion of the acceptance of the Japanese surrender in Indo China. The French may wish to take the question up directly with those governments.

Ambassadors Winant [31] and Hurley [32] are being instructed to support any representations which their French colleagues may make to this end. Sent to Paris repeated to London and Chungking with the following opening:

"Please be guided by instructions contained in final paragraph of the following telegram which has been sent to Paris."

BYRNES

23. *Decisions of the People's Congress* *
   August 16, 1945

1. In Europe, Italian and German fascism is dead and the movement of new democracy is progressing.

After having played a great part in the annihilation of fascism in Europe, the Soviet Union declared war on Japan on August 8, 1945, resolute to wage, together with the Allies, the decisive battle against the fascists in Asia.

The Japanese fascists have surrendered unconditionally. The Allied forces will soon arrive at wherever the Japanese troops are stationed.

The movement of national liberation and new democracy has grown in strength and scope all over the world.

2. In our country, Japanese power is falling to pieces. Availing itself of the opportunity, the Insurrection Committee, created by the General Committee of the Viet Minh Front, has ordered our Liberation forces to disarm the routed Japanese troops and to widen their sphere of activity.

3. The People's Congress appeals to the whole people and revo-

---

* *Source: Breaking Our Chains: Documents on the Vietnamese Revolution of August 1945* (Hanoi: Foreign Languages Publishing House, 1960), pp. 68–70.

[31] John G. Winant, Ambassador to the United Kingdom.

[32] General Patrick J. Hurley, Ambassador to the Republic of China.

lutionary organizations to rise up, unite together in good time and struggle for the carrying out of the following ten points: [33]

a. To seize power and build up a Democratic Republic of Viet Nam on the basis of complete independence.

b. To arm the people. To develop the Viet Nam Liberation Army.

c. To confiscate the property of the invaders and the traitors, nationalize it or distribute it to the poor according to the case.

d. To abolish the old system of taxation established by the French and the Japanese, to set up an equitable and rational one.

e. To promulgate democratic rights:

Human rights

Rights to property

Civil rights: universal suffrage, democratic freedoms (freedom of conscience, thought, speech, association, and movement, equality between nationalities and the sexes).

f. To re-distribute communal land equitably, to reduce land rent and interest, defer payment of loans and organize relief.

g. To promulgate labour regulations: eight-hour-work-day, minimum wages and establishment of social insurance.

h. To build up the national economy, develop agriculture and found the National Bank.

i. To organize national education, to fight illiteracy, popularize and make compulsory primary education. To build up a new culture.

j. To maintain good relations with the Allies and the weak and small nations with a view to winning their sympathy and support.

4. The People's Congress decided upon the setting up of the Viet Nam National Liberation Committee to lead our revolution for national liberation to victory. The Committee is tantamount to the Provisional Government of Viet Nam, pending the founding of an official government. This committee will, on behalf of the people, take in hand relations with foreign countries, and the direction of all internal affairs.

5. We are in an emergency and must act in good time. The National Liberation Committee gives the Insurrection Committee full power of command.

6. The Japanese defeat will not of itself bring independence to our country. Numerous obstacles and difficulties will crop up. We must be clear-headed and resolute. Clear-headed in avoiding all that can harm our cause and resolute to win complete independence. In the present

---

[33] Sometimes referred to as the "Ten Point Viet Minh Policy."

post-war international situation, a people that is united and determined to demand its independence will certainly win it. We will be victorious.

24. *Letter from Emperor Bao Dai to General Charles de Gaulle* *
   August 18, 1945 — *Bao Đại a VN se Frenchman,*

I address myself to the people of France, to the country of my youth. I address myself as well to its chief and liberator, and I wish to speak as a friend rather than as Chief of State.

You have suffered too much during four deadly years not to understand that the Vietnamese people, who have a history of twenty centuries and an often glorious past, no longer desire and can no longer endure any foreign domination or government.

You would understand still better if you could see what is happening here, if you could feel the will for independence which has been smoldering in the hearts of all and which no human force can hold in check any longer. Even if you were to come to reestablish French government here it would not be obeyed: each village would be a nest of resistance, each former collaborator an enemy, and your officials and your colonists themselves would ask to leave that unbreathable atmosphere.

I beg you to understand that the only means of safeguarding French interests and the spiritual influence of France in Indochina is to recognize unreservedly the independence of Viet-Nam and to renounce any idea of re-establishing French sovereignty or French administration here in any form.

We would be able to understand each other so easily and to become friends if you would stop hoping to become our masters again.

In making this appeal to the well known idealism of the French people and to the great wisdom of their leader, we hope that the peace and

* *Source:* Philippe Devillers, *Histoire du Viêt-Nam de 1940 à 1952* (Paris: Editions du Seuil, 1952), p. 138, citing *Viêt-Nam Tan Bao,* Hué, August 20, 1945; copyright 1952, reprinted by permission of Editions du Seuil and The Bobbs-Merrill Company, Inc. Translation by the editor. An identical French text of this document is in Jean Sainteny, *Histoire d'une Paix Manquée: Indochine 1945–1947* (Paris: Amiot-Dumont, 1953), pp. 108–109. On August 20, Emperor Bao Dai wrote President Truman, who was soon to meet with de Gaulle. Bao Dai stated: "The French people must yield to the principle of equity which the powerful American nation has proclaimed and defends. France must recognize this with good grace in order to avoid the disaster of a war breaking out on the territory of our country." Bao Dai asked the President to transmit the same letter to the governments of Britain, China, and Russia. A text appears without citation in Chester L. Cooper, *The Lost Crusade: America in Vietnam* (New York: Dodd, Mead & Company, 1970), p. 46.

[handwritten marginalia: Truman paid no attention! he got other.]

the joy which has come for all the peoples of the world will be equally ensured to all the inhabitants of Indochina, native as well as foreign.

BAO DAI

25. *Bao Dai's Rescript on His Abdication* *
   August 26, 1945

The happiness of the Vietnamese people!

The independence of Viet-Nam!

To achieve these aims, We have declared ourselves ready for all sacrifices, and We desire that Our sacrifice be beneficial to the Fatherland.

Considering that the union of all Our compatriots at this moment is a necessity for Our Fatherland, We reminded Our people on August 22: "At this decisive hour of the national history, union signifies life and division death."

In view of the mighty democratic impulse which is developing in the North of Our Realm, We fear that a conflict between the North and the South would be inevitable if We await the opening of a National Congress to come to Our decision. We are aware that this conflict, if it ever took place, would plunge all Our people into suffering and present a good opportunity to the invaders.

We cannot keep ourselves from a certain feeling of melancholy at the thought of Our glorious ancestors who fought without respite for 400 years in order to extend Our country from Thuan-Hoa to Ha-tien. We cannot keep from feeling a certain regret at the thought of Our twenty years of rule, during which We have been in an impossible position to render any appreciable service to Our country.

In spite of that, and strong in Our convictions, We have decided to abdicate, and We hand over power to the democratic Republican Government.

* *Source:* Philippe Devillers, *Histoire du Viêt-Nam de 1940 à 1952* (Paris: Editions du Seuil, 1952), pp. 139–140; copyright 1952, reprinted by permission of Editions du Seuil and The Bobbs-Merrill Company, Inc. Translation by the editor. There are a number of English language texts of this document available from Viet Minh sources, but the translations are generally poor. The Devillers text appears to be the best available. There is also some question as to the date of the Rescript, some sources giving it as August 24 or 26. It seems likely that it was drafted on August 24, the day the Privy Council telegraphed the Viet Minh in Hanoi to inform them of Bao Dai's willingness to abdicate. The Viet Minh delegation to accept the abdication arrived in Hué on August 25, and apparently the Rescript was approved and signed later that day. See Ellen J. Hammer, *The Struggle for Indochina* (Stanford, Cal.: Stanford University Press, 1954), pp. 103–104.

At the moment of leaving Our throne, We have only three wishes to express:

1. We request the new government to take care of the dynastic temples and royal tombs.

2. We request the new government to treat fraternally all the parties and groups who have fought for the independence of the country, even though they do not closely follow the popular movement; this is to give them the opportunity to participate in the reconstruction of the country and to show them that the new regime is founded on the absolute union of the entire population.

3. We invite all the parties and groups, all the classes of society as well as the royal family,[34] to join together to support without reservation the democratic Government in order to consolidate the national independence.

As for us, We have known much bitterness during twenty years of rule. Henceforth We are happy to be a free citizen in an independent country. We will not permit anybody to abuse Our name or the name of the royal family to sow discord among Our compatriots.

Long live the independence of Viet-Nam.

Long live our Democratic Republic.

Hué, Kien-trung Palace, August 25, 1945

(Signed) BAO DAI

---

[34] Footnote in the original: "A message to the imperial family follows the rescript: 'Having adopted the slogan "the people before all" and having declared that I prefer to be a simple citizen of an independent State than king of a subjugated nation, I have decided to abdicate and to turn over power to a government capable of directing all the forces of the country toward the conclusion of national independence and the amelioration of the lot (lit., the pursuit of happiness) of our compatriots.'

" 'Independence for the country. Happiness for the people. For these eight words, and during 80 years, so many of our brothers and our sisters have sacrificed their life in the jungle, the forests, and the prisons that compared to the sacrifices of these thousands of heros and heroines my abdication is only a very little thing.'

" 'That is why I am sure that after having read my last rescript, given on the occasion of my abdication, all my relatives will place their duty toward the Fatherland before their love for our Family, and will unite closely with our compatriots in order to help the Democratic Government consolidate the independence of the country. It is only in this generous manner that they will demonstrate their loyalty toward me and their love for the ancestors.' Signed: BAO DAI."

26. *Telegram to the Department of State from Max W. Bishop,
Secretary of the American Commission at New Delhi* *
August 29, 1945

FROM BISHOP

Extension of SEAC (Southeastern Asia Command) theater to include Indochina south of 16 degrees, early dispatch of SEAC (Southeastern Asia Command) military mission to Dalat/Saigon, and SEAC (Southeastern Asia Command) plans to establish a "control commission" at Saigon make it highly desirable that I be able to inform General Wheeler [35] of American policy toward and objectives in regard to Indochina and of role if any which Department may wish American personnel to play in order to attain implementation of policies.

Immediate problems appear to fall mainly into two categories: (A) war problems, liquidation of Jap forces and their return to Japan and (B) occupation problems, preservation of order, restoration of civil govt., protection American interests, obtaining intelligence, etc. Department's guidance requested by telegraph.

MERRELL

27. *Telegram from the Department of State to Max W. Bishop,
Secretary of the American Commission at New Delhi* †
August 30, 1945

FOR BISHOP

US has no thought of opposing the reestablishment of French control in Indochina (REURTEL 709, August 29) and no official statement by US GOVT has questioned even by implication French sovereignty over Indochina. However, it is not the policy of this GOVT to assist the French to reestablish their control over Indochina by force and the willingness of the US to see French control reestablished assumes that French claim to have the support of the population of Indochina is borne out by future events.

* *Source:* Telegram No. 709, dated August 29, 1945, from the American Commission at New Delhi to the Secretary of State; declassified and released to the editor by the Department of State, August 1969.

† *Source:* Telegram No. 657, dated August 30, 1945, from the Secretary of State to the American Mission at New Delhi; declassified and released to the editor by the Department of State, July 1969.

[35] Lt. General R. A. Wheeler, U.S. Army, Chief of Staff to Admiral Mountbatten.

Under (A) the role of American personnel should not exceed the Allied effort to complete the surrender of Japanese forces.

Under (B) American personnel should act as observers to keep US GOVT fully informed.

BYRNES [36]

28. *Declaration of Independence of the Democratic Republic of Viet-Nam* *
   September 2, 1945

All men are created equal. They are endowed by their Creator with certain inalienable rights, among these are Life, Liberty and the pursuit of Happiness.

This immortal statement was made in the Declaration of Independence of the United States of America in 1776. In a broader sense, this means: All the peoples on the earth are equal from birth, all the peoples have a right to live, to be happy and free.

The Declaration of the French Revolution made in 1791 on the Rights of Man and the Citizen also states: "All men are born free and with equal rights, and must always remain free and have equal rights."

Those are undeniable truths.

Nevertheless, for more than eighty years, the French imperialists, abusing the standard of Liberty, Equality and Fraternity, have violated our Fatherland and oppressed our fellow-citizens. They have acted contrary to the ideals of humanity and justice.

In the field of politics, they have deprived our people of every democratic liberty.

They have enforced inhuman laws; they have set up three distinct political regimes in the North, the Centre and the South of Viet Nam

Ho was ashamed the equality *Obama — he personally had always been denied*

---

* *Source: Breaking Our Chains: Documents on the Vietnamese Revolution of August 1945* (Hanoi: Foreign Languages Publishing House, 1960), pp. 94–97. Several typographical errors in the original have been corrected. There are numerous English texts of the Declaration of Independence from Viet Minh and North Vietnamese sources. The one reproduced here, which also appears verbatim in Volume III of Ho Chi Minh's *Selected Works* (4 vols., Hanoi: Foreign Languages Publishing House, 1961–1962), pp. 17–21, is apparently the version now accepted as official. The others differ in wording rather than in substance, although the wording is, if anything, stronger in some other versions (e.g., Vietnam News Service, *Vietnam: A New Stage in Her History* [Bangkok: A "Vietnam News" Publication, June 1947], pp. 3–5). The Declaration was read publicly by Ho Chi Minh at a rally in Ba Dinh Square in Hanoi on September 2; its inclusion in Ho's *Selected Works* would seem to indicate that he was the principal author.

[36] James F. Byrnes, Secretary of State.

in order to wreck our national unity and prevent our people from being united.

They have built more prisons than schools. They have mercilessly slain our patriots; they have drowned our uprisings in rivers of blood.

They have fettered public opinion; they have practised obscurantism against our people.

To weaken our race they have forced us to use opium and alcohol.

In the field of economics, they have fleeced us to the backbone, impoverished our people and devastated our land.

They have robbed us of our ricefields, our mines, our forests and our raw materials. They have monopolized the issuing of bank-notes and the export trade.

They have invented numerous unjustifiable taxes, and reduced our people, especially our peasantry, to a state of extreme poverty.

They have hampered the prospering of our national bourgeoisie; they have mercilessly exploited our workers.

In the Autumn of 1940, when the Japanese fascists violated Indochina's territory to establish new bases in their fight against the Allies, the French imperialists went down on their bended knees and handed over our country to them.

Thus, from that date, our people were subjected to the double yoke of the French and the Japanese. Their sufferings and miseries increased. The result was that from the end of last year to the beginning of this year, from Quang Tri province to the North of Viet Nam, more than two millions of our fellow-citizens died from starvation. On the 9th of March, the French troops were disarmed by the Japanese. The French colonialists either fled or surrendered; showing that not only were they incapable of "protecting" us, but that, in the span of five years, they had twice sold our country to the Japanese.

On several occasions before the 9th of March, the Viet Minh League urged the French to ally themselves with it against the Japanese. Instead of agreeing to this proposal, the French colonialists so intensified their terrorist activities against the Viet Minh members that before fleeing they massacred a great number of our political prisoners detained at Yen Bay and Cao Bang.

Notwithstanding all this, our fellow citizens have always manifested towards the French a tolerant and humane attitude. Even after the Japanese putsch of March 1945, the Viet Minh League helped many Frenchmen to cross the frontier, rescued some of them from Japanese jails and protected French lives and property.

From the autumn of 1940, our country had in fact ceased to be a French colony and had become a Japanese possession.

After the Japanese had surrendered to the Allies, our whole people rose to regain our national sovereignty and to found the Democratic Republic of Viet Nam.

The truth is that we have wrested our independence from the Japanese and not from the French.

The French have fled, the Japanese have capitulated, emperor Bao Dai has abdicated. Our people have broken the chains which for nearly a century have fettered them and have won independence for the Fatherland. Our people at the same time have overthrown the monarchic regime that has reigned supreme for dozens of centuries. In its place has been established the present Democratic Republic.

For these reasons, we, members of the Provisional Government, representing the whole Vietnamese people, declare that from now on we break off all relations of a colonial character with France; we repeal all the international obligations that France has so far subscribed to on behalf of Viet Nam and we abolish all the special rights the French have unlawfully acquired in our Fatherland.

The whole Vietnamese people, animated by a common purpose, are determined to fight to the bitter end against any attempt by the French colonialists to reconquer their country.

We are convinced that the Allied nations which at Teheran and San Francisco have acknowledged the principles of self-determination and equality of nations, will not refuse to acknowledge the independence of Viet Nam.

A people who have courageously opposed French domination for more than eighty years, a people who have fought side by side with the Allies against the fascists during these last years, such a people must be free and independent.

For these reasons we, members of the Provisional Government of the Democratic Republic of Viet Nam, solemnly declare to the world that Viet Nam has the right to be a free and independent country— and in fact it is so already. The entire Vietnamese people are determined to mobilize all their physical and mental strength, to sacrifice their lives and property in order to safeguard their independence and liberty.

Hanoi, the Second of September 1945
Ho Chi Minh, President

Tran Huy Lieu	Vo Nguyen Giap
Chu Van Tan	Pham Van Dong
Duong Duc Hien	Nguyen Van To
Nguyen Manh Ha	Cu Huy Can *Poet?*
Pham Ngoc Thach	Nguyen Van Xuan
Vu Trong Khanh	Dao Trong Kim
Vu Dinh Hoe	Le Van Hien

29. *Report to the Combined Chiefs of Staff by the Supreme Allied Commander, South East Asia [Extracts]* *

[The portions of Vice-Admiral Mountbatten's Report included here are those of particular relevance to British activities in Viet-Nam in late 1945.]

19. At the Potsdam Conference, the Combined Chiefs of Staff had allotted to S.E.A.C. [South East Asia Command] that part of French Indo-China lying south of 16° North,[37] and by this arbitrary division the northern half of the country was occupied by Chinese forces. My specific instructions from the Chiefs of Staff were to secure control of the Supreme Headquarters of the Japanese Expeditionary Forces of the Southern Regions: the Headquarters of Field Marshal Count Terauchi, which was now located in Saigon. The Chiefs of Staff laid down, however, that my forces were not to occupy more of F.I.C. [French Indo-China] than would be necessary to ensure this control; and that they should be withdrawn as soon as their military task— the round-up and disarming of the Japanese, and the Recovery of A P.W.I. [Allied Prisoners of War and Internees]—was completed. I was told that French forces, with Civil officials, would be responsible for the administration of the country, Civil administration being carried out by the French even in the key areas in which my forces would be operating.

20. This policy was agreed in the documents that General [Jacques]

* *Source:* Vice-Admiral The Earl Mountbatten of Burma, *Post Surrender Tasks: Section E of the Report to the Combined Chiefs of Staff by the Supreme Allied Commander South East Asia, 1943–1945* (London: Her Majesty's Stationery Office, 1969), pp. 285–289, 298. Written in July 1947, the bulk of the report (Sections A through D) was made public in 1950. Portions of Section E were made public in 1965, and Section E in its entirety was made public in 1969.

37 Footnote in the original: "See Map 40 (between pages 283–284)." See also Document 21.

Leclerc,[38] representing the French Government, presented to General M[a]cArthur at Tokyo; but while willing to comply with the terms of General Order No. 1,[39] the French authorities asserted their sovereignty over F.I.C., and reserved the right to take whatever measures they might consider necessary—while keeping the Allied powers informed. This attitude was supported by His Majesty's Government in an agreement made with the French Government concerning F.I.C.[40]

21. As soon as the staging-post at Bangkok was secured, forces had been flown into F.I.C., control of Field Marshal Terauchi's Headquarters established, and the S.A.C.S.E.A. [Supreme Allied Commander South East Asia] Commission set up. The Commission, under Major-General [Douglas D.] Gracey, had been formed at Rangoon, where the Field Marshal's representatives had attended, so as to be able to transmit my orders to Japanese Supreme Headquarters: on the 15th September, the day following its establishment in Saigon, the Commission held its first plenary session with Field Marshal Terauchi. Reassuring leaflets been dropped over Saigon before the initial fly-in. I had decided to bring in 20 Indian Division; with a Naval Port Party, a staging-post, and two R.A.F. Tactical Squadrons, with Air H.Q. established in Saigon. On the 13th September the fly-in of a brigade of 20 Indian Division had begun, and our troops had taken over the guarding of the airfield [41] on the same day.

22. The day before the S.A.C.S.E.A. Commission was set up, the Chiefs of Staff had telegraphed that my authority, responsibility, and activities in F.I.C. were strictly limited and temporary. This policy would have been welcome if French forces had been on hand for supporting French responsibilities; but adequate French forces, which had been promised to me at Potsdam, were not yet available. The only French resources I could make immediately available to General Leclerc were some 1,000 troops of the 5th Colonial Infantry Regiment (Regiment d'Infanterie Coloniale) [42] in Ceylon, and certain French warships, including the battleship *Richelieu*. The 9th and 3rd Colonial Infantry Divisions (Divisions d'Infanterie Coloniale) [43] had been de-

[38] Footnote in the original: "Who, in August, had been appointed C.-in-C. of the French forces in S.E.A.C., in succession to General Blaizot."

[39] See Note 30, p. 45.

[40] Information on this agreement is not available. It appears to be an earlier agreement than the October 9 exchange of letters described in Document 31.

[41] Now Tan Son Nhut airfield at Saigon.

[42] Footnote in the original: "Commonly known as the 'Cinquiéme R.I.C.' "

[43] Footnote in the original: "Commonly known as the 'Neuvième D.I.C.' and the 'Troisième D.I.C.,' respectively."

tailed for F.I.C.; but they were both still in Europe, and inadequately equipped. The 1st Far East Brigade (Brigade d'Extrême-Orient), which was in Madagascar, was also destined for F.I.C.; but General Leclerc did not wish it to be phased in until after the arrival of the 9th D.I.C. —which was not to be until the first week in November. For the next six weeks, therefore, the only troops available to the French authorities outside the key areas in Southern F.I.C., would be the 1,000 troops of the 5th R.I.C., and a force of some 500 French released prisoners of war and local inhabitants.

23. On the 19th September, I signalled the Chiefs of Staff, urging them to speed up the arrival of French reinforcements: for two days previously the Annamite Independence Movement in F.I.C. (Viet Minh) had announced that Bao Dai, Emperor of Annam, had abdicated in August; and that the Annamite administration which had been set up at Hanoi (in Northern F.I.C.) was now the independent Republic of Viet Nam.[44] A strong Independence Movement had existed in F.I.C. before the war, and had been a continual source of difficulty to the French authorities. During the occupation, this movement had been fostered by the Japanese; and the situation had been aggravated by the fact that the French administration of the country had been in the hands of representatives of the puppet government at Vichy. The spectacle of France's betrayal had greatly undermined French prestige in her colony: particularly in view of the fact that the Vichy administration in F.I.C. had at all times collaborated openly with the enemy. In March 1945, when the collapse of Germany, and the Vichy regime, seemed imminent, the Japanese had decided to assume complete control: this had caused resistance from the French Army in F.I.C., small elements of which had fought their way out into China—the remainder, however, had been placed in prisoner of war camps, and French civilians had been either interned or placed under severe restrictions. With the defeat of Japan, the Annamite Independence Movement had at once set up an administration at Hanoi, which was now under Chinese occupation; and it was this administration of the Viet Minh party that was now declared an independent Republic.

[44] The Revolution had, of course, taken place in August and the DRV had been proclaimed on September 2. There was, however, apparently a delay before the DRV obtained control of communication facilities in Hanoi. The earliest DRV materials the editor has been able to locate in radio monitoring reports are items transmitted through the Hanoi Telegraph Service on September 19. It seems probable, therefore, that Admiral Mountbatten simply was not aware of the earlier events, particularly in the confusion accompanying the end of the war.

24. Outside the key areas, the Viet Minh were in complete control in Southern F.I.C. The French Government had offered the Annamites the attainment of self-government by stages; but the latter had declared their intention of achieving immediate independence—if necessary, by force. On the 2nd September, before the arrival of S.E.A.C. forces, a serious riot had taken place, which had only been prevented from assuming grave proportions by the courageous action of released British and Australian prisoners of war, who were unarmed, and of the few R.A.P.W.I. [Released Allied Prisoners of War and Internees] Control officers who had already been flown in. On the 17th September, the day on which the independence of the Viet Nam republic was declared, the Viet Minh closed the markets in Saigon and a boycott of all French employers was enforced. Sporadic fighting took place in the town; but this was mainly unpolitical, and was engaged in by hooligans profiting from the prevailing atmosphere of unrest. The seriousness of the situation, however, lay in the fact that no legal writ ran; and that the Viet Minh party (who claimed to be in control) were taking no steps to see that order was maintained.

25. On the 21st September, Major-General Gracey posted a proclamation in all relevant languages,[45] in Saigon and the adjoining port of Cholon, stating that it was his firm intention to ensure with strict impartiality that the transition from war to peace conditions should be carried out, throughout Southern F.I.C., with the minimum of dislocation to public services, legitimate business and trade; and with the least interference with the normal peaceful activities and vocations of the people. Calling on all citizens to cooperate to the fullest extent, the proclamation warned all wrong-doers (and especially looters and saboteurs of public and private property) that they would be summarily shot. No demonstrations or processions would be permitted; no public meetings would take place; no arms of any kind, including sticks, staves, bamboo spears, etc., would be carried—except by British and Allied troops and by such other military and police as had been specially authorised to do so.

26. While appreciating that the military situation in Saigon was grave, with only a small Allied force available and the river not yet

---

[45] Text in Great Britain, Parliament, Papers by Command, *Documents Relating to British Involvement in the Indo-China Conflict, 1945–1965* (London: Her Majesty's Stationery Office, Cmnd. 2834, 1965), pp. 52–53. This paragraph contains a detailed summary of the proclamation.

open,[46] I felt that this proclamation—addressed, as it was, to the whole of Southern F.I.C., and not merely to the key points—was contrary to the policy of His Majesty's Government; and since proclamations of this nature may well appear to be initiated by Government policy, I warned Major-General Gracey that he should take care to confine operations of British/Indian troops to those limited tasks which he had been set. At the same time, I approved the military measures which he proposed to take: these consisted in the first place of bringing home more strictly to Field Marshal Terauchi his personal responsibility for ensuring that the Japanese obeyed their orders; Major-General Gracey further proposed to empl[o]y Japanese troops for keeping the northern approaches to Saigon clear, moving British/Indian troops out to the approaches—and finally, he proposed to extend and consolidate his perimeter as soon as the remainder of 20 Indian Division arrived. (The categorical orders to Field Marshal Terauchi had the desired effect; and in the future the Japanese were to fulfil their obligations satisfactorily).

27. After consultation with General [William] Slim [47] and with General Leclerc (who, with his staff, was still at my Headquarters [48]), and in view of further reports from Major-General Gracey at Saigon, I telegraphed to the Chiefs of Staff on the 24th September that I considered that Major-General Gracey, in issuing his proclamation, had acted with courage and determination in an extremely difficult situation; with as yet inadequate forces. In my opinion, if the riots he feared had developed, the safety of the small British/Indian force and of the French population might have been compromised, since the river and port were not yet open. I informed the Chiefs of Staff that, as I saw it, two courses were now open:

(*a*) to implement the proclamation and to retain responsibility for civil and military administration throughout Southern F.I.C.;

[46] Footnote in the original: "Minesweeping and surveying of the sea approaches, the anchorage at Cap St. Jacques [Vung Tao], and the river to Saigon, had been completed, and sea communications opened, by the 28th September."

[47] Commander of British forces in Burma.

[48] Footnote in the original: "I had asked General Leclerc not to go forward until Major-General Gracey was ready for him. He readily agreed, and volunteered to serve under his orders, on arrival, until such time as I turned over to him the command of any part of F.I.C."

(*b*) to limit my responsibility solely to the control of the Japanese Supreme Headquarters.

28. I pointed out that the first course, which would include my directly controlling all French forces and Civil Affairs until such time as General Leclerc advised me that he could take over, would entail the potential employment of British and French troops throughout Southern F.I.C., to maintain order in support of the French Government. This course, which in practice would require a full British/Indian Division to implement it, was not in accordance with my present instructions. The second course, by which the High Commissioner of the French Republic [49]—or, in his absence, the senior Commander of the French forces, acting as his delegate—would have to be instructed by the French Government to exercise civil and military authority outside the key areas, would entail the re-affirmation by General Leclerc in the name of the French Republic of the proclamation already issued; since in my opinion it would be dangerous now to revoke it.

29. General Leclerc, however, while welcoming and supporting Major-General Gracey's proclamation (even though only one brigade of 20 Indian Division was as yet available for implementing it) was not prepared to re-affirm the proclamation in the name of the French Republic, until the 9th D.I.C. had arrived and he had ample forces at his disposal. I asked the Chiefs of Staff for a policy ruling, as to which of the two courses I had outlined was to be adopted: recommending, for my part, that the second course should be put into effect at the earliest date by which the French Government was prepared to take over. Any British forces which might subsequently remain in F.I.C., I suggested, should not be under French command, and should have the sole duty of maintaining control of Field Marshal Terauchi's Headquarters.

30. In the meantime, on the 23rd September, Major-General Gracey had agreed with the French that they should carry out a *coup d'état;* and with his permission, they seized control of the administration of Saigon and the French Government was installed. Considerable fighting took place in the city that night; but British/Indian troops had taken over the security of all important positions. On the 24th, the Annamites staged a determined assault on the power station, while unsuccessful attempts were also made to sabotage the radio and the

[49] Admiral Thierry d'Argenlieu, then in India. Admiral d'Argenlieu, a Carmelite monk, was designated by General de Gaulle as National Commissioner for the Pacific in 1941 and was named High Commissioner for Indochina in August 1945.

water supply. On the 26th, Lieut.-Colonel P. Dewey, of the U.S. Office of Strategic Services,[50] was shot dead while motoring through the outskirts of Saigon, and his body removed by the Annamites. It was clear that the whole military position was deteriorating, and might well prove beyond the capacity of the only brigade of 20 Indian Division that had as yet arrived.

31. On the 28th September, when the situation in Saigon appeared very serious, I called a meeting with Major-General Gracey and Colonel [Jean Henri] Cédille [*sic*] [51] at Singapore, in the presence of the Secretary of State for War: [52] at which I made it clear to Colonel Cédille that I considered it vitally important that negotiations between the French and the Annamites should start as soon as possible. I requested him to meet the Viet Minh representatives; and he informed me that, with Major-General Gracey's concurrence, he had for three days been trying to do so. At this meeting, the Secretary of State confirmed my impression that it was the policy of His Majesty's Government not to interfere in the internal affairs of French Indo-China.

32. On the 1st October, I received a telegram from the Chiefs of Staff, altering my instructions and informing me that I was to use British/Indian troops to give assistance to the French throughout the interior of Southern F.I.C., so long as this did not prejudice my primary responsibility for Saigon. I passed these instructions on to Major-General Gracey, while impressing on him that British/Indian troops were still to be used only in a preventive role and not in an offensive one. On the same day, Major-General Gracey and Mr. H. N. Brain (a member of my political staff whom I sent to F.I.C., until a permanent Political Adviser to Major-General Gracey arrived from England) [53] held a first meeting with representatives of the Viet Minh party, and stated British policy. The Viet Minh agreed to a cease-fire order, which the British undertook to ensure that the French carried out. Meetings between the French and the Annamites were held on the 3rd and the 6th October; but on this day the armistice was broken by the Annamites, who opened fire on British/Indian troops in Saigon. Two days later, 20 Indian Division H.Q. was established at Saigon and H.Q.

---

[50] Footnote in the original omitted.

[51] Footnote in the original: "French Civil Adviser to Major-General Gracey, and Governor-designate of Cochin-China." The correct spelling is "Cédile."

[52] Footnote in the original: "The Rt. Hon. J. J. Lawson, who was visiting the British troops in India and S.E.A.C."

[53] Footnote in the original: "Mr. Brain was relieved a few weeks later by Mr. E. W. Meiklereid."

Allied Land Forces, French Indo-China (A.L.F.F.I.C.); and in the next ten days the remainder of the Division arrived.

33. On the 9th October, Major-General Gracey, General Leclerc, and Colonel Cédille met me at Rangoon to discuss the situation; and I again urged the importance of further negotiation with the Annamites. During our meeting, news was received that the Annamites had again broken the armistice; and as it seemed clear that the Viet Minh spokesmen were incapable of ensuring that agreements into which they entered would be honoured, I ordered that strong action should be taken by the British/Indian forces to secure further key-points, and to widen and consolidate the perimeter of these areas. At the same time, I insisted that further attempts to negotiate must continue.

[Two paragraphs on developments in Cambodia are omitted.]

36. The arrival of General Leclerc in F.I.C. [on October 8] raised the question of when Vice-Admiral d'Argenlieu, the High Commissioner-designate, should go there. The latter had visited me at Kandy [Ceylon] in the first week of September, and I had asked him then not to go until General Leclerc had got to F.I.C. and reported that the time was propitious. This General Leclerc did shortly after his own arrival; and on the 30th October Vice-Admiral d'Argenlieu arrived at Saigon to take up his appointment of High Commissioner for French Indo-China, and nominal Commander of the French forces in the theatre—in this respect, under the operational command of Major-General Gracey.

[A section on Indonesia is omitted.]

[83.] Outside Java, the state of affairs in South-East Asia gave no cause for anxiety. In French Indo-China the situation had cleared up by the end of the year: the 9th D.I.C. had arrived, and the 3rd D.I.C. was expected to arrive soon. I had taken Field Marshal Terauchi's personal surrender on the 30th November at Saigon; and had subsequently held discussions with Vice-Admiral d'Argenlieu, Major-General Gracey, General Leclerc, Rear-Admiral Auboyneau (Naval C.-in-C. Afloat), and Rear-Admiral Graziani (Naval C.-in-C. Ashore). On the 1st January, Vice-Admiral d'Argenlieu and I issued a joint statement, announcing that the French authorities assumed full responsibility for military commitments in F.I.C.; and on the 28th January, command of all French forces in the country passed from Major-General Gracey (who then left French Indo-China) to General Leclerc; while command of the British/Indian forces which remained passed to a reduced S.A.C.S.E.A. Inter-Service Mission established under Brigadier M.S.Q. Maunsell, late Chief of Staff of the S.A.C.S.E.A. Commission No. 1. The Commission itself ceased to exist.

[Two further paragraphs on withdrawal of British forces from Indochina, and the balance of the report are omitted.]

30. *Telegram from the Foreign Minister of the Democratic Republic of Viet-Nam to the Prime Minister of Great Britain ** *September 26, 1945*

Foreign Minister of Viet-Nam Republic to Premier Attlee, London.

The release of French prisoners of war with arms and ammunitions leading to the French attack against Saigon and the arrests of members of the Peoples Committee constitutes a great violation of our national rights and is an offense to our national dignity, a non-fulfilment of the mission placed on Commander British Forces in South Indo-China by the United Nations, a failure in the carrying out of the Atlantic Charter [54] and non-observation of attitude of neutrality by the British Disarmament Forces. We therefore lodge a most emphatic protest against such smoke-screening of French aggression and express earnest hope that you would interfere on basis full respect for the independence of Viet-Nam Republic.

31. *Telegram to the Secretary of State from Ambassador Jefferson Caffery in Paris † October 12, 1945*

6006. My 5964, October 10.[55] Last night's semi-official *Le Monde* gives further details re Franco-British agreement on Indochina.[56] *Le*

* *Source:* Great Britain, Parliament, Papers by Command, *Documents Relating to British Involvement in the Indo-China Conflict 1945–1965* (London: Her Majesty's Stationery Office, Cmnd. 2834, 1965), p. 53.

† *Source:* United States, Department of State, *Foreign Relations of the United States, 1945* (9 vols., Washington: Government Printing Office, 1967–1969), Vol. VI, p. 314. The agreement was concluded by an exchange of letters between Foreign Secretary Ernest Beven and René Massigli, French Ambassador in London, on October 9. The editor has not been able to locate a complete authentic text, although portions of the agreement were broadcast by Radio Saigon on November 3, 1945, 4:45 A.M., E.S.T. Ambassador Caffery's message appears to give an accurate summary.

54 Footnote in the original omitted.

55 Footnote in the original: "Not printed."

56 See the Source Note to this document.

Monde states agreement will not be published at this time but that principal provisions are known.

In the agreement French Civil Administration is recognized as sole authority in that part of Indochina south of 16th parallel. Only exceptions result from presence of British troops in this part of Indochina and these exceptions do not affect principles of agreement. *Le Monde* adds agreement is designed to determine relations between French Civil Administration and British military authorities and provides that British Commander will not intervene in civil affairs except through French authority. Latter in Turkey [*turn*] [57] agree to fulfill any requests arising from presence of British troops. Agreement provides British troops will only be there temporarily for purpose of enforcing terms of Jap surrender and to assure repatriation of Allied prisoners and civilian internees.

It is again emphasized that cordial atmosphere of negotiations was indication of solidarity of Franco-British relations in that part of world.

Sent Department as 6006, repeated London as 748.

CAFFERY

32. *Speech by John Carter Vincent, Director of the Office of Far Eastern Affairs, Department of State [Extract]* *
   October 20, 1945

[Mr. Vincent's speech, "The Post-War Period in the Far East," was made to the Foreign Policy Association Forum on "Between War and Peace," in New York. Only the two paragraphs directly relevant to Indochina are printed here.]

In southeast Asia a situation has developed to the liking of none of us, least of all to the British, the French, the Dutch, and, I gather, to the Annamese and Indonesians. With regard to the situation in French Indochina, this Government does not question French sovereignty in that area. Our attitude toward the situation in the Dutch East Indies is similar to that in regard to French Indochina. In both these areas, however, we earnestly hope that an early agreement can be reached between representatives of the governments concerned and the Annamese and Indonesians. It is not our intention to assist or participate

* *Source:* United States, Department of State, *Bulletin,* XIII (October 21, 1945), p. 646.
   [57] In the original.

in forceful measures for the imposition of control by the territorial sovereigns, but we would be prepared to lend our assistance, if requested to do so, in efforts to reach peaceful agreements in these disturbed areas.

In a statement issued by Secretary Hull on March 21, 1944, entitled "Bases of the Foreign Policy of the United States," [58] there occurs the following paragraph in regard to "dependent peoples": "There rests upon the independent nations a responsibility in relation to dependent peoples who aspire to liberty. It should be the duty of nations having political ties with such peoples . . . to help the aspiring peoples to develop materially and educationally, to prepare themselves for the duties and responsibilities of self-government, and to attain liberty." This continues to be American policy.

33. *Statement by the Secretary of State for Foreign Affairs of Great Britain, Right Hon. Ernest Bevin, in the House of Commons* * *October 24, 1945*

MR. BEVIN: In Indo-China, as in Java, the Japanese followed a policy of encouraging the growth of nationalism, and with Japanese backing and arms nationalist groups were able in August last to establish what has become known as the Viet Nam Republic, comprising the coastal territories of Tonkin, Annam and Cochin China. After the Japanese general surrender, responsibility for disarming and controlling all Japanese forces and for releasing and evacuating Allied prisoners of war and internees in Southern Indo-China up to the boundary between South East Asia Command and the China theatre, which for operational purposes had been established along the parallel of 16° N., devolved on forces under Admiral Mountbatten's command.

Unfortunately, in fulfilling the primary task entrusted to him, the British Force Commander in Indo-China, General Gracey, found himself obliged to contend with continual looting and attacks by Annamite armed bands on French civilians and property and with conflicts between these bands and the French forces under his command. On General Gracey's advice, the senior French officer agreed to meet Annamite representatives and arrangements were made for a truce to run from 2nd October. In face of the evident inability of the Annamite

* *Source:* Great Britain, *Parliamentary Debates (Hansard)*, Fifth Series, House of Commons, Vol. 414 (October 24, 1945), cols. 2149–2150. Mr. Bevin's statement was in the form of a written answer to a question.

[58] Footnote in the original: "*Bulletin* of Mar. 25, 1944, p. 275."

leaders to exercise effective control over their own armed forces, General Gracey warned them on 8th October that should their forces break the truce he would have no option but to take whatever steps might be necessary to ensure the proper execution of his task. There has been sporadic fighting involving British forces in the outskirts of Saigon.

As stated by the Prime Minister in reply to a Question on the situation in Java on 17th October,[59] His Majesty's Government do not desire to be unnecessarily involved in the administration or in the political affairs of non-British territories, and their object is to withdraw British troops as soon as circumstances permit. As the House is no doubt aware, the French Government, in a declaration of policy issued on 24th March last,[60] promised a wide measure of autonomy to Indo-China, and I should like to take this opportunity of informing the House that this liberal attitude on the part of the French Government has been reflected in the very conciliatory manner in which the local French representatives have dealt with the Annamite leaders. There has also been close and friendly co-operation between the British and French Commanders. In the meanwhile, every effort is being made to expedite the movement of French troops to Saigon in sufficient numbers to enable them to take over from the British forces.

34. *Communiqué Issued by the Central Committee of the Indochinese Communist Party* *
   November 11, 1945

1. Whereas, in consideration of the given historical situation, both internationally and internally, the present moment is precisely an exceptional occasion for Viet Nam to reconquer her unitary independence;

2. Whereas, in order to complete the Party's task in this immense movement of the Vietnamese people's emancipation, a national union conceived without distinction of class and parties is an indispensable factor;

* *Source:* I. Milton Sacks, "Marxism in Viet Nam," in Frank N. Trager, ed., *Marxism in Southeast Asia: A Study of Four Countries* (Stanford, Cal.: Stanford University Press, 1959), p. 158, citing *La République,* Hanoi, November 18, 1945. Reprinted by permission of the RAND Corporation. The communiqué was also broadcast by Hanoi Radio in French Morse, November 12, 1945, 7:30 A.M., E.S.T.

59 Great Britain, *Parliamentary Debates (Hansard),* Fifth Series, House of Commons, Vol. 414 (October 17, 1945), cols. 1152–1153.

60 Document 16.

3. Wishing to prove that the Communists, in so far as they are advance guard militants of the Vietnamese people, are always ready to make the greatest sacrifices for national liberation, are always disposed to put the interest of the country above that of classes, and to give up the interests of the Party to serve those of the Vietnamese people;

4. In order to destroy all misunderstandings, domestic and foreign, which can hinder the liberation of our country, the Central Executive Committee of the Indochina Communist Party in meeting assembled on November 11, 1945, has decided to voluntarily dissolve the Indochina Communist Party.

Those followers of Communism desirous of continuing their theoretical studies will affiliate with the Indochina Association of Marxist Studies.

CENTRAL COMMITTEE INDOCHINA COMMUNIST PARTY
November 11, 1945

Franco-Vietnamese War and Formation of a Rival Viet-Nam January 1946–December 1949

CHAPTER III

Franco-Vietnamese Negotiations and the Outbreak of Hostilities

January 1946-January 1947

Introduction

The period of the Viet-Nam crisis beginning in 1946 and ending in 1949 was unique in that there was very little involvement by powers other than the Democratic Republic of Viet-Nam (DRV) and France, although toward the end of 1949 the Indochina war began to develop into a major international issue. The year 1946 saw the attempt to reconcile French and Vietnamese positions, an attempt which failed because the objectives of the two parties were mutually exclusive, particularly on the status of Cochin China. At the end of the year hostilities erupted, because of intransigence on both sides, and were to continue for eight long years.

The critical year began with both the Viet Minh and the French attempting to consolidate their positions. In the North, the election of a national assembly, originally scheduled for November 8, had been postponed to January 6 under Chinese pressure. The elections, although not free by Western standards and with the results as reported by the Viet Minh open to some question, demonstrated that the mood of the country was one of support for the Viet Minh or, more properly, for independence. Chinese pressure subsequently forced the pro-Chinese nationalists and the Viet Minh to cooperate in the formation of a new coalition government in February.

France also had to deal with the Chinese, who hoped to use their grasp on northern Indochina as a bargaining counter. Negotiations between the two powers culminated with the conclusion of a series of agreements on February 28. The most important for French purposes was an exchange of letters with attached Minute which provided for

French relief of Chinese forces north of the sixteenth parallel (Document 35). In turn, China obtained French renunciation of exterritoriality in China and an "Agreement Concerning Sino-Indochinese Relations" which gave China major trade concessions.[1] The evacuation of Chinese troops, originally to be completed by the end of March, dragged on into the summer and was marred by numerous incidents between French and Chinese forces.

French negotiations with the DRV to permit the peaceful return of French forces to the North had begun in secret in September 1945. The long and difficult negotiations finally bore fruit on March 6 with the signature of a "Preliminary Convention," by which France recognized the DRV as a "free State having its own government, parliament, army and finances, and forming part of the Indochinese Federation and the French Union," and pledged a referendum to determine whether Cochin China should become part of Viet-Nam. The DRV in turn agreed to the return of French troops to the North (Document 36).

The agreements in Hanoi were less than wholly satisfactory to both sides, and almost immediately each began to interpret them in its own way. A major difference arose over the status of Cochin China. France took the position that the March 6 agreement did not imply French recognition of the right of the Hanoi government to rule all Viet-Nam, and there were indications that Paris planned to establish an "independent" government in Cochin China. Continued guerrilla fighting in the South coupled with friction between French and Vietnamese in the North to produce increasing discontent with the March 6 agreement among the Vietnamese population.[2] The DRV also attempted to obtain international recognition on the basis of the March 6 Convention; a

[1] Text of the Agreement on exterritoriality is in France, *Journal Officiel de la République Française, Lois et Décrets,* May 19, 1946, pp. 4315–4317; the "Agreement on Sino-Indochinese Relations" is in *ibid.,* p. 4315, and, translated, in Allan B. Cole, ed., *Conflict in Indochina and International Repercussions: A Documentary History, 1945–1955* (Ithaca, N.Y.: Cornell University Press, 1956), pp. 7–9.

[2] The Agreement had not been well received by the population of Hanoi, and both Ho Chi Minh and Vo Nguyen Giap found it necessary to explain its terms and the Government's reason for signing it at a March 7 mass meeting; substantial extracts from their statements are in Philippe Devillers, *Histoire du Viêt-Nam de 1940 à 1952* (Paris: Editions du Seuil, 1952), pp. 228–231, citing *Quyet Chieng* (Hué), March 8, 1946. Ho, in particular, put all his prestige behind the agreement: "I, Ho Chi Minh, have always led you on the road to liberty, I have fought for the independence of our Fatherland all my life. You know that I would prefer to die than ever betray the country. I swear to you that I have not betrayed you!" (*ibid.,* p. 231).

telegram to the Prime Minister of the United Kingdom (Document 37) was probably typical of those sent to a number of states.

From April 17 to May 11 France and the DRV held a "preliminary" conference at Dalat as a precursor to "definitive" negotiations to be held subsequently in Paris. The Dalat Conference established a mixed commission to work for an end to hostilities in the South but accomplished little else beyond demonstrating the depth of disagreement between France and the DRV. During May, High Commissioner d'Argenlieu proceeded with the creation of an "independent" regime in Cochin China, and on May 30 he recognized the Republic of Cochin China "as a free state having its own government, parliament, army and finances, and forming part of the Indochinese Federation and the French Union." [3] On June 3 Colonel Jean Henri Cédile, French Commissioner for Cochin China, and Dr. Nguyen Van Thinh signed the "Franco-Cochinchinese Convention" setting forth the organization and power of the new government (Document 38). The Foreign Ministry of the DRV protested the new status for Cochin China in a strongly worded statement on June 10 (Document 39).

Ho Chi Minh and the DRV delegation to the "definitive" negotiations in Paris had departed Viet-Nam on May 31 and arrived in Paris to find France in the midst of a political crisis stemming from the rejection by referendum of the draft French constitution.[4] This and disagreement over the preliminary arrangements delayed the opening of the Franco-Vietnamese Conference until July 6. Disagreement persisted after the opening of the Conference at Fontainebleau, with the two sides able to reach agreement only on some economic and financial matters. Neither was willing to relax its position on political questions. The Conference was then dealt a mortal blow by High Commissioner d'Argenlieu, who decided to call a second Dalat Conference, opening August 1, to discuss the future of Indochina. The DRV was not invited to participate, on the grounds that it had already expressed its views and now it was the turn of the other Indochinese peoples to do so. The DRV protested and on August 1 broke off negotiations (Document 40).

Attempts continued, however, to reach some agreement, even lim-

[3] Devillers, *Histoire du Viêt-Nam,* p. 270; compare with the language of paragraph 1 of the March 6 Preliminary Convention, Document 36.
[4] The crisis had been foreshadowed in January when General de Gaulle resigned as Premier. One effect of this move was to allow officials in Indochina freedom by default to make policy decisions without close supervision from Paris.

ited, outside the formal conference framework. Agreement on a *modus vivendi* covering economic and financial matters was reached on the night of September 9 but was then repudiated by Pham Van Dong, head of the DRV delegation, which left for home. Finally, on September 14, Ho Chi Minh, who had remained in Paris, reached agreement with Premier Georges Bidault and Marius Moutet, Minister for Overseas France, on a Joint Declaration (Document 41) and a *modus vivendi* (Document 42). Although these confirmed agreement on certain economic and financial matters, and provided once more for a cessation of hostilities in the South, they skirted the vital issues of Cochin China and of the status of Viet-Nam within the French Union.

Ho Chi Minh returned to Viet-Nam in October to find that the Viet Minh position had been consolidated. The army was more than doubled, and the opposition parties had been suppressed. Former Emperor Bao Dai had departed for exile in Hong Kong. The DRV National Assembly met on October 28 and was completely dominated by Viet Minh members. On November 8 it approved the Constitution of the Democratic Republic of Viet-Nam (Document 43) by a vote of 240 to 2.[5] The Constitution made no mention of ties with France nor of membership in the Indochinese Federation.

Relations with France now worsened rapidly. The French attempted to control imports and exports at Haiphong, thus depriving the DRV of needed revenue, and High Commissioner d'Argenlieu sealed off Cochin China from official DRV representatives. The DRV responded by establishing a semiclandestine "Executive Committee for Nam-bo," which the French were unable to suppress, refused to put their armed forces under overall French command as provided in the March 6 Convention, and attempted to substitute their own currency for the Indochinese piastre.

Fighting between French and Vietnamese forces broke out at

---

[5] In 1950 Pham Van Dong stated: "Our Republic possesses a constitution adopted by the National Assembly elected at the beginning of 1946. This fundamental law, however, has never been promulgated, because several of its provisions require for their application the cessation of the state of war" (Ellen J. Hammer, *The Struggle for Indochina* [Stanford, Cal.: Stanford University Press, 1954], p. 178n, citing Léo Figuères, *Je Reviens du Viêt-Nam Libre* [Paris: Imp. J. London, 1951], p. 122). According to Donald Lancaster, the Assembly, before adjourning on November 14, decided not to require the Government to put the Constitution into effect: *The Emancipation of French Indochina* (New York: Oxford University Press, 1961), p. 169.

Haiphong and Lang Son on November 20. It was brought to a halt on November 22, but the following day the French ordered Viet Minh forces to evacuate the Chinese quarter of Haiphong. When the Viet Minh refused, the French moved in. Refugees fleeing the fighting into the open country were fired upon by the cruiser *Suffren* with heavy casualties.[6] Despite appeals for calm, Vo Nguyen Giap, the Vietnamese Commander, and General Morlière, the French Commander in Tonkin, were unable to stabilize the situation, and the Vietnamese in Hanoi began erecting barricades, digging tunnels, and making simliar military preparations. Attempts to improve the situation were unavailing, and on the evening of December 19 fighting broke out between French and Viet Minh forces in Hanoi. The following day Ho Chi Minh issued an appeal for a general uprising,[7] and fighting spread throughout Viet-Nam.

The outbreak of war in Indochina caused great concern in Paris, and the new Socialist-coalition Government of Premier Léon Blum decided to send M. Marius Moutet, the Minister for Overseas France, to Indochina on a mission of investigation. On December 23 Premier Blum outlined French policy in a statement to the National Assembly; [8] he expressed determination to avoid war but reaffirmed equal determination to cope with violence and restore order. Despite a number of proposals from the Viet Minh to return to the *status quo ante,* the two sides had moved too far apart for either to accept a meaningful compromise with the other.[9]

[6] This brief account is based on Bernard B. Fall, *The Two Viet-Nams* (2nd rev. ed., New York: Frederick A. Praeger, 1967), pp. 75–76. Fall disagrees with other accounts (i.e., Hammer, *The Struggle for Indochina,* p. 183) according to which the French fired upon and destroyed the Vietnamese quarter of Haiphong.

[7] Text in Ho Chi Minh, *Selected Works* (4 vols., Hanoi: Foreign Languages Publishing House, 1961–1962), Vol. III, pp. 81–82.

[8] Text of Blum's statement in *Journal Officiel de la République Française, Débats Parlementaires, Assemblée Nationale,* Session of December 23, 1946, pp. 320–321. See also Moutet's January 7, 1947, radio statement in Saigon, in French Press and Information Service (New York), *News From France,* Second Year, No. 1 (January 9, 1947), pp. 10–11.

[9] Documentation on "The Interest of the United States in Nationalist Opposition to the Restoration of French Rule in Indochina" will be published in United States, Department of State, *Foreign Relations of the United States, 1946* (7 vols. and others forthcoming, Washington: Government Printing Office, 1969–), Vol. VIII.

35. *Exchange of Letters between China and France Relating to the Relief of Chinese Troops by French Troops in North Indochina [Extracts]*
February 28, 1946

His Excellency Mr. Jacques Meyrier, French Ambassador, to His Excellency Dr. Wang Shih-chieh, Minister of Foreign Affairs, Chungking, 28 February 1946 *

Sir:

I have the honour to confirm to Your Excellency that the French Command is prepared to assume entire responsibility for guarding the Japanese prisoners, the maintenance of order and security, and the protection of Chinese nationals in the territories of the Indochinese Union to the north of the 16th degree of latitude and to propose for this purpose that the relief of Chinese troops by French troops be carried out upon the following bases:

The relief of Chinese troops stationed in Indochina to the north of the 16th degree of latitude shall begin between 1 and 15 March and should be completed at the latest on 31 March. The Chinese and French Military Staffs shall come to an agreement within the scope of the conversations now taking place at Chungking, with respect to the procedure for carrying out this operation.

Any units of the Chinese Army which are to be moved by sea but may not be able to embark after the relief will be regrouped in the stationing areas adjacent to the ports of embarkation, it being agreed that their evacuation shall be carried out as rapidly as physical conditions may permit. These areas shall be defined by local agreement between the Chinese and French Commands. With regard to the Chinese units which are to be withdrawn by other routes, their movements shall be governed by local agreement between the Chinese and French Commands.

I should be grateful if you would be good enough to inform me whether the Chinese Government agrees to the arrangements referred to above.

I avail myself of this opportunity to renew to Your Excellency the assurance of my highest consideration.

(Signed) JACQUES MEYRIER

* *Source:* United Nations, *Treaty Series*, No. 14 (1948), pp. 155–157.

[Dr. Wang Shih-chieh's letter of February 28, accepting the arrangements outlined in Ambassador Meyrier's letter, is omitted.]

MINUTE *

With reference to the exchange of letters of this date relative to the relief by French troops of the Chinese troops in northern Indochina, it is understood that the Chinese military authorities will not oppose the rearmament of the French troops in the Hanoi citadel, at the time of the relief, so that they may be in a position to assume effectively the responsibilities which fall to them by the fact of that relief.

MEYRIER

36. *Franco-Vietnamese Preliminary Convention and Annex* †
March 6, 1946

Between the High Contracting Parties hereafter designated: on the one side, the Government of the French Republic, represented by M. [Jean] Sainteny, delegate of the High Commissioner of France, properly commissioned by Admiral d'Argenlieu, the High Commissioner of France, depositary of the powers of the French Republic; and on the other side, the Government of Viet-Nam, represented by its President, M. Ho Chi Minh, and the special delegate of the Council of Ministers, M. Vu Hong Khanh, it is agreed as follows:

1. The French Government recognizes the Republic of Viet-Nam

---

* *Source:* France, Direction de la Documentation, *Principaux Textes de Politique Internationale de l'Année 1946* (Paris: 1955), p. 36. Translation by the editor. The Minute annexed to the exchange of letters does not appear in the version of the agreement registered with the United Nations in 1948.

† *Source:* France, Direction de la Documentation, *Principaux Textes de Politique Internationale de l'Année 1946* (Paris: 1955), p. 42. Translation by the editor. Another official version of the Annex omits subparagraph 2c and substitutes paragraph 3 for it. Paragraph 4 is numbered as Paragraph 3. See France, Direction de la Documentation, *Notes Documentaires et Etudes,* No. 548 (February 15, 1947), pp. 4–5. The same version appears in Philippe Devillers, *Histoire du Viêt-Nam de 1940 à 1952* (Paris: Editions du Seuil, 1952), pp. 225–226. The version used here also appears in Jean Sainteny's own account, *Histoire d'une Paix Manquée: Indochine 1945–1947* (Paris: Amiot-Dumont, 1953), pp. 182–184. This version is probably correct, being taken from a later official version and being corroborated by Sainteny's own account. The *Notes Documentaires et Etudes* version also lists General Raoul Salan and Vo Nguyen Giap as signatories of the Annex. This also appears to be in error. Sainteny does not mention Vo Nguyen Giap as one of the people present at the ceremony of signature; General Salan was present.

as a free State having its own government, parliament, army and finances, and forming part of the Indochinese Federation and the French Union.

Concerning the unification of the three "Ky," [1] the French Government agrees to accept [*entériner*] the decisions taken by the population consulted by referendum.

2. The Government of Viet-Nam declares itself prepared to receive the French army amicably when, in conformity with international agreements, it relieves the Chinese forces.

An agreement annexed to this Preliminary Convention will settle the means by which the relief operations will be effected.

3. The provisions formulated above will enter into force immediately. Immediately after the exchange of signatures each of the High Contracting Parties will take all necessary measures to bring about an immediate cessation of hostilities, to maintain the military forces in their respective positions, and to create the favorable climate necessary to the immediate opening of frank and friendly negotiations.

These negotiations will deal in particular with the diplomatic relations of Viet-Nam with foreign states, with the future status of Indochina, and with the French economic and cultural interests in Viet-Nam.

Hanoi, Saigon or Paris may be chosen as the site of the conference.

Done at Hanoi, March 6, 1946
SAINTENY
HO CHI MINH
VU HONG K[H]ANH

Agreement Annexed to the Preliminary Convention

Between the High Contracting Parties designated in the Preliminary Convention, it is agreed as follows:

1. The relief forces will be composed:

a. of 10,000 Vietnamese with their Vietnamese officers and non-commissioned officers responsible to the military authorities of Viet-Nam;

b. of 15,000 French, including the French forces presently located on the territory of Viet-Nam north of the 16th parallel. Said elements must be composed entirely of Frenchmen from the Metropole with the exception of troops charged with guarding Japanese prisoners.

These forces as a whole will be placed under the French supreme

[1] I.e., the three divisions of Viet-Nam: Tonkin, Annam, and Cochin China. In Viet Minh usage the three divisions were usually referred to as "Bac-bo," "Trung-bo," and "Nam-bo," respectively.

command, assisted by Vietnamese representatives. The advance, stationing and employment of these forces will be defined during a Staff Conference between the representatives of the French and Vietnamese commands which will be held upon the landing of French units.[2]

Mixed commissions will be created at all levels in order to ensure liaison in a spirit of friendly cooperation between French and Vietnamese forces.

2. French elements of the relief forces will be divided into three categories:

a. The units charged with guarding Japanese prisoners of war. These units will be sent home as soon as their mission ceases to exist, after the evacuation of the Japanese prisoners, and in any event within a maximum of ten months.

b. The units charged, in cooperation with the Vietnamese army, with ensuring the maintenance of public order and the security of Vietnamese territory. One fifth of these units will be relieved each year by the Vietnamese army, this relief being, therefore, effectively completed after five years.

c. The units charged with the defense of naval and air bases. The duration of the mission entrusted to these units will be defined in subsequent conferences.

3. In the places where the French and Vietnamese troops are garrisoned, cantonments, clearly delimited, will be assigned to them.

4. The French Government undertakes not to use Japanese prisoners for military purposes.

Done at Hanoi, March 6, 1946

SAINTENY

HO CHI MINH

VU HONG K[H]ANH

37. *Telegram from Ho Chi Minh to the Prime Minister of the United Kingdom * *
March 18, 1946

I beg to inform your Excellency that on 6th March, 1946, a preliminary agreement [3] has been signed between representatives of France

* *Source:* Great Britain, Parliament, Papers by Command, *Documents Relating to British Involvement in the Indo-China Conflict 1945–1965* (London: Her Majesty's Stationery Office, Cmnd. 2834, 1965), p. 55.

[2] Text of the subsequent staff agreement of April 3 is in France, Direction de la Documentation, *Notes Documentaires et Etudes,* No. 548 (February 15, 1947), pp. 5–6.

[3] Document 36.

and Viet-Nam. In this agreement France recognises the Democratic Republic of Viet-Nam as a free State. Friendly and sincere negotiations began immediately after the signature of the agreement. On behalf of the Viet-Nam people and Government I respectfully request the Government of Great Britain to recognise the Democratic Republic of Viet-Nam as a free State. We are firmly convinced that acknowledgement by your Government of our Republic will be an important step towards the materialisation of Atlantic and San Francisco [4] charters and will be highly contributive to the maintenance of world security while it will open a new era of co-operation between the British Commonwealth and our nation. Respectfully.

38. *Franco-Cochinchinese Convention* *
June 3, 1946

Convention [between France and Cochin China] determining the broad lines of the organization of powers in the Provisional Government of the French Republic of Cochin China and its relations with the Commissioner of the French Republic in Cochin China.

I. THE HEAD OF THE PROVISIONAL GOVERNMENT

He has the title of President of the Provisional Government of the Republic of Cochin China.

The President of the Provisional Government is elected by the Cochin China Advisory Council [5] by a two-thirds majority.

The President of the Provisional Government chooses the Ministers, who are responsible to him.

He presides over the Council of Ministers.

He appoints all officials of the Republic of Cochin China, on the suggestion of the responsible ministers. Under the authority of the President, the ministers are charged with the responsibility to assure the good management of their departments and the observation of discipline at all levels of the administrative hierarchy.

However, the appointment of the heads of the technical departments requires the prior approval of the Commissioner of the French Republic in Cochin China.

* *Source:* France, Direction de la Documentation, *Notes Documentaires et Etudes,* No. 554 (February 22, 1947), pp. 7–8. Translation by the editor.

[4] Footnote in the original omitted.

[5] The Cochin China Advisory Council was established by High Commissioner d'Argenlieu on February 4; it was composed of four Frenchmen and eight Vietnamese. Seven of the eight Vietnamese, however, were naturalized French citizens.

Province Chiefs are appointed by the President. The Commissioner of the French Republic is informed in advance of their designation.

The President signs the texts of regulations, decrees and decisions.

II. THE COMMISSIONER OF THE FRENCH REPUBLIC IN COCHIN CHINA

1. He is the representative of France and of the Indochinese Federation in Cochin China.

a. In this capacity and in agreement with the Cochinchinese Government, he sees to the maintenance of internal and external security. He may, in the event the defense of the territory so requires, and subject to the requirements of pacification action underway, requisition the French armed forces stationed in Cochin China.

b. He sees to the protection of French nationals, property and interests, and those of foreigners and Indochinese from other countries of the Federation.

2. He is the Advisor to the Provisional Government.

In this capacity, the Head of the Provisional Government and the members of the Government shall receive him in private and personal audience whenever he requests.

He may, on the invitation of the Government, attend meetings of the Council of Ministers.

He recommends French officials and technicians required for the smooth functioning of public services. The conditions of their utilization will be defined subsequently by mutual agreement.

III. THE COUNCIL OF MINISTERS

There are nine ministerial departments: [6]

Ministry of the Interior	Ministry of Public Works, Communications and Transport
Ministry of Defense	
Ministry of Justice	Ministry of Agriculture
Ministry of Finances	Ministry of Commerce and Industry
Ministry of National Education	Ministry of Public Health, Labor and Social Security.

The organization of the Ministry of Justice will be the subject of a subsequent convention.

There are three Under-Secretaries of State:

[6] Some versions of the Convention state that it provided for only eight ministerial departments, with the Ministry of Agriculture and the Ministry of Commerce and Industry combined into one. The version of the Convention given here, and a subsequent official version (in France, Direction de la Documentation, *Principaux Textes de Politique Internationale de l'Annee 1946* [Paris: 1955], pp. 92–93) list nine departments and that version is accepted as probably correct.

Under-Secretary of State for internal security.

Under-Secretary of State for the security of the capital.

Under-Secretary of State for Communications and Transportation.

The Council of Ministers decides the general policy of the Government. Its deliberations are secret.

IV. THE COCHIN CHINA ADVISORY COUNCIL

In agreement with the Advisory Council, the Provisional Government will decide on the enlargement of that assembly and the means of that enlargement.

The Government reports on its activity to the Council.

The Council votes the budget of Cochin China. The power to propose expenses is the function not of the Council but of the Government.

V. ADMINISTRATIVE ORGANIZATION OF THE PROVISIONAL GOVERNMENT

The transfer of services within the jurisdiction of the Commissioner of the French Republic in Cochin China to the ministries which will be responsible for their operation will be settled by accords between the Commissioner of the French Government in Cochin China and the Provisional Government.

For the time being these services will remain organized in their present form except for modifications decided by mutual agreement.

The officials presently in service will keep their positions. Plans for relief and repatriation presently in effect will remain applicable.

The fiscal and financial organization for Cochin China will be the subject of a special agreement.[7]

Questions not covered by this Convention will be the subject of special agreements.

VI. TERRITORIAL ORGANIZATION

The territorial organization will remain unchanged except for modification decided by mutual argeement between the Commissioner of the French Republic in Cochin China and the Provisional Government.

VII. [CONCLUSION]

This Convention is provisional. It may be modified by agreement reached between the Commissioner of the French Republic in Cochin China and the Provisional Government, subject to the approval of the French High Commissioner for Indochina.

Done at Saigon, June 3, 1946

J. H. CÉDILE   DR. NGUYEN VAN T[H]INH

[7] Signed on August 28. Text in France, Direction de la Documentation, *Notes Documentaires et Etudes,* No. 554 (February 22, 1947), pp. 8–9.

39. *Protest by the Foreign Minister of the Democratic Republic of Viet-Nam against the Creation of the Provisional Government of Cochin China* *
June 10, 1946

The establishment of the Provisional Government of the Free Republic of Cochin China could have no other aim than to set up a governmental and administrative apparatus with powers of coercion over the population in order to prejudice the outcome of the referendum provided by the Convention of March 6 [8] by means of autonomy granted in advance of that referendum.

In the name of the whole Vietnamese people our Government protests with this note against such a violation of the March 6 Convention. We solemnly declare that we will not recognize as qualified to speak in the name of Cochin China any other than those representatives designated by an election which is freely and sincerely endorsed by the Governments of France and Viet-Nam.

Our Government declares that it considers the convention recently concluded between Colonel Cédile, Commissioner of the Republic in Cochin China, and Dr. Nguyen Van Thinh, Premier of the Provisional Government of the free Republic of Cochin China, as null and void.

On the eve of the sincere and friendly negotiations which will shortly begin in Paris, the Government of Viet-Nam draws the attention of the French Government to the fact that the creation of the Provisional Government of Cochin China has caused great indignation among the entire Vietnamese people and is not likely to contribute to the maintenance of the "favorable climate," already realized to some extent, which is so necessary for peace negotiations.

40. *Communiqué Issued by the Fontainebleau Conference* †
August 1, 1946

The Political Committee of the Fontainebleau Conference, meeting in plenary session on August 1, heard a new protest by M. Pham Van

---

* *Source:* The Institute of International Studies (Milan), *Relazioni Internazionali*, Vol. X, No. 2 (June 22, 1946), p. 15. Translation by the courtesy of Mr. Alexander A. L. G. Zampieron. This protest was in the form of a note from the Foreign Minister of the DRV to the French Foreign Ministry.

† *Source:* France, Ministère de la France d'Outre-Mer, *Bulletin d'Information*, No. 82 (August 26, 1946), p. 5. Translation by the editor.

[8] Document 36.

Dong against the Federal Conference which opens today in Dalat,[9] a protest to which M. Max André responded.

The Chairmen of the two delegations have decided, by mutual agreement, to publish these documents as follows:

PROTEST BY M. PHAM VAN DONG

On July 26, I addressed to the Chairman of the French Delegation a protest in the name of our delegation relative to the so-called federal conference of Dalat. So far we have had no response on this subject. It is for that reason that we consider it necessary to take a definite position.

Gentlemen, in the name of the Vietnamese delegation I have the honor to remind you of our intervention of July 26 on the subject of the so-called federal conference which should meet in Dalat this very day. We want to state our position before the Fontainebleau Conference today. We find ourselves with the following alternatives. Either it is the French authorities in Cochin China who decide the fate of Cochin China, southern Annam,[10] the High Plateaux,[11] and the statute of the Indochinese Federation, in which case the Convention of March 6 [12] ceases to have any purpose and our Conference at Fontainebleau no longer has any reason for being. Or else the Convention of March 6 should be applied, in which case only the Fontainebleau Conference is qualified to discuss all those problems. Our dignity requires that we extricate ourselves from this equivocal situation and in consequence suspend our work until the equivocation is cleared up.

RESPONSE BY M. MAX ANDRÉ

M. Chairman, I want to repeat what I said earlier when I received your protest of July 20 [*sic*], which I have transmitted to our Government. This question of the so-called Dalat Conference is not within the scope of our Conference. I am able only to transmit your protest and your declaration to our Government. If you so desire, we will suspend the meeting and then, should the occasion arise, I will examine with you when and under what conditions we should resume it.

---

[9] For details on the Dalat Conference, see France, Haut Commissariat en Indochine, Direction Federale de l'Information, *Conférence Préparatoire de Dalat sur le Statut de la Féderation Indochinoise dans l'Union Française 1er–13 Août 1946* (Saigon: 1946?).

[10] I.e., that part of Annam south of the 16th parallel; a delegation from "Southern Annam" was present at the Dalat Conference.

[11] I.e., the highland regions of South Viet-Nam.   [12] Document 36.

41. *Joint Declaration of the Government of the French Republic and the Government of the Democratic Republic of Viet-Nam* *
September 14, 1946

The Government of the French Republic and the Government of the Democratic Republic of Viet-Nam are firmly decided to continue, in a spirit of reciprocal confidence, the policy of agreement and cooperation initiated by the Preliminary Convention of March 6, 1946,[13] and expressed during the Franco-Vietnamese Conferences at Dalat and Fontainebleau.

Convinced that this policy alone corresponds to the permanent interests of the two countries and to the democratic traditions which they espouse, the two Governments, while reaffirming their faith in the Convention of March 6, 1946, which remains in force, deem that the moment has come to mark a new advance in the development of relations between France and Viet-Nam pending the time when circumstances permit the conclusion of a complete and definitive agreement.

In a spirit of friendship and mutual understanding, the Government of France and the Government of the Democratic Republic of Viet-Nam have proceeded to the signature of a *modus vivendi* [14] providing, within the framework of limited agreements, provisional solutions to the principal questions of immediate interest which exist between France and Viet-Nam.

Concerning the referendum provided by the Preliminary Convention of March 6, the two Governments reserve the right to fix the date and the methods at a later time.

They are convinced that the totality of the measures contained in the *modus vivendi* will contribute to the establishment, in the near future, of a climate of calm and of confidence permitting the early continuation of definitive negotiations.

They believe, therefore, that it is possible to contemplate the resumption, in January 1947, of the labors which have just been accomplished at the Franco-Vietnamese Conference at Fontainebleau.

At Paris
September 14, 1946

* *Source:* France, Direction de la Documentation, *Notes Documentaires et Etudes,* No. 412 (September 19, 1946), p. 2. Translation by the editor.
[13] Document 36.   [14] Document 42.

42. *Franco-Vietnamese* Modus Vivendi *
September 14, 1946

Article 1

Vietnamese nationals in France and French nationals in Viet-Nam will enjoy the same freedom of domicile as the nationals of the host country, as well as the freedoms of opinion, education, commerce, movement, and all democratic liberties in general.

Article 2

French property and businesses in Viet-Nam will not be subjected to stricter regulation than that accorded to the property and businesses of Vietnamese nationals, particularly with regard to fiscal matters and labor legislation. This equality of status will be accorded on the basis of reciprocity to the property and businesses of Vietnamese nationals in the territories of the French Union.

The status of French property and businesses in Viet-Nam may be modified only by mutual agreement between the French Republic and the Democratic Republic of Viet-Nam.

All French property requisitioned by the Government of Viet-Nam, or of which individuals or businesses may have been deprived by Vietnamese authorities, will be returned to its proprietors and rightful owners. A mixed commission will be designated to decide the methods of this restitution.

Article 3

With a view to resuming henceforth the cultural relations which France and Viet-Nam are equally desirous of developing, French educational institutions of various levels will be able to function freely in Viet-Nam. They will apply official French curricula. By special agreement, these institutions will be given the buildings necessary to their operation. They will be open to Vietnamese students.

Scientific research and the establishment and operation of scientific institutes are open to French nationals throughout Vietnamese territory. Vietnamese nationals will enjoy the same privilege in France.

The Institut Pasteur will be restored to its rights and property. A

* *Source:* France, Direction de la Documentation, *Notes Documentaires et Etudes,* No. 412 (September 19, 1946), pp. 1–2. Translation by the editor.

mixed commission will decide the conditions under which the Ecole Française d'Extrême-Orient will resume its activity.

Article 4

The Government of the Democratic Republic of Viet-Nam will give priority to French nationals whenever it needs advisors, technicians, or experts. The priority accorded to French nationals will cease to be operative only in the event that France cannot furnish the requested personnel.

Article 5

As soon as the problem of monetary harmonization is resolved, a single and identical currency will be legal tender in the territories under the authority of the Democratic Republic of Viet-Nam and in the other Indochinese territories.

This currency is the Indochinese piastre, presently issued by the Bank of Indochina pending the creation of an Institute of Issue.

The statute of the Institute of Issue will be studied by a mixed commission on which all the members of the Federation will be represented. This commission will also have the function of coordinating currency and exchange. The Indochinese piastre is part of the Franc zone.

Article 6

Viet-Nam forms a customs union with the other countries of the Indochinese Federation. In consequence there will be no internal tariff barriers, and the same tariffs will be applied everywhere to entry into and departure from Indochinese territory.

A coordinating committee for customs and foreign commerce, which may in addition be the same as that for currency and exchange, will study the necessary measures of application and will prepare the customs organization for Indochina.

Article 7

A mixed coordinating committee for communications will study the necessary measures to reestablish and improve communications between Viet-Nam and the other countries of the Indochinese Federation and the French Union: land, sea, and air transportation; postal, telephonic, telegraphic, and radio-electronic communications.

Article 8

Pending the conclusion between the French Government and the Government of the Democratic Republic of Viet-Nam of a definitive agreement settling the question of the diplomatic relations of Viet-Nam with foreign countries, a mixed Franco-Vietnamese commission will determine the arrangements to be taken to fix Vietnamese consular representation in the neighboring countries and the relations of Viet-Nam with foreign consuls.

Article 9

Anxious to assure in Cochin China and in southern Annam the restoration as soon as possible of the public order so indispensable to free development of democratic liberties as well as the resumption of commercial transactions, and conscious of the happy consequences which the cessation of all acts of hostility and violence by both sides would have in this connection, the French Government and the Government of the Democratic Republic of Viet-Nam mutually agree on the following measures:

a. All acts of hostility and violence on both sides will be halted.

b. Agreements between the French and Vietnamese general staffs will settle the conditions of application and control of measures decided by mutual agreement.

c. It is specified that the prisoners presently held for political motives will be freed with the exception of those prosecuted for crimes and offenses under generally accepted law [*de droit commun*].

The same will apply to prisoners taken in the course of military operations.

Viet-Nam guarantees that no prosecution will be instituted and no act of violence tolerated against anyone by reason of his sympathy or loyalty to France. Reciprocally, the French Government guarantees that no prosecution will be undertaken and no acts of violence tolerated against anyone by reason of his sympathy for Viet-Nam.

d. The enjoyment of the democratic liberties defined in Article 1 will be reciprocally guaranteed.

e. A stop will be put to unfriendly propaganda by both sides.

f. The French Government and the Government of the Democratic Republic of Viet-Nam will cooperate to render harmless the nationals of former enemy powers.

g. A person designated by the Government of the Democratic Republic of Viet-Nam and approved by the French Government will be accredited to the High Commissioner to establish the cooperation indispensable for the execution of this agreement.

Article 10

The Government of the French Republic and the Government of the Democratic Republic of Viet-Nam agree to seek together the conclusion of special agreements on all questions which may arise between them, with a view to drawing the bonds of friendship closer and preparing the way for a general definitive treaty. Negotiations toward that end will be resumed as soon as possible and at the latest in January 1947.

Article 11

All the provisions of this *modus vivendi,* drawn up in duplicate, will enter into force on October 30, 1946.

Done at Paris, September 14, 1946

For the Provisional Government of the French Republic, the Minister for Overseas France
(Signed) MARIUS MOUTET

For the Government of the Democratic Republic of Viet-Nam, the President of the Government
(Signed) HO CHI MINH

43. *Constitution of the Democratic Republic of Viet-Nam* *
    November 8, 1946

Preamble

The August Revolution regained the independence of our Fatherland, the liberty of our people and founded the Democratic Republic.

After 80 years of struggle, the Vietnam people threw off the colonial yoke and, at the same time, abolished the internal feudal regime.

The nation entered upon a new stage in its history.

From now on our people face the tasks of preserving the integrity of

* *Source:* Vietnam News Service, *Vietnam: A New Stage in Her History* (Bangkok: A "Vietnam News" Publication, June 1947), pp. 11–22. Numerous typographical and several grammatical errors in the original have been corrected.

our territory, achieving full independence and building up the country on democratic foundations!

Being entrusted by the nation with the task of drafting the first Constitution of the Democratic Republic of Vietnam, the National Assembly is deeply conscious that the Constitution, to embody the glorious achievements of the Revolution, should be based on the following principles:

> The union of all the people without distinction of race, clan [class], creed, wealth or sex;
>
> The guaranteeing of democratic liberties;
>
> The establishment of a true people's government.

Permeated by the spirit of unity symbolized in the struggle of the entire nation and manifested in an enlarged and enlightened democratic regime, Vietnam now goes forward confidently in consonance with the progressive movements of the world and the peaceful aspirations of mankind.

Chapter I
GENERAL PROVISIONS

Article 1. Vietnam is a Democratic Republic.

All power in the country belongs to the people of Vietnam without distinction of race, class, creed, wealth or sex.

Article 2. The territory of Vietnam composed of *Bac-Bo* or Northern Vietnam, *Trung-Bo* or Central Vietnam, and *Nam-bo* or Southern Vietnam, is one and indivisible.

Article 3. The national flag of Vietnam is red, centered with a five-pointed golden star.

The national anthem of Vietnam is the "Tien Quan Ca." [15]

The Capital of Vietnam is Hanoi.

Chapter II
THE DUTIES AND RIGHTS OF THE CITIZENS
A. DUTIES

Article 4. It is the duty of every citizen:

> to defend the country;
>
> to abide by the Constitution;
>
> to observe the laws.

Article 5. All Vietnamese citizens are liable for military service.

B. RIGHTS

---

[15] Text of the national anthem is in Allan B. Cole, ed., *Conflict in Indo-China and International Repercussions: A Documentary History, 1945–1955* (Ithaca, New York: Cornell University Press, 1956), pp. 39–40.

Article 6. All Vietnamese citizens enjoy equal rights in the economic, political and cultural fields.

Article 7. All Vietnamese citizens are equal before the law and enjoy equal opportunity to participate in the administration and in national construction, each according to his or her abilities and character.

Article 8. Besides enjoying full and equal rights, the ethnical minorities are to receive every help and encouragement to enable them to reach the common level of advancement as speedily as possible.

Article 9. Women enjoy full and equal rights with men under the Constitution in every respect.

Article 10. Vietnamese citizens enjoy:

Freedom of speech,

Freedom of the press,

Freedom of assembly and meeting,

Freedom of religion,

Freedom to reside and travel in the country or to go abroad.

Article 11. Vietnamese citizens may not be arrested and detained except under the law, and their residence and correspondence are inviolable.

Article 12. The rights of property and possession of Vietnamese citizens are guaranteed.

Article 13. The rights and interests of both manual and intellectual workers are guaranteed.

Article 14. Aged and infirm Vietnamese citizens unfit to work are to be assisted by the state. And the education of children is to be provided for.

Article 15. Primary education is compulsory and free of charge. In local primary schools, the ethnical minorities have the right to learn in their own language.

Poor students are to be helped by the Government.

Private schools are free to operate; they have to conform to the educational programme provided by the Government.

Article 16. Foreigners who immigrate owing to their struggle for Democracy and Freedom are granted the right of asylum in Vietnam.

C. ELECTION—REVOCATION—VETO

Article 17. The mode of elections to all popular representative state bodies is first and primarily through universal suffrage by free, direct and secret ballot.

Article 18. All Vietnamese citizens from the age of 18 upwards, without distinction of sex, have the right to vote except lunatics and those deprived of civic rights.

Candidates must be qualified electors, at least 21 years of age, and be able to read and write the Vietnamese language. Citizens on military duty have the right to vote and to stand for elections on a par with all other citizens.

Article 19. The method and procedure of polling is to be determined by law.

Article 20. All citizens have the right to recall their elected representatives according to Articles 41 and 61.

Article 21. All citizens have the right to decide on constitutional issues and all problems affecting the destiny of the nation according to Articles 32 and 70.

Chapter III

THE PEOPLE'S PARLIAMENT [16]

Article 22. The People's Parliament is the body entrusted with supreme powers in the Democratic Republic of Vietnam.

Article 23. The People's Parliament decides all questions of common national interest such as the enactment of laws, the sanctioning of budgets and the ratification of agreements entered into with foreign countries.

Article 24. Parliamentary elections are to be held normally once every three years, there being ordinarily one parliamentary representative for every 50,000 inhabitants.

The number of parliamentary representatives for up-country areas where there are ethnical minorities and for big cities will be determined by law.

Article 25. A member of the People's Parliament represents not only his own constituency but the entire nation as well.

Article 26. The People's Parliament determines if necessary on the validity of elections and accepts the resignation of its members.

Article 27. The People's Parliament shall elect from its members its own President and two Vice-Presidents along with twelve permanent and three substitute members to form its Permanent Committee. The President and Vice-Presidents of the People's Parliament will assume the functions of Chairman and Vice-Chairmen of the Permanent Committee respectively.

Article 28. The People's Parliament shall meet twice a year on being convoked by the Permanent Committee (about May and November).

The Permanent Committee, when it deems necessary, may summon the People's Parliament to an extraordinary meeting.

---

[16] Subsequently the "People's Parliament" was generally termed the "National Assembly," and the "Permanent Committee" was called the "Standing Committee." This terminology was used in the 1960 Constitution.

The Permanent Committee shall summon the People's Parliament if at least a third of all the members of the latter so desire or if, in exceptional circumstances, the Government requires it to do so.

Article 29. At every meeting of the People's Parliament at least half of its total membership shall constitute a quorum. To declare war, the decision must be taken by at least a two-third majority.

Article 30. The meeting of the People's Parliament is open to the public. The press is allowed to report all deliberations and decisions arrived at.

In exceptional cases the People's Parliament is entitled to hold a secret meeting.

Article 31. The President of the Democratic Republic of Vietnam shall promulgate all bills, measures and laws which have been passed by the People's Parliament not later than ten days after they have been voted upon. However within this interval of time, the President of Vietnam may ask the People's Parliament to re-consider their decision. The President is obliged to publish any revised decision of the People's Parliament.

Article 32. Any matter vitally concerning the nation's destiny must be presented to the nation for final decision, if agreement by at least two thirds of the People's Parliament has been obtained to this effect.

The mode of procedure for arriving at this final decision will be fixed by the law.

Article 33. The People's Parliament may dissolve itself with the consent of at least two thirds of all its members. The Permanent Committee, in the name of the People's Parliament, shall proclaim such dissolution.

Article 34. When the People's Parliament dissolves, whether the period of its normal duration be expired or not, its functions shall be assumed by the Permanent Committee until a new Parliament is elected.

Article 35. Two months before the normal expiration of the People's Parliament, the Permanent Committee shall announce re-elections. These re-elections must be carried out within these two months before the expiration of the People's Parliament.

When the People's Parliament voluntarily dissolves, the Permanent Committee immediately proclaims re-elections. These re-elections must be carried out within two months after dissolution.

The Permanent Committee must convoke the new Parliament at the latest one month after elections.

If the term of office of the People's Parliament expires during such crises as war time, the Permanent Committee is allowed to prolong their functioning for an indefinite time; however, the People's Parliament must be re-elected not later than six months after the end of such crises.

Article 36. During the time that the People's Parliament does not meet, the Permanent Committee is entitled:

    a. to vote on bills and decrees and other such projects proposed by the Government. All such decisions are to be presented to the People's Parliament at its next meeting, in order to get them approved, rescinded or modified;

    b. to convoke the People's Parliament;

    c. to control and criticize the Government.

Article 37. To be valid and binding, all the Permanent Committee's decisions must be accepted by more than half of its members.

Article 38. If the People's Parliament cannot meet, the Permanent Committee and the Government are together entitled to decide upon war or peace.

Article 39. After the report of the Permanent Committee on its working, which is to be presented at the beginning of every session, a vote of confidence in the Permanent Committee may be proposed, if requested by not less than a fourth part of the total members of the People's Parliament. In case of no-confidence, the whole Permanent Committee must resign.

Out-going members of the last Permanent Committee are eligible for re-election.

Article 40. The Government may not ordinarily arrest or pass sentence on any of the members of the People's Parliament without the prior permission of the People's Parliament or in case it is not meeting, of the Permanent Committee.

A member of the People's Parliament may not be prosecuted for a speech or opinion expressed during the sessions.

In case of flagrant breaches of the common laws, the Government may arrest a member of the People's Parliament, but it has to report to the Permanent Committee within twenty-four hours; the Permanent Committee or the People's Parliament will decide on the validity of such arrest.

When a member of the People's Parliament loses his right to vote, he loses at the same time all his rights and privileges as a member of the People's Parliament.

Article 41. If the People's Parliament receives a request from at least a fourth part of the electors of any constituency to recall their parliamentary representative, it must consider the question. And if at least two thirds of all the members of the People's Parliament agree to dismiss this parliamentary representative, he must resign.

Article 42. The honorarium of the members of the People's Parliament will be determined by law.

Chapter IV
THE GOVERNMENT

Article 43. The highest executive authority of the whole nation is the Government of the Democratic Republic of Vietnam.

Article 44. The Government consists of the President of the Democratic Republic of Vietnam, the Vice-President and the Cabinet. The Cabinet consists of the Prime Minister, the other Ministers and Under-Secretaries and, if need be, a Deputy Prime Minister.

Article 45. The President of the Democratic Republic of Vietnam is chosen from among the members of the People's Parliament and elected by a majority of at least two thirds of all its members.

If during the first vote, the requisite majority is not reached, the second vote shall decide by a relative majority. The President of Vietnam is elected for five years and may be re-elected for consecutive terms. One month before the expiration of his functions, the Permanent Committee must summon the People's Parliament to elect a new President.

Article 46. The Vice-President of Vietnam is elected by the People's Parliament in the same way as the President. The length of his tenure of office is the same as that of the People's Parliament.

The Vice-President assists the President. In case the President dies or resigns, the Vice-President temporarily replaces him. The new President must be elected subsequently within two months.

Article 47. The President of Vietnam chooses the Premier from the People's Parliament and presents his appointment to the People's Parliament for approval.

If the choice is approved by the People's Parliament, the new Premier may nominate all the Ministers from among the People's Parliament and presents the nominated list to the People's Parliament for approval.

The Under-Secretaries may be chosen from outside the People's Parliament and must be introduced by the Premier to the Government's Council for approval.

The members of the Permanent Committee are not allowed to participate in the Cabinet.

Article 48. In case of a Ministerial vacancy, the Premier in agreement with the Permanent Committee, appoints immediately a temporary substitute pending approval by the People's Parliament.

Article 49. The President of the Vietnam Democratic Republic:

   a. represents the Nation;

   b. is invested with the command of the whole nation's armed forces, appoints or dismisses commanders of the land army, navy and air forces;

   c. signs decrees appointing the Premier, members of the Cabinet and high officials of the Government;

   d. presides over the Government's Council;

   e. promulgates all laws decided by the People's Parliament;

   f. confers decorations or honorific diplomas;

   g. decrees special amnesties;

   h. signs agreements with foreign nations;

   i. assigns representatives of Vietnam to foreign countries and receives foreign representatives;

   j. declares war or peace according to Article 38.

Article 50. The President of Vietnam Republic is above the law unless he betrays the nation.

Article 51. In case the President, the Vice-President or a Cabinet member are prosecuted for treason, the People's Parliament will set up a special tribunal for their trial.

Arrest and legal prosecution of a member of the Cabinet for common law delinquencies must be previously agreed upon by the Government's Council.

Article 52. The Government is empowered to:

   a. execute laws and decrees of the People's Parliament;

   b. propose bills or laws to the People's Parliament;

   c. suggest emergency bills or laws to the Permanent Committee while the People's Parliament is not meeting;

   d. annul orders and decisions of all subordinate administrative organs, if need be;

   e. appoint or dismiss officials in its administrative organs and technical branches;

   f. execute mobilization orders and take all measures required for national security;

   g. draft and present the annual budget.

Article 53. Every decree of the Government must bear the signature of the President of the Vietnam Republic and the signatures of one or several other Ministers concerned as well.

These Ministers are responsible to the People's Parliament.

Article 54. Any Minister, on a successful motion of no-confidence against him by the People's Parliament, must resign. The whole Cabinet is not jointly responsible for individual Ministers.

The Premier is responsible for the Cabinet's policy. A no-confidence motion may be deliberated on by the Parliament only when proposed by the Premier, the Permanent Committee or a fourth part of the whole People's Parliament.

Within a space of 24 hours after the People's Parliament has passed a no-confidence motion on the Cabinet, the President of the Vietnam Republic is entitled to propose that the no-confidence motion be re-examined by the People's Parliament.

The second deliberation must be held, at the latest, 48 hours after the first one. Subject to the preceding qualification, the Cabinet must at once resign on a no-confidence motion being passed against it.

Article 55. All Ministers have to answer, either orally or in writing, to all relevant questions of the People's Parliament or the Permanent Committee. At the latest they must answer within the space of ten days after receiving questions.

Article 56. When the People's Parliament dissolves, whether its normal duration be expired or not, the Cabinet exercises power till a new People's Parliament meets.

Chapter V
PEOPLES'S COUNCIL AND EXECUTIVE COMMITTEE

Article 57. From the executive point of view, Vietnam comprises three main administrative units (*"bo"*s), namely Northern, Central and Southern. Each *bo* is divided into provinces and cities, provinces and cities into prefectures and districts, and prefectures and districts into villages and quarters.

Article 58. In each province, main city, village and quarter there is a People's Council elected by direct universal suffrage.

These administrative units elect their own Executive Committee.

In *bo* and districts or prefectures, there are only Executive Committees. A *bo*'s Executive Committee is elected by the People's Councils of its respective provinces and cities. District and prefectural Executive Committees are elected by their respective village and quarter People's Councils.

Article 59. The People's Councils decide upon questions peculiar to their own localities. These decisions must not conflict with orders issued by higher authorities.

Executive Committees must:

a. carry out orders issued by higher authorities;

b. execute decisions of their own People's Councils after these decisions have been approved by higher authorities;

c. manage the administrative machinery in their own localities.

Article 60. An Executive Committee is responsible to higher authorities as well as to its own People's Council.

Article 61. The members of People's Councils and Executive Committees may be compelled to resign; correct procedure for the purpose will be determined by law.

Article 62. A Government Act will determine the details of the organization of People's Councils and Executive Committees.

Chapter VI
THE JUDICIARY ORGANS

Article 63. The judiciary organs of Vietnam consist of:

a. A Supreme Court of Appeal,

b. Appeal Courts,

c. Provincial and Prefectural Courts.

Article 64. All judges are appointed by the Government.

Article 65. All criminal cases must be attended by a People's Jury who either profer advice if the case be one of "misdemeanour," or give verdicts with the judge if the case be one of "felony."

Article 66. The national minorities may use their own language before the Tribunal.

Article 67. The trial sessions must be held in public unless extraordinary circumstances preclude such procedure. All accused are allowed to conduct their own defence or plead with the assistance of an advocate.

Article 68. It is forbidden to torture, strike or ill-treat accused persons and prisoners.

Article 69. While trying cases, the judges have to discharge their functions in conformity with the law. No other authority is allowed to interfere with the functions of the judiciary.

Chapter VII
AMENDMENT OF THE CONSTITUTION

Article 70. Amendments to a part or to the whole Constitution are subject to the following conditions:

a. the amendments must be requested by at least a two third majority of the whole People's Parliament;

b. the People's Parliament must elect a committee to draft the amendments;

c. the amendments, when thus ratified by the People's Parliament, must be put before the whole nation for final approval.

CHAPTER IV

The Formation of
a Rival Viet-Nam

February 1947-December 1949

Introduction

During the three years following the outbreak of hostilities between
France and the Democratic Republic of Viet-Nam (DRV), both sides
hardened their positions. At first it appeared that negotiations might
be possible, but that hope evaporated during the course of 1947, and
by the end of 1949 it was clear that there was no immediate possibility
of a peaceful resolution of the conflict. The gulf between the two sides
was further extended by the French decision, in the summer of 1947,
to endorse the formation of an anti-Communist national government
centering on former Emperor Bao Dai. Formation of that government,
and the nominal reunification of Viet-Nam under its authority, was
accomplished during 1948 and 1949, while the Viet Minh moved closer
to open identification with the Communist bloc.

As the war spread throughout Viet-Nam following the events of
December 1946, French forces were able to establish control over the
principal towns and communication routes, but Viet Minh guerrilla
units operated almost at will in the countryside. In Paris a coalition
government under Paul Ramadier replaced the Blum government in
January, and the new Premier reaffirmed the determination of France
to respond firmly to Viet Minh military action while also expressing
French willingness to see a resolution of the conflict on the basis of
Vietnamese reunification and independence within the French Union
and the Indochinese Federation. But after the events of December
1946 the French were distrustful of the Viet Minh, and the Viet Minh
in turn were suspicious of France, particularly so long as High Commissioner d'Argenlieu shaped policy. Despite a series of peaceful

declarations by both sides, it was impossible to open meaningful negotiations. The conflict attracted passing attention from the United States when Secretary of State Marshall, in a February 7 press conference, expressed the hope that "a pacific basis of adjustment of differences could be found." [1]

At the beginning of March the French Cabinet replaced High Commissioner d'Argenlieu with Emile Bollaert, a Socialist member of Parliament. Later in the month the Government's policy was supported by the National Assembly.[2] Shortly after his arrival in Saigon, High Commissioner Bollaert received a new peace initiative in the form of a message from the DRV Foreign Minister, Hoang Minh Giam (Document 44). Paris agreed to send an emissary, Paul Mus, to inform the Viet Minh of French conditions for peace. Meeting with Ho Chi Minh on May 12, Mus delivered conditions [3] which were unacceptable to the Viet Minh (Document 46). The failure of the Mus mission marked the end of immediate hopes for an end to the war through negotiations, and France turned toward a policy of military victory supported by efforts to establish a pro-French nationalist government which would accept "independence" as defined by France and act as a counterweight to the Viet Minh. Bollaert's speech in Hanoi on May 15 (Document 45) indicated the new turn of policy.

France focused her attention on former Emperor Bao Dai, now in exile in Hong Kong, who was also acquiring support from various

[1] *The New York Times*, February 8, 1947, p. 2. On February 6, 1947, United States Ambassador Jefferson Caffery in Paris took up with Foreign Minister Georges Bidault the substance of a Department of State instruction which contained a phrase to the effect that the United States would be opposed to the replacement of the French colonial administration in Indochina by organizations whose "philosophy of life and government" would be contrary to the interests of the United States. The Department of State instruction remains unavailable, but very likely will be published in the pertinent volume of *Foreign Relations of the United States* for 1947. See also the speech delivered by Etienne Fajon to the 11th Congress of the French Communist Party later in 1947, in Monique Lafon, ed., *Le Parti Communiste Français dans la Lutte Contre le Colonialisme* (Paris: Editions Sociales, 1962).

[2] In voting on the Government's policy as well as in voting military credits for the war, Communist cabinet members voted with the Government while the rank and file abstained. Communist members were expelled from the Cabinet on May 4 after refusal to support the Government's economic policy.

[3] The French conditions, as reported by Mus, were: (1) surrender by the Viet Minh of all their arms; (2) free movement of French troops throughout Viet-Nam; (3) concentration of Vietnamese troops within determined perimeters; (4) surrender of all hostages; and (5) surrender of all non-Vietnamese personnel serving with the Viet Minh forces. See Paul Mus, *Viêt-Nam: Sociologie d'une Guerre* (Paris: Editions du Seuil, 1952), p. 315.

nationalist elements, including Ngo Dinh Diem, who turned to him as an alternative to both France and the Viet Minh. Bollaert was instructed to make a "final offer" to the Viet Minh, which was contained in the speech he delivered at Ha Dong on September 10 (Document 47). Delegates of the various political groups gathered around Bao Dai in Hong Kong were disappointed by many aspects of the speech but urged him to adopt it as the basis for his own negotiations with the French, as the spokesman of non-Communist Vietnamese nationalism. The former Emperor responded affirmatively to their advice on September 18 (Document 48).

The Viet Minh response to the Bollaert speech was wholly negative. Their international position seemed stronger; an indication of Soviet support for their struggle was given by Andrei Zhdanov in his speech at the founding meeting of the Communist Information Bureau (Cominform) on September 22 (Document 49). Ho Chi Minh denounced the Bollaert speech on September 23 (Document 50). By this time the DRV was almost completely an underground movement, conducting guerrilla warfare from bases in the mountains and jungles of Viet-Nam. There was, until the end of 1949, little active participation in international affairs. The DRV did maintain "news service" operations in Bangkok and Rangoon as well as in New York and, until the end of 1948, in Paris. DRV delegates did participate actively in the "First Asian Relations Conference" in New Delhi in March and April 1947, and in the famous "Calcutta Conference" in February 1948 where they reportedly urged the virtues of revolution and armed struggle. For the most part, however, active and open international activity until after the Communist victory in China was overwhelmingly that between France and the Bao Dai regime.

Three-way negotiations now began between France, Bao Dai, and General Nguyen Van Xuan, the new President of the Cochin China government. Bao Dai met with Bollaert on December 7 in Ha Long Bay, but the joint declaration and secret protocol [4] which Bao Dai signed on that occasion were rejected by his advisors. On December 23 France officially confirmed its decision to ignore Ho Chi Minh and to treat Bao Dai as the true spokesman of Vietnamese nationalism (Document 51), although the latter had made clear that he would demand at least as much as Ho had demanded in 1946. France's position was strengthened by indications that the United States was moving toward

[4] Texts not available.

support of the French fight against "international Communism" as represented by the DRV.[5]

In March 1948, France finally agreed to the formation of a "Provisional Central Government" under General Xuan. Bao Dai refused to take an official role in the project but did endorse Xuan's effort to rally nationalist support. On June 5 Xuan met with Bollaert and Bao Dai on board the cruiser *Duguay-Trouin* in Ha Long Bay and signed the agreement establishing the Provisional Government of Viet-Nam (Document 52). The agreement was denounced by Ho Chi Minh (Document 53). The French Government officially endorsed the agreement on August 19, in a statement made to the National Assembly by Premier André Marie (Document 54). But the Ha Long Bay Agreement did not appreciably improve the situation in Viet-Nam: many nationalists, including Ngo Dinh Diem, refused to support it and the failure of France to grant complete independence drove others to the Viet Minh.

As 1949 began, the situation was growing increasingly difficult for France. The Viet Minh continued to consolidate its position in the countryside and French internal opposition to the war was mounting. It appeared essential to bring Bao Dai actively into the nationalist government, but the former Emperor demanded a more real independence and unity than had been given. Agreement was finally reached, and on March 8 Bao Dai and President Auriol of France exchanged letters at the Elysée Palace setting forth detailed arrangements (Document 55), in terms much the same as the DRV had refused at Fontainebleau in 1946.

Since the Elysée Agreements were not to come into effect until after the reunification of Cochin China with the rest of Viet-Nam, France initiated the procedure required by the Constitution to change the status of a French territory.[6] In March the National Assembly passed a law creating an elected territorial assembly (with very limited suffrage) in Cochin China which, on April 23, adopted a motion in favor of the reattachment of Cochin China to Viet-Nam. The law modifying the status of Cochin China (Document 56) was approved by the National

[5] See William Buillet, "The Saddest War," *Life,* Vol. 23 (December 29, 1947), pp. 64–69; extracts are in Allan B. Cole, ed., *Conflict in Indo-China and International Repercussions: A Documentary History, 1945–1955* (Ithaca, N.Y.: Cornell University Press, 1956), pp. 83–84.

[6] See Document 55, "Explanatory Letter from President Auriol to H.M. Bao Dai" (Section I), p. 126.

Assembly on May 21 and promulgated by President Auriol on June 4. The Elysée Agreements came into effect on June 7, and Bao Dai set about forming the new government of the State of Viet-Nam. But many of the most prominent Vietnamese nationalists refused to associate themselves with the new government. After Ngo Dinh Diem refused to become Premier, Bao Dai finally was forced to assume the post himself (Document 58). At the end of the year France and the State of Viet-Nam approved 27 additional agreements on various matters of mutual concern not covered specifically by the Elysée Agreements.[7]

The Indochina war became a major internal political issue in France during the fall. Opposition to the war was spearheaded by the Communists and Socialists, while the right wing criticized the French Government for giving away its colonial empire and privileges. The thinking of a large portion of public opinion was reflected in a press conference statement made by General de Gaulle on November 14:

France should remain in Indochina, she should remain there for Indochina, for, without the presence and the assistance of France, the independence, the security, and the development of Indochina would surely be compromised. Moreover, the more time that passes the better one sees that the events in Indochina are only part of a whole. In reality, it is a matter of knowing whether Asia is going to remain free. At a time when it is necessary for the free world to cooperate with free Asia, I do not see why France should not cooperate with Indochina.[8]

It was now also that Indochina began to acquire significance as an international issue for the first time since the spring and summer of 1945. The United States had greeted the implementation of the Elysée Agreements hopefully (Document 57). The Soviet Union condemned "the puppet 'government' formed with the blessings of the Americans." [9] More importantly, the victory of the Chinese Communists during 1949 brought a power friendly to the Viet Minh to the northern frontiers of Indochina and accelerated the drift of the DRV toward full Communist status. Fear of Chinese Communist action in Southeast Asia and elsewhere had become a factor in Western concerns during the summer, and was expressed by Secretary of State Acheson in July:

[7] Texts in Haut Commissariat de France en Indochine et Gouvernement du Vietnam, *Accords Franco-Vietnamiens du 8 Mars 1949: Conventions d'Application* (Saigon?: 1950?).

[8] France, Ministère de la France d'Outre-Mer, *Bulletin d'Information de la France d'Outre-Mer*, No. 138 (December 1949), p. 17.

[9] "Struggling Vietnam," *Literaturnaya Gazeta* (June 22, 1949); extracts in Cole, *Conflict in Indo-China*, pp. 85–86.

Should the Communist regime [in China] lend itself to the aims of Soviet Russian imperialism and attempt to engage in aggression against China's neighbors, we and the other members of the United Nations would be confronted by a situation violative of the principles of the United Nations Charter and threatening international peace and security.[10]

In November, Viet Minh representatives attended the "Trade Union Conference of Asian and Australasian Countries" in Peking, where Liu Shao-chi presented the Chinese model of revolution as one which might well be followed by other peoples in Asia, including the Vietnamese (Document 59).

44. *Message from Foreign Minister Hoang Minh Giam of the Democratic Republic of Viet-Nam to the French Government, Delivered to High Commissioner Emile Bollaert* *
April 19, 1947

Viet-Nam is fighting for its unity and independence. France, Premier Ramadier has declared, is not opposed to that unity and independence. The interest of the two peoples is to collaborate fraternally within the French Union, an association of free peoples who understand each other and who are friends with each other. In continuing, the war can only increase the hate, entail new sacrifices of human life, and aggravate the situation of French businesses and the Vietnamese economy, without resolving the problem of Franco-Vietnamese relations.

The French Government, by the nomination of a new French High Commissioner in Indochina, seems to have indicated the desire to orient its policy with regard to Viet-Nam on a new road, worthy of the New France. I am convinced that the motion of the National Council of the Socialist Party, dated March 21, 1947,[1] resolving to let no opportunity pass to engage in negotiations with Viet-Nam, expresses

* *Source:* Philippe Devillers, *Histoire du Viêt-Nam de 1940 à 1952* (Paris: Editions du Seuil, 1952), pp. 385–386, citing Délégation de la République Démocratique du Viêt-Nam en France, Service d'Information, Bureau de Paris, *Messages de Paix addressés par le Président Ho-Chi-Minh au Peuple et au Gouvernement français* (Paris: 1947); copyright 1952, reprinted by permission of Editions du Seuil and The Bobbs-Merrill Company, Inc. Translation by the editor. Emphasis in the original. This message was received by M. Bollaert on April 26.

[10] Letter, dated July 30, 1949, to President Truman, transmitting the "white paper," *United States Relations with China, with Special Reference to the Period 1944–1949,* reprinted in *The China White Paper: August 1949* (Stanford, Cal.: Stanford University Press, 1967), p. xvii.

[1] Reported in *Le Monde,* March 22, 1947, p. 3.

not only the feelings of the French Socialists but those of all the people of France. In order to prove the sincere attachment of Viet-Nam to peace and its friendship for the people of France, *the Vietnamese Government proposes to the French Government the immediate cessation of hostilities and the opening of negotiations with a view to a peaceful solution of the conflict.*

45. High Commissioner Bollaert: Speech in Hanoi [Extracts] *
    May 15, 1947

Two months ago I had the honor of being chosen by the Government of the French Republic to represent France in Indochina. Today I want to tell you, with what may seem to be brutal frankness, my views on the Franco-Vietnamese problem and the measures which I think should be taken to solve the present difficult situation so that this land may at last be restored to calm, happiness and prosperity.

I want to make one statement at the outset, because everything else hinges upon it: France will remain in Indochina and Indochina within the French Union. This is the first principle of our policy and it would be prejudicial to the interests of peace if the slightest doubt on this matter were allowed to arise in anyone's mind. The continued presence of France in this country is now and henceforth a fact that realists must not leave out of their considerations.

Any man whose judgment is not warped by hatred will acknowledge that we have rights and legitimate interests in Indochina. We have sown much seed there and we are not ashamed to say that we do not wish to be cheated out of the harvest. We do not feel that we have fallen short of our responsibilities and we do not intend to give up, because France has not the right to fail.

We shall remain. The French political parties are unanimously resolved that France shall not be dispossessed. The Constitution, adopted by the National Constituent Assembly, approved by the French people and promulgated on October 27th, 1946, makes the French Union, of which Indochina is an integral part, an institution of the Republic. The French Union thus gains a constitutional basis which precludes any notion of abandonment.

However, the maintenance of French presence in Indochina does not

* *Source:* French Press and Information Service (New York), *News from France,* Second Year, No. 23 (June 12, 1947), pp. 3–4, 7. Subheadings are omitted. The official French text of this speech is in France, Direction de la Documentation, *Notes Documentaries et Etudes,* No. 638 (June 7, 1947), pp. 1–3.

mean the oppression of its people. It must not prevent this country from being happy and free. We hope it will provide a stimulus, a ferment of new activities for all those who wish to derive some benefit from it. We do not intend it to act as an impediment, nor an affront to the legitimate patriotism of the Indochinese peoples, who have a right to their place in the sun. The French Parliament, of which I have the honor to be a member, will see to this. Indeed it considers one of its chief tasks to be the organization of the French Union to safeguard both the interests of France and of the member States, by ensuring the harmonious development of all in accordance with the general lines of world development.

[The bulk of the speech, dealing with the characteristics of the French Union and the advantages which will accrue to the Indochinese nations from membership in it, is omitted. Bollaert remarked that "Now, through the fault of a few men, one Indochinese people is suffering," and went on to explain how peace might be restored.]

Let them send us representatives of all their parties—I say "all their parties" because France does not recognize that any one party has the exclusive right to speak in the name of the Vietnamese people. We hope that they may all work together for the reconstruction of their country in their own way and protected from totalitarian domination. Indeed, it is only in an atmosphere free from strain, distrust and restrictions, that political life, which is still disturbed, can be resumed in the Viet Nam (I hope this may be soon) and develop through the honest open functioning of liberal institutions. France, however great her desire to see calm restored to this devastated land, is firmly resolved that the democratic principles which have always guided her, shall never be betrayed.

[The concluding paragraphs, emphasizing Bollaert's sincerity, are omitted.]

46. *Ho Chi Minh: Letter to the Vietnamese People after the Meeting with Paul Mus, Representative of the French High Commissioner* * 2
May 25, 1947

Compatriots,
Armymen, militamen, and self-defence guards throughout the country.

* *Source:* Ho Chi Minh, *Selected Works* (4 vols., Hanoi: Foreign Languages Publishing House, 1961–1962), Vol. III, pp. 111–113. This letter also appeared

Up to now, our entire people have waged the Resistance war for five months. Our southern compatriots have waged the Resistance war for twenty months.

The French have shed much blood, our people have made no less sacrifices;

For the sake of humanity and peace, for the maintenance of the sympathy with France, our Government has proposed to the French Government to find ways and means to stop war by negotiations on the basis of our people's aspirations for unity and independence.

But the French colonialist militarists are used to atrocity, inhumanity and impoliteness. They hold our Army and people in contempt. They put forth arrogant and unacceptable conditions.

They asked us

1. to surrender them all our weapons,

2. to give the French Army freedom to move everywhere in our country, etc.

This means that they want us to surrender. They want to strangle our Fatherland. They want us to give them a free hand to burn down villages, plunder our property, massacre our people, rape women, and destroy temples, pagodas and churches. This means that they want all our compatriots and our offspring to kneel down and bow our heads and be their everlasting slaves.

Compatriots!

Armymen, militiamen and self-defence guards!

We are determined not to let our mothers, fathers and relatives be killed by them. We are determined not to let our wives and sisters be violated by them. We are determined not to let our churches, villages and our people's property be plundered by them.

We are determined not to be enslaved.

Therefore, on behalf of the Government, I call on all my compatriots to make every effort in taking part in the Resistance and help the Army to fight the enemy.

───────────

in Viet-Nam American Friendship Association, Viet-Nam News Service (New York), *Release* (June 14, 1947), p. 1, with slightly different wording.

2 Footnote in the original: "On March 6, 1947, the bellicose reactionary French colonialists appointed Bollaert as French High Commissioner in Indo-China to replace D'Argenlieu. Apparently Bollaert seemed mild and ready to negotiate in order to settle the 'Viet Nam–France conflict', but actually he continued D'Argenlieu's predatory policy and was 'determined not to give up the French interests in Indo-China'. After successive defeats, Bollaert was recalled to France towards the end of October 1948."

I order that all armymen, militiamen and self-defence guards be determined to fight, to go forward and kill the enemy.

Each citizen must be a fighter. Each village must be a fortress.

We must be determined to sacrifice ourselves in struggle in order to smash the colonialist militarists and reconquer unity and independence.

Compatriots!

Fighters!

Our Fatherland is calling on us. Victory is awaiting us. March forward, march forward!

The long-term Resistance will certainly win!

Long live united and independent Viet Nam!

47. *High Commissioner Bollaert: Speech at Ha Dong [Extracts] * September 10, 1947*

During my recent visit to France, I was given the mission of explaining the ideas of the Government of the Republic. It is, therefore, my duty to address the whole Vietnamese people.

As you know, our Government has more than once shown its desire to bring to a successful conclusion in the Annamite lands a peace effort that is as dear to France as to Indochina. It has not swerved in this purpose and the fact that peace has not yet become a reality is not its fault. True, peace has been the object of certain démarches, but these démarches have never been accompanied by the slightest guarantees. In particular, our Government has waited in vain for assurances that the hostages taken would be returned to us, that our friends and fellow-citizens would be protected in their person and property, and that French presence in Indochina and the French Union was neither contested nor threatened. On the other hand, we have been asked on many occasions to make known in what spirit we intended to solve the Indochinese problem and to outline in detail a constructive policy capable of ending the present conflict and ensuring a better future to these ravaged lands.

It is this desire that we wish to satisfy today here in Hadong, in this

* *Source:* French Press and Information Service (New York), *Document* (September 10, 1947), pp. 1–2, 6–7. Subheadings are omitted. The official French text of this speech is in France, Direction de la Documentation, *Notes Documentaires et Etudes,* Hors Serie No. 117 (September 13, 1947); and in France, Ministère de la France d'Outre-Mer, *Bulletin d'Information,* No. 110 (September 22, 1947), pp. 10–15.

burned Tonkinese city whose ruins are still haunted by memories of terror,[3] by calling upon the Vietnamese people, the entire Vietnamese people, to be the judge of our good will and by showing them that, if they but wish it, they can put an end to their sufferings tomorrow.

First, I wish to make a statement about what has so often been represented to us as the principal aspiration of the Vietnamese peoples: freedom within the French Union and the Union of the three "Ky." [4] This freedom is the basis of future relations between France and the peoples of Indochina. It has no other limitations than those imposed by the adherence of these territories to the French Union.

France seeks neither conquest nor reconquest and has renounced any idea of directly or indirectly administering these territories; we are ready to restore to qualified governments the exercise of public authority and for this purpose offer them as much assistance as they deem necessary from our functionaries and technicians. Each of the Indochinese peoples will determine its mode of existence in conformity with its own genius. It will organize its own representative institutions, judicial system, educational system, public welfare agencies and hospitals, without the slightest interference on the part of France. Thus, the peoples of Indochina will take into their own hands control over, and responsibility for, their destiny. And it is our heartfelt hope that this will be in their best interests.

Believing that these populations have a right to prosperity and happiness, France will not only leave their economic development unhampered; she will facilitate it by giving them markets for their goods and access to her own riches. We pledge ourselves, as is fitting between free and equal States, to respect both in the spirit and in the letter, the moral dignity of each of these peoples and each of their individual members.

With regard to the peoples of Viet Nam, this freedom has an even more basic implication: France is not taking any position on the problem of the Union of the three "Ky"; this is an internal Vietnamese problem which must be solved by the populations concerned. France is not proposing a solution; she has no preference for any one of the many solutions that can be envisaged. However, she can and must insist that the Union not be created by constraint and according to totalitarian formulas which are universally condemned. She very properly expects

---

[3] Ha Dong was almost totally destroyed in fighting between French and Viet Minh forces during the spring of 1947.

[4] See Note 1, p. 78.

and will see to it that, if a Union is created as the result of a formal expression of the popular will, the local peculiarities, which have made of these lands in their traditional form such an harmonious whole, are not repudiated, and that the amalgamation of the Annamite lands, to which France is not in the least opposed, is based, not on the interests of one of them, but on the mutual confidence and friendship of all.

[Three paragraphs on the necessity for respect of democratic principles are omitted; a long section on the advantages and attributes of the French Union (facilitation of the development of its members, international relations and national defense, internal relations of the Indochinese states and economic coordination, and the role of the High Commissioner of the French Republic) is omitted.]

France demands nothing beyond what is required for the fulfillment of certain binding obligations that she has assumed, nothing that is not essential to the very existence of the French Union. While she wishes to be as conciliatory as possible in the application of these fundamental principles, she does not intend to allow them to be dissociated from each other. The offer I am formulating on behalf of the Government of the Republic, constitutes an indivisible whole that must be accepted or rejected in its entirety. We have no intention of bargaining; this would be unworthy of so noble a cause. Moreover, I am firmly convinced, in all good faith, that our proposal is of a nature to satisfy all the patriots of this country. Is not freedom, as we have defined it, the embodiment of the formula which, we are told, expresses the fervent aspirations of the Vietnamese people?

We must now find out whether certain declarations were sincere or, as I am loathe [*sic*] to believe, whether they were intended to mask other designs. For my part, I consider that, since we are satisfying such profound aspirations, it is all the more senseless to prolong hostilities. We can only build solidly upon a foundation of peace and a happy future cannot take shape amidst the prevailing disorder.

In the meantime, what do we see around us? Where peace reigns, in those Indochinese countries that have freely accepted the regime we propose, happiness and prosperity are returning. Why should they not return throughout the entire territory? We must lay down our arms.

I hope that the Vietnamese people, whose traditional wisdom and diplomatic finesse I well know, will at this juncture select to represent them men capable of carrying the negotiations to a successful conclusion. They will have the best chance of success if they can inspire confidence. Need we conceal the fact that the instigators of the December 19th uprising have lost much of their standing with the French people? They themselves must be aware that certain methods they have employed have shocked public opinion all over the world. If these methods are continued, deep anxiety will be aroused concerning the fate of those patriots—and, despite the efforts made to minimize their number, they are many—who have not flocked to the banner of the Viet Minh, because they have a different conception of patriotism.

In bringing up this question of confidence, I am not speaking from the standpoint of feeling only, but of the real advantage the Viet Nam has to gain. It is quite impossible that the disrepute into which some of its leaders have fallen through their participation in party conflicts —of which they were the first prisoners—could work to the advantage of the Vietnamese people, when the time comes to conclude the separate agreements which may be negotiated.

For that matter, peace will never be securely established if it is the work of a single party.

Once all the healthy forces of Viet Nam unite in the government of the country, the adjustment of Franco-Vietnamese relations will become an easy matter. By responding wholeheartedly to the wholehearted offer of the French people, the Vietnamese nation will affirm its political maturity. It is, therefore, to all political, religious and social groups that I address this last appeal. All patriots, whatever their tendency, must have the courage to proclaim their political ideal and assume their share of responsibility in the reconstruction of their country. The broader the bases of the young states associated within the French Union the more stable will be their autonomy and the more durable the peace.

It is toward peace that I ask you to lift your eyes, a radiant peace that can transform this gutted town into a joyful city whose inhabitants will return at the end of their day's work to a rebuilt and improved home where, surrounded by their well-fed family, they can enjoy the rest they deserve.

It depends upon you to win such a peace.

48. *Proclamation by Bao Dai* *
September 18, 1947

People of Viet-Nam! In order to avoid the shedding of blood by my compatriots I renounced the throne of my fathers.[5] As you wanted to entrust the responsibility for your destiny to new masters, I voluntarily stood aside. I abdicated and I took the road of exile so as not to be an obstacle to that experiment which, in your opinion, would bring you happiness. I am in exile in a foreign land, where I am at this moment, but I am able to follow, sometimes with hope and often with melancholy, the development of these recent and terrible pages of our history. I am fully aware of your hopes. I follow your torments, your sufferings. Despite the dictatorship which tries to stifle your voices, I hear today your appeals and your cries of distress. You outline the picture of your misery for me, and you present to me the balance sheet of the disasters suffered by our dear Viet-Nam after the two-year experience during which your masters held the absolute exercise of power. Thus your hopes of happiness vanished little by little, hopes which a clever propaganda in an instant awakened in your hearts. In your distress you come to me. You appeal to my authority to bring peace to our country, ravaged by war and torn by internal dissension, a peace such as is appropriate between free and equal States, an internal peace within security. You urge me to be your negotiator with France, who, by the voice of its very distinguished representative in Viet-Nam, High Commissioner Bollaert, asked you, in specific terms in his speech at Ha Dong,[6] to designate the personalities having your confidence.

Responding to your appeal I accept the mission which you entrust to me and am ready to enter into contact with the French authorities.

With them I will examine in all objectivity the propositions which were made to us. To begin with, I hope to obtain for you the independence and unity conforming to your aspirations, to arrive at accords of reciprocal guarantee, and to be able to affirm to you that the ideal for which you have fought in a fierce resistance is fully attained. Then I will bring you my authority to arbitrate the conflict which has you all turned one against the other, for once our goal is

---

* *Source:* France, Direction de la Documentation, *Notes Documentaires et Etudes,* No. 752 (October 30, 1947), p. 7, citing *Le Populaire d'Indochine,* No. 469 (September 19, 1947). Translation by the editor.
  [5] See Document 25.   [6] Document 47.

attained nothing should continue to stand in the way of the return of peace.

I want you to maintain that productive peace which will give you prosperity and security. Time will soothe the passions. In union, we Vietnamese will reconstruct our beautiful country on new bases, drawing our vigorous forces from our powerful traditions.

49. *Andrei Zhdanov: "The International Situation," Speech Delivered at the Founding Meeting of the Communist Information Bureau [Extracts]* *
September 22, 1947

[The first portion of the speech reproduced here is the section of Part I, "The Post-War World Situation," which is directly relevant to Soviet attitudes and policy toward Indochina.]

World War II aggravated the crisis of the colonial system, as expressed in the rise of a powerful movement for national liberation in the colonies and dependencies. This has placed the rear of the capitalist system in jeopardy. The peoples of the colonies no longer wish to live in the old way. The ruling classes of the metropolitan countries can no longer govern the colonies on the old lines. Attempts to crush the national liberation movement by military force now increasingly encounter armed resistance on the part of the colonial peoples and lead to protracted colonial wars (Holland-Indonesia, France-Viet Nam).

[The second portion of the speech reproduced here is the section of Part II, "The New Post-War Alignment of Political Forces and the Formation of Two Camps: the Imperialist and Anti-Democratic Camp, and the Anti-Imperialist and Democratic One," which is directly relevant to Soviet attitudes and policies toward Indochina.]

The cardinal purpose of the imperialist camp is to strengthen imperialism, to hatch a new imperialist war, to combat Socialism and democracy, and to support reactionary and anti-democratic pro-fascist regimes and movements everywhere.

In the pursuit of these ends the imperialist camp is prepared to rely on reactionary and anti-democratic forces in all countries, and to support its former adversaries in the war against its wartime allies.

* *Source:* Communist Information Bureau, *For a Lasting Peace, For a People's Democracy*, No. 1 (November 10, 1947), p. 2.

The anti-fascist forces comprise the second camp. This camp is based on the U.S.S.R. and the new democracies. It also includes countries that have broken with imperialism and have firmly set foot on the path of democratic development, such as Rumania, Hungary and Finland. Indonesia and Viet Nam are associated with it; it has the sympathy of India, Egypt and Syria. The anti-imperialist camp is backed by the labour and democratic movement and by the fraternal Communist parties in all countries, by the fighters for national liberation in the colonies and dependencies, by all progressive and democratic forces in every country. The purpose of this camp is to resist the threat of new wars and imperialist expansion, to strengthen democracy and to extirpate the vestiges of fascism.

50. *Ho Chi Minh: Appeal on the Occasion of the Second Anniversary of the Resistance in Nam-bo (South Viet-Nam) [Extracts]** *September 23, 1947*

[The first five paragraphs of the statement, congratulating the fighters in the South and stressing determination to fight for unification and national independence, are omitted.]

Recently, after two years of our national resistance [the representative of France],[b] speaking to us as master to servant, as victor to vanquished, declared that the French will not recognize our independence, will not allow us to have a diplomatic representation and a national

* *Source:* Broadcast by Viet-Nam News Agency in English Morse, September 23, 1947, 8:00 A.M., E.S.T. It has been impossible to obtain a reliable complete text of this important statement. The broadcast version printed here has gaps in it which have been filled from versions found elsewhere.

A text appears in Ho Chi Minh, *Messages of President Ho Chi Minh to the Southern People* (Hanoi: Foreign Languages Publishing House, 1956), pp. 7–9. That version, however, was edited to omit the paragraphs replying to High Commissioner Bollaert's September 10 speech, and the wording throughout is much different from the broadcast version, probably because of differences in translation. Extracts from this version which were used to fill gaps in the broadcast text are enclosed in brackets and indicated by superscript "a."

Extracts from the appeal, including the paragraphs responding to Bollaert's speech, appear in France, Ministère de la France d'Outre-Mer, *Bulletin d'linformation,* No. 112 (October 20, 1947), pp. 26–27. Extracts from this version which were used to fill gaps in the broadcast text are enclosed in brackets and indicated by superscript "b."

An extract from the appeal, including the paragraphs rejecting Bollaert's offer, is contained in Viet-Nam American Friendship Association, Viet-Nam News Service (New York), *Release* (October 14, 1947), p. 1.

army of our own, and made clear that the French authorities would pursue [the same policy as d'Argenlieu] [b] regarding the unity of our land.[7]

Furthermore, they tried to get past our national assembly and our government. They planned to set up a puppet regime in our country and to use Vietnamese people to fight Vietnamese people. We certainly shall not accept those humiliating conditions and we shall fight to the bitter end for complete independence and unity.

We are willing to cooperate with the French people like friends and equals. But we are also determined to fight to the very last end in order to smash down enemy attempts at enslaving our people for a second time. Victory will be ours because we are 20 million people fighting for freedom, for the safeguard of our Fatherland, for a just cause.

On this solemn occasion, I urgently appeal to those who, for some reason or other, have been led astray by the enemy to go back to their Fatherland. Whatever your motive, may be you are the true-born sons of Viet-Nam. I am confident that you [will not have the courage to carry on helping the enemy to plunge our people again into a miserable and shameful life].[a] I cannot stand by and see our own people divided in an internal fratricidal war.

I hope you shall repent without delay and I pledge that the Fatherland of our People and our Government shall always be tolerant to those who have strayed. When next you will go back to the Fatherland you will be greeted forgetfully, like straying sons.

Dear people and freedom fighters, the hearts of Ho Chi Minh and the Government, the national Army, and the entire people are always with you, watching you, loving you. Let us march forth unitedly, hand in hand with each other. Victory to our long-draw-out resistance! Viet-Nam, united and independent!

Signed: Ho Chi Minh

51. *Communiqué Issued by the French Government* * December 23, 1947

The Government has taken note of the fact that Ho Chi Minh has not answered the offers to negotiate made in M. Bollaert's speech [8] to

* *Source:* French Press and Information Service (New York), *News from France,* Fourth Year, No. 12 (September 15, 1949), p. 5. A slightly different version of this communiqué appears in Philippe Devillers, *Histoire du Viêt-Nam de 1940 à 1952* (Paris: Editions du Seuil, 1952), p. 421.

[7] The reference is to High Commissioner Bollaert's speech at Ha Dong on September 10, Document 47.

[8] Document 47.

all the political groups in Viet Nam and that the Viet Minh radio has refused to consider these offers. Consequently, the Government has decided to give the French High Commissioner in Indochina full powers to carry on, outside Ho Chi Minh's Government, all activities and negotiations necessary for the restoration of peace and freedom in the Vietnamese countries.

52. *The Ha Long Bay Agreement* *
   June 5, 1948

In the presence of His Majesty Bao Dai,

M. Emile Bollaert, Councillor of the Republic, High Commissioner of France for Indochina, acting in the name of the Government of the French Republic,

And M. Nguyen Van Xuan, President of the Provisional Government of Viet-Nam, assisted by M. Nghiem Xuan Thien and M. Dang Huu Chi, M. Phan Van Giao, M. Nguyen Khoa Toan and M. Dinh Xuan Quang, M. Tran Van Huu and M. Le Van Hoach, representing respectively North Viet-Nam, Central Viet-Nam, and South Viet-Nam,

Made the following declaration:

1. France solemnly recognizes the independence of Viet-Nam, to whom falls hereafter the task of freely realizing its unity. On its part, Viet-Nam proclaims its adherence to the French Union as a State associated to France. The independence of Viet-Nam has no other limits than those imposed upon it by its adherence to the French Union.

2. Viet-Nam undertakes to respect the rights and interests of French nationals, constitutionally to ensure respect for democratic principles, and to give priority to French advisors and technicians for the needs of its internal administration and its economy.

3. As soon as a Provisional Government is constituted, the representatives of Viet-Nam will conclude with the representatives of the French Republic the various necessary special agreements of a cultural, diplomatic, military, economic, financial, and technical nature.

Done in double original, at Ha Long Bay, June 5, 1948.

BAO DAI   EMILE BOLLAERT
NGUYEN VAN XUAN
NGHIEM XUAN THIEN, DANG HUU CHI,
PHAM VAN GIAO, NGUYEN KHOA TOAN,
DINH XUAN QUANG, TRAN VAN HUU, LE VAN HOACH

* *Source:* France, *Journal Officiel de la République Française, Lois et Décrets* (March 14, 1953), p. 2409. Translation by the editor.

53. *Ho Chi Minh: Declaration on the "Puppet Government" Created
by the French Authorities* *
June 1948

Since September 23, 1945, French colonial interests have waged a
full-scale war of aggression against the Vietnam people with the object
of destroying the sovereignty and independence of the Democratic Republic of Vietnam. The entire Vietnam people have successfully resisted
French armed forces and are determined to struggle in defense of the
unity and independence of the Fatherland until final victory is achieved.

The French authorities have now taken the step of setting up a puppet government which is prepared to commit every treason against the
Vietnam people.

The Government of the Democratic Republic of Vietnam reserves
the right to judge these traitors in conformity with the legal code of
the Vietnam state.

In the name of the Government and the people of the Democratic
Republic of Vietnam I hereby declare null and void any agreement
which may be signed by these puppets with any foreign powers.

54. *Premier André Marie: Declaration to the National Assembly* †
August 19, 1948

[Premier André Marie's statement was made in response to several interpellations on the Indochinese question submitted for discussion in the National
Assembly.]

PREMIER ANDRÉ MARIE: Ladies, Gentlemen, the Government asks
the National Assembly to postpone the interpellations, of which it has
just been informed.

But, so that the postponement may be decided by you in full knowledge of the reason, the Government wishes to inform you in terms
whose brevity will, in its opinion, usefully serve clarity, of the position
which it intends to take with regard to the grave problem of Indochina.

* *Source:* Viet-Nam American Friendship Association (New York), *Information Bulletin,* July 1, 1948, p. 1. Several grammatical mistakes in the original
have been corrected. The exact date of the Declaration cannot be ascertained.

† *Source:* France, *Journal Officiel de la République Française, Débats Parlementaires, Assemblée Nationale,* Session of August 19, 1948, p. 5998. Translation by the editor.

The Government expresses the gratitude of the nation to the members of the French forces in the Far East and salutes the memory of those who have fallen in order to re-establish peace. (*The deputies on the left, in the center and on the right rise and applaud at length.*) [9]

THE CHAIRMAN: M. Premier, I desire to associate the National Assembly with the so legitimate homage you have just rendered to our troops in the Far East and to the victims. (*Renewed applause on the same benches.*)

THE PREMIER: The Government pays homage to the action of the High Commissioner of France.

His untiring efforts to restore peace have reached an important stage: the conclusion of the agreements of December 7, 1947,[10] and of June 5, 1948,[11] which have defined the principles on which France intends to base her association with the Vietnamese people.

The Government gives its complete and solemn endorsement to these principles.

On the one hand, faithful to the mission of France which consists, in the words of the Constitution, of "leading the peoples of whom she has charge to the liberty of self-government and of democratically administering their own affairs," the Government intends to associate the States of Indochina in full equality and independence within the French Union; to them henceforth falls the responsibility to assure their harmonious development.

On the other hand, the Government considers that the present regime of Cochin China no longer corresponds to current necessity and that the populations themselves should determine freely their final status within the framework of the French Union. (*Applause on the left and on various benches in the center.*)

The Government renews the appeal of the High Commissioner to all the spiritual and political groupings in Viet-Nam (*Applause on the left and on various benches in the center*) to cooperate on this basis in the work of independence and peace.

The Government expresses the ardent wish that there therefore be made possible, as soon as circumstances permit, the organization of a popular vote and the creation of a permanent government, providing the institutions of a democratic State exercising the functions of a free

[9] This did not include the Communists, who are referred to as the "extreme left."

[10] Subsequently renounced by Bao Dai; texts not available.

[11] Document 52.

State over the whole of its territory. (*Applause on the left, the center and on various benches of the right.*)

55. The Elysée Agreements: Exchange of Letters between President Auriol of France and H.M. Bao Dai [Extracts] *
March 8, 1949

LETTER FROM PRESIDENT AURIOL TO H.M. BAO DAI

SIRE,

You have very properly expressed the desire to see the principles established by the Joint Declaration made on June 5, 1948,[12] in Ha Long Bay by M. Emile Bollaert, High Commissioner of France in Indochina, and General Nguyen Van Xuan, President of the Central Provisional Government of Viet-Nam, in the presence of Your Majesty, confirmed and stated precisely with regard to the Unity and the Independence of Viet-Nam.

This desire coincides with that of the French Government which, after discussing the matter in the Council of Ministers, requested me, in my capacity as President of the French Union, to proceed by exchange of letters with Your Majesty to the conclusion of an agreement for the purpose of defining more accurately, for their application, the principles of the Declaration of June 5.

It will be incumbent on the Government of Your Majesty, on the one hand, to conclude with the High Commissioner of France in Indochina the special or provisional conventions which will determine the relations between the French Union and Viet-Nam, taking into account the principles established in the present exchange of letters and the present state of affairs, pending the reestablishment of peace and order; and, on the other hand, to prepare, with the Representative of France and in liaison with the Royal Governments of Laos and Cambodia, the necessary regulations implied by the present agreements.

On this basis and in these circumstances, in the name of the Government of the French Republic I confirm my agreement to the following provisions:

---

* *Source:* France, Direction de la Documentation, *Notes et Etudes Documentaires,* No. 1147 (June 20, 1949), pp. 3–5, 8, 13–14. Translation by the editor.
12 Document 52.

I. UNITY OF VIET-NAM

Notwithstanding previous treaties of which she might have taken advantage, France solemnly reaffirms her decision to pose no obstacle in law or in fact to the inclusion of Cochin China within Viet-Nam, defined as formed by the union of the territories of Tonkin (North Viet-Nam), Annam (Central Viet-Nam), and Cochin China (South Viet-Nam).

But the reattachment of Cochin China to the rest of Viet-Nam can be considered as legally established only after free consultation of the populations concerned or of their representatives.

The whole of the provisions of the present agreement will be valid only in the case of the effective and legal reattachment of Cochin China to the rest of Viet-Nam.

To that end, the Government of the French Republic undertakes to implement the procedures provided by the Constitution.[13]

As soon as the procedure provided above is completed, the French Government will definitively recognize the Unity of Viet-Nam as it has just been defined.

The French Government renounces the right to take advantage of the special status conferred by royal ordinances on the three cities of Hanoi, Haiphong, and Tourane.

The administration of the non-Vietnamese populations whose historical home is located in the territory of Viet-Nam as it has just been defined and who have always traditionally been dependent on the Crown of Annam, will be made the subject of special statutes granted to the representatives of these populations by H.M. the Emperor.[14] These statutes will be determined in agreement with the Government of the French Republic which has, in this matter, special obligations toward these populations. The statutes should at the same time guarantee the paramount rights of Viet-Nam and the free development of these populations in respect for their traditions and their customs.

II. DIPLOMATIC QUESTIONS

The foreign policy of the French Union, within the framework of which Viet-Nam exercises its rights through its delegates to the High

[13] See the "Explanatory Letter from President Auriol to H.M. Bao Dai" (Section I), p. 126.
[14] Bao Dai never officially reassumed the title of "Emperor" but referred to himself only as "Head of State."

Council and by its diplomacy as hereafter defined, will be examined and coordinated under the direction and the responsibility of the Government of the French Republic in the High Council of the Union, where the Government of Viet-Nam will be represented by its freely chosen delegates.

For the implementation of the above general rules in matters of foreign policy, H.M. the Emperor will join the activity of his diplomacy to that of the French Union.

The chiefs of foreign diplomatic missions in Viet-Nam will be accredited to the President of the French Union and to H.M. the Emperor of Viet-Nam.

The chiefs of the Vietnamese diplomatic missions, who the Government of Viet-Nam will designate in agreement with the Government of the French Republic to represent it in foreign States, will receive letters of credence issued by the President of the French Union and initialed by H.M. the Emperor of Viet-Nam.

The countries in which Viet-Nam will be represented by a diplomatic mission will be determined after agreement with the French Government.

The unity of the international policy of the French Union in these States will be ensured both by preconcerted general directives, the High Council of the French Union being informed, and transmitted by the Government of the Republic to the Government of Viet-Nam, as well as by direct contacts which the French and Vietnamese diplomats will establish among themselves. In other States, Viet-Nam will be represented by the diplomatic missions of the Government of the French Republic, which may include representatives of Viet-Nam.

Viet-Nam is empowered to negotiate and to sign agreements relative to its own interests, on the express condition that before any negotiation it will submit its proposals to the Government of the Republic for examination in the High Council and that the negotiations be conducted in coordination with the diplomatic missions of the Republic. A favorable decision of the High Council will be necessary in order for agreements thus concluded to become final.

The Government of the French Republic is prepared, on the request of the Government of Viet-Nam, to intercede for the opening of Vietnamese consulates in the foreign countries where Viet-Nam considers itself to have special interests.

In the States where Viet-Nam has a diplomatic mission, the Vietnamese consuls will carry on their activity under the direction and the control of the chief of that mission, in liaison with the chief of the diplomatic post of the Government of the French Republic; in other States the Vietnamese consuls will act under the direction and control of the head of the diplomatic post of the Government of the French Republic.

The Government of the French Republic undertakes to present and to support the candidacy of Viet-Nam for membership in the United Nations when it fulfills the general conditions laid down by the Charter for admission to that organization.[15]

III. MILITARY QUESTIONS

Viet-Nam has its own national army charged with the maintenance of order and internal security, and with the defense of the Empire. In this last case, it is supported if necessary by the forces of the French Union. The Vietnamese army likewise participates in the defense of the frontiers of the French Union against all foreign enemies.

The total strength of the Vietnamese national army and that of the army of the French Union stationed in Viet-Nam will be fixed by a special agreement, in such a manner that in time of war the total of the means available will be able to assure effectively the defense of the territory of Viet-Nam and of the French Union.

The Vietnamese army is composed of Vietnamese nationals officered by Vietnamese officers; French instructors and technical advisors will be placed at the disposal of Viet-Nam.

The Vietnamese officers and non-commissioned officers will be trained in the Vietnamese military schools and, if necessary, in French schools, where they will be admitted without any discrimination. To facilitate cooperation in time of war, the internal composition of the Vietnamese army will be as close as possible to that of the army of the French Union.

The Vietnamese army will be dependent on the budget of the Government of Viet-Nam. Orders for materiel will be made by the Government of Viet-Nam to the French Government.

In order to contribute effectively to the defense of the French Union, the army of the French Union is stationed on the territory of Viet-Nam in bases and garrisons whose nomenclature, limits, and status will be made the subject of a special agreement. In any event, this status will be such as to permit these forces completely to fulfill their mission

[15] The application was submitted on December 17, 1951: United Nations document A/2023 and S/2446. A more detailed application was submitted on August 7, 1952: United Nations Document A/2168 and S/2756. For disposition of the application, see Document 82.

while completely respecting the principle of Vietnamese national sovereignty. They will be able to circulate freely between the bases and garrisons which are assigned to them according to the terms and conditions which will be specified in the aforesaid military convention. According to the principle of total cooperation within the French Union, they will include Vietnamese elements whose rules of recruitment will also be determined by the aforesaid convention.

In order to assure immediately effective joint action in time of war, a permanent military committee composed of officers of the general staffs of the two armies will be established in peacetime to prepare a plan of joint defense and military cooperation between the national army and the army of the French Union; it will be able if necessary to serve in peacetime as the organ of permanent liaison between the two armies. The methods for composition and operation of this military committee in time of peace will appear in the special convention annexed to the Franco-Vietnamese Treaty.

In time of war, the totality of the means of defense, consisting particularly of the Vietnamese army and the army of the French Union, will be pooled, and the Military Committee will form the nucleus of a mixed general staff whose direction and command will be in the hands of a French general officer in charge of the theater of operations principally affecting Viet-Nam and one of whose chiefs of staff will be Vietnamese.

IV. INTERNAL SOVEREIGNTY

The Government of Viet-Nam will exercise in their totality the attributions and prerogatives which derive from its internal sovereignty. It will conclude with the High Commissioner of France in Indochina the special or provisional agreements which, taking circumstances into account, will determine the means of transfer to Viet-Nam of the powers previously exercised by the French authority.

The Government of Viet-Nam will call in by priority nationals of the French Union each time it needs advisors, technicians or experts in the departments, public establishments, or the enterprises of a public character concerning the defense of the French Union.

The priority accorded to nationals of the French Union will cease only in the event that the French Government is unable to furnish the requested personnel. The methods of application of this provision will be specified in a subsequent text.

No French citizen, no national of the French Union, will be allowed to be a part of a Vietnamese administrative service without having obtained the prior authorization or agreement of the representative of the

French Union, and in turn no Vietnamese will be allowed to belong to a French administrative service or an administrative service of the French Union without having obtained the authorization or agreement of his Government in advance.

[Section V, "Judicial Questions," Section VI, "Cultural Questions," and Section VII, "Economic and Financial Questions," are omitted. All provide a privileged position for French nationals and French interests in Viet-Nam and for the conclusion of further conventions to regulate specific matters. The "Economic and Financial" section also provides for unity of the three Indochinese states in economic and financial matters, with the specifics to be determined by a subsequent Indochinese Conference. This Conference was held at Pau during the second half of 1950.]

[CONCLUSION]

Legal instruments will be exchanged in Saigon between Your Majesty and the High Commissioner of France in Indochina. The Agreement will enter into force on the date of that exchange.[16]

The Joint Declaration of June 5 and the present agreements, as well as the complementary conventions which they require, will be submitted for approval to the French Parliament and to Vietnamese authorities qualified to frame the act provided for by Article 61 of the Constitution of the French Republic.[17]

The Government of the Republic and myself are convinced that the rapid implementation by Your Majesty and the representative of France, in a spirit of mutual confidence and of reciprocal good will, of the foregoing dispositions will contribute effectively to the re-establishment of peace in Viet-Nam, freely united to France in equality and friendship.

I ask Your Majesty kindly to accept the assurances of my highest consideration.

VINCENT AURIOL

For the President of the Republic:

[16] June 14, 1949, was the date of the formal exchange.

[17] Article 61 reads: "The position of the Member States in the French Union shall appear for each of them in the act defining its relations with France" (Allan B. Cole, ed., *Conflict in Indo-China and International Repercussions: A Documentary History, 1945–1955* [Ithaca, N.Y.: Cornell University Press, 1956], p. 12). The Elysée Agreements were never ratified by a Vietnamese body so constituted. French ratification of the Ha Long Bay Agreement and the Elysée Agreements was accomplished by Law No. 50-142 of February 2, 1950, in France, *Journal Officiel de la République Française, Lois et Décrets*, February 2, 1950, p. 1192.

The President of the Council of Ministers,
                    HENRI QUEUILLE
The Keeper of the Seals, Minister of Justice,
                    ROBERT LECOURT

[The letter from Bao Dai to President Auriol, agreeing to the letter above, is omitted.]

EXPLANATORY LETTER FROM PRESIDENT AURIOL TO H.M. BAO DAI

SIRE,

As was anticipated during the negotiation of the Franco-Vietnamese agreement signed in Paris on March 8, 1949, I have the honor to give Your Majesty in this letter the additional details which He requested on certain special points of that text.

I. UNITY OF VIET-NAM

1. The reuniting of South Viet-Nam to the rest of the Empire will be accomplished according to the following procedure:

Vote by the French Parliament of the law creating the Representative Territorial Assembly of South Viet-Nam provided for by Article 77 of the French Constitution and charged to give its opinion on the changing of the status of the territory in question;[18]

Vote by the Representative Territorial Assembly of South Viet-Nam on the changing of the status referred to above and the integration of South Viet-Nam with the rest of the Empire;[19]

Vote by the French Parliament of the law provided for in Article 75 of the French Constitution sanctioning the changing of the status of Cochin China.[20]

The National Assembly will be consulted according to the procedure of urgency as soon as the Representative Territorial Assembly of South Viet-Nam has made its opinion known.

2. The agreement of the Government of the French Republic provided for on the subject of the special statutes granted to the non-Vietnamese populations whose historical home is situated on the territory of Viet-Nam is required at the time of the granting of the said statutes and for all subsequent modifications.

[18] The law was passed on March 12; text in France, *Journal Officiel, Lois et Décrets,* March 14–15, 1949, p. 2644.

[19] The vote of the Assembly approving the status change took place on April 23; text of the motion in *Journal Officiel, Assemblée Nationale, Documents Parlementaires, Annexes aux Procès-Verbaux des Séances,* 1949, Annex No. 7158, May 17, 1949, p. 754.

[20] Document 56.

The text of these statutes will determine the means of application by the parties in question. The French Government does not envisage the submission of the Vietnamese administration to a special materiel control.

II. DIPLOMATIC QUESTIONS

1. The number of delegates from Viet-Nam to the High Council of the Union will be determined subsequently, in agreement with the Government of Viet-Nam.

2. The Government of the French Republic is in agreement that Viet-Nam be immediately represented by diplomatic missions in the following countries: Holy See, China, Siam.

However, if, on account of the events which presently affect China, Viet-Nam judges it preferable to be allowed another post, the Government of the French Republic will see no objection to China being replaced by India in the above list.[21]

Any revision or extension of the present article may be effected only in agreement with the Government of the French Republic.

3. The Vietnamese diplomats who will be included in the French diplomatic missions will be designated by the Government of Viet-Nam and commissioned by the Government of the French Republic.

They will be most especially charged to attend to matters concerning Viet-Nam.

They will be able to correspond with their Government under cover of the Chief of the French diplomatic mission, it being understood that French is the official language of the post.

4. These provisions apply equally to Vietnamese Consuls in the countries where, in the absence of Vietnamese diplomatic representation, they conduct their activity under the direction of the Chief of the French diplomatic mission.

5. The "liaison" with the diplomatic missions of the French Republic at the time of negotiations undertaken by Viet-Nam for the purpose of concluding and signing agreements relative to its particular interests implies not the obligatory existence of mixed Franco-Vietnamese delegations but the establishment in each case of a system of reciprocal information which, while leaving to the Vietnamese mission its full liberty of action and responsibility, permits, if necessary, the diplomacy of the French Union to support and help the Vietnamese mission in any difficulties and any serious incidents which might arise during the negotiations.

[21] This was later done, but diplomatic representation was not established as India did not recognize the State of Viet-Nam. In addition, the State of Viet-Nam was authorized to establish diplomatic relations with the United Kingdom and the United States after they extended recognition in February 1950.

I ask Your Majesty kindly to accept the assurances of my highest consideration.

VINCENT AURIOL

For the President of the Republic:
The President of the Council of Ministers,
HENRI QUEUILLE
The Keeper of the Seals, Minister of Justice,
ROBERT LECOURT

56. *Law Modifying the Status of Cochin China* *
   June 4, 1949

On the recommendation of the Assembly of the French Union,

The National Assembly and the Council of the Republic have deliberated,

The National Assembly has adopted,

The President of the Republic promulgates the law whose terms follow:

Article 1. Within the framework established in Article 60 of the Constitution of the French Republic [22] and on the recommendation made, in its session of April 23, 1949, by the Territorial Assembly of Cochin China,[23] the status of Cochin China is modified in the terms provided in the following article.

Article 2. The territory of Cochin China is reattached to the Associated State of Viet-Nam in accordance with the terms of the joint declaration of June 5, 1948,[24] and the declaration of the French Government of August 19, 1948.[25]

Cochin China in consequence ceases to have the status of an overseas territory.

Article 3. In the event of a change in the status of Viet-Nam, the status of Cochin China shall be the subject of a new deliberation by the assemblies as provided in Article 75 of the Constitution (Title VIII: The French Union).[26]

* *Source:* France, *Journal Officiel de la République Française, Lois et Décrets,* June 5, 1949, p. 5502. Translation by the editor.

[22] "The French Union shall comprise, on the one hand, the French Republic, which shall include Metropolitan France and the overseas Departments and Territories, and, on the other hand, the Member States and Territories." See Allan B. Cole, ed., *Conflict in Indo-China and International Repercussions: A Documentary History, 1945–1955* (Ithaca, N.Y.: Cornell University Press, 1956), p. 12.

[23] See Note 19, p. 126.   [24] Document 52.   [25] Document 54.

[26] "The status of the members of the Republic and of the French Union shall be subject to change.   [continued on page 129]

The present law will be enforced as a law of the State.

Done at Toulon, June 4, 1949.

VINCENT AURIOL

For the President of the Republic:

The President of the Council of Ministers,

HENRI QUEUILLE

The Minister of Overseas France,

PAUL COSTE-FLORET

57. *United States Reaction to the Elysée Agreements: Statement by the Department of State * *
    June 21, 1949

The formation of the new unified state of Vietnam and the recent announcement by Bao Dai that the future constitution will be decided by the Vietnamese people[27] are welcome developments which should serve to hasten the reestablishment of peace in that country and the attainment of Vietnam's rightful place in the family of nations.

The United States Government hopes that the agreements of March 8 between President Auriol and Bao Dai,[28] who is making sincere efforts to unite all truly nationalist elements within Vietnam, will form the basis for the progressive realization of the legitimate aspirations of the Vietnamese people.

58. *H.M. Bao Dai: Proclamation to the Vietnamese People †*
    July 2, 1949

Compatriots! International events and the internal situation of our country demand the immediate formation of a national government ca-

* *Source:* United States, Department of State, *Bulletin,* XXI (July 18, 1949), p. 75.

† *Source:* France, Direction de la Documentation, *Bulletin Quotidien de Presse Etrangère,* No. 1317 (July 5, 1949), p. 1. Translation by the editor.

"Changes in status and passage from one category to another, within the framework fixed by Article 60, may result only from a law voted by the Parliament, after consultation with the Territorial Assemblies and the Assembly of the Union" (Cole, *Conflict in Indo-China,* p. 14).

[27] See "H.M. Bao-Dai's Message to the Vietnamese People Delivered in Saigon, 14th June 1949," in *Accords Franco-Vietnamiens du 8 Mars 1949: The Franco-Vietnamese Agreement of March 8th, 1949* (Saigon: Imprimerie Française d'Outre-Mer, 1949?) [In French and English], pp. 41–44. This publication also contains several other documents relevant to the Elysée Agreements.

[28] The Elysée Agreements, Document 55.

pable of taking in hand the destiny of the nation and carrying out the initial measures necessary to consolidate our independence.

Great powers have demonstrated their sympathy for our people and have expressed the hope that our country will take its place in the concert of free and democratic nations. The coming months will see the fate of our country decided.

From this day on I myself will direct the affairs of state. General Nguyen Van Xuan will assist me as Vice President and Minister of National Defense. As soon as the people are in a position freely to express their will, the agreements of March 8 [29] will be submitted to constitutional processes and the people will decide conclusively the political statute of the State.

The higher interest of the nation requires the union of all men of good will: let each do his duty.

59. *Liu Shao-chi: Speech at the Opening Session of the Trade Union Conference of Asian and Australasian Countries, Peking [Extracts]* * *November 16, 1949*

[Opening paragraphs on the proposed work of the Conference and the economic basis of colonialism are omitted.]

* *Source:* Broadcast by Peking, New China News Agency, in English Morse, November 23, 1949, 9:30 A.M., E.S.T. The November 18 speech to the meeting by the Vietnamese representative, Luu Duc Pho [Le Duc Tho?], was broadcast by Peking, New China News Agency, in English Morse, November 19, 1949, 1:40 P.M., E.S.T., *prior* to the broadcast of the Liu Shao-chi speech. The Vietnamese address was concerned primarily with endorsement of the principles of the Conference and of the international trade union movement, and with condemnation of the labor movement in the United States. It did, however, contain the following paragraphs endorsing the Liu Shao-chi speech:

"Dear comrades, this conference is going to pronounce death on divisionism and proclaim the inalienable rights of workers. But it is now for all Asian trade union organizations to struggle hard for their implementation. We neither overestimate the reactionary forces nor underestimate them. In Asia, the decisive victory of the Chinese working class and the Chinese people has already dealt them a mortal blow. But in a good many places, particularly in the countries of Southeast Asia where they intend to reinforce their bases, they are still quite strong.

"The path of the 475 millions of Chinese people is the path to be taken for eventually defeating them. The essential principles were already defined in words clear enough by Comrade Liu Shao-chi in his opening speech. These principles must serve as the compass for all the workers of Southeast Asia who wish to fight and triumph, especially in us, the workers of Viet-Nam, now engaged in a similar armed struggle."

[29] The Elysée Agreements, Document 55.

After the victory of the Second World War, owing to the defeating of the three imperialist states, Germany, Japan and Italy, and the weakening of the two others, Britain and France, the national liberation movement of the colonies and semicolonies has been developing more rapidly in scope and strength. As a result of this development, China has been able to achieve a great victory in the unprecedentedly large-scale people's war of liberation against imperialism and its lackeys, the Kuomintang reactionaries, and to liberate one quarter of the world population.

The war of national liberation in Viet-Nam has liberated 90 percent of her territory; the war of national liberation in Burma and Indonesia is now developing; the partisan warfare against imperialism and its lackeys in Malaya and the Philippines has been carried on over a long period; and armed struggles for emancipation have also taken place in India. In Japan, the progressive labor movement and the progressive people's movement against the conversion of Japan into a colony by American imperialism are developing. The movement of the Korean people against Syngman Rhee, puppet of American imperialism, and for the establishment of a unified people's democratic republic of Korea cannot be halted. The labor movements and national liberation movements in Siam and the Near East countries as well as in Australasia are also growing.

Standing by the side of the powerful development of the national liberation and labor movements in these colonies and semicolonies are the mighty Soviet Union, the new democracies, and the forces of peace and democracy all over the world. Therefore, it can be fully anticipated that these movements will persist, develop, and attain final victory. The national liberation movement and the people's democratic movement in the colonies and semicolonies will never stop short of complete victory. Their struggles are entirely righteous. They should, and will, win victory. The great victory of the Chinese people has set them the best example.

The imperialists had been compelled during the war to promise the colonial and semicolonial peoples the freedom to form their own independent states after the war and choose a system for themselves according to their own will. No sooner had the war concluded, however, than the imperialists went back on their promises and trained their guns on the colonial and semicolonial peoples who demanded independence. They undermined peace and curbed the national independence movement of the colonies and the semicolonies by armed forces. In view of this, it is wholly justifiable for the colonial and semicolonial peoples to conduct armed struggles for their own national independence against imperialist armed attacks.

The armed struggles of the colonies and semicolonies in resisting imperialist attacks to win national independence are a mighty force in strengthening and defending world peace, just as the victory of the Chinese people's war of liberation has greatly strengthened the forces of world peace and democracy. The fighters of the national liberation wars of Viet-Nam, Burma, Indonesia, Malaya, and the Philippines have acted entirely correctly. They have merely applied the methods employed by the imperialists in conquering the colonies on the imperialists themselves.

[One paragraph on the necessity for wars of national liberation as a prelude to improving the workers' livelihood is omitted.]

The path taken by the Chinese people in defeating imperialism and its lackeys and in founding the People's Republic of China is the path that should be taken by the peoples of the various colonial and semicolonial countries in their fight for national independence and people's democracy.

The path which led the Chinese people to victory is expressed in the following formula:

1. The working class must unite with all other classes, political parties, and [under?]ground organizations and individuals who are willing to oppose the oppression of imperialism and its lackeys, form a broad and Nation-wide united front and wage a resolute fight against imperialism and its lackeys.

2. This Nation-wide united front must be led by and built around the working class, which opposes imperialism most resolutely, most courageously, and most unselfishly, and its party, the Communist Party, with the latter as its center, it must not be led by the wavering and compromising national bourgeoisie or the petty bourgeoisie and their parties.

3. In order to enable the working class and its party, the Communist Party, to become the center for uniting all the forces throughout the country against imperialism, and to competently lead the national united front to victory, it is necessary to build up through long struggles a Communist Party which is armed with the theory of Marxism-Leninism, which understands strategy and tactics, practices self-criticism and strict discipline, and is closely linked with the masses.

4. It is necessary to set up wherever and whenever possible a national army which is led by the Communist Party, and is powerful and skillful in fighting the enemies. It is necessary to set up the bases on which the liberation army relies for its activities, and to make the mass struggles in the enemy-controlled areas and the armed struggles to coordinate with each other. Armed struggle is the main form of struggle for the national liberation struggles of many colonies and semicolonies.

This is the basic way followed and practiced in China by the Chinese people in winning their victory. This way is the way of Mao Tse-tung, which may also be the basic way for winning emancipation by the people of other colonial and semicolonial countries where similar conditions prevail.

[The balance of the speech is omitted. In it, Liu Shao-chi states that any way other than the one he has outlined would be a mistake for the peoples of the colonial and semicolonial countries, and gives a detailed presentation of the reason for adoption of this particular strategy. He emphasizes the necessity for the working class to "unite with the peasantry and establish a strong alliance between workers and peasants."]

PART THREE

The Internationalization
of the War in Viet-Nam
January 1950–October 1953

CHAPTER V

Great Power Involvement

January 1950-January 1951

Introduction

From January 1950 to November 1953 the war in Viet-Nam developed into a major international crisis as outside powers became involved in the struggle and Viet-Nam became the scene of an indirect but potentially explosive confrontation between the Communist bloc and the Western world. Great power involvement also reinforced the deepening ideological rift within Viet-Nam itself. The external powers became involved during early 1950 as the two Vietnamese states, the Democratic Republic of Viet-Nam (DRV) and the State of Viet-Nam, sought and obtained international diplomatic recognition. Later the same year the outbreak of the Korean war had its impact on the Viet-Nam crisis as both the Communist world and the West came to view Indochina as a second front in the active military confrontation between the two power blocs.

The DRV drift toward alignment with the Soviet bloc reached a new and decisive stage in January 1950. On January 14 Ho Chi Minh issued a declaration appealing for diplomatic recognition and support (Document 60). The following day Foreign Minister Hoang Minh Giam telegraphed DRV recognition of the Chinese People's Republic (CPR); Chinese Foreign Minister Chou En-lai responded on January 18 with formal recognition of the DRV (Document 61).

The process of international recognition for the State of Viet-Nam was underway at the same time. In November 1949 the French had asked the United Kingdom, and presumably other Western powers as well, to extend diplomatic recognition to the three Associated States of Indochina.[1] During January 1950 President Truman sent Ambassador-

---

[1] Text not available; see Document 66.

at-Large Philip Jessup on a political evaluation mission to Southeast Asia; during his visit to Viet-Nam Jessup delivered a note to Bao Dai expressing American recognition of "increased sovereignty" in the State of Viet-Nam (Document 62). France was jolted on January 30 when the Soviet Union extended diplomatic recognition to the DRV (Document 63), an action which France protested on January 31 (Document 64). Secretary of State Acheson commented on the Soviet decision the following day (Document 65). On February 2 France formally ratified the agreements previously concluded with the three Associated States. Great Britain then extended diplomatic recognition on February 7 (Document 66) and the United States did likewise (Document 67).

During the spring first Nguyen Phan Long and then Tran Van Huu succeeded Bao Dai as Prime Minister, but the State of Viet-Nam continued unable to rally wide popular support, and political infighting and instability increased. At the same time the Viet Minh tightened their identification with the Communist bloc. In April, Tran Van Giau, a veteran Communist now director of the Viet-Nam Information Bureau, described the DRV as a "People's Democracy," although pointing out that Viet-Nam was at a lower level of development than the people's democracies of Eastern Europe.[2] The Viet Minh also began to expand their efforts into the other countries of Indochina, supporting the formation of the "Khmer Issarak" ("Free Khmer") movement in Cambodia in April and the "Neo Lao Itsala" ("Free Laos Front") in Laos in August.

The United States moved rapidly toward active support for the French war effort. Following conversations with French officials in Paris, Secretary of State Acheson on May 8 announced that the United States would give both economic and military aid to France and the Associated States (Document 68). On May 24 the United States delivered identical notes to the governments of France and the Associated States informing them of the establishment of an economic aid program (Document 69).

The Indochinese conflict took on a new character with the outbreak of the Korean War in June. Both sides, Western and Communist, viewed the Korean struggle as part of a larger situation which included Indochina, as was indicated by statements made during the first weeks of the war (Document 70). Ho Chi Minh reacted strongly to the Amer-

[2] Interview broadcast by the Vietnamese News Agency (VNA) in English Morse, April 4, 1950, 1300 G.M.T.

ican policy of assistance to France (Document 71). After the onset of the Korean War Washington began more and more to deal directly with the Bao Dai government, bypassing France. This policy was a source of irritation to the French and caused the Viet Minh to direct increasing hostility against the United States, as Document 71 indicates. For the next several years the Korean war had a significant impact on American policy, both because it contributed to the perceived threat of "aggressive Communism" in Asia and because the South Korean experience gradually led American policy-makers to conclude that Communist activities could be countered effectively only by independent governments relying primarily on their own armed forces.

In May Premier Tran Van Huu of the State of Viet-Nam was able to gain French approval for Vietnamese diplomatic representation in Washington and London. During June, delegations from the three Associated States arrived in France for negotiations on the "interstate structure" of Indochina. The "Conference of the Associated States" at Pau was to drag on until December, marked both by Indochinese distrust of the French and Cambodian distrust of the Vietnamese.

For the Viet Minh, the fifth anniversary of the August Revolution was the occasion for an increasingly overt identification with Communism. Credit for the successful revolution in 1945 was given to the Indochinese Communist Party: "If the Communist Party did not exist, it is certain that there would be no August Revolution nor Democratic Republic of Viet-Nam." [3] Numerous statements emphasized the close identification of the DRV with the Soviet bloc and the necessity to conduct an armed struggle on the Chinese model to consolidate independence and build a prosperous Viet-Nam.

In the new situation created by the Korean War, the Western powers considered Indochina along with other questions at a September Foreign Ministers' meeting in London, but details of the discussions were not made public. In October a French delegation had further talks with American officials in Washington, and the United States agreed to provide additional military assistance (Document 72).

During the fall, Viet Minh troops, trained and armed with Chinese assistance, abandoned guerrilla tactics for a series of victorious attacks on French positions along the Chinese frontier. Heavy French losses,

[3] "Documents and Directives Prepared for Cadres on the August Revolution Anniversary," broadcast by VNA in Vietnamese Morse, August 10, 1950, 0500 G.M.T.

particularly at Cao Bang, caused consternation in Paris. The Government's Indochina policy was the subject of bitter debates in the National Assembly on October 19 and November 22. The military events of the fall may have affected the negotiations at the Pau Conference which, despite continued frictions among the participants, managed to conclude its work on November 27 with agreement on ten quadripartite conventions, signed on December 16.[4]

The French Government decided to rectify the military situation through the creation of a Vietnamese army which could eventually relieve French forces. A military convention [5] was signed with the State of Viet-Nam on December 8, by which Viet-Nam agreed to raise four divisions during 1951, and Vietnamese military forces were placed under the command of Bao Dai and the Vietnamese Ministry of National Defense. Bao Dai, in turn, delegated command of military operations to the French commander in Indochina. Shortly thereafter, on December 23, the three Associated States, France, and the United States signed a Mutual Defense Assistance Agreement, providing for materiel for the national armies as well as assistance for the French Expeditionary Corps.[6]

France also appointed General Jean de Lattre de Tassigny as both High Commissioner and Commander-in-Chief in Indochina. Of all the Frenchmen who served there between 1945 and 1954, de Lattre (known unofficially as "Le Roi Jean" for his imperious manner) was the most dynamic and the most controversial. He won a significant victory over regular Viet Minh forces at Vinh Yen in January 1951 and set about the construction of a defense line to protect the vital Red River delta of Tonkin. During the same month Premier René Pleven visited Washington, where his discussions with President Truman resulted in a promise of further American aid (Document 73).

[4] Texts of the Pau Agreements are in France, Direction de la Documentation, *Notes et Etudes Documentaires,* No. 1425 (January 24, 1951), pp. 3–38.

[5] Text not available.

[6] The text of the Military Assistance Agreement is in United Nations, *Treaty Series,* No. 185 (1954), pp. 4–10. It is in standard form for such agreements and deals primarily with the mechanics of provision and control of assistance.

60. *Declaration of the Government of the Democratic Republic of Viet-Nam to the Governments of the Countries All over the World* * 1
January 14, 1950

After the August 1945 Revolution had overthrown the domination of the Japanese and French imperialists in Viet Nam, the Democratic Republic of Viet Nam was established. On September [2], 1945, the Provisional Government of the Democratic Republic of Viet Nam read its Declaration of Independence 2 to the Vietnamese people and the world. On March 3, 1946, the Vietnamese National Assembly elected the Government of Viet Nam.

On September 23, 1945, the French colonialists attacked south Viet Nam. After that France signed with Viet Nam on March 6, 1946 the Preliminary Agreement,3 and on September 14, 1946, the Modus Vivendi.4 But the French colonialists have carried on their unjust war in defiance of the peaceful aspirations of the French people. They have set up the puppet Bao Dai Government and used it as a tool to invade Viet Nam and deceive the world.

Determined to safeguard their national independence from the French colonialists the Vietnamese people and army are fighting heroically and are nearing final victory. Throughout these years of resistance, Viet Nam has won the sympathy and support of the people of the world. The Government of the Democratic Republic of Viet Nam declares to the Governments of the countries of the world that it is the only lawful Government of the entire Vietnamese people. On the basis of common interests, it is ready to establish diplomatic relations with the Governments of all countries which respect the equality, territorial sovereignty and national independence of Viet Nam in order to contribute to safeguarding peace and building world democracy.

* *Source:* Ho Chi Minh, *Selected Works* (4 vols., Hanoi: Foreign Languages Publishing House, 1961–1962), Vol. III, pp. 191–192. This Declaration appears in a number of contemporary sources with slightly different wording but no significant differences in meaning.

1 Footnote in the original: "After this Declaration was issued, the Governments of People's China, the Soviet Union and afterwards the other People's Democracies successively recognized the Government of the Democratic Republic of Viet Nam and established diplomatic relations with it. Since then the Democratic Republic of Viet Nam has officially sided with the socialist camp headed by the Soviet Union. This was a most important political success which created conditions for the other successes of the Vietnamese people's resistance."

2 Document 28.   3 Document 36.   4 Document 42.

61. *Recognition of the Democratic Republic of Viet-Nam by the People's Republic of China* *
    January 15 and 18, 1950

MESSAGE TO FOREIGN MINISTER CHOU EN-LAI FROM
FOREIGN MINISTER HOANG MINH GIAM
(JANUARY 15, 1950)

Considering the statement issued by the Central People's Government of China on October 1, 1949,[5] the Government and people of the Democratic Republic of Viet-Nam hereby declare that they formally recognise the Central People's Government of the People's Republic of China headed by Chairman Mao Tse Tung. In order to strengthen the friendly relations and cooperation, the Government of the Democratic Republic of Viet-Nam has decided to establish official diplomatic relations and exchange ambassadors with the Central People's Government of China.

MESSAGE TO FOREIGN MINISTER HOANG MINH GIAM FROM
FOREIGN MINISTER CHOU EN-LAI
(JANUARY 18, 1950)

I am greatly honoured to receive your telegram dated January 15, 1950, which requested the establishment of diplomatic relations with the People's Republic of China.

I hereby inform you, Mr. Minister, that the Central People's Government of the People's Republic of China regards the Government of the Democratic Republic of Viet-Nam as the legal government representing the will of the Viet-Nam people, and that the Central People's Government of the People's Republic of China is willing to establish diplomatic relations with the Government of the Democratic Republic of Viet-Nam and to exchange ambassadors, so as to consolidate the relations between the two countries and to strengthen their friendship and cooperation.

---

* *Source:* New China News Agency, *Daily News Release*, No. 261 (January 19, 1950), pp. 79–80. A Vietnamese ambassador (Hoang Van Hoan), however, did not take up duties in Peking until April 1951, and China did not have overt diplomatic representation in the DRV until after the Geneva Conference in 1954.

5 The formal proclamation of the Chinese People's Republic (CPR), in which the Chinese appealed for diplomatic recognition from countries which had broken relations with the Nationalist regime.

62. *United States Recognition of Increased Sovereignty in the State of Viet-Nam: Note from United States Ambassador-at-Large Philip C. Jessup to H.M. Bao Dai ***
January 27, 1950

The Secretary of State, Dean Acheson, has instructed me to express to Your Majesty the gratification of the United States Government at the assumption by Your Majesty of the powers transferred by the French Republic at the beginning of this year,[6] and its confident best wishes for the future of the State of Viet Nam with which it looks forward to establishing a closer relationship. My Government believes that both the people of Viet Nam and the people of France are to be congratulated on this development.

The Secretary of State also asked me to express his personal hopes that Your Majesty will succeed in his present endeavors to establish stability and prosperity in Viet Nam, which, Your Majesty may be assured, my Government is following with close attention.

63. *Recognition of the Democratic Republic of Viet-Nam by the Soviet Union* †
January 30, 1950

To the Minister of Foreign Affairs of the Democratic Republic of Viet-Nam, Mr. Hoang Minh Giam:

The Government of the Union of Soviet Socialist Republics hereby acknowledges the receipt of the appeal of President Ho Chi Minh, dated January 14, 1950,[7] proposing to all governments the establishment of diplomatic relations.

Having examined the proposal of the Democratic Republic of Viet-

---

* *Source:* United States, Department of State, *American Foreign Policy 1950– 1955: Basic Documents* (2 vols., Washington: Government Printing Office, 1957), Vol. II, pp. 2363–2364.

† *Source:* France, Direction de la Documentation, *Bulletin Quotidien de Presse Etrangère*, No. 1492 (February 1, 1950), p. 2, citing Radio Moscow, January 31, 1950. Translation by the editor. The message is also in *Pravda*, January 31, 1950. There was no Vietnamese ambassador in the Soviet Union until April 1952. A Soviet ambassador did not take up his duties in the Democratic Republic of Viet-Nam until after the Geneva Conference in 1954.

[6] By the conventions signed on December 30, 1949; for citation, see Note 7, p. 104.

[7] Document 60.

Nam, and taking into consideration the fact that the Democratic Republic of Viet-Nam represents the overwhelming majority of the population of the country, the Soviet Government has made the decision to establish diplomatic relations between the Soviet Union and the Democratic Republic of Viet-Nam and to proceed to the exchange of ambassadors.

On the order of the Government of the U.S.S.R., the Minister of Foreign Affairs of the U.S.S.R:

A. VYSHINSKY

64. *French Government Protest against Soviet Recognition of the Democratic Republic of Viet-Nam* * *January 31, 1950*

The French Government learned, through the publication of a communiqué by TASS,[8] that the Government of the U.S.S.R. had taken the decision to recognize the insurgent government led by Ho Chi Minh as the Government of Viet-Nam.

Such a decision violates the principles of international law since the sole legitimate government of Viet-Nam is the government formed by H.M. Bao Dai, to which the French Government has transferred the rights of sovereignty which it previously held.

By encouraging Ho Chi Minh's insurrectionary movement, as is evidently the intention of the Soviet Government, this decision can only make the return of peace to Viet-Nam more difficult.

It is thus gravely injurious to the vital interests of the Vietnamese people.

In taking the initiative which has just been announced, the Government of the U.S.S.R. commits toward France an act whose character and consequences cannot be underestimated.

For all these reasons, the French Government raises an official protest against a decision which is of a nature to seriously impair Franco-Soviet relations.

---

* *Source:* France, Direction de la Documentation, *Bulletin Quotidien de Presse Etrangère,* No. 1493 (February 2, 1950), p. 1. Translation by the editor. The French protest was in the form of a note handed to the Soviet ambassador in Paris. It was returned to the French Foreign Ministry with a note stating that the Soviet Government "does not consider it possible to accept a note of this kind."

8 Document 63.

65. *Secretary of State Dean Acheson: Statement on Soviet Recognition of the Democratic Republic of Viet-Nam* *
    February 1, 1950

The recognition by the Kremlin of Ho Chi Minh's Communist movement in Indochina comes as a surprise. The Soviet acknowledgement of this movement should remove any illusions as to the "nationalist" nature of Ho Chi Minh's aims and reveals Ho in his true colors as the mortal enemy of native independence in Indochina.

Although timed in an effort to cloud the transfer of sovereignty by France to the legal Governments of Laos, Cambodia, and Viet Nam, we have every reason to believe that those legal governments will proceed in their development toward stable governments representing the true nationalist sentiments of more than 20 million peoples of Indochina.

French action in transferring sovereignty to Viet Nam, Laos, and Cambodia has been in process for some time. Following French ratification, which is expected within a few days,[9] the way will be open for recognition of these legal governments by the countries of the world whose policies support the development of genuine national independence in former colonial areas.

Ambassador Jessup has already expressed to Emperor Bao Dai our best wishes for prosperity and stability in Viet Nam and the hope that closer relationship will be established between Viet Nam and the United States.[10]

66. *Note Delivered by the British Ambassador at Paris to the French Ministry of Foreign Affairs* †
    February 7, 1950

In their note of the 25th November, 1949,[11] to His Majesty's Embassy, the Ministry of Foreign Affairs stated that the French Gov-

* *Source:* United States, Department of State, *Bulletin,* XXII (February 13, 1950), p. 244.

† *Source:* Great Britain, Parliament, Papers by Command, *Documents Relating to British Involvement in the Indo-China Conflict 1945–1965* (London: Her Majesty's Stationery Office, Cmnd. 2834, 1965), p. 56.

[9] It took place the following day, February 2, by Law 50-142: text in France, *Journal Officiel de la République Française, Lois et Décrets,* February 2, 1950, p. 1192.

[10] Document 62.   [11] Text not available.

ernment would appreciate recognition as early as possible of the Government of His Majesty Bao Dai in Viet-Nam by His Majesty's Government in the United Kingdom.

2. The Ministry of Foreign Affairs stated moreover that the status of the Kingdoms of Laos and Cambodia under the Franco-Laotian and Franco-Cambodian treaties of the 19th July, 1949,[12] and the 8th November, 1949,[13] respectively was very similar to that of Viet-Nam, in particular in so far as concerned their relations with foreign States.

3. His Majesty's Government in the United Kingdom have noted with pleasure the transfer of certain powers to the Government of Viet-Nam which took place at Saigon on 30th December, 1949,[14] and the ratification of 2nd February, 1950,[15] by the French Government of the agreement between President Auriol and His Majesty Bao Dai of the 8th March, 1949,[16] and of the Franco-Laotian and Franco-Cambodian treaties referred to above. They also note that it is the intention of the French Government to transfer further powers to the Governments of Viet-Nam, Laos and Cambodia after an inter-State conference to be held in the near future.[17]

4. His Majesty's Government in the United Kingdom have accordingly decided to recognise the status of Viet-Nam, Laos and Cambodia as Associate States within the French Union and to recognise the Governments of His Majesty Bao Dai, His Majesty Sisavang Vong and His Majesty Norodom Sihanouk as the Governments of these states. His Majesty's Consul-General at Saigon has been granted the personal rank of Minister.

67. *United States Recognition of Viet-Nam, Laos, and Cambodia:*
    Statement by the Department of State *
    February 7, 1950

The Government of the United States has accorded diplomatic recognition to the Governments of the State of Viet Nam, the Kingdom of Laos, and the Kingdom of Cambodia.

---

* *Source:* United States, Department of State, *American Foreign Policy 1950–1955: Basic Documents* (2 vols., Washington: Government Printing Office, 1957), Vol. II, pp. 2364–2365.

[12] Text in France, *Journal Officiel de la République Française, Lois et Décrets,* March 14, 1953, pp. 2407–2409.

[13] Text in *ibid.,* pp. 2404–2407.   [14] For citation, see Note 7, p. 104.

[15] By Law 50-142.   [16] The Elysée Agreements, Document 55.

[17] The Pau Conference; see the Introduction to this chapter.

The President, therefore, has instructed the American consul general at Saigon to inform the heads of Government of the State of Viet Nam, the Kingdom of Laos, and the Kingdom of Cambodia that we extend diplomatic recognition to their Governments and look forward to an exchange of diplomatic representatives between the United States and these countries.[18]

Our diplomatic recognition of these Governments is based on the formal establishment of the State of Viet Nam, the Kingdom of Laos, and the Kingdom of Cambodia as independent states within the French Union; this recognition is consistent with our fundamental policy of giving support to the peaceful and democratic evolution of dependent peoples toward self-government and independence.

In June of last year, this Government expressed its gratification [19] at the signing of the France-Viet Namese agreements of March 8,[20] which provided the basis for the evolution of Viet Namese independence within the French Union. These agreements, together with similar accords between France and the Kingdoms of Laos and Cambodia, have now been ratified by the French National Assembly and signed by the President of the French Republic. This ratification has established the independence of Viet Nam, Laos, and Cambodia as associated states within the French Union.

It is anticipated that the full implementation of these basic agreements and of supplementary accords which have been negotiated and are awaiting ratification will promote political stability and the growth of effective democratic institutions in Indochina. This Government is considering what steps it may take at this time to further these objectives and to assure, in collaboration with other like-minded nations, that this development shall not be hindered by internal dissension fostered from abroad.

The status of the American consulate general in Saigon will be raised to that of a legation, and the Minister who will be accredited to all three states will be appointed by the President.

---

[18] The text of the letter delivered to H.M. Bao Dai in Dalat on February 9 by the U.S. Chargé d'Affaires, Edmund Gullion, is in France, Ministère de la France d'Outre-Mer, *Bulletin d'Information de la France d'Outre-Mer*, No. 141 (March, 1950), pp. 25–26. Similar letters were later delivered in Vientiane and Phnom Penh.

[19] Document 57.   [20] The Elysée Agreements, Document 55.

68. *Secretary of State Acheson: Statement on United States Aid to the Associated States* *
   May 8, 1950

The [French] Foreign Minister [21] and I have just had an exchange of views on the situation in Indochina and are in general agreement both as to the urgency of the situation in that area and as to the necessity for remedial action. We have noted the fact that the problem of meeting the threat to the security of Viet Nam, Cambodia, and Laos which now enjoy independence within the French Union is primarily the responsibility of France and the Governments and peoples of Indochina. The United States recognizes that the solution of the Indochina problem depends both upon the restoration of security and upon the development of genuine nationalism and that United States assistance can and should contribute to these major objectives.

The United States Government, convinced that neither national independence nor democratic evolution exist in any area dominated by Soviet imperialism, considers the situation to be such as to warrant its according economic aid and military equipment to the Associated States of Indochina and to France in order to assist them in restoring stability and permitting these states to pursue their peaceful and democratic development.

69. *Note from the American Chargé d'Affaires at Saigon* [22] *to the Chiefs of State of Viet-Nam, Laos, and Cambodia, on Provision of Economic Aid* †
   May 24, 1950

I have the honor to inform you that the Government of the United States has decided to initiate a program of economic aid to the States of Cambodia, Laos, and Vietnam. My Government has reached this decision in order to assist Cambodia, Laos, and Vietnam to restore stability and pursue their peaceful and democratic development.

* *Source:* United States, Department of State, *American Foreign Policy 1950– 1955: Basic Documents* (2 vols., Washington: Government Printing Office, 1957), Vol. II, p. 2365. This statement was issued in Paris, where Secretary Acheson was attending a Western Foreign Ministers' meeting.

† *Source:* United States, Department of State, *American Foreign Policy 1950– 1955: Basic Documents* (2 vols., Washington: Government Printing Office, 1957), Vol. II, pp. 2365–2366.

21 Robert Schuman.   22 Edmund Guillion.

With these purposes in mind, the United States Government is establishing, with headquarters in Saigon and associated with the United States Legation, a special economic mission to Cambodia, Laos, and Vietnam. This mission will have the responsibility of working with the Governments of Cambodia, Laos, and Vietnam and with the French High Commissioner in developing and carrying out a coordinated program of economic aid designed to assist the three countries in restoring their normal economic life. The members of the American economic mission will, at all times, be subject to the authority of the Government of the United States and will not become a part of the administrations of the Associated States.

The Government of the United States recognizes that this American assistance will be complementary to the effort made by the three Associated States and France, without any intention of substitution. American aid is designed to reinforce the joint effort of France and the Governments and peoples of Cambodia, Laos, and Vietnam, on whom rests the primary responsibility for the restoration of security and stability.

United States economic aid will be granted in accordance with separate bilateral agreements between each of the Associated States and the United States of America.[23] The approval of these agreements will be subject to legal conventions existing between the Associated States and France. Initial economic aid operations, however, may begin prior to the conclusion of these agreements.

The United States Government is of the opinion that it would be desirable for the three governments and the French High Commissioner to reach agreement among themselves for the coordination of those matters relating to the aid program that are of common interest. The American economic mission will maintain contact with the three Associated States, with the French High Commissioner in Indochina and, if desired, with any body which may be set up by the Associated States and France in connection with the aid program.

Mr. Robert Blum has been appointed Chief of the United States special economic mission to Cambodia, Laos, and Vietnam.

Identical letters are being addressed today to the governments of Cambodia, Laos, Vietnam and the President of the French Union.

[23] The Agreement of September 7, 1951, between the United States and the State of Viet-Nam is in United Nations, *Treaty Series*. Vol. 174 (1953), pp. 172–184.

70. *Viet-Nam and the Korean Crisis: American, Chinese, and Soviet Statements [Extracts]*
June 27–July 4, 1950

[All three of the statements from which extracts are presented here dealt primarily with the Korean War and only secondarily with other areas, such as Viet-Nam. In each case only those portions directly relevant to Viet-Nam are printed; the major portions, dealing with Korea, are omitted.]

I. STATEMENT BY PRESIDENT TRUMAN, JUNE 27, 1950 *

The attack upon Korea makes it plain beyond all doubt that communism has passed beyond the use of subversion to conquer independent nations and will now use armed invasion and war. It has defied the orders of the Security Council of the United Nations issued to preserve international peace and security. . . .

I have similarly directed acceleration in the furnishing of military assistance to the forces of France and the Associated States in Indochina and the dispatch of a military mission to provide close working relations with those forces.

I know that all members of the United Nations will consider carefully the consequences of this latest aggression in Korea in defiance of the Charter of the United Nations. A return to the rule of force in international affairs would have far-reaching effects. The United States will continue to uphold the rule of law.

II. STATEMENT BY FOREIGN MINISTER CHOU EN-LAI OF THE
    CHINESE PEOPLE'S REPUBLIC, JUNE 28, 1950 †

On behalf of the Central People's Government of the People's Republic of China I declare that Truman's statement of the 27th and the actions of the American navy [in moving to the coast of Taiwan] constitute armed aggression against the territory of China, and total violation of the United Nations Charter. This violent, predatory action by the U.S. government comes as no surprise to the Chinese people but only increases their wrath; because the Chinese people have, over a long period, constantly exposed all the conspiratorial schemes of American imperialism for aggression against China and grabbing Asia by

* *Source:* United States, Department of State, *American Foreign Policy 1950– 1955: Basic Documents* (2 vols., Washington: Government Printing Office, 1957), Vol. II, pp. 2539–2540.

† *Source:* New China News Agency, *Daily News Release*, No. 420 (June 30, 1950), p. 187.

force. All that Truman's statement does is openly expose his premeditated plan and put it into practice. In fact the attack by the puppet Korean government of Syngman Rhee on the Korean People's Democratic Republic at the instigation of the U.S. government was a premeditated move by the United States, designed to create a pretext for the United States to invade Taiwan, Korea, Viet-Nam and the Philippines. It is precisely a further act of intervention by American imperialism in the affairs of Asia. . . .

The Central People's Government of the People's Republic of China calls on all peoples throughout the world who love peace, justice and freedom and especially on all the oppressed nations and peoples of the East, to rise as one and halt the new aggression of American imperialism in the East. Such aggression can be completely defeated if we do not yield to threats but resolutely mobilise the broad masses of the people to take part in the struggle against the war-makers. The Chinese people express their sympathy and respect to the people of Korea, Viet-Nam, the Philippines and Japan who are similarly victims of U.S. aggression and are similarly fighting against it. The Chinese people firmly believe that all the oppressed nations and peoples of the East are undoubtedly capable of burying the vicious and hated American imperialist war-makers once and for all in the great flames of struggle for national independence.

III. STATEMENT BY A. A. GROMYKO, DEPUTY MINISTER OF FOREIGN AFFAIRS OF THE SOVIET UNION, JULY 4, 1950 *

President Truman stated in addition that he had issued an instruction that the so-called "military assistance" to France in Indochina be accelerated. This statement of Truman shows that the Government of the United States has embarked on a course of kindling war against the people of Viet Nam for the sake of supporting the colonial regime in Indochina, thereby demonstrating that it is assuming the role of gendarme of the peoples of Asia.

Thus, President Truman's statement of 27 June means that the Government of the United States has violated peace and has gone over from a policy of preparing aggression to direct acts of aggression simultaneously in a whole number of countries in Asia. Thereby the Government

* *Source:* United Nations, Security Council, Document S/1603 (letter dated 13 July 1950 from the Representative of the U.S.S.R. to the United Nations Secretary-General, transmitting the statement of July 4, 1950, by Deputy Minister of Foreign Affairs A. A. Gromyko), pp. 7–8.

of the United States has trampled underfoot its obligations to the United Nations in strengthening peace throughout the world, and has acted as a violator of peace.

71. *Ho Chi Minh: Answers to Questions Put by the Press Regarding*
     U.S. Intervention in Indochina * [24]
     July 25, 1950

Question: What is, Mr. President, the present situation of the U.S. imperialists' interventionist policy in Indo-China?

Answer: The U.S. imperialists have of late openly interfered in Indo-China's affairs. It is with their money and weapons and their instructions that the French colonialists have been waging war in Viet Nam, Cambodia and Laos.

However, the U.S. imperialists are intensifying their plot to discard the French colonialists so as to gain complete control over Indo-China. That is why they do their utmost to redouble their direct intervention in every field—military, political and economic. It is also for this reason that the contradictions between them and the French colonialists become sharper and sharper.

Question: What influence does this intervention exert on the Indochinese people?

Answer: The U.S. imperialists supply their henchmen with armaments to massacre the Indochinese people.

They dump their goods in Indo-China to prevent the development of local handicrafts.

Their pornographic culture contaminates the youth in areas placed under their control.

They follow the policy of buying up, deluding and dividing our people. They drag some bad elements into becoming their tools and use them to invade our country.

* *Source:* Ho Chi Minh, *Selected Works* (4 vols., Hanoi: Foreign Languages Publishing House, 1961–1962), Vol. III, pp. 208–210. A typographical error in the original has been corrected.

[24] Footnote in the original: "So far the U.S. imperialists have helped the French colonialists to invade Indo-China. In 1950, while the Resistance carried out by the people of Viet Nam, Cambodia and Laos was developing favourably in every respect, the U.S. imperialists intervened directly in the affairs of Indo-China. Their generals, colonels, spies, senators, businessmen and even missionaries, came to Viet Nam in great number. They immediately set up the Military Aid Advisory Group (M.A.A.G.) in order directly to conduct the war in Indo-China. At the same time, they increased their military aid to the French colonialists and covered the major part of the war budget of Indo-China. They have become the dangerous enemy of the Indochinese peoples."

Question: What measure shall we take against them?

Answer: To gain independence, we, the Indochinese people, must defeat the French colonialists, our enemy number one. At the same time, we will struggle against the U.S. interventionists. The deeper their interference the more powerful are our solidarity and our struggle.

We will expose their manoeuvres before all our people, especially those living in areas under their control.

We will expose all those who serve as lackeys for the U.S. imperialists to coerce, deceive and divide our people.

The close solidarity between the peoples of Viet Nam, Cambodia and Laos constitutes a force capable of defeating the French colonialists and the U.S. interventionists. The U.S. imperialists failed in China, they will fail in Indo-China.

We are still labouring under great difficulties but victory will certainly be ours.

72. *Statement by the Department of State Regarding Franco-American Conversations* *
    October 17, 1950

In the course of conversations which have taken place during the last few days between Dean G. Acheson, Secretary of State; John W. Snyder, Secretary of the Treasury; George C. Marshall, Secretary of Defense; and William C. Foster, Economic Cooperation Administrator, on behalf of the United States, and Jules Moch, Minister of Defense, and Maurice Petsche, Minister of Finance, on behalf of France, a review has been made of the United States contribution to the implementation of the French rearmament program within the framework of the North Atlantic Treaty Organization. This review has included the question of additional United States military aid to Indochina.

The United States Government has expressed the view that a military effort of the general magnitude and character planned by the French Government would be a vital contribution to the defensive strength of the North Atlantic area. Out of the sums appropriated by the United States Congress under the Mutual Defense Assistance Act, for fiscal years 1950 and 1951,[25] about 5 billion dollars have been earmarked

---

* *Source:* United States, Department of State, *American Foreign Policy 1950–1955: Basic Documents* (2 vols., Washington: Government Printing Office, 1957), Vol. I, pp. 1668–1669.
25 Footnote in the original omitted.

for military equipment to be delivered to the European members of the North Atlantic Treaty Organization. France has been assigned by far the largest single part of these amounts.

In addition, the United States Congress has appropriated for military assistance in the Far East approximately one-half billion dollars. In view of the importance of the operations in Indochina, the major part of this sum is being used to provide military equipment, including light bombers, for the armed forces both of France and of the Associated States of Indochina.

This assistance will provide a very important part of the equipment required by the forces contemplated for activation in 1951 in France and for current operations in Indochina. Deliveries of equipment are being expedited and, with respect to Indochina, a particularly high priority has been assigned.

Moreover, the following agreement has been reached during the talks with respect to production assistance:

(a) On an interim basis, and within the funds already appropriated under the Mutual Defense Assistance Act by the Congress for the fiscal year 1951, the Government of the United States will make available in support of the French Government's increased military production program assistance in the amount of 200 million dollars, these funds to be obligated prior to June 30, 1951.

(b) The final amount of American assistance to support the expanded French defense effort will, subject to future provision of funds by the Congress, be determined on the basis of multilateral discussions within the framework of the North Atlantic Treaty Organization directed toward an equitable distribution among all the North Atlantic Treaty members of the economic burdens of the common rearmament effort.

73. *Communiqué by the President of the United States and the Premier of France [Extract]* * 26
January 30, 1951

The President and the Prime Minister exchanged views on the broad subject of international affairs and they touched upon all the questions

* *Source:* United States, Department of State, *American Foreign Policy 1950–1955: Basic Documents* (2 vols., Washington: Government Printing Office, 1957), Vol. I, pp. 1669–1670.
26 Issued after conversations between President Truman and Premier René Pleven during M. Pleven's visit to Washington on January 29-30, 1951.

that are of common interest to France and the United States. Once again they found that there exists a fundamental identity of views between the two countries.

The President and the Prime Minister reaffirmed their belief that the principle of collective security, embodied in the Charter of the United Nations, is the chief bulwark of world peace and of the independence and survival of free societies in the world. They agreed that, in conformity with this principle, aggression must not be rewarded or the menace of aggression appeased. It is in this spirit that the President and the Prime Minister examined the means to assure coordinated action and turned to the more detailed questions as set forth below.

The President and the Prime Minister found themselves in complete agreement as to the necessity of resisting aggression and assisting the free nations of the Far East in their efforts to maintain their security and assure their independence.

The situation in Korea was discussed and they concurred that every effort must be exerted to bring about an honorable solution there. Until that end can be accomplished, resistance by United Nations forces to aggression must continue. Both France and the United States will support action directed toward deterring aggression and toward preventing the spread of hostilities beyond Korea.

With regard to Indochina, the Prime Minister described the heavy responsibilities borne by France in that area and the great cost, both in lives and money, she has paid in resisting the Communist onslaught in order to maintain the security and independence of the Associated States, Vietnam, Cambodia and Laos. The Prime Minister declared that France was determined to do its utmost to continue this effort. The President informed the Prime Minister that United States aid for the French Union forces and for the National Armies of the Associated States will continue, and that the increased quantities of material to be delivered under the program authorized for the current fiscal year will be expedited.

The President and the Prime Minister agreed that continuous contact should be maintained between the interested nations on these problems.

[The balance of the communiqué, dealing with European matters and the common desire for peace through negotiations, is omitted.]

CHAPTER VI

Overt Communism in Indochina

February-March 1951

Introduction

Early 1951 saw the emergence of open Communism in Viet-Nam as the leaders of the Viet Minh took steps to confirm their adherence to the Communist world and Communist ideology. Whatever the reasons for the Viet Minh action, it went a long way toward destroying any lingering possibility of compromise not only with the French but with anti-Communist Vietnamese nationalists as well. The international events of 1950 had made the Indochina war a struggle between the two "camps" into which both Communists and the West saw the world divided, and, indirectly, between the leaders of those two "camps," the Soviet Union and the United States. For both sides the conflict acquired elements of an ideological crusade, and after March 1951 the conflict assumed many of the characteristics of a crusade internally as well as internationally.

From February 11 to February 19 the "founding Congress" of the "Viet Nam Lao Dong Dang" or "Viet-Nam Workers' Party" (VWP) was held "somewhere in North Viet-Nam." The "new" party was the former Indochinese Communist Party (ICP), dissolved in 1945,[1] reconstituted under another name after its six-year underground existence as the "Indochinese Association for the Study of Marxism." In the long political report he delivered at the opening session of the Congress (Document 74) Ho Chi Minh not only set forth the aims of the party but justified many of the policies adopted in 1945 and 1946. At the end of the Congress, on February 19, the VWP adopted its Manifesto (Document 75) and its Program, or Platform (Document 76). Both documents made clear that the VWP was a Marxist-Leninist Party affiliated with the world Communist movement and that the

[1] See Document 34.

party was the directing force of the Vietnamese revolution. The Congress confirmed in their offices the leaders who had held power continuously since the beginning of World War II, with Ho Chi Minh as Chairman and Truơng Chinh as General Secretary.

The formation of the VWP was followed, on March 3, by the opening of the "Congress to Merge the Viet Minh and Lien Viet Fronts" under the chairmanship of Ho Chi Minh. The Viet Minh Front, which had spearheaded the revolutionary movement since 1941, had lost much of its coalition character through overwhelming domination by Communists and the purging of most non-Communist leaders. Thus the leadership sought to broaden its base, and reassert the unity of the various groups opposing the French, through the merger of the Viet Minh with the somewhat amorphous Lien Viet Front ("The League for the National Union of Viet-Nam") which had been formed in 1946 as an organization complementary to, and supportive of, the Viet Minh. The new "United National Front" (known, still, as the "Lien Viet Front") [2] adopted a program (Document 77) which clearly showed the dominant influence of the VWP.

Having thus reorganized its activities in Viet-Nam, the VWP now further extended its action in the rest of Indochina. The struggle in Viet-Nam had spilled over into neighboring Cambodia and Laos. In the former state the Viet Minh had established bases in the sparsely inhabited northeastern countryside and were supporting the anti-French and anti-Royalist Khmer Issarak ("Free Cambodian") Front. In Laos the Viet Minh had been, since 1945, supporting the Pathet Lao.

In January 1951 the Viet-Nam News Agency announced that during the previous November representatives of the "United Fronts" of Viet-Nam, Laos, and Cambodia (the Viet Minh in Viet-Nam, the "Neo Lao Itsala" [or "Lao Issara"] in Laos, and the Khmer Issarak in Cambodia) had met and issued a statement calling for formation of a "Joint United Front" of the three countries in the common struggle against "French imperialists and American interventionists." [3] In early March 1951, immediately after formation of the new Lien Viet Front, Lien Viet leaders met with leaders of the Lao Issara and Khmer Issarak in a "Joint Conference." The Conference formed a "Joint

[2] Although after this point "Viet Minh" became inaccurate as a blanket term to cover the Communist-dominated part of the Vietnamese revolutionary movement, the term has become so widely accepted that it will continue to be used here for the sake of convenience and clarity.

[3] The text of the Joint Statement of November 22, 1950, was broadcast by Viet-Nam News Agency in English Morse, January 22, 1951, 1030 G.M.T.

United Front" whose Manifesto (Document 78) was published the same day.

74. *Ho Chi Minh: Political Report Read at the Second National Congress of the Viet-Nam Workers' Party [Extracts]* *
February 11, 1951

[Because of its great length, only the most interesting extracts of this important speech can be reprinted here, and no attempt is made to summarize the portions of the speech which are not included.]

Thanks to the clear-sighted and resolute leadership of our Party, and the solidarity and enthusiasm of the entire people within and without the Viet Minh Front, the August Revolution was successful.
Comrades,
Not only the toiling classes and people but also the oppressed people in other countries can be proud that this is the first time in the revolutionary history of colonial and semi-colonial peoples in which a party, only fifteen years of age [in 1945] has led the revolution to success and seized power throughout the country.
On our part, we must bear in mind that our success was due to the great victory of the Soviet Red Army which had defeated fascist Japan, to the friendly assistance of international solidarity, to the close unity of our entire people and to the heroic sacrifice of our revolutionary predecessors.

. . . . .

We were independent for hardly one month when the British troops entered the South. They allegedly came to disarm the Japanese army, but were in reality an expeditionary corps helping the French colonialists in their attempt to re-occupy our country.
The Kuomintang troops entered the North under the same pretext, but actually they had three wicked aims: to annihilate our Party, to smash the Viet Minh Front, to help the Vietnamese reactionaries overthrow the people's power in order to set up a reactionary government under their sway.
In the face of that grave and pressing situation, our Party did everything possible to keep itself in existence, to work and develop, to give

* *Source:* Ho Chi Minh, *Selected Works* (4 vols., Hanoi: Foreign Languages Publishing House, 1961–1962), Vol. III, pp. 245, 247–249, 266–267. The complete text of this speech is also available in Bernard B. Fall, ed., *Ho Chi Minh on Revolution: Selected Writings, 1920–1966* (New York: Frederick A. Praeger, 1967), pp. 206–227.

discreet and more effective leadership in order to have the time gradually to consolidate the forces of the people's power and to strengthen the National United Front.

At that time the Party could not hesitate: hesitation meant failure. The Party had to make quick decisions and take measures—even painful ones—to save the situation. The greatest worry was about the Party's proclamation of voluntary dissolution.[1] But in reality it went underground.

And though underground, the Party continued to lead the administration and the people.

We recognise that the Party's declaration of dissolution (actual withdrawal into the underground) was a good measure.

In spite of many a big difficulty, the Party and the Government guided our country through dangerous rapids and implemented many points in the programmes of the Viet Minh Front:

> Holding the General Elections to elect the National Assembly and chart the Constitution,
>
> Building and consolidating the people's power,
>
> Annihilating the Vietnamese reactionaries,
>
> Building and strengthening the people's army and arming the people,
>
> Elaborating labour laws,
>
> Reducing land rent and interest rates,
>
> Building people's culture,
>
> Broadening and consolidating the national united front (setting up of the All Viet Nam Union).[2]

Mention should be made of the Preliminary Agreement of March 6, 1946,[3] and the Modus Vivendi of September 14, 1946,[4] because they were considered as ultra-rightist and caused much grumbling. But in the opinion of our comrades and compatriots in the South they were correct. Indeed they were, because our comrades and compatriots cleverly availed themselves of this opportunity to build up and develop their forces.

Lenin said that even if a compromise with bandits was advantageous to the revolution, he would do it.

We needed peace to build our country, and therefore we made

[1] Document 34.

[2] The Lien Viet Front, created on May 27, 1946, to broaden the national base of the government. The group was founded by "27 prominent nationalists," including pro-Viet Minh members of the nationalist VNQDD and Dong Minh Hoi parties.

[3] Document 36.   [4] Document 42.

concession to maintain peace. Although the French colonialists broke their word and unleashed war, nearly one year of temporary peace gave us time to build up our basic forces.

When the French deliberately provoked war, we could no longer put up with them, and the nation-wide war broke out.

. . . . .

We do not fear difficulties. But we must foresee and clearly see difficulties and be prepared and ready to overcome them.

With the solidarity and unity of mind, the determination and indomitable spirit of our Party, Government and entire people, we will certainly overcome all difficulties in order to gain complete victory.

The October Revolution was victorious. The building of socialism in the Soviet Union has been successful. The Chinese Revolution has been successful. These great successes have opened the way to success for our revolution and that of many other countries in the world.

We have a great and powerful Party. It is great and powerful thanks to Marxism-Leninism, to the constant efforts of all our Party members, and to the love, confidence and support of our army and people as a whole.

We have the most clear-sighted and worthy elder brothers and friends of mankind—comrade Stalin and comrade Mao Tse-tung.

That is why I am convinced that we will fulfil the following heavy but glorious tasks:

> To found a most powerful party, the Viet Nam Workers' Party,
>
> To carry out the Resistance till complete victory,
>
> To build a new democratic Viet Nam,
>
> To contribute to the defence of democracy in the world and a lasting peace.

75. *Manifesto of the Viet-Nam Workers' Party* *
February 19, 1951

Dear fellow countrymen and women!

The world of today is clearly divided into two camps:

There is the anti-democratic imperialist camp led by the American imperialists and composed of imperialist states and reactionary governments, lackeys of imperialism. They plan to seize the lands of other peoples in order to dominate the world; to suppress the national liberation movements of the peoples; to destroy world peace and de-

* *Source: People's China*, III, No. 9 (May 1, 1951), Supplement, pp. 2–3.

mocracy and to provoke a third world war which would plunge mankind into darkness and misery.

There is the anti-imperialist democratic camp headed by the Soviet Union and composed of the countries of Socialism and People's Democracy, of the oppressed peoples, and of the working people and progressives in capitalist countries. This camp is striving to carry on the work of national construction; it is struggling for national liberation, for the defence of national independence and the maintenance of world peace and democracy; and it seeks to enhance the unity, progress and happiness of mankind.

That the democratic camp has become stronger than the imperialist camp is clearly shown by the fact that the Soviet Union is daily growing more prosperous and powerful; that the work of national construction is swiftly moving ahead in the People's Democracies; that the Chinese People's Revolution has been victorious; and that the Korean people are waging a successful struggle.

Our country and our people stand in the democratic camp.

The French colonialists stand in the imperialist camp. They want to plunder our land. In this they have the all-out assistance of the American imperialists. Our people, who definitely do not want to be enslaved, are determined to fight in defence of their land and homes. They are now preparing for an early general counter-offensive.

The forces of our Resistance spring from the people. Over 90 per cent of our people are working people, that is, the workers, peasants and intellectual workers. Thus, the working people are the main driving force of our armed Resistance and of our national construction.

The central task of the working class and the working people of Viet-Nam now is to unite the entire people, to carry the War of Resistance to complete victory, to build an independent, united, democratic, strong and prosperous Viet-Nam, and to fully realise People's Democracy so as to gradually advance towards Socialism. In order to fulfil this task, the working class and the working people of Viet-Nam must have a vanguard army, a general staff, a powerful, clear-sighted, determined, pure and thoroughly revolutionary political party: the Viet-Nam Lao Dong Party.[5]

The Viet-Nam Lao Dong Party will be composed of the most patriotic, the most enthusiastic, the most revolutionary workers, peasants and intellectual workers. It will be comprised of those who are determined to serve the Motherland, to serve the people, to serve

5 The "Viet-Nam Lao Dong Party" is the Viet-Nam Workers' Party.

labour, who place the overall interests of the country and the people above their own personal interests and who set the example in the War of Resistance and in national construction.

The theoretical foundation of the Party is Marxism-Leninism.

The principle of organisation of the Party is democratic centralism.

The discipline of the Party is a strict, voluntary discipline.

The policy of the Party aims to serve the interests of the country and the people.

The law governing the development of the Party is criticism and self-criticism.

The present main tasks of the Viet-Nam Lao Dong Party are: to unite and lead the working class, the working people and the whole Viet-Nam nation in their liberation struggle; to wipe out the aggressive French colonialists and defeat the American interventionists; and to lead the War of Resistance of the people of Viet-Nam to complete victory, thereby making Viet-Nam a genuinely independent and united country.

The Viet-Nam Lao Dong Party fully supports the government of the Viet-Nam Democratic Republic, unites and co-operates closely with other parties and organisations in the Lien Viet Front (the Viet-Nam League of National Union—Ed.) [6] with a view to fully realising People's Democracy in all fields—political, economic, social and cultural.

The Viet-Nam Lao Dong Party stands for the safe-guarding of the legitimate interests of all strata of the people.

Special care shall be taken to raise the material standard of living and cultural level of the army which is fighting for the defence of the country against the enemy and which has been enduring the greatest hardships.

The workers who are production fighters in enterprises shall have their living conditions improved and take part in the running of enterprises.

The peasants who are production fighters in the rural areas shall benefit from the reduction of land rent and interest rates, and from appropriate agrarian reforms.

The intellectual workers shall be encouraged and assisted to develop their abilities.

[6] In the original. Presumably this refers to the "new" Lien Viet Front, created by the merger of the old Lien Viet Front and the Viet Minh Front on March 3. That "new" Front had not been created at the time the Manifesto was adopted but had been formed by the time the Manifesto was made public at the end of March.

Small-scale traders and small workshop owners shall be assisted to develop their trade and handicrafts.

The national bourgeoisie shall be encouraged, assisted and guided in their undertakings in order to contribute to the development of the national economy.

The right of patriotic landlords to collect land rent in accordance with law shall be guaranteed.

National minorities shall be given every assistance and shall enjoy perfect equality of all rights and duties.

Effective help shall be extended to women so as to achieve equality between men and women.

Followers of all religions shall enjoy freedom of belief and worship.

Overseas citizens of Viet-Nam in foreign countries shall be given protection.

The lives and properties of foreign residents in Viet-Nam shall be protected. In particular, Chinese nationals, if they so desire, shall be allowed to enjoy the same rights and perform the same duties as citizens of Viet-Nam.

In the sphere of external affairs, the Viet-Nam Lao Dong Party recommends that the people of Viet-Nam closely unite with and help the peoples of Cambodia and Laos in their struggle for independence, and, jointly with them, liberate the whole of Indo-China; actively support the national liberation movements of oppressed peoples; closely unite with the Soviet Union, China and other People's Democracies; and closely ally themselves with the peoples of France and of the French colonies so as to contribute to the anti-imperialist struggle for the defence of world peace and democracy.

Fellow countrymen and women!

The Viet-Nam Lao Dong Party will carry on the glorious historic mission of all the revolutionary parties which have preceded it, and will develop the heroic revolutionary traditions of the people of Viet-Nam.

The Viet-Nam Lao Dong Party is resolved to overcome all difficulties and to struggle to the end in order to bring independence, freedom and happiness to the whole people and at the same time to liberate the working people.

Fighters in the regular people's army, the local people's armies and people's militia and guerrillas! Compete with one another in annihilating the enemy and scoring military victories!

Workers, peasants, intellectual workers, and all fellow countrymen and women, compete with one another in increasing food production, and in developing your creative abilities and inventiveness in order to serve the Resistance and national construction.

All compatriots at home and abroad! Unite closely around the People's Government of the Viet-Nam Democratic Republic, the Viet-Nam Lao Dong Party and the leader of the people, of the working class and working people of Viet-Nam—President Ho Chi Minh!

The Viet-Nam Lao Dong Party earnestly requests other organisations sincerely to criticise Party cadres and rank and file members and the policy of the Party, so that it can make constant progress and act in accordance with the wishes of the people.

Confident in the efforts of all Party members, in the support of the workers and the response from the entire people, the Viet-Nam Lao Dong Party will certainly fulfil its tasks:

To lead the Resistance to complete victory;

To develop the People's Democratic regime;

To contribute to the defence of World Peace and Democracy;

To march towards Socialism.

THE VIET-NAM LAO DONG PARTY

76. *Platform of the Viet-Nam Workers' Party **
   February 19, 1951

Chapter One
THE WORLD AND VIET-NAM

1. The end of the Second World War brought the collapse of German, Italian and Japanese fascism. While capitalism entered a period of grave crisis, the Soviet Union became more prosperous and powerful with each passing day, and the democratic movement daily gained in

* Source: *People's China*, III, No. 9 (May 1, 1951), Supplement, pp. 4–8. To the best of the editor's knowledge, neither this document nor the VWP Manifesto (Document 75) is available from a DRV source in complete text in a Western language. The texts used here are "unofficial" translations of both documents in full texts, although the language from which they were translated is not clear. The Vietnamese News Agency (VNA) apparently issued at least portions of both documents in English: extracts from the Platform are in New China News Agency, *Daily News Release*, No. 656 (March 27, 1951), pp. 97–99; and extracts from the Manifesto are in *ibid.*, No. 657 (March 28, 1951), pp. 101–102. The platform also appears, in Russian translation, in O. A. Arturov, ed., *Demokraticheskaya Respublika Vietnam: Konstitutsia, Zakonodatelnia Akti, Dokumenti* (Moscow: Izdatelstvo Innostrannoi Literaturi, 1955), pp. 33–46, citing "Manifesto and Programme of the Workers' Party of Viet-Nam" (published by the Central Committee of the Workers' Party of Viet-Nam, 1951), in Vietnamese.

strength. The world divided into two camps: the anti-imperialist, democratic camp headed by the Soviet Union, and the anti-democratic, imperialist camp led by the United States.

The democratic camp has become stronger while the imperialist camp has become weaker day by day. With the victory of the Chinese People's Revolution and with the founding of the German Democratic Republic, the balance of power was changed further in favour of the democratic camp.

At the present time, the American imperialists and their accomplices are making frenzied preparations for a third world war and are expanding their war of aggression. The danger of a new world war has become apparent. The central task of the working class and the peoples of the world at present is to struggle for the defence of peace. Under the leadership of the Soviet Union, the world peace camp is strongly opposing the imperialist warmongers. The peace movement has become stronger and more widespread than ever before in history. If the imperialists ever start a third world war, they will be signing their own death warrant.

2. After the Second World War, thanks to the victory of socialism over fascism, the people's democratic revolution spread and achieved victory in several countries of Eastern Europe and the Far East. A number of People's Republics were established and broke away from the imperialist system.

The people's democratic regimes have day by day become more consolidated and are developing and laying the basis of Socialism: People's Democracy, under the present historic conditions of the world, is in many countries a transitional stage towards Socialism.

3. A striking characteristic of the world scene since the end of the Second World War is the widespread liberation movement which gains in strength day by day and which is shaking the very foundations of imperialism. The liberation movement has become an integral part of the world-wide movement for peace and democracy and against the imperialist warmongers.

The British, French, Dutch and other imperialists are using various cunning means to deceive the colonial peoples, such as granting them pseudo-independence, buying over the reactionary feudal landlords and bourgeois compradores, attempting to split the ranks of these peoples so as to maintain their rule over their colonies. The American imperialists are striving to turn the colonies of other countries into markets for their own goods and into their aggressive military bases.

However, the colonial and semi-colonial peoples are becoming more and more convinced that the only path to national liberation is that of national unity, close alliance with other peoples in the world and unremitting, persistent armed struggle under the leadership of the working class. Experience shows that any oppressed people that faithfully takes this path is assured of victory.

4. Viet-Nam is an outpost of the democratic camp in Southeast Asia. The Viet-Nam revolution is a part of the world-wide movement for national liberation and for the defence of peace and democracy. In their struggle for their own independence and freedom, the people of Viet-Nam contribute to the maintenance of world peace and to the development of People's Democracy in Southeast Asia.

Thanks to the efforts of all the people of Viet-Nam and the progress of the democratic camp, especially the gigantic victory of the Chinese people, the Viet-Nam revolution will surely achieve success.

Chapter Two
VIET-NAM SOCIETY AND THE VIET-NAM REVOLUTION

1. Prior to the French imperialist conquest, Viet-Nam society was a feudal society. After the establishment of French domination, Viet-Nam became an exclusive market, a source of raw materials and man-power, an object of usurious exploitation, and a military base for the French colonialists.

After the First World War, the French mining industry and light industries were expanded in Viet-Nam. The Viet-Nam feudal regime began to totter. The working class of Viet-Nam was formed and matured quickly. Capitalism in Viet-Nam came into being but was unable to develop owing to the domination of French capital.

French colonial policy made Viet-Nam completely dependent on France. It hampered the development of the productive forces of Viet-Nam. It combined the forms of capitalist oppression and exploitation with those of feudal oppression and exploitation, driving the people of Viet-Nam, especially the workers and peasants, into the darkest misery. For this reason, the people of Viet-Nam never ceased to struggle for independence and democracy.

In 1930, the Communist Party of Indo-China was founded. Since then the hegemony of the revolution has been exclusively in the hands of the working class of Viet-Nam.

During the Second World War, the Japanese occupied Viet-Nam. Under the yoke of Japanese and French fascism, the people of Viet-

Nam were subjected to untold sufferings. Many uprisings broke out. Guerrilla bases were established and developed. The People's Rule was set up in the liberated area of the uplands of North Viet-Nam after the *coup d'etat* of March 9, 1945. (The Japanese displaced the French in Indo-China on March 9, 1945—Ed.) [7]

As a whole, however, Viet-Nam society was still a colonial and semi-feudal society.

In 1945, under the crushing blows of the Soviet Red Army, the Japanese fascists surrendered. Under the leadership of President Ho Chi Minh and the Communist Party of Indo-China, the Viet-Minh League together with the people of Viet-Nam launched a successful general uprising. The Democratic Republic of Viet-Nam was founded.

But the French imperialists invaded Viet-Nam once again in the hope of restoring their old colonial rule. The nation-wide, all-out and protracted War of Resistance of the people of Viet-Nam began.

The American imperialists made the utmost efforts to help the French colonialists. However, as a result of the unity and single-mindedness of our people and the heroic struggle of our army, the French colonialists were able to occupy temporarily only a part of our territory. In fighting for liberation and in realising democratic reforms in all fields—economic, political, social and cultural—Viet-Nam has stepped on to the path of People's Democracy.

Today, Viet-Nam society is, therefore, a society which is popular-democratic and partly colonial and semi-feudal in character.

The people of Viet-Nam earnestly desire a People's Democracy. The colonial regime has been a scourge to the whole of the people. The remnants of feudalism and semi-feudalism hamper the progress of the new Viet-Nam and have been a heavy burden to the peasants who are the majority of the people of Viet-Nam. The entire people of Viet-Nam demand independence and freedom, and are determined never to be enslaved again. The great majority of the people of Viet-Nam—the peasants—need land.

The fundamental task of the Viet-Nam revolution, therefore, is: to drive out the imperialist aggressors; to gain complete independence and unity for the people, to wipe out the colonial regime in the temporarily enemy-occupied areas and uproot the remnants of feudalism and semi-feudalism so that the tillers may have land; to develop People's Democracy; and to lay the foundations of Socialism.

The motive forces of the Viet-Nam revolution at present are the

[7] In the original.

people comprising primarily the workers, peasants, petty bourgeoisie and national bourgeoisie, followed by the patriotic and progressive personages and landlords. The basic mass of the people consists of the workers, peasants and intellectual workers (intellectual workers belong to various strata of the people, mostly to the petty bourgeoisie). The leading class in the Viet-Nam revolution is the working class.

From the point of view of the basic tasks it aims to fulfil and because its motive forces are the people led by the working class, the Viet-Nam Revolution is at present a national people's democratic revolution.

This national people's democratic revolution will lead Viet-Nam towards Socialism. The road towards Socialism is a road of protracted struggle which will pass through several stages.

In the present stage, the Viet-Nam revolution is spearheaded against the imperialist aggressors. It is necessary to rally all the forces of the people, to consolidate the national united front to carry on the protracted Resistance against the imperialist aggressors and their lackeys. At the same time, it is necessary to improve the living conditions of the people, especially the working people, so that the people can take a still more active part in the Resistance.

The main task at the present stage is to fight against imperialist aggression. The other tasks must be carried out so as to contribute to the fullfilment of this main task.

Chapter Three
POLICY OF THE VIET-NAM LAO DONG PARTY

The Viet-Nam Lao Dong Party is resolved to fulfil the mission of liberating the people of Viet-Nam, to curb the influence of feudalism so as to further eradicate feudal and semi-feudal remnants, to develop People's Democracy, to build an independent, united, democratic, prosperous and powerful Viet-Nam and lead it towards Socialism.

During and immediately after the War of Resistance, the Viet-Nam Lao Dong Party stands for the realisation of the following policies aimed to give a powerful impetus to the Resistance to achieve complete victory, and to lay the basis for the building up of a prosperous and powerful state.

1. FIGHTING TO COMPLETE VICTORY

The entire people of Viet-Nam are resolved to fight to the end in order to wipe out the French colonialists, defeat the American interventionists, punish the traitors and gain complete independence and unity for the Motherland.

The War of Resistance of the people of Viet-Nam is a people's war, with the characteristics of a nation-wide, all-out and protracted war. It must pass through three stages: a defensive stage, a stage in which the opposing forces approach a balance and a stage of counter-offensive.

The central task of the Resistance from the present time till final victory is to complete the preparations for and to launch a victorious general counter-offensive. In order to win complete victory, it is necesary to mobilise manpower, material and financial resources for the War of Resistance in accordance with the slogan "All for the front, all for victory!" and continually to replenish the Resistance forces of the people. At the same time, the following strategic directives of the Resistance must be strictly observed:

> All political, economic and cultural work must aim at ensuring military victories, and the military struggle must be coordinated with the political, economic and cultural struggle;

> Fighting at the front against the enemy must be closely coordinated with guerrilla fighting and sabotage in the enemy's rear;

> The War of Resistance of the people of Viet-Nam must be closely co-ordinated with the armed Resistance of the peoples of Laos and Cambodia and with the world-wide struggle for peace and democracy.

2. Consolidating the People's Rule

The political power in our country is a democratic power of the people, that is, of the workers, peasants, petty bourgeoisie, national bourgeoisie, and patriotic and progressive personages and landlords. The form of this power is the People's Democratic Republic. Its content is the People's Democratic Dictatorship: democratic towards the people, dictatorial towards the imperialist aggressors and traitors.

The People's Rule relies on the national united front based on the alliance between the workers, peasants and intellectual workers, and is under the leadership of the working class.

The organisational principle of the People's Rule is democratic centralism.

Our People's Rule owes its strength to the active participation and support of the people, to the leadership of the working class, and to the assistance rendered by the Soviet Union, China and other People's Democracies. Thus, in order to consolidate our People's Rule, we must:

> Continually consolidate the links between the state power and the popular masses;

Increase the number of workers, peasants and women participating in the government organisations, particularly in the People's Councils;

Put into effect a genuine People's Democratic constitution; [8]

Strengthen the Party's leadership in government organisations of all levels;

Consolidate Viet-Nam's friendly relations with the Soviet Union, China and other People's Democracies.

3. Consolidating the National United Front

The National United Front of Viet-Nam unites all political parties, organisations and patriotic persons irrespective of class, nationality, religion, or sex in the common struggle for Resistance and national construction.

The National United Front is one of the pillars of the People's Rule. It has the task of mobilising, organising, educating and leading the people to implement the policy of the government, and of informing the government of the people's aspirations and proposals.

The Viet-Nam Lao Dong Party co-operates closely with all the political parties, organisations and personages in the National United Front according to the following principles:

Sincere solidarity and friendly mutual criticism for the sake of common progress;

Joint action and consultation in the struggle for a common programme;

[8] This is the first formal public mention by the Viet Minh that the Constitution adopted on November 8, 1946 (Document 43) was not adequate. Presumably the point in the VWP Program here calls for a constitution modeled after that of the East European People's Democracies. During the period following the public appearance of the VWP and the promulgation of its Program there were various calls for constitutional revision. For instance, on April 3, 1951, the "Liaison Bureau of the 5th Interzone National Assembly Delegates" called for a new constitution, said to be in preparation by the National Assembly Standing Committee, to be presented at the third session of the National Assembly (which had not met since the second session in November 1946). According to this source, "The Viet-Nam Constitution was created during a period in which the French colonialists were frantically preparing to occupy Central and North Viet-Nam. Due to other weak points, principally because a gang of traitors depended upon the strength of Chiang Kai-shek's Kuomintang to carry out their activities, a progressive character was lacking, and consequently, the Constitution was not clearly defined" (Voice of South Viet-Nam, in Cochinchinese at dictation speed, May 4, 1951, 1000 G.M.T.). Despite the constitutional activity during 1951, and a revival of similar activity after 1954, a new Constitution was not adopted until the fall of 1959.

Long-term co-operation during and after the protracted War of Resistance.

In order to consolidate the national united front, we must complete the merger of the Viet-Minh and the Lien Viet; [9] consolidate the alliance of workers, peasants and intellectual workers as a solid basis for the Front; mobilise all circles of the bourgeoisie and the landlords to participate actively in the Lien Viet Front; develop the organisations of the Front in the temporarily enemy-occupied areas, in the areas inhabited by religious groups and by the national minorities; consolidate the Party's leadership in the national united front, etc.

4. BUILDING UP AND DEVELOPING THE PEOPLE'S ARMY

The Viet-Nam Army is a people's army organised, maintained and assisted by, and fighting for the people. It is national, popular and democratic in character.

Its discipline is strict and voluntary. While fighting it carries on widespread political work, strengthening the unity of purpose between officers and men and between the army and the people, and strives to carry out propaganda work among enemy troops with a view to breaking down their morale.

In order to build up and develop the people's army, we must develop the local people's armed militia groups and guerrillas in the villages so as continually to replenish our regular army. At the same time, we must capture the enemy's arms, ammunition and food supplies so as partly to solve our equipment and supply problems.

5. DEVELOPING THE ECONOMY

Our economic policy now is: to increase production so as to meet the demands of the War of Resistance and to raise the living standard of the people, benefiting both the governm[e]nt and private individuals, and both Labour and Capital.

In the present stage, while special attention must be paid to the development of agriculture, we must develop industry, handicrafts and home trade, we must establish and develop trade relations with friendly countries, and lay the basis for a state economy and the development of co-operative economy. With regard to the national bourgeoisie, our Party encourages, assists and guides it in its enterprises.

In the financial field, we advocate increasing the national income through increased production, reducing expenditures through economies and putting into practice the system of democratic contributions.

[9] See Document 77.

As regards the enemy's economy, we urge planned sabotage and blockade in ways beneficial to the Resistance and the people, and confiscation of the imperialist aggressors' and traitors' properties and the putting of these properties at the disposal of the People's Rule.

6. CARRYING OUT AGRARIAN REFORM

Our agrarian policy at present aims mainly at carrying out the reduction of land rent and interest, as well as other reforms such as:

Regulation of the land-rent system;

Provisional allocation of the land formerly owned by the imperialists and traitors to the poorer peasants and families of disabled ex-servicemen and war dead;

Re-distribution of communal lands;

Appropriate use of land belonging to absentee landlords and of wastelands, etc.

These reforms must be thoroughly carried out so as to improve the living conditions of the peasants and to mobilise the majority of the people, that is, the peasants, to participate actively in the armed Resistance, to increase production and ensure supplies.

In order to carry out these reforms thoroughly, our Party must organise and awaken the great peasant masses and give steady leadership to the peasant movement.

We must carry out this agrarian policy step by step, according to local circumstances. In South Viet-Nam where land is more concentrated than in North and Central Viet-Nam, the agrarian policy of the Party must be carried out more vigorously than in North and Central Viet-Nam.

We must prepare the conditions for gradually giving each peasant his own plot of land.[10]

7. DEVELOPING CULTURE AND EDUCATION

In order to train new men and new cadres and to push forward the war of Resistance and national construction, it is necessary to wipe out the remnants of colonial and feudal culture and education, and develop a national, scientific and popular culture and education.

Thus the task of Viet-Nam culture and education at the present stage is:

---

[10] For a number of decrees on DRV agrarian policy during the period of the Resistance War, see O. A. Arturov, ed., *Demokraticheskaya Respublika Vietnam: Konstitutsia, Zakonodatelnia Akti, Dokumenti* (Moscow: Izdatelstvo Innostrannoi Literaturi, 1955), Section V, "Documents on the Questions of Agrarian Reform and Economic Construction," pp. 154–229. Documents are in Russian.

To develop the people's hatred for the imperialist aggressors, and to develop their genuine patriotism and spirit of internationalism;

To develop the best of the people's national culture and at the same time to study the progressive culture of the world, especially of the Soviet Union and of China; to develop the culture of the national minorities;

To develop the people's science, technique and art;

To mobilise the people to observe a new way of life;

To liquidate illiteracy, reform the educational system and develop vocational schools.

8. THE PARTY'S STAND TOWARDS RELIGION

The Viet-Nam Lao Dong Party respects and guarantees the freedom of religious belief of the people.

It opposes the French imperialists' policy of utilising religion to deceive the people and to split the National United Front of Viet-Nam.

9. THE PARTY'S POLICY TOWARDS THE NATIONALITIES

All the peoples living in Viet-Nam's territory are equal in rights and duties. They must unite with and help one another in order to carry forward the armed Resistance and national construction.

Our Party resolutely opposes narrow-minded nationalism and is determined to smash the plots of the imperialists and traitors to sow hatred among the people and divide them.

Our Party seeks to raise the living standards of the national minorities, to help them progress in all spheres of activity, to ensure their participation in the government and the use of their own language for their education in their own areas.

10. THE PARTY'S POLICY CONCERNING THE TEMPORARILY ENEMY-OCCUPIED AREAS AND THE NEWLY-LIBERATED AREAS

We attach the same importance to the work in enemy-occupied areas as to that in the liberated areas.

The work in the enemy-occupied areas consists in bringing about a broad unity between all strata of the people, intensifying and extending guerrilla warfare, building up and consolidating the People's Rule, destroying the puppet administrations and shattering the ranks of the puppet troops, mobilising the people to struggle against the enemy's oppression and exploitation, and co-ordinating action in enemy-occupied areas and liberated areas.

With regard to the lackeys of the enemy, we recommend the punishment of the leading unrepentant traitors and clemency towards those people who have been misled but who seek to atone for their mistakes and return to the side of the Motherland.

With regard to the newly-liberated areas, we must pay great attention to the realisation of unity among the whole population, to the question of ensuring the people's security, to vigilance against traitors and their extermination, to rehabilitation of the economy.

11. EXTERNAL POLICY

Viet-Nam's external policy must be based on the principle of mutual respect for national independence and territorial integrity, equality of rights and defence of world peace and democracy.

Consequently, it is necessary for Viet-Nam to consolidate her friendly relations with the Soviet Union, China and other People's Democracies, to actively support the national liberation movements of colonial and semi-colonial countries and to establish diplomatic relations with all countries that are willing to respect Viet-Nam's national sovereignty on the basis of freedom, equality and mutual benefit.

We stand for broadening the sphere of the people's diplomatic activities.

We stand for the protection of Viet-Nam nationals in foreign countries.

12. OUR POLICY TOWARDS LAOS AND CAMBODIA

The people of Viet-Nam must unite closely with the peoples of Laos and Cambodia and give them every assistance in the common struggle against imperialist aggression, for the complete liberation of Indo-China and for the defence of world peace.

In the common interests of the three peoples, the people of Viet-Nam are willing to enter into long-term co-operation with the peoples of Laos and Cambodia, with a view to bringing about an independent, free, strong and prosperous federation of the states of Viet-Nam, Laos and Cambodia, if the three peoples so desire.[11]

13. OUR POLICY TOWARDS FOREIGN NATIONALS

Those foreign nationals who respect Viet-Nam law are assured of the safety of their lives and properties, and they have the right to reside and carry on business in Viet-Nam.

Foreign nationals belonging to the People's Democracies, especially overseas Chinese in Viet-Nam, are allowed to enjoy the same rights

[11] For steps toward implementation of Indochinese "federation," see Document 78.

and perform the same duties as citizens of Viet-Nam if they so desire, subject to the approval of the government of their own country and of the Viet-Nam People's Government.

14. THE STRUGGLE FOR WORLD PEACE AND DEMOCRACY

To fight for the defence of world peace and democracy is an international task of the people of Viet-Nam. To fight against the imperialist aggressors is the most active means whereby our people can fulfil this task.

We recommend that the people of Viet-Nam co-ordinate their War of Resistance with the struggles of other peoples of the world, and especially with those of the peoples of France and the French colonies.

15. PATRIOTIC EMULATION

The patriotic emulation campaign is a nation-wide movement reaching into all branches of activity and mainly aiming at checking three enemies: illiteracy, famine and foreign aggression.

The army, rural areas, enterprises, schools and organisations are the main places where the emulation campaign is to be carried out.

We recommend that emulation heroes and labour fighters be promoted so as to mobilise the entire people to take part in the War of Resistance and national construction.

77. *Program of the United National (Lien Viet) Front* *
March 3, 1951

INTERNATIONAL SITUATION

Since the end of World War II the Soviet Union has become an increasingly prosperous and powerful state; people's democratic states are springing up one after the other; the national-liberation movement in colonial and semi-colonial countries is becoming continuously stronger; and the fight of the peoples of the capitalist countries is growing more and more.

After the Second World War, fascist Germany, Italy and Japan

* *Source:* O. A. Arturov, ed., *Demokratischeskaya Respublika Vietnam: Konstitutsia, Zakonodatelnia Akti, Dokumenti* (Moscow: Izdatelstvo Innostrannoi Literaturi, 1955), pp. 47–56, citing "The Lien Viet Front, Manifesto, Program, Charter" (Lien Viet Edition, 1951), in Vietnamese. Translation from the Russian by courtesy of Dr. Herbert L. Sawyer. The editor has been unable to find a complete text of the Lien Viet program, other than the one translated here, in a Western language. The Viet Minh radio broadcast only portions of it.

dropped out of the number of the great imperialist powers; and English and French imperialism declined at the same time that American imperialism, having acquired fabulous wealth during the war, became the leader of imperialism. And beyond that the narrow markets of the capitalist world shrunk still further. The capitalist economy, especially in the United States, is facing a growing economic crisis.

As a result of all this the world was divided into two camps: the democratic camp, led by the Soviet Union, and the imperialist camp led by the United States.

In order to compensate for the losses which they suffered in World War II, and to avoid an economic crisis, the imperialists are now using all possible means for the ever greater exploitation of the peoples of their own countries and of their colonies, and are inciting aggressive wars in various parts of the world. The American imperialists and their satellites are broadening regional wars and are feverishly preparing for a third world war. They want to plunge mankind into a new, bloody war.

By contrast the peace-loving democratic camp, endeavoring to assure the happiness of the peoples, is filled with determination to fight against the warmongers.

The world-wide movement in defense of peace is growing and broadening. Under the leadership of the Soviet Union, the forces of peace and democracy united in a powerful peace front. The victory of the Chinese revolution and the Korean people's successful war of liberation show that the democratic camp is stronger than the imperialistic camp. Therefore, in the event that the imperialists ignite a third world war they will be destroyed.

Fighting for independence, democracy and peace, Viet-Nam stands firmly in the ranks of the camp of peace and democracy. The imperialists invaded Viet-Nam, Laos and Cambodia and intend to turn these three countries into their own bases for aggression against the Chinese People's Republic. Nonetheless, the camp of peace and democracy will be victorious, and without doubt the revolution in Viet-Nam, Laos and Cambodia is triumphing.

THE INTERNAL SITUATION IN VIET-NAM

In the course of several millennia of its history, Viet-Nam was an independent state. The French colonizers seized it in 1862. In 1940 Japanese domination was added to French domination.

In March of 1945 the Japanese overthrew the French colonizers and turned Viet-Nam into their own colony. In the course of more than eighty years of colonial domination the Vietnamese people never stopped its fight for independence and freedom. In August of 1945, thanks to the close unity of the Viet Minh Front, the Vietnamese people began a victorious general uprising, seized power, overthrew the monarchical-bureaucratic regime, established the Democratic Republic of Viet-Nam and moved towards the creation of a people's-democratic order.

On September 23, 1945, the French invaders, supported by the British imperialists, again attacked South Viet-Nam. The Vietnamese people immediately arose in a war of resistance. On December 19, 1946, the war spread over the entire territory of Viet-Nam, and thus for more than five years the Vietnamese people has carried on a heroic struggle.

The French colonizers, relying on American weapons, planned a lightning attack and expected a quick victory but met with failure. They resorted to all possible political intrigues in order to defeat the Vietnamese people. On the one hand, they resorted to barbaric destruction of people, to arson, pillage and violence. On the other hand, they employed deceit and promises, and granted Viet-Nam a fictitious independence. They created the puppet government of Viet-Nam, used the so-called "autonomous states" of Nung and Thai as well as the Catholics, forcibly recruited soldiers for the puppet forces with the aim of dividing the ranks of the resistance and forcing the Vietnamese to murder one another. However, all of these devices failed completely. The Vietnamese people remained closely unified and filled with determination to continue the struggle.

Since 1950 the American imperialists have been openly involved in the Franco-Viet-Nam War and now are directly guiding the French colonialists in their aggression against Viet-Nam, Laos and Cambodia. However, there are contradictions between the French and American imperialists, and in addition the anti-war movement in France is growing stronger and it is arising in America. Peoples of the world are branding both the French and American imperialists with shame.

By contrast, the Vietnamese people under the leadership of Ho Chi Minh are marching forward in solid ranks, unanimous in their determination to carry out a national, comprehensive and prolonged resistance. At first the Viet Minh (The Viet-Nam Independence League) alone united the masses of the people, but then, along with the Lien Viet (The National Union of Viet-Nam), which was formed in 1946, it continually broadened the united national front. Subsequently the

Viet Minh and the Lien Viet merged into a united front—the Lien Viet United Front—thereby making national unity still stronger and the victory of the resistance movement in Viet-Nam still more certain.

At the beginning of 1950, the Democratic Republic of Viet-Nam was recognized by the Soviet Union, China and the other People's Democracies. At the end of 1950, the People's Army of Viet-Nam liberated five provinces and broke the blockade established by the French imperialists along the northern border—the border of Viet-Nam with the Chinese People's Republic.

Thus, notwithstanding American help, the French colonizers were forced to go over from the offense to the defense. Fighting without foreign help, but being closely united and filled with determination, the Vietnamese people went over from defensive to offensive actions. American imperialism, by increasing its aid to the French colonialists, can create new difficulties for the resistance war in Viet-Nam, but the final victory unquestionably will belong to the Vietnamese people.

ARMED RESISTANCE AND NATIONAL CONSTRUCTION

With regard to Viet-Nam's current international and internal situation, the United National Front declares that the most evil enemies of the Vietnamese people are the French colonialists and the American interventionists, and that traitors must suffer the appropriate punishment. They are not only trying to destroy the independence and unity of Viet-Nam and hinder the development of Vietnamese society, but also to undermine peace in the entire world.

Therefore, in the present stage the revolutionary tasks of the Vietnamese people consist of the following: to destroy the French colonizers, to smash the American interventionists and to punish traitors; to strengthen and develop the people's democratic order; to unite its struggle with the forces of the international movement in defense of peace; to create an independent, united, democratic, free, powerful and flourishing Viet-Nam; and to cooperate with other peoples of the world in the task of consolidating a durable peace.

For the accomplishment of these tasks the Lien Viet Front supports the unification of all patriotic organizations and individuals, regardless of sex, nationality, religion and class, into a united national bloc serving as the basis of a people's-democratic state, in the interests of accomplishing the following policy of armed resistance and national construction.

I. Armed Resistance

1. Resolutely to support a policy of nationwide and protracted resistance until complete victory.

2. To mobilize all human reserves and material and financial resources for conducting the war of resistance in accordance with the slogan "Everything for the front, everything for victory!" and at the same time continuously to strengthen the resistance movement.

3. Simultaneously to accomplish armed resistance and national construction, at the same time directing the latter at fulfilling the most immediate tasks of the armed resistance struggle which are necessary to hasten victory.

II. In the Political Field

1. To strengthen the broad united national front, consisting of workers, peasants, the petty bourgeoisie, the national bourgeoisie and the patriotic and progressive elements among the notables and the landlords; to strengthen the basis of this bloc—a union of the working class, the peasantry and the intelligentsia; to establish ties between the people of the territory occupied by the enemy and the population of the liberated provinces; to support ties with Vietnamese living abroad for the purpose of carrying out to the end the armed resistance and national construction.

2. To strengthen the people's power, which belongs to the working class, the peasantry, the intelligentsia, the petty bourgeoisie, the national bourgeoisie, and also to the patriotic landlords, and which is based on the union between the workers, the peasants and the intelligentsia. This people's power is democratic for the people and dictatorial with respect to the imperialistic aggressors and traitors.

3. To guarantee political and socio-economic rights to all Vietnamese citizens: human rights such as freedom of political views and religion, freedom of choice of residence and movement; political rights such as the right to elect and be elected, to participate in the administration of the state, and other democratic freedoms such as freedom of speech, press, organization, assembly, etc.; economic rights such as the freedom of enterprise, personal property and inheritance.

4. To guarantee equality between men and women and equality of nationalities in economic, cultural, social and other relations.

III. In the Military Field

1. To create a powerful people's army capable of withstanding foreign aggression, destroying traitors and defending the people's power.

2. To strengthen and develop local armed forces, the people's militia and guerrilla partisan detachments and transform them into a powerful reserve of the regular army.

3. To arm the popular masses and to carry out the people's war.

4. To combine closely the armed struggle with political, economic and cultural-enlightenment struggle. To closely coordinate military operations at the front with the partisan war and with the battle in the enemy's rear and in territory temporarily occupied by the enemy.

IV. In the Economic Field

1. To develop the national economy and production so as to satisfy the needs of the war and to raise the people's standard of living. To mobilize all levels of the population in active participation in a campaign for increasing production on the basis of mutual benefit for the state and for private persons, capital and labor. To create a state economy, to develop cooperation and encourage private economic activity.

2. To implement an agrarian policy, the aim of which is the improvement of the living conditions of the peasants who constitute the basic part of the population, the increasing of agricultural production and the guaranteeing of the food supply. To develop agriculture. To consider the legimate rights of both landowners and tenants. To bring about a lowering of land rents and interest on loans, to confiscate lands which earlier belonged to traitors and French colonialists, and temporarily transfer them to the peasants. To redistribute public lands and to use properly the empty lands and those of the absentee landlords.

3. To develop industry and trade, to broaden the activity of small merchants, tradesmen and the national bourgeoisie, and to render them every assistance.

4. To create an independent and durable financial system. To raise national income by increasing production and lowering expenditures through economies. To democratize the tax system.

5. To undermine the enemy's economy so as to advance the resistance movement and benefit the people's interest.

6. To establish close economic relations with the people's democracies, especially with China.

V. In the Field of Culture and Enlightenment

1. To root out the slavish and antiquated ideology of the colonizers and feudalists; to struggle against the corrupt and reactionary ideological influence of the imperialist warmongers.

2. To develop all that is best in the national culture, and to study the progressive world culture.

3. To develop national science, technology, art and literature.

4. To create a new, national, people's culture so as to instill into the entire people a feeling of love for the Fatherland, for mankind, for labor and science, and to instill respect for public property.

5. To liquidate illiteracy, to create a new democratic system of education, to educate the younger generation and to encourage the development of talents.

VI. In the Social Field

1. To pass and observe labor legislation and to create a system of social insurance.

2. To surround with attention and concern the servicemen, the wounded, invalid soldiers, and the families of those who perished for the motherland.

3. To surround with concern pregnant women, children, the aged and invalids.

4. To organize social insurance and to develop a national health administration.

5. To observe hygiene and to encourage the development of physical culture in order to strengthen the health of our people.

6. To develop "The movement for a new life." [12]

VII. In the Field of Religious Relations

1. To respect the freedom of religion and creed for everyone.

2. To struggle against the policy of the imperialists and the plots of the traitors who are endeavoring to use religion for the purpose of dividing our people.

VIII. On the Nationalities of the Highland Regions

1. All people born on Vietnamese soil have equal rights and obligations and must unite and help each other in the task of armed resistance and national construction.

2. To struggle against the enemy's policy of "divide and rule." To come out decisively against any thoughts and actions directed towards inciting national differences between the populations of the mountains and the plains regions, and differences between separate peoples of the mountain regions.

3. To help the peoples of the mountain regions achieve progress in all fields, especially in raising their standard of living, in involving them in the administration of the state, and in the development of the national culture.

[12] Footnote in the original: "A social organization putting as its task the comprehensive improvement of the workers' lives. Ed."

IX. On Foreigners Residing in Viet-Nam

1. The lives and property of all foreigners residing in Viet-Nam who observe the laws and respect the national sovereignty of Viet-Nam come under the protection of the law; foreigners residing in Viet-Nam have the right to choose their place of residence and employment.

2. Foreigners who are citizens of democratic countries recognizing the Government of the Democratic Republic of Viet-Nam, especially Chinese, can, if they desire, take advantage of the laws and fulfill obligations on an equal footing with Vietnamese citizens with the agreement of the appropriate governments.

3. Protection and help is guaranteed to foreigners who, struggling for freedom, democracy and peace, are seeking asylum in Viet-Nam.

X. Foreign Affairs

1. To support friendly relations, on the basis of equality, with all peoples of the world respecting the independence of Viet-Nam and supporting the defense of peace throughout the world.

2. To strengthen relations with the Soviet Union, China and other People's Democracies.

3. To establish friendly relations with the peoples of Laos and Cambodia on a mutually voluntary basis and on a basis of equality and mutual assistance with the objective of completing the struggle for independence.

4. To broaden diplomatic contacts. To strengthen and develop the contacts of Vietnamese people's organizations with the people's organizations of other countries, especially China and France.

5. To defend the interests of Vietnamese residing abroad.

XI. The Struggle for Peace

1. To intensify the war of resistance as a means of active defense of peace in the entire world.

2. To encourage in the army and among the population the desire to struggle in defense of peace throughout the world.

3. To coordinate the resistance movement of the Vietnamese people with the struggle of all peoples in defense of peace, especially with the struggle of the French people and the oppressed peoples.

XII. Patriotic Emulation

1. To carry out a campaign of patriotic emulation in the task of destroying the aggressor, preventing hunger, liquidating illiteracy and achieving success in the construction of the nation.

2. To honor and reward leaders in patriotic emulation.

78. *Manifesto of the Joint United Front of Viet-Nam, Laos, and Cambodia* *
March 11, 1951

The Joint Conference of Viet-Nam, Laos, and Cambodia, attended by delegates of the three National United Fronts of Viet-Nam, Laos, and Cambodia—Lien Viet Front in Viet-Nam, Khmer Issarak Front in Cambodia, and Lao Issara Front in Laos—at its meeting on March 11, 1951, after examining the situation in the world and in Viet-Nam, Laos, and Cambodia, and relations between these three peoples in the struggle against aggression, unanimously declares:

1. The French colonialists and American interventionists are making all-out attempts to conquer Viet-Nam, Cambodia, and Laos, and to enslave these three peoples once again. But the regimes they have set up in Viet-Nam, Cambodia, and Laos are merely puppet regimes, and the independence they have bestowed on these three countries is but a fake independence. The American interventionists are not only plotting to turn these three countries into their colonies but also to use them as bases for aggression on China, for suppressing of the liberation movement of the peoples in Southeast Asia, and for plunging the world into a new war.

2. In the face of the common enemies, the Joint Conference of Viet-Nam, Laos, and Cambodia has set up an alliance between the peoples of Viet-Nam, Cambodia, and Laos on the basis of free choice, equality, mutual assistance, and mutual respect of national sovereignty, with the aim of wiping out the French colonialists, defeating the American interventionists, and punishing the traitorous puppets, and gaining genuine independence for the three peoples and contributing to the maintenance of world peace.

The Conference has elected a Joint Committee of Viet-Nam, Cambodia, and Laos, with a view to strengthen friendly relations and realize mutual assistance between the three peoples.

* *Source:* Broadcast by Viet-Nam News Agency in English Morse, April 23, 1951, 1000 G.M.T. The Manifesto was adopted by a "Joint Conference" held on March 11, shortly after the formation of the Lien Viet Front in Viet-Nam. Viet-Nam was represented by the veteran Communist revolutionary Ton Duc Thang, who later became Vice President (and, after the death of Ho Chi Minh in September 1969, President) of the DRV. Laos was represented by Prince Souphanouvong, and Cambodia by Sieu Heng (reputedly also a member of the Viet Minh). The Conference also adopted a Resolution, calling for the formation of the Joint United Front: text broadcast by Viet-Nam News Agency in English Morse, April 23, 1951, 1000 G.M.T.

3. The Conference calls on the people of Viet-Nam to unite ever more closely in the Lien Viet Front, on the people of Cambodia to unite more closely in the Khmer Issarak Front, and the people of Laos to unite more closely in the Lao Issara Front, so as to strengthen the alliance between Viet-Nam, Laos, and Cambodia, to bring early victory to the resistance of these three peoples, to consolidate and develop the national and people's power in the three countries.

The Conference calls on peoples of the world and the oppressed peoples to support the alliance between Viet-Nam, Laos, and Cambodia, so that it can fulfill the task of defending justice and gaining freedom. The Conference firmly believes that world peace will certainly be victorious and that the three peoples of Viet-Nam, Cambodia, and Laos will surely achieve genuine independence.

CHAPTER VII

The Western Reaction and the American Commitment

March 1951-October 1953

Introduction

Following the open identification of the Viet Minh with Communism, there was a hardening of Western, particularly American, determination to oppose "Communist aggression" in Indochina as well as in Korea. American aid increased so greatly that by the end of 1953 the United States was assuming more than half the cost of the war. Chinese assistance to the Viet Minh as well as increasing Soviet support made the Viet-Nam war a true international crisis by the end of this period. Nonetheless there were indications that a peaceful resolution of the struggle might be possible in the wake of the Korean armistice.

At the end of April 1951, President Auriol of France visited Washington where he and President Truman discussed, among other matters, "the present situation in Indochina where French forces and the forces of the Associated States (of Indochina) are successfully opposing Communist aggression." [1] Simultaneously France accelerated the creation of a Vietnamese army, and Bao Dai in July signed an ordinance decreeing general mobilization. At the beginning of September the United States and Viet-Nam concluded an Economic Cooperation Agreement.[2]

In September General de Lattre visited the United States for lengthy conversations with the Joint Chiefs of Staff. He also addressed the National Press Club, linking the struggle in Indochina to the security of the free world (Document 79). He obtained United States agreement to accelerated delivery of military supplies (Document 80).

[1] The text of the Joint Communiqué of March 29, 1951, is in United States, Department of State, *American Foreign Policy 1950–1955: Basic Documents* (2 vols., Washington: Government Printing Office, 1957), Vol. I, p. 1672.

[2] Text in United Nations, *Treaty Series*, Vol. 174 (1953), pp. 172–184.

The end of 1951 saw the first major debate on Indochina policy in the French National Assembly since 1950, with opposition to the Government led by Pierre Mendès-France. Subsequently, in a January 3, 1952, statement to the Council of the Republic, Jean Letourneau, Minister of State for the Associated States, said the Government was hopeful that, if negotiations for a cease-fire in Korea proved successful, "joint conversations would be able to start in order to achieve a complete solution for Southeast Asia." [3] The next week the United States and the State of Viet-Nam concluded an agreement on mutual security.[4]

Following the death of General de Lattre (of natural causes) on January 11, Jean Letourneau was appointed High Commissioner, resident in Indochina, while retaining his post in the French cabinet. General Raoul Salan, who had long experience in Indochina and was later to win notoriety in Algeria, was named Commander-in-Chief of French forces. John Foster Dulles, then an advisor to the State Department but to become Secretary of State in less than a year, spoke in Paris on May 5; he referred to Indochina as "the key to Southeast Asia" and said that "the loss of Indochina to the gain of Communism would put other regions in grave danger." [5]

At the beginning of June, Bao Dai dismissed Premier Tran Van Huu and replaced him with Nguyen Van Tam. That same month High Commissioner Letourneau visited Washington, where his discussions with American officials produced agreement on further increases in American aid (Document 81). Indochina was debated in the Security Council of the United Nations in September during consideration of applications for membership in the world body (Document 82). The Soviet Union proposed membership for the DRV and opposed it for the Associated States, but none of the Indochinese states was admitted.

October 1952 saw a major Viet Minh attack in northwest Tonkin, followed by an offensive into Laos. The alarming military situation was discussed at the December meeting of the North Atlantic Council in Paris, where a resolution supporting the French effort was adopted (Document 83). Only a month later the new American administration of President Eisenhower took office, and the new Secretary of State, John Foster Dulles, indicated the tenor of American policy by citing

[3] France, *Journal Officiel de la République Française, Débats Parlementaires, Conseil de la République*, Session of January 3, 1952, p. 100.

[4] The text of the exchange of notes of December 1951 and January 1952 is in United Nations, *Treaty Series*, Vol. 205 (1955), pp. 128–138.

[5] Summary and extracts in France, Direction de la Documentation, *Chroniques d'Outre-Mer: Etudes et Informations*, No. 6 (June 1952), pp. 58–59.

the Soviet "drive to get Japan" through control of the "rice bowl" of Southeast Asia.[6] Shortly thereafter French Premier René Mayer visited Washington. The United States had become impatient with the failure of France to inflict a decisive defeat on the Viet Minh and, as a condition for continued aid, began to take a more active role in the planning of the French military effort as was indicated by the joint communiqué issued on March 28 (Document 84).[7]

At the end of April the Viet Minh suddenly ceased their advance on Luang Probang in Laos and retired to Viet-Nam, leaving behind a Lao revolutionary government at Sam Neua. The Western powers had been thoroughly unsettled by the entire affair, and it stimulated further American support for the French effort. On May 9 the French Government named General Henri Navarre as Commander-in-Chief in Indochina, with Maurice Dejean as High Commissioner. Only two days later the Government devalued the Indochinese piastre relative to the French franc, without advance consultation with the Associated States, thus producing considerable ill-feeling on the part of the latter.

During May the French Government fell, initiating a political crisis lasting until June 26 when Joseph Laniel, a conservative Independent, was able to form a ministry. Confronting Indochina as his most immediate problem, Laniel dismissed Jean Letourneau as Minister for the Associated States and, on July 3, informed the Associated States that France was prepared to "perfect" their independence (Document 85). On July 6 a spokesman for the Department of State said that the United States "welcomed" the French offer and pledged its "wholehearted support."[8] Foreign Minister Georges Bidault visited Washington in July for talks with Secretary Dulles and the acting British Foreign Minister. In addition to discussing the situation in Indochina and the French military plan (the "Navarre Plan") (Document 86), the three powers also decided to invite the Soviet Union to a "Big Four"

[6] Speech of February 7, "A Survey of Foreign Policy Problems," in United States, Department of State, *Bulletin*, XXVIII (February 9, 1953), pp. 212–216.

[7] An April 26, 1953, memorandum from the United States to France reportedly reaffirmed the principle of an increase in American aid but posed certain conditions, including "that the French Government would adopt a program capable, in every aspect, of ensuring military success in Indochina" (Philippe Devillers and Jean Lacouture, *End of a War: Indochina, 1954*, Alexander Lieven and Adam Roberts, trans. [New York: Frederick A. Praeger, 1969], p. 34n, citing para. 5, sub-para. C of the April 26 memorandum as quoted in *Le Monde*, July 26, 1953). This was the immediate origin of the French military plan known as the "Navarre Plan." The editor has been unable to obtain a complete official text of the memorandum, which remains classified by the United States.

[8] Reported in *The New York Times*, July 7, 1953, p. 3.

conference to discuss European problems. That decision was the first
step toward the 1954 conferences at Berlin and Geneva which were to
be of such great importance for Indochina.

The conclusion of the Korean Armistice on July 27, in the somewhat relaxed international atmosphere which followed the death of
Stalin, increased the attention given to Indochina. President Eisenhower's views were expressed in his remarks to the Governors' Conference in Seattle on August 5 (Document 87). On September 2, in
a St. Louis speech, Secretary Dulles took a tough line on possible Chinese intervention in Indochina while leaving the door open for negotiations (Document 88). He amplified his views on political talks at
a news conference the following day (Document 89). At the end of
the month a Franco-American communiqué gave details on additional
American aid (Document 90).

Meanwhile France had begun negotiations with the State of Viet-
Nam for the transfer of those governmental services remaining under
French control. While Bao Dai and Premier Tam were negotiating in
Paris, nationalists in Viet-Nam, including Ngo Dinh Nhu (the younger
brother of Ngo Dinh Diem), organized an unofficial "National Congress" to manifest their desire to have a voice in negotiations with
France as well as in internal affairs. The Congress, meeting in
Saigon in September, degenerated into an indictment of France and
Bao Dai. Bao Dai then decided to summon an "official" National Congress; it met in Saigon from October 12 through 17 for the ostensible
purpose of informing Bao Dai of the desires of the people with regard
to relations with France. But this Congress too was highly nationalistic
and adopted strong resolutions on the subject of independence (Document 91).

The actions of the National Congress caused consternation in Paris,
where many saw them as a betrayal of the French effort in Indochina.
The matter was raised in the National Assembly, and Paris protested to
Bao Dai. On October 27 Premier Laniel found it necessary to state the
Government's policy to the National Assembly; he took a strong stand
on relations with the State of Viet-Nam and, more importantly, under-
lined French willingness to negotiate a solution to the war if the opportunity should arise (Document 92). In an atmosphere of increasing
discontent with the war, the Assembly endorsed the Government's policy only by the narrow margin of 315 to 257.

While France was shaken by these events and by the opening of a
new Viet Minh offensive in Laos, she continued to receive support from

her allies. The Foreign Ministers of the three Western powers, meeting in London on October 18, discussed the situation:

The French Foreign Minister [9] gave an account of the military results obtained thus far in Indo-China, as well as the progress made in negotiations with the Associated States in order to carry out the French declaration of July 3.[10] The three Ministers agreed that the successful conclusion of this war will be an essential step toward the reestablishment of peace in Asia begun by the armistice in Korea.[11]

79. *General Jean de Lattre de Tassigny: Speech Made to the National Press Club in Washington [Extracts]* *
    September 20, 1951

[The first three and one-half pages of the speech are omitted. In them General de Lattre described the wars in Korea and in Indochina as "the same fight, in the same war against the same enemy," and presented an explanation and defense of the independence granted to the Indochinese states.]

Why, then, is there still war in Indochina, now that all the objectives of Indochinese nationalism have been attained?

It is because the war declared six years ago by the Vietminh did not have independence as its real objective but rather the installation of Communism: it is because this war tried to eliminate all that was French in order to enslave Indochina in the most terrible of dominations. The mask of nationalism has helped to fool many Vietnamese, many Frenchmen and Americans, into allowing the Communist party in Indochina, as in the countries of Eastern Europe, to implant its police little by little, to organize its propaganda, to liquidate its opponents.

Today, the Vietminh throws off its mask.

The Indochinese Communist party, which was disbanded in 1944 [sic], has recently been officially reconstituted; all workers have been grouped in a syndicate which is actually a branch of the Communist party, the whole army is in the hands of political commissars.

The situation has the advantage of being clear. Well, the patriots

* *Source:* French Press and Information Service (New York), *Document,* No. 61 (September 1951), pp. 4–5. Emphasis in the original.
  [9] Georges Bidault.   [10] Document 85.
  [11] Text in United States, Department of State, *American Foreign Policy 1950–1955: Basic Documents* (2 vols., Washington: Government Printing Office, 1957), Vol. I, pp. 1467–1468.

who at the beginning had cooperated with the Vietminh are pulling away from it, even at the price of the greatest risks; they rally to the legitimate Government which now has in its favor the prestige of independence, an authority capable of affirming itself, the guarantee of France's power, victorious once again, and the friendship and help of America.

The Governments of the Associated States are gradually increasing their popular support. Elections have just been held in Cambodia and in Laos; they will be held in Viet Nam, as pacification succeeds. On the other hand, His Majesty Bao Dai has recently outlined a whole program of social measures, which will transform Viet Nam into a true democracy, and also of economic measures which will permit its reconstruction and development.

These reforms which are already being applied in the recently pacified zones of the Tonkin delta will give to a people deceived by Communism a new patrimony to defend against it. They will be a complement to the Decree of Mobilization signed on July 15 [1] which shows the will of Viet Nam to fight the war to the end because it knows now that it is *its* war, for the protection of *its* independence against Communism.

Gentlemen, if France is fighting this war with the Associated States, it is to fulfill the obligations she has undertaken when she created the French Union. It is also true to the spirit of the United Nations for the defense of the world's liberty.

It is because in this war, Gentlemen, Indochina is not the only stake, Southeast Asia and even the whole of Asia is at stake. Tonkin is the main redoubt, the keystone to the whole structure.

Today there is in the world a city whose importance is great, it is the capital of Tonkin: Hanoi. Morally this city has become, in the eyes of all peoples of Southeast Asia, the test of the will and of the power to stop Communism. Militarily its loss would open to the Communist invasion the road to Bangkok, to Singapore, and many other roads that you can easily guess. Gentlemen, Hanoi today is for the free world of

---

[1] "With a view to hastening the re-establishment of peace and order in the national territory, the Government will mobilize the whole of the means and resources of the nation. The Premier is empowered to prescribe, by decree of the Council of Ministers, all the measures which he shall judge compatible with the general situation in order to ensure each day a larger and more effective participation of the national potential in the defense of liberty and the restoration of peace" (State of Viet-Nam, High Commission in Paris, *Vietnam,* No. 7 [August 1, 1951], p. 6). Translation by the editor.

Southeast Asia both the Bastogne of December 1944 and the Berlin of June 1947 [*sic*].

And the loss of Southeast Asia would mean that Communism would have at its disposal essential strategic raw materials, that Japanese economy would forever be unbalanced and that the whole of Asia would be threatened.

Once Tonkin is lost, there is really no barrier left before Suez, and I leave to your imagination how defeatism and defeat would grow as time goes by, how Communist fifth columns would get into the game in every country as a strong external Communist force applied pressure on its frontiers.

But the fall of Asia would mean the end of Islam, which has two-thirds of its faithful in Asia; it would mean an upheaval in North Africa; it would mean that the strategic bases for the defense of Europe are in jeopardy. In what situation would Europe find herself, flanked in this way, and remaining as a last clear patch at the end of an immense red continent?

Some of you gentlemen perhaps think that I am presumptuous and that I take the place where I am stationed for the center of the world. No, I am not presumptuous, because I do not say that it is sufficient to protect Indochina to safeguard Asia, but I do say that it would probably be sufficient to lose Indochina to lose Asia. And that is quite a lot, don't you think?

[The balance of the speech is omitted. In it General de Lattre outlined the military successes by the French forces since the defeats in the fall of 1950 and the progress being made in the building of national armies, for which he appealed for additional American aid.]

80. *Statement by the Departments of State and Defense on Military Aid to France and the Associated States* *
    September 23, 1951

Discussions which have been going on for the past week between General of the Army, Jean de Lattre de Tassigny, French High Commissioner in Indochina and Commander in Chief of the French Union Forces in Indochina, and officials of the Departments of Defense and State were concluded September 22 in an atmosphere of cordiality and unity of purpose.

* *Source:* United States, Department of State, *American Foreign Policy 1950–1955: Basic Documents* (2 vols., Washington: Government Printing Office, 1957), Vol. II, pp. 2366–2367.

The participants were in complete agreement that the successful defense of Indochina is of great importance to the defense of all Southeast Asia. United States officials stated that General de Lattre's presentation of the situation in that area had been invaluable to them and had demonstrated that United States and French policies in the Associated States were not at variance.

In the course of the discussions with the Department of Defense, the military-aid program for Indochina was reexamined, with the result that considerable improvement will be made in the rate of deliveries of many items of equipment. General de Lattre has been advised that the question of additional aid for the French and Vietnamese forces in Indochina in the fiscal year 1952 program is under study by the United States Government.

81. *Communiqué Regarding Discussions on the Defense of Indochina between Representatives of the United States, France, Viet-Nam, and Cambodia* *
June 18, 1952

Mr. Jean Letourneau, Minister in the French Cabinet for the Associated States in Indochina, has just concluded a series of conversations with U.S. Government officials from the Department of State, Department of Defense, the Office of Director for Mutual Security, the Mutual Security Agency, and Department of the Treasury. The Ambassadors of Cambodia and Viet-Nam have also participated in these talks.

The principle which governed this frank and detailed exchange of views and information was the common recognition that the struggle in which the forces of the French Union and the Associated States are engaged against the forces of Communist aggression in Indochina is an integral part of the world-wide resistance by the Free Nations to Communist attempts at conquest and subversion. There was unanimous satisfaction over the vigorous and successful course of military operations, in spite of the continuous comfort and aid received by the Communist forces of the Viet-Minh from Communist China. The excellent performance of the Associated States' forces in battle was found to be a source of particular encouragement. Special tribute was paid to the 52,000 officers and men of the French Union and Associated States'

* *Source:* United States, Department of State, *American Foreign Policy 1950–1955: Basic Documents* (2 vols., Washington: Government Printing Office, 1957), Vol. II, pp. 2367–2368.

armies who have been lost in this six years' struggle for freedom in Southeast Asia and to the 75,000 other casualties.

In this common struggle, however, history, strategic factors, as well as local and general resources require that the free countries concerned each assume primary responsibility for resistance in the specific areas where Communism has resorted to force of arms. Thus the United States assumes a large share of the burden in Korea while France has the primary role in Indochina. The partners, however, recognize the obligation to help each other in their areas of primary responsibility to the extent of their capabilities and within the limitations imposed by their global obligations as well as by the requirements in their own areas of special responsibility. It was agreed that success in this continuing struggle would entail an increase in the common effort and that the United States for its part will, therefore, within the limitations set by Congress, take steps to expand its aid to the French Union. It was further agreed that this increased assistance over and above present U.S. aid for Indochina, which now approximates one third of the total cost of Indochina operations, would be especially devoted to assisting France in the building of the national armies of the Associated States.

Mr. Letourneau reviewed the facts which amply demonstrate the determination of the Associated States to pursue with increased energy the strengthening of their authority and integrity both against internal subversion and against external aggression.

In this connection Mr. Letourneau reminded the participants that the accords of 1949,[2] which established the independence within the French Union of Cambodia, Laos and Viet-Nam, have been liberally interpreted and supplemented by other agreements, thus consolidating this independence. Mr. Letourneau pointed out that the governments of the Associated States now exercise full authority except that a strictly limited number of services related to the necessities of the war now in progress remain temporarily in French hands. In the course of the examination of the Far Eastern economic and trade situation, it was noted that the Governments of the Associated States are free to negotiate trade treaties and agreements of all kinds with their neighbors subject only to whatever special arrangements may be agreed between members of the French Union.

It was noted that these states have been recognized by thirty-three foreign governments.

The conversations reaffirmed the common determination of the par-

[2] For Viet-Nam, the Elysée Agreements, Document 55.

ticipants to prosecute the defense of Indochina and their confidence in a free, peaceful and prosperous future for Cambodia, Laos, and Viet-Nam.

Mr. Letourneau was received by the President, Mr. Acheson, and Mr. Foster, as Acting Secretary of Defense. Mr. John Allison, Assistant Secretary of State for Far Eastern Affairs, acted as Chairman of the U.S. Delegation participating in the conversations.

82. *Debate in the Security Council on Admission of the Indochinese States to Membership in the United Nations [Extracts] **
September 19, 1952

[Only the most interesting paragraphs of the long debate on the admission of the Indochinese states to the United Nations are reproduced here.]

[MR. MALIK (Union of Soviet Socialist Republics) (*translated from Russian*)]:

11. The French Minister for Foreign Affairs submitted to the Council three applications for membership in the United Nations, from Bao Dai's Vietnam, the Kingdom of Laos and the Kingdom of Cambodia,[3] which were established in Indo-China by French ruling circles with the help and assistance of the ruling circles in the United States. The mere fact that a special official statement by a French Minister was needed for the submission of these applications to the United Nations gives a true idea of the kind of "States" these are and of their degree of independence or, more properly, of the extent to which they are dependent and puppet States.

12. As early as 29 December 1951, the Security Council received a telegram from the Government of the Democratic Republic of Vietnam

* *Source:* United Nations, Security Council, *Verbatim Records,* Seventh Year, 603rd Meeting (September 19, 1952), pp. 2, 8–9, 19. In a subsequent meeting of the Council, the applications of the Associated States for membership in the United Nations were defeated by Soviet veto.

[3] The initial application by the State of Viet-Nam, of December 17, 1951, is United Nations, Security Council, document S/2446. A more detailed application, submitted on August 7, 1952, is document S/2756. The Cambodian application of June 15 is document S/2672, and the Lao application of June 30 is document S/2706. The latter two were endorsed by letters from the French Foreign Minister, in documents S/2675 and S/2706 respectively. The French draft resolutions for the admission of Viet-Nam, Laos, and Cambodia, dated September 2, 1952, are documents S/2758, S/2759, and S/2760 respectively.

containing an application for the admission of the Republic to membership in the United Nations [*S/2466*].[4] This telegram, which was issued as a Security Council document, formally apprised the Council that the Democratic Republic of Vietnam had applied for membership as early as 22 November 1948 [*S/2780*] [5] and that the Government of that Republic had even then declared that it was the sole legitimate government of Vietnam, that it wished to confirm that it assumed the obligations laid down in the United Nations Charter, and that it would fulfil those obligations.

. . . . .

46. In the light of these facts, it is not difficult to understand the establishment of Franco-American puppets in Indo-China and the attempt, moreover, to have them admitted to the United Nations. The purpose is clear. The ruling circles in the United States intend to use them as a screen behind which the United States could openly and publicly send its forces to participate in the aggressive war against the people of Vietnam. Their purpose is to engage in a colonial war against the Indo-Chinese people under the same conditions and using the same methods as the United States aggressors are using in their war against the Korean people, namely, by enlisting the support of the armed forces of other colonial Powers dependent upon them, the emblem and flag of the United Nations being used as a screen for their colonial war.

47. As early as 1950, the representative of France, in one of his communications to the United Nations, published as a United Nations document, stated officially that the French armed forces in Indo-China were doing exactly what the American armed forces were doing in Korea, i.e., engaging in an aggressive colonial war against the peoples of Asia. This official admission by the French representative may be found in document S/1586.[6]

48. To admit Bao Dai's Vietnam, headed by the royal puppet Bao Dai, who first obeyed the French, then the Japanese, then the French again and now the Americans and the French, and likewise to admit

[4] Telegram to the Secretary General from Foreign Minister Hoang Minh Giam, dated December 29, 1951 (United Nations, Security Council, document S/2466).

[5] Letter to the Secretary General from Tran Ngoc Danh, Chairman of the DRV Delegation in Paris, dated November 22, 1948 (United Nations, Security Council, document S/2780). This document was dated September 17, 1952; it is unclear why the initial DRV application was not circulated until almost four years after its submission.

[6] Letter, dated July 7, 1950, from the Permanent Representative of France to the Secretary General concerning the Security Council resolution of June 27, 1950, (S/1511) on the Korean crisis.

Laos and Cambodia, headed by puppet kings—protégés of the foreign interventionists—would be a national insult to the people of Indo-China in view of their courageous struggle for freedom and national independence. It would be a most wrongful international act.

49. The only State which can conceivably be considered for admission to membership in the United Nations is the free and independent State of Indo-China, the Democratic Republic of Vietnam, the government of which stated in its official application for admission to membership in the United Nations, on 29 December 1951, that it is the only legitimate government of Vietnam. It was acknowledged as such by France under the treaty of 1946,[7] which the French representative now disavows.

. . . . .

52. In view of these circumstances, the USSR delegation objects to and will vote against the admission to the United Nations of the three puppet régimes which have been hastily set up in Indo-China by the foreign interventionists for aggressive purposes and in order to deprive the peoples of Indo-China of freedom and independence.

53. At the same time, the USSR delegation supports the application of the Government of the Democratic Republic of Vietnam—the only legitimate government of Vietnam and one based on widespread popular support—concerning the admission of the Democratic Republic of Vietnam to membership in the United Nations.

54. In support of this application, the USSR delegation has submitted a formal proposal for the admission of the Democratic Republic of Vietnam to membership in the United Nations [*S/2773*] [8] and will press for the adoption of this proposal.

. . . . .

104. THE PRESIDENT: As there are no further speakers, I shall put to the vote the draft resolution, set forth in document S/2773, on the application of the Democratic Republic of Vietnam for admission to membership in the United Nations.

A vote was taken by show of hands, as follows:

In favour: Union of Soviet Socialist Republics.

Against: Brazil, Chile, China, France, Greece, Netherlands, Pakistan,

---

[7] I.e., the Preliminary Franco-Vietnamese Convention of March 6, 1946, Document 36.

[8] United Nations, Security Council, document S/2773, dated September 15, 1952, "Draft Resolution Concerning the Application of the Democratic Republic of Viet-Nam for Admission to Membership in the United Nations."

Turkey, United Kingdom of Great Britain and Northern Ireland and the United States of America.

The draft resolution was rejected by 10 votes to 1.

105. MR. AUSTIN (United States of America): I will not detain the Council. I merely wish to give an explanation of the vote of the United States against the Soviet Union draft resolution contained in document S/2773. In the opinion of the United States, this so-called, Republic is not a State. It does not measure up to the commonly accepted test of statehood. It has no established capital. It is simply a name given by [the] Vietminh to their armed rebellion against recognized authority. In the opinion of my Government, no discussion or consideration is needed to reach the conclusion that the Security Council should reject, as it has done, the Soviet Union draft resolution which attempts to give this so-called application the status of a true request by a State for membership in the United Nations.

83. *Resolution Adopted by the North Atlantic Council **
December 17, 1952

The North Atlantic Council

Recognizes that resistance to direct or indirect aggression in any part of the world is an essential contribution to the common security of the free world;

HAVING BEEN INFORMED at its meeting in Paris on the 16th December of the latest developments in the military and political situation in Indo-China;

Expresses its wholehearted admiration for the valiant and long continued struggle by the French forces and the armies of the Associated States against Communist aggression; and

Acknowledges that the resistance of the free nations in South-East Asia as in Korea is in fullest harmony with the aims and ideals of the Atlantic Community;

And therefore agrees that the campaign waged by the French Union forces in Indo-China deserves continuing support from the NATO governments.

* *Source:* United States, Department of State, *American Foreign Policy 1950–1955: Basic Documents* (2 vols., Washington: Government Printing Office, 1957), Vol. II, pp. 2368–2369.

84. *Communiqué Regarding Franco-American Discussions [Extracts]* *
    March 28, 1953

1. Representatives of the United States and France, meeting in Washington, today concluded a detailed review of a wide range of problems which face both governments in Europe, the Far East and the Near East. Peace will always remain the basic policy of the United States and France. The discussions, therefore, centered on measures for obtaining peace where there is fighting and for consolidating peace where threats exist.

2. It was agreed, in the absence of any tangible proof to the contrary, that recent developments in the Soviet Union [9] had not changed the basic nature of the threat confronting the free world. The representatives of both countries were in full agreement on the necessity of concerting their efforts so as to defeat Communist aggression in the Far East and to strengthen the defenses of the free countries in the West. They remain convinced that true peace can be achieved and maintained only by constructive efforts of all free nations.

3. It was recognized that Communist aggressive moves in the Far East obviously are parts of the same pattern. Therefore, while the full burden of the fighting in Indochina falls on the forces of the French Union including those of the Associated States, and similarly the United States bears the heaviest burden in Korea, the prosecution of these operations cannot be successfully carried out without full recognition of their interdependence. This in turn requires the continuation of frequent diplomatic and military consultation between the two Governments.

The French Government reasserted its resolve to do its utmost to increase the effectiveness of the French and Associated States forces in Indochina, with a view to destroying the organized Communist forces and to bringing peace and prosperity to her free associates within the French Union, Cambodia, Laos and Viet-Nam. The Ambassadors of Viet-Nam and Cambodia were present and participated in this phase of the discussions.

* *Source:* United States, Department of State, *American Foreign Policy 1950–1955: Basic Documents* (2 vols., Washington: Government Printing Office, 1957), Vol. I, pp. 1672–1675. The French Ministers participating in the conversations were Premier René Mayer; Foreign Minister Georges Bidault; Finance Minister Maurice Bourgès-Manoury; and Jean Letourneau, Minister of State for the Associated States.
  [9] I.e., the death of Stalin.

Advantage was taken of this meeting to continue discussion of plans prepared by the High Command in Indochina for military action there. These plans are being developed with a view to achieving success in Indochina and are being given intensive study so as to determine how and to what extent the Unted States may be able to contribute matériel and financial support to their achievement.

Obviously any armistice which might be concluded in Korea by the United Nations would be entered into in the hope that it would be a step toward peace. It was the view of both Governments, however, that should the Chinese Communist regime take advantage of such an armistice to pursue aggressive war elsewhere in the Far East, such action would have the most serious consequences for the efforts to bring about peace in the world and would conflict directly with the understanding on which any armistice in Korea would rest.

[Two sections dealing with matters other than Indochina are omitted.]

6. The French delegation explained the economic and budgetary implications for France of carrying out her defense programs in Europe as well as in the Far East.

[The concluding three sections, dealing with matters other than Indochina, are omitted.]

85. *Declaration of the French Government to the Associated States* * *July 3, 1953*

The Government of the French Republic, meeting in Council of Ministers, has conducted an examination of French relations with the Associated States of Indochina.

It considers that the time has come to adapt the agreements they have concluded with France to the position which, with her full support, they have been able to secure in the community of free peoples.

Respectful of national traditions and human freedoms, France, during nearly a century of cooperation, has led Cambodia, Laos and Viet-

---

* *Source:* France, Direction de la Documentation, *Bulletin Quotidien* (*Textes du Jour et Pressé Etrangère*), No. 2515 (July 6, 1953), p. 1. Translation by the editor. This declaration was read, on July 4, to diplomatic representatives of the Associated States by Premier Joseph Laniel. The response of the State of Viet-Nam, in a communiqué issued on July 6, is in State of Viet-Nam, High Commission in Paris, *Viet Nam*, No. 55 (July 15, 1953), p. 4 [in French]. On July 12, Premier Nguyen Van Tam officially replied in a note which expressed willingness to begin negotiations; text in *ibid.,* No. 56 (August 1, 1953), p. 3 [in French].

Nam to the full flowering of their individuality and has maintained their national unity.

By the agreements of 1949,[10] she recognized their independence and they agreed to associate themselves with her in the French Union.

The Government of the Republic today wants to make a solemn declaration.

During the four year period which has passed since the signature of the agreements, the brotherhood in arms between the armies of the French Union and the national armies of the Associated States has been further strengthened, thanks to the development of these national armies which each day are taking a more important part in the struggle against the common enemy.

During the same period the civil institutions of the three nations have put themselves in a position to assume the totality of the powers belonging to modern States, while the international audience accorded to their governments has expanded to include the majority of the countries which make up the United Nations.

In these circumstances, France considers that there are grounds to perfect the independence and sovereignty of the Associated States of Indochina by assuring, in agreement with each of the three interested governments, the transfer of the powers which she has continued to hold in the interests of the States themselves because of the perilous circumstances resulting from the state of war.

The French Government has decided to invite each of the three governments to reach agreement with it on the settlement of the questions which each of them may deem it necessary to raise in the economic, financial, judicial, military and political fields, respecting and safeguarding the legitimate interests of each of the contracting parties.

The Government of the Republic expresses the hope that agreement on these various points will strengthen the friendship which unites France and the Associated States within the French Union.

86. *Communiqué by the Foreign Ministers of the United States, the United Kingdom, and France (Washington) [Extracts] * July 14, 1953*

The Foreign Minister of France, M. Georges Bidault, the Acting Foreign Secretary of the United Kingdom, the Marquess of Salisbury,

* *Source:* United States, Department of State, *American Foreign Policy 1950– 1955: Basic Documents* (2 vols., Washington: Government Printing Office, 1957), Vol. I, pp. 1463–1464, 1466–1467.

10 For Viet-Nam, the Elysée Agreements, Document 55.

and the Secretary of State of the United States, Mr. John Foster Dulles, met and consulted together at Washington from July 10 to 14, 1953.

I.

In the course of their consultations, they reviewed a wide range of common problems of concern to the three Governments. The topics considered have been diverse, but the entire conference has been inspired by one dominant purpose. That has been to seek solutions fulfilling the common hope of their governments and peoples for peace, freedom, and justice. They are certain that these same aspirations are shared by peoples everywhere.

The three Ministers are convinced that solid foundations for peace can be built only by constructive action to end oppression and remove causes of instability and sources of conflict. Those who genuinely want peace must seek to restore liberty, hope, and human dignity. In their meetings the Ministers have sought answers to existing problems consistent with these principles.

This has been the spirit leading to their conclusions on the future of Europe, the restoration of German unity and of Austrian independence, and the establishment of peace in Korea and Indochina. The same spirit inspires their desire to see true liberty restored in the countries of Eastern Europe. In each case, they have sought means offering the greatest hope of satisfying the general desire for freedom, security, and well-being. They believe that their proposed solutions will help to achieve that stability based on consent which alone can reduce tension and guarantee a durable peace.

It is the earnest hope of the three Ministers that the Soviet Union will approach outstanding problems in the same spirit. In so doing the Soviet Union would contribute to a lasting peace assuring the security of all.

[Omitted are Section II, dealing with NATO; Section III, dealing with the building of a European Community; and Section IV, dealing with the German and Austrian questions. Section IV included the statement that, in order to bring about an end to the division of Germany, "The three Governments have therefore decided, in consultation with the German Federal Government, to propose a meeting in the early autumn of the Foreign Ministers of France, the United Kingdom, the United States of America, and the USSR to discuss directly the first steps which should lead to a satisfactory solution of the German problem, namely, the organization of free elections and the establishment of a free all-German government." This statement was the basis for the calling of the Berlin Conference of January and February, 1954.]

V.

The three Ministers reviewed the situation in the Far East.

In reviewing the Korean situation the three Ministers reaffirmed their admiration for the gallantry of the United Nations forces, including the indomitable forces of the Republic of Korea, defending the free world's cause. They reaffirmed their strong support of the efforts of the United Nations Command to conclude an early armistice consistent with the United Nations' aims and the determination of their governments to continue to work toward that end.[11] They agreed to pursue every effort to assist the stouthearted and sorely tried Koreans to reunite peacefully under institutions of their own choosing.

They considered that, in existing circumstances and pending further consultation, the common policies of the three Powers towards Communist China should be maintained. They resolved that, if the Communists should renew their aggression in Korea after an armistice and again threaten the principles defended by the United Nations, their governments would as members of the United Nations again support the restoration of peace and security.[12]

The Foreign Ministers were of the opinion that an armistice in Korea must not result in jeopardizing the restoration or the safeguarding of peace in any other part of Asia. They hope that any armistice accepted by the United Nations would be a step forward in the cause of peace everywhere, and in particular in the Far East.

The current situation in Indochina was examined. The three Foreign Ministers paid tribute once again to the heroic efforts and sacrifices of the soldiers of the French Union, be they from France, Vietnam, Cambodia, Laos or other parts of the Union. They agreed that the struggle in defense of the independence of these three nations against aggressive Communism is essential to the Free World, and they exchanged views on various measures to hasten a satisfactory outcome and the restoration of peace in Indochina.

The Foreign Ministers of the United Kingdom and the United States noted with great satisfaction the proposal of the French Government to open discussions with each of the Governments of Cambodia, Laos, and Vietnam with a view toward completing their sovereignty and independence.[13] They agreed that this initiative was a most important and auspicious step toward perfecting a free association of these four

[11] Footnote in the original omitted.   [12] Footnote in the original omitted.
[13] Document 85.

nations, since the internal security and stability of the Associated States are best safeguarded by freely established constitutional regimes.

They noted that the French Union offers a harmonious and flexible framework within which the mutual interest of the participants may be guaranteed and their individual interests reconciled. They are convinced that the objective of the French Government is to perfect with the Associated States that mutually desirable cohesion which is indispensable to the success of the common struggle for the independence of the three states and which is therefore of fundamental importance to the security of the whole of Southeast Asia.

87. *President Eisenhower: Remarks at the Governors' Conference, Seattle [Extract]* *
    August 4, 1953

[Discussing federal problems and the role of state and local government in their solution, President Eisenhower made the following statement on Indochina as an example of problems in the foreign field.]

I could go on enumerating every kind of problem that comes before us daily. Let us take, though, for example, one simple problem in the foreign field. You have seen the war in Indochina described variously as an outgrowth of French colonialism, and its French refusal to treat indigenous populations decently. You find it again described as a war between the communists and the other elements in southeast Asia. But you have a confused idea of where it is located—Laos, or Cambodia, or Siam, or any of the other countries that are involved. You don't know, really, why we are so concerned with the far-off southeast corner of Asia.

Why is it? Now, first of all, the last great population remaining in Asia that has not become dominated by the Kremlin, of course, is the sub-continent of India, including the Pakistan government. Here are 350 million people still free. Now let us assume that we lose Indochina. If Indochina goes, several things happen right away. The Malayan peninsula, the last little bit of the end hanging on down there, would be scarcely defensible—and tin and tungsten that we so greatly value from that area would cease coming. But all India would be outflanked.

* *Source:* United States, Archives, *Public Papers of the Presidents of the United States: Dwight D. Eisenhower, 1953* (Washington: Government Printing Office, 1960), pp. 540–541.

Burma would certainly, in its weakened condition, be no defense. Now, India is surrounded on that side by the Communist empire. Iran on its left is in a weakened condition. I believe I read in the paper this morning that Mossadegh's [14] move toward getting rid of his parliament has been supported and of course he was in that move supported by the Tudeh, which is the Communist Party of Iran. All of that weakening position around there is very ominous for the United States, because finally if we lost all that, how would the free world hold the rich empire of Indonesia? So you see, somewhere along the line, this must be blocked. It must be blocked now. That is what the French are doing.

So, when the United States votes $400 million to help that war, we are not voting for a giveaway program. We are voting for the cheapest way that we can to prevent the occurrence of something that would be of the most terrible significance for the United States of America—our security, our power and ability to get certain things we need from the riches of the Indonesian territory, and from southeast Asia.

88. *Secretary of State Dulles: Statement to the American Legion, St. Louis [Extract]* *
    September 2, 1953

We do not make the mistake of treating Korea as an isolated affair. The Korean war forms one part of the worldwide effort of communism to conquer freedom. More immediately it is part of that effort in Asia.

A single Chinese-Communist aggressive front extends from Korea on the north to Indochina in the south. The armistice in Korea, even if it leads to a political settlement in Korea, does not end United States concern in the western Pacific area. As President Eisenhower said in his April 16 speech,[15] a Korean armistice would be a fraud if it merely released Communist forces for attack elsewhere.

In Indochina a desperate struggle is in its eighth year. The outcome affects our own vital interests in the western Pacific, and we are already

* *Source:* United States, Department of State, *American Foreign Policy 1950–1955: Basic Documents* (2 vols., Washington: Government Printing Office, 1957), Vol. II, pp. 2370–2371. The complete text of the speech is in United States, Department of State, *Bulletin,* XXIX (September 14, 1953), pp. 339–342.

[14] Mohammad Mosaddeq, Prime Minister of Iran from 1951 until his overthrow on August 19, 1953.

[15] "The Chance for Peace," Address before the American Society of Newspaper Editors, Washington, in United States, Department of State, *American Foreign Policy 1950–1955: Basic Documents* (2 vols., Washington: Government Printing Office, 1957), Vol. I, pp. 65–71.

contributing largely in material and money to the combined efforts of the French and of Viet-Nam, Laos, and Cambodia.

We Americans have too little appreciated the magnitude of the effort and sacrifices which France has made in defense of an area which is no longer a French colony but where complete independence is now in the making. This independence program is along lines which the United States has encouraged and justifies increased United States aid, provided that will assure an effort there that is vigorous and decisive.

Communist China has been and now is training, equipping, and supplying the Communist forces in Indochina. There is the risk that, as in Korea, Red China might send its own army into Indochina. The Chinese Communist regime should realize that such a second aggression could not occur without grave consequences which might not be confined to Indochina. I say this soberly in the interest of peace and in the hope of preventing another aggressor miscalculation.

We want peace in Indochina, as well as in Korea. The political conference about to be held relates in the first instance to Korea. But growing out of that conference could come, if Red China wants it, an end of aggression and restoration of peace in Indochina. The United States would welcome such a development.

89. *Secretary of State Dulles: Statement on the Possibility of Peace Talks in Indochina* *
   September 3, 1953

Asked at his press conference on September 3 whether his St. Louis speech [16] *was subject to conflicting interpretation as to whether the United States was willing to include the question of a possible restoration of peace in Indochina at the Korean political conference, Secretary Dulles made the following reply:*

I do not think that I ever said that these political talks would necessarily be limited exclusively to Korea. We have said that the conference as originally set up, in our opinion, should be limited to Korea. But also I think I have made clear that, if matters at that conference go well and the Chinese Communists show a disposition to settle in a reasonable way such a question as Indochina, we would not just on technical grounds say, "No, we won't talk about that."

* *Source:* United States, Department of State, *Bulletin,* XXIX (September 19, 1953), pp. 342–343.
[16] Document 88.

Of course, any discussions which dealt with Indochina would have to have a different participation than the conference which dealt with Korea. For example, the Republic of Korea is an indispensable party to a conference such as is projected about Korea. But Korea would not be an indispensable party to discussions about Indochina. So that in effect it would not be the same conference. Certainly in any discussion about Indochina, for example, the three Associated States of Viet-Nam, Laos, and Cambodia would be necessary parties. They are not parties to the Korean conference. What we mean is that if the atmosphere, insofar as it may be contributed to by Communist China, seemed to be conducive for the settlement of the Indochina war, we would not be opposed to that.

90. *Franco-American Communiqué on Additional United States Aid for France and Indochina* *
   September 30, 1953

The forces of France and the Associated States in Indochina have for 8 years been engaged in a bitter struggle to prevent the engulfment of Southeast Asia by the forces of international communism. The heroic efforts and sacrifices of these French Union allies in assuring the liberty of the new and independent states of Cambodia, Laos and Vietnam has [*sic*] earned the admiration and support of the free world. In recognition of the French Union effort the United States Government has in the past furnished aid of various kinds to the Governments of France and the Associated States to assist in bringing the long struggle to an early and victorious conclusion.

The French Government is firmly resolved to carry out in full its declaration of July 3, 1953,[17] by which is announced its intention of perfecting the independence of the three Associated States in Indochina, through negotiations with the Associated States.

The Governments of France and the United States have now agreed that, in support of plans of the French Government for the intensified prosecution of the war against the Viet Minh, the United States will make available to the French Government prior to December 31, 1954

---

* *Source:* United States, Department of State, *American Foreign Policy 1950–1955: Basic Documents* (2 vols., Washington: Government Printing Office, 1957), Vol. II, pp. 2371–2372. This communiqué reflects decisions reached during the Foreign Ministers' Conference in July (see Document 86) and subsequently approved by the American government in their details.

[17] Document 85.

additional financial resources not to exceed $385 million. This aid is in addition to funds already earmarked by the United States for aid to France and the Associated States.

The French Government is determined to make every effort to break up and destroy the regular enemy forces in Indochina. Toward this end the government intends to carry through, in close cooperation with the Cambodian, Laotian, and Vietnamese Governments, the plans for increasing the Associated States forces while increasing temporarily French forces to levels considered necessary to assure the success of existing military plans. The additional United States aid is designed to help make it possible to achieve these objectives with maximum speed and effectiveness.

The increased French effort in Indochina will not entail any basic or permanent alteration of the French Government's plans and programs for its NATO forces.

91. *Resolutions Adopted by the National Congress of the State of Viet-Nam* *
    October 15–17, 1953

I
The Independence of Viet-Nam
October 15, 1953

Considering that only complete Independence satisfies the thousand year old and sacred aspirations of the Vietnamese people;

Considering that complete Independence is the first of the conditions necessary for the establishment of Franco-Vietnamese relations on the basis of the equality and sovereignty of the two States;

Considering that complete Independence is the essential condition for ending the war and hastening the return of peace to Viet-Nam;

THE NATIONAL CONGRESS:

Representing all classes of the Vietnamese population and animated by the same desire for independence;

RECOMMENDS:

1. The proclamation of Viet-Nam as a completely independent State,

* *Source:* State of Viet-Nam, High Commission in Paris, *Viet Nam,* No. 61 (October 17, 1953), pp. 12–13. Translation by the editor. Actual publication of this issue of the magazine (normally published biweekly) was probably delayed to include the resolutions of the National Congress.

with full internal and external sovereignty in the same manner as all independent countries according to the definition of international law;

2. The abrogation of the treaties and conventions concluded between France and Viet-Nam up to the present and the abolition of the present status of the Montagnard Lands.

II
The Association of Viet-Nam with France
October 16, 1953

Considering that in the present historical circumstances free and independent nations tend to join together and to cooperate for the maintenance of Independence and reciprocal liberty and to safeguard the peace of the world;

Considering that an association between peoples can be solid and useful only if it is established on the basis of complete liberty and perfect equality and with mutual respect of their reciprocal interests;

Considering that the French Union as defined by the French Constitution of 1946 is hardly compatible with the status of an independent country;

Considering that the prime interest of a people consists of its freedom to decide all the matters which concern it;

THE NATIONAL CONGRESS DECLARES:

1. That independent Viet-Nam would be unable to participate in in French Union in its present form; [18]

2. After the transfer to Viet-Nam of all the powers still held by the French authorities, and after the liquidation of the old Institute of Issue which was the Bank of Indochina, Viet-Nam will sign with France, on a basis of equality and according to the circumstances, treaties of alliance according to the needs of the two countries and for a period to be determined;

---

[18] As originally drafted, this paragraph read: "Viet-Nam will not participate in the French Union as it is defined by the French Constitution of 1946, this conception being incompatible with the principle of sovereignty of the member states." It was then modified, after heated discussion, with the revised first part, "Considering that the French Union as it is defined by the French Constitution of 1946 is incompatible with the status of an independent country," placed in the preamble to the resolution, and the revised second part, "The National Congress declares that independent Viet-Nam would be unable to participate in the French Union," placed as paragraph 1 of the body of the resolution. After some further discussion, paragraph 1 was modified into its final form. See State of Viet-Nam, High Commission in Paris, *Vietnam*, No. 62 (November 1, 1953), p. 5 [in French].

3. All these treaties must be approved by the National Assembly elected by universal suffrage;

4. No negotiations, no proposals or decisions concerning Viet-Nam may take place or be taken in international conferences without the agreement of the National Government of Viet-Nam.

III
The Choice of Delegates for Future Negotiations
October 17, 1953

THE NATIONAL CONGRESS:

Affirms its total confidence in His Majesty, the Chief of State,[19] and requests him to proceed himself with the choice of the members of the Delegation, from among the members of the Congress and from among qualified personalities not included in the Congress, in order to realize the complete Independence of Viet-Nam.

IV
Complete Confidence in His Majesty Bao Dai
October 17, 1953

THE NATIONAL CONGRESS:

Places its complete confidence in His Majesty to direct the forthcoming negotiations with a view to realizing the complete independence of Viet-Nam and forming with France a union freely agreed upon, respecting the sovereignty of the two nations and assuring the reciprocity of their rights and obligations;

Expresses its thanks to the French Republic and to the Government of the United States for the aid supplied to Viet-Nam in its efforts to consolidate its national independence.

92. *Premier Joseph Laniel: Policy Statement in the National Assembly [Extracts]* *
   October 27, 1953

[Two extracts of this long but important speech are included here. The first deals with French reaction to the resolutions adopted by the Vietnamese National Congress (Document 91), particularly the resolution on "The

---

* *Source:* France, *Journal Officiel de la République Française Débats Parlementaires, Assemblée Nationale,* Session of October 27, 1953, pp. 4602–4603, 4606–4607. Translation by the editor.
   [19] Bao Dai.

Association of Viet-Nam with France." The introductory paragraphs are omitted.]

The Government had the right and the duty not to be satisfied with explanations [from the Vietnamese] minimizing the incident without having first definitely settled the question which that incident—whether well or poorly reported, whether grossly exaggerated or not—had suddenly raised before French conscience.

Yes or no, did our Vietnamese partner hold to a loyal attitude? Yes or no, did he hold to the language of sincerity? Yes or no, were we in the process of playing a game of fools? Right or wrong, an uneasiness was born which required before all else a clear explanation between the Vietnamese authorities and us.

I am able to say to the Assembly that we have hidden nothing of our feeling from the Chief of State and the Government of Viet-Nam.

In a communication which was sent to them several days ago,[20] we reminded them not only of the services rendered, not only of our reciprocal engagements, but also, and especially, of the fact that the French Government would be justified, if they were to challenge the very idea of the French Union, to consider herself free of her own obligations, notably those concerning the military responsibilities which she takes upon herself. (*Applause on the right.*)

France will never abandon her friends, but she would have no reason to prolong her sacrifices if the meaning of those sacrifices were disdained or betrayed by the very people for whom she had agreed to make them. (*Applause on the right, in the center, on the extreme right and on certain benches of the left.*)

[Premier Laniel went on to explain that the National Congress did not truly reflect the attitudes of the Vietnamese people and that Viet-Nam was fulfilling its obligations. After a lengthy discussion of French military policy, Premier Laniel then came to the subject of French policy on negotiations in the situation prevailing after the conclusion of the Korean armistice.]

I now come to the most vehement criticism which is made of us on certain benches and which may be summarized thus:

"What are you waiting for in order to make peace? Enough talking of war, we must negotiate. France is exhausting herself in vain in this unpopular conflict. The wise thing is to stop the drain as soon as possible."

[20] Extracts from the French note of October 22 and from the Vietnamese reply of November 16 are in State of Vietnam, High Commission in Paris, *Vietnam*, No. 64 (December 1, 1953), p. 3 [in French].

I have very sincerely asked myself this question. Here is my answer.

Certainly it is preferable to negotiate. No one ever makes war for the pleasure of making war, especially for seven years. It would be unthinkable for anyone in this Assembly to imagine that the French Government does not think of peace as its supreme objective in this affair.

But to make peace there must be at least two, and those who talk of peace and of negotiations have said nothing so long as they have not said with whom we should negotiate, with whom we should make peace.

With China? As a matter of course, whatever happens we will never disregard the loyalty which we owe to our allies, but, subject to that reservation, negotiations with China in order to facilitate the settlement of the war in Viet-Nam would not appear in our eyes as a pact with the devil.

France has given the most concrete proof of the sincerity of her intentions toward Viet-Nam. That proof is the recognition of total independence, the acceptance of the unity sanctioned by the vote of the French Parliament concerning Cochin China.[21]

It is impossible to think that Vietnamese nationalists, even Communists, would freely have chosen to prolong the war, to continue the devastation of their country, after what France did to comply with the aspirations of Vietnamese patriotism.

Everything is happening as if the great Communist powers forced the Viet Minh to continue the war. The war, for true Vietnamese nationalists, can no longer have national objectives.

I know of no Franco-American agreement which limits our freedom of negotiation or which could hinder our efforts for peace. Undoubtedly there are secret agreements which oblige the Viet Minh, in exchange for the arms which they are receiving, to use them so long as the Communist camp estimates that is in its interest.

Nevertheless, why should we now think that the chances of a solution are greater today than a year ago? It is because a major change has taken place since then. That change is the one which results from the armistice in Korea.

That armistice is the sign that the Communist world, when it is certain that it cannot gain a military victory without the danger of risking a general conflict, accepts at least a pause, at least a truce.

For, what do we see since the armistice? Until last August the

[21] Document 56.

keynote of Russian and Chinese propaganda was the total victory of the Viet Minh and the crushing of the imperialists.

Since then numerous allusions to the possibility of negotiations have been made in Moscow and in Peking, in the press and on the radio.

In a speech given in the Kremlin on September 19, M. Malenkov indicated his desire to see the armistice in Korea become "the point of departure for new efforts designed to reduce international tension throughout the world, and particularly in the Far East." [22]

An analogous declaration was made on August 24 by M. Chou En-lai, Chinese Minister of Foreign Affairs.[23]

M. Foster Dulles, for his part, on several occasions publicly declared himself ready to participate in negotiations. In his speech delivered in St. Louis on September 2,[24] he declared that out of the political conference on Korea "there could grow, if Communist China wants it, the end of the aggression and the return of peace in Indochina." He confirmed that idea once again to the United Nations on September 24.[25]

The British Government has also, little by little, come around to that position.

Do I need to say what France thinks? Who among us would object to the idea of negotiations, in an international framework, to re-establish peace in Indochina?

Unfortunately there is someone who does not seem to agree: Ho Chi Minh, the General Staff of the Viet Minh, the little group of leaders of a movement which is no longer able to compromise.

They are caught in the trap of their ruthless struggle. Their sole passion seems to be to stimulate the morale of their troops, to keep them devoted to the idea of a war always longer, to put them on guard against what they call a "false peace," against what they denounce as a "false independence."

Numerous orators have said to us: it is with Ho Chi Minh that we must negotiate!

I reply to them simply this: at the moment when Ho Chi Minh has

[22] Text in Communist Information Bureau, *For a Lasting Peace, For a People's Democracy*, September 25, 1953, pp. 1–2.

[23] Text in New China News Agency, *Daily News Release*, No. 1409 (August 25, 1953), p. 1.

[24] Document 88.

[25] Text in United States, Department of State, *American Foreign Policy 1950–1955: Basic Documents* (2 vols., Washington: Government Printing Office, 1957), Vol. I, pp. 350–359.

just declared, on September 2,[26] that only his total victory can lead to peace, at the moment when he bases so great a hope on his autumn campaign, is it at this moment that France should ask him his conditions for peace?

But, aside from Ho Chi Minh and his General Staff, what about all those who obey them, more or less duped or terrorized by them? What about the thousands of men in their army, who would tomorrow go their own way if the moral and material hold of their chiefs were relaxed?

Certainly it is necessary to try to detach these men from the Viet Minh, to attract them toward the true Vietnamese patriots.

Certainly we are ready to facilitate national reconciliation over there, national reconciliation without which there could not be a free and independent Viet-Nam. The young army which trains its cadres in the schools at Dalat, the representative regime which Emperor Bao Dai envisages, must receive one day in a peaceful amalgamation all the Vietnamese of good will from wherever they may come. France, it must be understood, prays for that day.

In this spirit, my Government is ready, beginning today, to avail itself of all opportunities to make peace, whether they occur in Indochina or on the international plane. But if the Government is willing to study every constructive proposition, it is a matter of course, obviously, that it will be able to do that only in full agreement with the Associated States which it has recognized, aids, sustains and had recognized by thirty-three free nations. Any other position would be contrary to the honor of France and of the French Union, personified in Indochina—and never forget it—by the heroic combatants of all races who were able, by their sacrifices, to make that Union a living and durable reality. (*Applause on the right, on the extreme right, in the center and on certain benches of the left.*)

We are not carrying on a crusade or a war of extermination.

If one day Ho Chi Minh and his group recognize the impossibility of winning and the futility of the struggle, if they wish to renounce it, if they show themselves disposed to make proposals, then it will be incumbent upon the French Government and other interested Governments, particularly the Governments of the Associated States, to consult with each other, to examine those proposals, to evaluate them and

[26] "Appeal on the Occasion of the August Revolution and National Day," in Ho Chi Minh, *Selected Works* (4 vols., Hanoi: Foreign Languages Publishing House, 1961–1962), Vol. III, pp. 392–399.

to reserve for them the response which, by mutual agreement, they appear to require.

But it is still a matter only of very uncertain eventualities. Our duty is to consider realities.

I have thus arrived, ladies and gentlemen, at the deep conviction, shared by the entire Government, that there is no policy in Indochina other than that which I have just defined.

Let us try to imagine another one. Of what would it consist? Our interpellators proceed by negative criticisms, but what other, constructive, policy do they propose?

We are fighting so that tomorrow Viet-Nam, a member of the French Union, will not be subjected to a tyranny which would make a vain word of the independence we have given. We want the Vietnamese people to be able freely to give themselves the regime, the institutions, of their own choice and we desire that those who put their confidence in the word of France not be threatened in their life and property.

We want the immense work that France has accomplished to be preserved.

How can we imagine that our country should fail in her mission in this part of the world?

It is then that the sacrifice of our dead would become worthless, if today we allow territories to pass under the despotism of a world imperialism, territories of prime importance because of their geographic position and which would quickly serve as the point of departure for other conquests, in the end putting in peril the security of France and her European allies.

And when we are told that this duty is contrary to our self-interest, that also is not true. Do you believe that we would retain our positions in Africa for very long if the whole of Asia became hostile to us?

There are options which are only mirages. One does not pick his duties.

[The closing paragraphs, appealing for Parliamentary unity in support of the Government, are omitted.]

PART FOUR

International Crisis
and the Geneva Conference
November 1953–July 1954

CHAPTER VIII

Preliminaries to Negotiations

November 1953-May 1954

Introduction

Although talk of negotiations in Indochina had become common after the Korean armistice in July 1953, at the beginning of November peace appeared distant. A new Viet Minh offensive was underway in northwestern Tonkin and Laos; as a counter move the French, on November 20, reoccupied Dien Bien Phu as a blocking position. The situation changed at the end of November when the Viet Minh evinced a willingness to talk with France This helped make possible "Big Four" agreement at Berlin in early 1954 on a conference to discuss both Korea and Indochina. As the date of the Geneva Conference neared during the spring, growing hopes for peace were shaken by the deteriorating military situation in Viet-Nam, where the battle of Dien Bien Phu was underway, and by threats of American intervention to bolster France.[1]

The major change in Viet Minh policy was shown at the opening session of the World Peace Council in Vienna on November 23 when Le Dinh Than, the representative of the Democratic Republic of Viet-Nam (DRV), stated:

[1] A case can be made that the Soviet Union and China applied pressure on the DRV in order to bring about negotiations. Unfortunately, adequate and reliable documentation on Soviet and Chinese policy during this period is largely unavailable except for press statements. For a detailed examination of events leading up to the Geneva Conference, with emphasis on Soviet policy but including analysis of the Chinese position, see Allan W. Cameron, "The Soviet Union and Vietnam: The Origins of Involvement," in W. Raymond Duncan, ed., *Soviet Policy in Developing Countries* (Waltham, Mass.: Ginn-Blaisdell, 1970), pp. 166–205. See also King C. Chen, *Vietnam and China, 1938–1954* (Princeton, N.J.: Princeton University Press, 1969), Chapters 5 and 6. A source for official Soviet statements during the Berlin Conference is indicated in the Source Note to Document 97.

The Korean war had already ended on the basis of peaceful negotiations. To stop the Viet-Nam war through peaceful negotiations is completely necessary and also possible. We Viet-Nam people long for peace, and we stand for an end to the Viet-Nam war and peaceful settlement of the Viet-Nam question by means of peaceful negotiations.[2]

On November 29 the Swedish newspaper *Expressen* printed a cabled interview with Ho Chi Minh, in which he offered to negotiate with France (Document 93). At the beginning of December, the DRV National Assembly, meeting for the first time since 1946, adopted a Communist-pattern agrarian reform law.[3] Two weeks later Ho Chi Minh linked land reform to successful conclusion of the war and reaffirmed DRV willingness to talk with France (Document 94).

In early December President Eisenhower, Prime Minister Churchill, and Premier Laniel discussed Indochina at the Bermuda Conference. According to the communiqué issued on December 7:

We reviewed the situation in the Far East. The immediate object of our policy continues to be the convening of the political conference provided for in the Korean Armistice agreement. This would provide the means for reaching a peaceful settlement of the Korean question and for making progress in restoring more normal conditions in the Far East and South East Asia.

In Indo-China we salute the valiant forces of France and of the three Associated States of Indo-China fighting within the French Union to protect the independence of Cambodia, Laos and Viet-Nam. We recognise the vital importance of their contribution to the defence of the free world. We will continue to work together to restore peace and stability in this area.[4]

But American officials showed a lack of enthusiasm for negotiations. On December 23 Vice President Nixon took a hard line on Indochina (Document 95), while six days later Secretary of State Dulles expressed reservations on Viet Minh "peace feelers" (Document 96).

Meanwhile, the "Big Four" powers had agreed to hold a Foreign Ministers' meeting in Berlin in January 1954. Although the primary

[2] Text in New China News Agency, *Daily News Release*, No. 1489 (November 27, 1953), pp. 304–305.

[3] The text of the Agrarian Reform Law, with amendments adopted in 1955, appears in *Agrarian Reform Law* (Hanoi: Foreign Languages Publishing House, 1955), pp. 13–59. The text of the basic law also appears in Allan B. Cole, ed., *Conflict in Indo-China and International Repercussions: A Documentary History, 1945–1955* (Ithaca, N.Y.: Cornell University Press, 1956), pp. 150–156.

[4] Text in United States, Department of State, *American Foreign Policy 1950–1955: Basic Documents* (2 vols., Washington: Government Printing Office, 1957), Vol. I, pp. 1468–1470.

focus of the Conference was on European problems, there were indications that Asian problems might also be discussed. At the opening session, on January 25, Foreign Minister Molotov of the Soviet Union called for a "Five Power" conference, including Communist China, to consider "measures to reduce international tension." That item was of particular concern to France, which was anxious to discuss an end to the war in Indochina in a multilateral context provided that such discussions were serious rather than just for propaganda purposes (Document 97).

During December and January the Viet Minh began to mass forces around Dien Bien Phu while continuing their advance into Laos. French attempts to counter the offensive resulted in dispersion of military strength and posed particular problems in aircraft maintenance. The United States then agreed to send a small number of aircraft technicians to Indochina. President Eisenhower indicated that they could not be considered combat troops and stated his personal opposition to heavy military involvement in Indochina (Document 98).

The Berlin Conference concluded on February 18, and although agreement on European matters was impossible the Foreign Ministers agreed to hold a conference, beginning in Geneva on April 26, to settle the Korean question and to discuss Indochina (Document 99). News of the Geneva Conference was welcomed in India where, on February 22, Prime Minister Nehru for the first time involved his nation in the Indochina situation by calling for a cease-fire in advance of the conference.[5] Nehru's statement stimulated a debate in the French National Assembly at the beginning of March. Premier Laniel stated the conditions under which France would be willing to conclude a cease-fire; [6] at the end of the debate the Government was supported, through the adoption of an order of the day endorsing negotiations to end the war (Document 100), by a majority of only 84 votes.

[5] Text in India, *Parliamentary Debates, Official Report, House of the People,* Part II, 6th Session, Vol. I, No. 6 (February 22, 1954), cols. 415–416.

[6] The conditions stated by Laniel were the following: (1) complete withdrawal of Viet Minh troops from Laos and Cambodia; (2) withdrawal of Viet Minh forces outside a "no man's land" surrounding the Red River Delta in Tonkin, such withdrawal to be strictly controlled; (3) Viet Minh forces in central Viet-Nam to be regrouped in specified zones; (4) Viet Minh forces in southern Viet-Nam (Cochin China) to be disarmed or evacuated; and (5) guarantees and means of control to be provided to prevent the Viet Minh from using a cease-fire to rearm or reinforce themselves during the period of negotiations which would follow. See France, *Journal Officiel de la République Française, Débats Parlementaires, Assemblée Nationale,* Session of March 5, 1954, pp. 714–715.

The battle for Dien Bien Phu began in earnest with Viet Minh attacks on March 13. The Viet Minh showed capabilities in artillery which were far greater than had been anticipated and which were to make the airfield unserviceable less than two weeks later. In that context General Paul Ely, Chief of the French General Staff, arrived in Washington on March 20, reportedly to tell the Americans that the situation in Indochina was grave and that massive American action would be required to retrieve it.

On March 10 President Eisenhower indicated that the United States would not become involved in the Indochina war without appropriate Congressional action (Document 101). Secretary Dulles, at a March 23 news conference, gave no indication of possible American military involvement but reaffirmed support for France (Document 102). At the end of the month, however, Ely's pessimistic report touched off a major debate within the Administration and the Congress as the United States found itself obliged to consider military intervention on behalf of its ally.

The new concerns were reflected in Secretary Dulles' speech of March 29 (Document 103). The possibility of American action caused uneasiness in London, where Foreign Secretary Anthony Eden instructed the British Ambassador in Washington to inform the United States that the British considered that "conditions for a favourable solution in Indo-China may no longer exist" and that it might be necessary to compromise with the Communists at Geneva.[7] At a meeting on April 3, ranking members of Congress expressed reluctance to endorse a proposed joint resolution approving limited military intervention, particularly after they found that the Joint Chiefs of Staff were split on the matter.[8] Dulles then reportedly proposed to the British and French that the concerned Western governments make a joint declaration prior to the Geneva Conference, warning of possible Allied action, while parallel attempts were made to recruit support for "united action" in Indochina.[9] It was in the context of such American attempts

[7] A partial text of Eden's message of April 1 is in Anthony Eden, *Full Circle* (Boston: Houghton Mifflin Company, 1960), p. 102.

[8] See the account in James A. Robinson, *Congress and Foreign Policy-Making* (Homewood, Illinois: The Dorsey Press, Inc., 1962), p. 53.

[9] Complete documentation on these proposals, as well as on many of the other events during the period preceding the Geneva Conference, is not available because of continued classification of the relevant documents by the governments involved. Extracts from President Eisenhower's letter of April 4 to Prime Minister Churchill, proposing the implementation of "united action" through formation of an ad hoc coalition of Western and Southeast Asian nations, appear in

to assist the French that President Eisenhower, at his April 7 news conference, used the "falling domino" analogy to describe the situation in Southeast Asia (Document 104).[10]

Secretary Dulles went to London on April 10 in the hope of winning the British to some form of "united action" in support of France; the communiqué issued on April 13, however, indicated that no action would be taken before the Geneva Conference (Document 105). Dulles then went to Paris, where a similar communiqué was issued (Document 106).

In an off-the-record statement to a gathering of newspaper editors on April 16, Vice President Nixon stated that if the situation required, the United States would have to send troops to fight the Communists in Indochina, that the United States could not afford another retreat in Asia.[11] On April 23, the NATO Foreign Ministers met in Paris; their final communiqué stated simply that "The [North Atlantic] Council paid tribute to the gallantry of the French Union forces fighting in Indochina. It expressed the hope that the Geneva Conference will have positive results." [12]

On the same day the French Government reportedly received a message from General Navarre in Indochina to the effect that only powerful American air intervention within the next few days could save Dien Bien Phu. Although the details of subsequent events are unknown, the French apparently appealed for American aid, which was tentatively offered contingent on British support. Foreign Secretary Eden returned to London and drafted a statement of the British position on Indochina (Document 107) which was approved by Prime Minister Churchill and the Cabinet on April 25. Two days later Churchill

---

Dwight D. Eisenhower, *The White House Years: Mandate for Change 1953–1956* (Garden City, N.Y.: Doubleday, 1963), pp. 346–347. In this letter the President also expressed the view that "our painstaking search for a way out of the impasse has reluctantly forced us to the conclusion that there is no negotiated solution of the Indochina problem which in its essence would not be either a face-saving device to cover a French surrender or a face-saving device to cover a Communist retirement." The editor has been unable to obtain a complete text of this letter, and was reluctant to print the available text with the numerous omissions which it appears to contain.

[10] The "Domino Theory" was not really new: for some of its forerunners, see Documents 79, 87, and 95.

[11] News report in *The New York Times,* April 17, 1954, pp. 1–2; a digest of the comments is in *ibid.,* April 18, 1954, p. 2. A complete official text is not available.

[12] Text in *American Foreign Policy 1950–1955: Basic Documents,* Vol. I, p. 1637.

reaffirmed that position in a statement to the House of Commons (Document 109). He also emphasized cooperation among Commonwealth countries, particularly to reassure India whose Prime Minister, Jawaharlal Nehru, had on April 24 once more appealed for a ceasefire and offered detailed suggestions on which a settlement at Geneva might be based.[13] The British stand effectively terminated any likelihood of immediate American intervention in Indochina, although the possibility of action by the United States was to be an implied threat throughout the Geneva negotiations.

Meanwhile, Franco-Vietnamese negotiations on "perfecting" the independence of Viet-Nam continued in Paris. Bao Dai felt that the French wanted to delay recognition of Viet-Nam's full independence until after the Geneva Conference. Thus, on April 25, the Imperial Cabinet issued a long communiqué defining Bao Dai's attitude toward the negotiations with France as well as on the Geneva Conference (Document 108). The communiqué caused a great stir in Paris, but three days later France and the State of Viet-Nam issued a joint declaration (Document 110) which confirmed agreement on two treaties to be signed in the near future.

Bao Dai had also been reluctant to allow participation by the State of Viet-Nam in the Geneva Conference, which he feared would produce results detrimental to Vietnamese interests. But after appeals from the three Western foreign ministers he agreed, on May 1, to discuss the matter. Following a meeting between Foreign Minister Nguyen Quoc Dinh and the three Western ministers on May 3, the State of Viet-Nam agreed to participate in the Indochina phase of the Geneva negotiations.[14]

The Korean phase of the Geneva Conference had begun on April 26, but it rapidly became clear that no progress was likely. Secretary Dulles announced he would leave Geneva even before discussions on Indochina began, entrusting American representation to Under Secretary of State Walter Bedell Smith. On May 6, just prior to Dulles' return to Washington, President Eisenhower summarized American policy on Indochina and the Geneva Conference (Document 111).

[13] Text in India, *Parliamentary Debates, Official Report, House of the People,* Part II, 6th Session, Vol. IV, No. 52 (April 24, 1954), cols. 5576–5583.

[14] The text of the communiqué issued after the meeting is in France, Direction de la Documentation, *Articles et Documents,* No. 051 (May 4, 1954), "Textes du Jour," p. 1.

93. *Ho Chi Minh: Interview Published in* Expressen, *Stockholm* *
   November 29, 1953

Question: The debate in the French National Assembly [1] has proved
that a great number of French politicians are for a peaceful settlement
of the conflicts in Viet Nam by direct negotiations with the Vietnamese
Government. This desire is spreading among the French people. Does
your Government and you welcome it?

Answer: The war in Viet Nam was launched by the French Government. The Vietnamese people are obliged to take up arms and have
heroically struggled for nearly eight years against the aggressors, to safeguard our independence and the right to live freely and peacefully.
Now, if the French colonialists continue their aggressive war, the
Vietnamese people are determined to carry on the patriotic resistance
until final victory. However, if the French Government has drawn a
lesson from the war they have been waging these last years and want
to negotiate an armistice in Viet Nam and to solve the Viet Nam
problem by peaceful means, the people and Government of the Democratic Republic of Viet Nam are ready to meet this desire.

Question: Will a cease fire or an armistice be possible?

Answer: A cessation of hostilities is possible, provided that the
French Government ends its war of aggression in Viet Nam. The
French Government's sincere respect for the genuine independence of
Viet Nam must be the basis of the armistice.

Question: Would you agree to a neutral country mediating to organise a meeting between you and the representatives of the High
Command of the other side? May Sweden be entrusted with this
responsibility?

Answer: If there are neutral countries who try to speed up a cessation of hostilities in Viet Nam by means of negotiations, they will be
welcomed. However, the negotiation for an armistice is mainly a concern of the Government of the Democratic Republic of Viet Nam and
the French Government.

* *Source:* Ho Chi Minh, *Selected Works* (4 vols., Hanoi: Foreign Languages
Publishing House, 1961–1962), Vol. III, pp. 408–410. The questions were telegraphed to Ho Chi Minh, via the DRV Embassy in Peking, by Mr. S. Löfgren,
Managing Editor of the newspaper *Expressen* in Stockholm. According to the
source from which this text was taken, Ho Chi Minh's telegram in reply was
dated November 26. Typographical errors have been corrected.
  [1] In October 1953; see Document 92.

Question: In your opinion, is there any other way to end the hostilities?

Answer: The war in Viet Nam has brought havoc to the Vietnamese people and at the same time caused countless sufferings to the French people, therefore the French people are struggling against the war in Viet Nam.

I have constantly showed my sympathy, affection and respect for the French people and the French peace fighters. Today not only is the independence of Viet Nam seriously jeopardised but the independence of France is also gravely threatened. On the one hand, the U.S. imperialists egg on the French colonialists to continue and expand the aggressive war in Viet Nam, thus weakening them more and more through fighting in the hope of replacing France in Indo-China; on the other, they oblige France to ratify the European defence treaty that is to revive German militarism.

Therefore the struggle of the French people to gain independence, democracy and peace for France and to end the war in Viet Nam, constitutes one of the most important factors to settle the Viet Nam question by peaceful means.

94. *Ho Chi Minh: Appeal on the Occasion of the Seventh Anniversary of the Nationwide Resistance War [Extract]* *
    December 19, 1953

[The three paragraphs of Ho Chi Minh's statement printed here are those relevant to the Viet Minh's position on negotiations.]

For the sake of national independence and world peace, our army and people have fought heroically and won great victories. With the solidarity of our people and the support of the French people and other peace-loving people, our armed resistance will certainly be victorious.

Because the French colonialists are dragging on their aggressive war, the Vietnamese people are determined to fight still harder in order to wipe out more enemy forces, to fight until final victory. However, if the French Government wants to reach a cease-fire in Viet Nam by means of negotiation and to solve the Vietnamese problem by peaceful means, the Vietnamese people and Government are ready to negotiate with it.

* *Source:* Ho Chi Minh, *Selected Works* (4 vols., Hanoi: Foreign Languages Publishing House, 1961–1962), Vol. III, p. 431. Emphasis in the original. The complete statement is on pp. 429–432.

To achieve national independence and peace, our army and people must *push forward the resistance war and carry out land reform.* These two tasks are closely linked with each other, because land reform will help increase the people's forces and guarantee victory for the resistance war, and to promote the resistance war is to guarantee success for land reform.

95. *Speech by Vice President Richard Nixon [Extract]* *
December 23, 1953

[This speech was made over radio and television by Vice President Nixon following his return from a long visit to Asia during the fall of 1953; the extract printed here is that of particular relevance to Indochina.]

Let us turn now to another area of the world—Indochina. And many of you ask this question: Why is the United States spending hundreds of millions of dollars supporting the forces of the French Union in the fight against communism in Indochina? I think perhaps if we go over to the map here, I can indicate to you why it is so vitally important. Here is Indochina. If Indochina falls, Thailand is put in an almost impossible position. The same is true of Malaya with its rubber and tin. The same is true of Indonesia. If this whole part of Southeast Asia goes under Communist domination or Communist influence, Japan, who trades and must trade with this area in order to exist, must inevitably be oriented toward the Communist regime. That indicates to you and to all of us why it is vitally important that Indochina not go behind the Iron Curtain.

Now I may say that, as far as the war in Indochina is concerned, I was there, right on the battlefield or close to it, and it's a bloody war and it's a bitter one. And may I make the position of the United States clear with regard to that war. The United States supports the Associated States of Indochina in their understandable aspirations for independence. But we know as they do that the day the French leave Indochina, the Communists will take over. We realize as they do that the only way they can assure their independence and the only way they can defend it is to continue the fight side by side with their partners in the French Union against the forces of Communist colonialism which would enslave them. And may I also say this, and this we should

* *Source:* United States, Department of State, *Bulletin,* XXX (January 4, 1954), p. 12.

never forget, the free world owes a debt of gratitude to the French and to the forces of the Associated States for the great sacrifices they are making in the cause of freedom against Communist aggression in Indochina.

Now, let me turn just briefly to another problem, and this is also a big problem. It's the problem of China. Because, as we look at China on the map, we can see that China is the basic cause of all of our troubles in Asia. If China had not gone Communist, we would not have had a war in Korea. If China were not Communist, there would be no war in Indochina, there would be no war in Malaya.

96. *Secretary of State Dulles: Statement at a Press Conference [Extract]* * *December 29, 1953*

[After commenting on the recent Viet Minh offensive into Laos, which he judged to be of limited military significance, Secretary Dulles made the following statement about the possibility of peace talks for Indochina.]

Now as to your questions of whether this [offensive in Laos] detracts from the sincerity of the highly publicized "peace feelers" of the Viet Minh,[2] whether this penetration is coordinated with Communist moves elsewhere, and whether it constitutes a threat to Thailand, let me say this: With respect to the "peace feelers," I have never thought there was much sincerity in them. So when you subtract nothing from nothing, you still have nothing.

It is not impossible that this move bears a relationship to the prospective meeting of the Foreign Ministers in Berlin.

97. *Foreign Minister Georges Bidault: Statement at the Third Session of the Berlin Conference [Extract]* † *January 28, 1954*

[This extract from M. Bidault's speech in response to Foreign Minister Molotov's proposal for a Five-Power Conference is the section which deals with French policy on international negotiations for peace in Indochina.]

* *Source:* United States, Department of State, *Bulletin*, XXX (January 11, 1954), p. 43.

† *Source:* Great Britain, Parliament, Papers by Command, *Documents Relating to the Meeting of Foreign Ministers of France, the United Kingdom, the Soviet Union and the United States of America, Berlin, January 25–February 18, 1954* (London: Her Majesty's Stationery Office, Cmd. 9080, 1954), pp. 29–30.

2 See Documents 93 and 94.

The Soviet Delegation has twice insisted that if operations in Korea have come to an end, the world owes this happy event to the Democratic Republic of Korea and to the Chinese People's Republic. In these circumstances it might be thought that these two countries had never had any other desire than to end hostilities.

Allow me to recall the fact that no less than two years have been needed, since the opening of the truce talks, to arrive at an armistice, and that a few days before the signing of the armistice the Sino-Korean forces were joining in vain in the most costly and bloody offensive; that before and during that period the Chinese People's Republic never ceased contributing to the arming and training of Viet-Minh troops; and that finally, since the signing of the Korean armistice, this provision of supplies has grown ever greater. In these conditions, is it to be wondered at that the French Government feels it has the right to demand proofs of the spirit of peace which has been so much eulogised? How can it be imagined that we can be convinced of this otherwise than by concrete evidence? Can it really be believed that the calling of a Five-Power Conference to examine, for example, the "causes of international tension," is justified by the very obstinacy with which the Chinese People's Republic continues its aggression against us?

Nevertheless the French Government, in its concern to see peace restored everywhere as quickly as possible, has never hesitated to proclaim that it is ready, from this very day, to seize every opportunity to make peace in Indo-China in full agreement with the Associated States. These words which I have just used are the very words which the Head of the Government of the French Republic used in his statement of October 27, 1953.[3] I repeat with him that the French Government is ready to seek every opportunity during the negotiations which must follow the signing of an armistice in Korea—I will go even further —every form of conversation which would allow real progress to be made in the restoration of peace would be welcome. But how can I believe in the will for peace of the Chinese People's Republic of which we hear so much when the battlefield brings us proof every day of the opposite desire? Nothing would be easier than for the Chinese People's Republic to convince us immediately of its peaceful intentions. It would not even be necessary to hold a Five-Power Conference for that purpose. The Soviet Delegation informed us yesterday that, according to circumstances, and the problems to be dealt with, Five-Power, Four-Power, Three-Power, and even Two-Power conversations might be in-

[3] Document 92.

dicated. I have always been ready to consider such conversations. But only when I am convinced by precise facts that I am not alone in desiring them.

I seek in vain, in the statements of which I made meticulous note yesterday, for any sign of this. Instead of these essential assurances I find nothing but a repetition of the need for holding a Five-Power Conference, a miraculous remedy for all the ills that flesh is heir to. We were told in the first place that there was no agreement among us on this Conference, and then that by means of an exchange of views we might succeed in defining the problems to be submitted to it. Once again I wish to repeat that I have never suggested that the situation in Korea or in South-East Asia necessitated a Five-Power Conference.

The real problem is therefore to determine exactly what the Soviet Delegation has in mind and at heart. If I am a good interpreter of their thoughts, I believe what they really want is the Five-Power Conference. For our part, our aim, inspired by the fervent hopes of the peoples, is to restore and assure peace in Asia while respecting the legitimate interests of all. If the aim of the Soviet Delegation is limited to a Conference at which the Chinese People's Republic would be a participant, we are forced to the reflection that this political plan on its procedured basis is by no means identical with the primary aim which it is our duty to seek and to achieve, which, I repeat, is called: peace through justice.

98. *President Eisenhower: Statements at a News Conference*
    [Extracts] *
    February 10, 1954

[The extracts printed here are two of the five questions and answers which dealt with Indochina.]

Q. Marvin Arrowsmith, Associated Press: Mr. President, to go back for a moment to that question on Indochina,[4] there seems to be some uneasiness in Congress, as voiced by Senator Stennis [5] for one, that sending these technicians to Indochina will lead eventually to our involvement in a hot war there. Would you comment on that?

---

* *Source:* United States, Archives, *Public Papers of the Presidents of the United States: Dwight D. Eisenhower, 1954* (Washington: Government Printing Office, 1960), pp. 250, 253.

[4] The earlier question dealt with the sending of aircraft technicians to Indochina; the President stated that they could not be considered combat troops.

[5] Senator John Stennis (D., Miss.).

THE PRESIDENT: I would just say this: no one could be more bitterly opposed to ever getting the United States involved in a hot war in that region than I am; consequently, every move that I authorize is calculated, so far as humans can do it, to make certain that that does not happen.

. . . . .

Q. Daniel Shorr, CBS Radio: Mr. President, should your remarks on Indochina be construed as meaning that you are determined not to become involved or, perhaps, more deeply involved in the war in Indochina, regardless of how that war may go?

THE PRESIDENT: Well, I am not going to try to predict the drift of world events now and the course of world events over the next months. I say that I cannot conceive of a greater tragedy for America than to get heavily involved now in an all-out war in any of those regions, particularly with large units.

So what we are doing is supporting the Vietnamese and the French in their conduct of that war; because, as we see it, it is a case of independent and free nations operating against the encroachment of communism.

99. *Final Communiqué Issued by the Foreign Ministers of the United States, France, the United Kingdom, and the Soviet Union at the Berlin Conference [Extract]* *
February 18, 1954

A meeting of the Foreign Ministers of the United States, France, the United Kingdom and the Soviet Union, Mr. John Foster Dulles, M. Georges Bidault, Mr. Anthony Eden and M. Vyacheslav Molotov, took place in Berlin between January 25 and February 18, 1954. They reached the following agreements:

(*a*) The Foreign Ministers of the United States, France, the United Kingdom and the Union of Soviet Socialist Republics, meeting in Berlin,

Considering that the establishment, by peaceful means, of a united and independent Korea would be an important factor in reducing international tension and in restoring peace in other parts of Asia,

Propose that a conference of representatives of the United States,

* *Source:* Great Britain, Parliament, Papers by Command, *Documents Relating to the Meeting of Foreign Ministers of France, the United Kingdom, the Soviet Union and the United States of America, Berlin, January 25–February 18, 1954* (London: Her Majesty's Stationery Office, Cmd. 9080, 1954), p. 180.

France, the United Kingdom, the Union of Soviet Socialist Republics, the Chinese People's Republic, the Republic of Korea, the People's Democratic Republic of Korea and the other countries the armed forces of which participated in the hostilities in Korea, and which desire to attend, shall meet in Geneva on April 26th for the purpose of reaching a peaceful settlement of the Korean question,

Agree that the problem of restoring peace in Indo-China will also be discussed at the conference, to which representatives of the United States, France, the United Kingdom, the Union of Soviet Socialist Republics, the Chinese People's Republic and other interested States will be invited.

It is understood that neither the invitation to, nor the holding of, the above-mentioned Conference shall be deemed to imply diplomatic recognition in any case where it has not already been accorded.

[Section (*b*), dealing with disarmament and European questions, is omitted.]

100. *Order of the Day Adopted by the French National Assembly* *
    March 9, 1954

The National Assembly,

Pays homage to the heroism of the fighting men of the French Expeditionary Corps in Indochina and bows before the sacrifice of those who during the past eight years have gloriously fallen in a just cause;

Expresses its satisfaction at the meeting on April 26, 1954, in Geneva, of a conference, whose object is to define the appropriate means for putting an end to the distressing conflict in Indochina;

Takes cognizance of the declarations of the Government [6] reaffirming its determination to avail itself of and to seek every solution capable of bringing about the cessation of the conflict as quickly as possible,

---

* *Source:* France, *Journal Officiel de la République Française, Débats Parlementaires, Assemblée Nationale,* Session of March 9, 1954, p. 764. Translation by the editor. The first paragraph of the Order of the Day was adopted unanimously with the exception of the Communists; the second paragraph was adopted 343 to 259; the third was adopted 343 to 259; and the final paragraph was adopted 374 to 234. A detailed breakdown of the voting is in *ibid.*, pp. 792–795. This Order of the Day has sometimes been described as endorsing negotiations with the Viet Minh, but in fact it would seem to endorse *any* negotiations designed to bring an end to the war, and most specifically the negotiations a*t* Geneva.

[6] Particularly Premier Laniel's statement of March 5, in France, *Journal Officiel de la République Française Débats Parlementaires, Assemblée Nationale,* Session of March 5, 1954, pp. 713–715. See Note 6, p. 219.

and of assuring peace and liberty in the Associated States, indissolubly united in the French Union;

Solemnly recalls that France is sustaining the armed struggle in Indochina by virtue of the provisions of the Constitution relative to the French Union, to which the Associated States have already voluntarily adhered, and that any repudiation of these provisions by the said States would relieve France of her obligations toward them while leaving her free to judge the measures that might be dictated by her interest, which is inseparable from that of the free world;

And, rejecting all amendment,

Proceeds with the business of the day.

101. *President Eisenhower: Statement at a News Conference [Extract]* * *March 10, 1954*

[The extract of the news conference printed here is the question and answer pertinent to American involvement in Indochina.]

Q. James J. Patterson, New York News: Mr. President, Senator Stennis [7] said yesterday that we were in danger of becoming involved in World War III in Indochina because of the Air Force technicians there. What will we do if one of those men is captured or killed?

THE PRESIDENT: I will say this: there is going to be no involvement of America in war unless it is a result of the constitutional process that is placed upon Congress to declare it. Now, let us have that clear; and that is the answer.

102. *Secretary of State Dulles: Statement at a News Conference* † *March 23, 1954*

I do not expect that there is going to be a Communist victory in Indochina. By that I don't mean that there may not be local affairs where one side or another will win victories, but in terms of a Communist domination of Indochina, I do not accept that as a probability.

---

* *Source:* United States, Archives, *Public Papers of the Presidents of the United States: Dwight D. Eisenhower, 1954* (Washington: Government Printing Office, 1960), p. 306.

† *Source:* United States, Department of State, *Bulletin,* XXX (April 5, 1954), pp. 512–513.

[7] Senator John Stennis (D., Miss.).

There is a very gallant and brave struggle being carried on at Dien-Bien-Phu by the French and Associated States Forces. It is an outpost. It has already inflicted very heavy damage upon the enemy. The French and Associated States Forces at Dien-Bien-Phu are writing, in my opinion, a notable chapter in military history. Dien-Bien-Phu is, as I say, an outpost position where only a very small percentage of the French Union forces is engaged and where a very considerable percentage of the forces of the Viet Minh is engaged.

Broadly speaking, the United States has, under its previously known policy, been extending aid in the form of money and materiel to the French Union Forces in Indochina. As their requests for materiel become known and their need for that becomes evident, we respond to it as rapidly as we can. Those requests have assumed various forms at various times. But I think that we have responded in a very prompt and effective manner to those requests.

If there are further requests of that kind that are made, I have no doubt that our military or defense people will attempt to meet them.

As soon as this press conference is over, I am meeting with Admiral Radford.[8] But so far I have not met General Ely,[9] and I do not know what requests he has made, if any, in that respect because that would be primarily a matter for the Defense people in any case. The policy has already been established so far as the political aspects of it are concerned.

We have seen no reason to abandon the so-called Navarre plan,[10] which was, broadly speaking, a 2-year plan which anticipated, if not complete victory, at least decisive military results during the fighting season which would follow the present fighting season, which is roughly a year from now.

As you recall, that plan contemplated a very substantial buildup of the local forces and their training and equipment. It was believed that under that program, assuming there were no serious military reversals during the present fighting season, the upper hand could definitely be achieved in the area by the end of the next fighting season. There have been no such military reverses, and, as far as we can see, none are in prospect which would be of a character which would upset the broad timetable and strategy of the Navarre plan.

·   ·   ·   ·   ·

8 Admiral Arthur W. Radford, Chairman of the Joint Chiefs of Staff.
9 General Paul Ely, French Chief of Staff, then in Washington.
10 Adopted by France during 1953 with the concurrence of the United States; named for General Henri-Eugene Navarre, French Commander in Indochina.

Asked whether that ruled out any possibility of a negotiated peace at Geneva, Mr. Dulles replied:

At any time if the Chinese Communists are willing to cut off military assistance and thereby demonstrate that they are not still aggressors in spirit, that would, of course, advance greatly the possibility of achieving peace and tranquility in the area. That is a result which we would like to see.

To date, however, I have no evidence that they have changed their mood. One is always hopeful in those respects, but so far the evidence seems to indicate that the Chinese Communists are still in an aggressive, militaristic, and expansionist mood.

103. *Secretary of State Dulles: Speech to the Overseas Press Club of America [Extracts]* *
March 29, 1954

This provides a timely occasion for outlining the Administration's thinking about two related matters—Indochina and the Chinese Communist regime.

[Section I, containing general comments on Indochina, and the first 4 paragraphs of Section II—*Communist Imperialism*—are omitted.]

Those fighting under the banner of Ho Chi Minh have largely been trained and equipped in Communist China. They are supplied with artillery and ammunition through the Soviet-Chinese Communist bloc. Captured material shows that much of it was fabricated by the Skoda Munition Works in Czechoslovakia and transported across Russia and Siberia and then sent through China into Vietnam. Military supplies for the Communist armies have been pouring into Vietnam at a steadily increasing rate.

Military and technical guidance is supplied by an estimated 2,000 Communist Chinese.[11] They function with the forces of Ho Chi Minh

* *Source:* United States, Department of State, *American Foreign Policy 1950–1955: Basic Documents* (2 vols., Washington: Government Printing Office, 1957), Vol. II, pp. 2373–2376.

[11] Whether or not Chinese Communist military advisors were present in Viet-Nam remains a matter of some dispute. At one point, in May 1954, the French High Command reportedly denied that there was any evidence of a Chinese combat presence: see *New Times* (Moscow), May 15, 1954, p. 32. This reputed announcement followed the release by the United States, on May 12, of an alleged Chinese "Handbook for Political Workers Going to Vietnam," dated December 15, 1952, published in *Far Eastern Notes*, No. 8 (May 7, 1954), pp. 7–11. The

in key positions—in staff sections of the High Command, at the division level and in specialized units such as signal, engineer, artillery and transportation.

In the present stage, the Communists in Indochina use nationalistic anti-French slogans to win local support. But if they achieved military or political success, it is certain that they would subject the people to a cruel Communist dictatorship taking its orders from Peiping and Moscow.

The Scope of the Danger

The tragedy would not stop there. If the Communist forces won uncontested control over Indochina or any substantial part thereof, they would surely resume the same pattern of aggression against other free peoples in the area.

The propagandists of Red China and Russia make it apparent that the purpose is to dominate all of Southeast Asia.

Southeast Asia is the so-called "rice bowl" which helps to feed the densely populated region that extends from India to Japan. It is rich in many raw materials, such as tin, oil, rubber and iron ore. It offers industrial Japan potentially important markets and sources of raw materials.

The area has great strategic value. Southeast Asia is astride the most direct and best developed sea and air routes between the Pacific and South Asia. It has major naval and air bases. Communist control of Southeast Asia would carry a grave threat to the Philippines, Australia and New Zealand, with whom we have treaties of mutual assistance.[12] The entire Western Pacific area, including the so-called "offshore island chain," would be strategically endangered.

President Eisenhower appraised the situation last Wednesday when he said that the area is of "transcendent importance." [13]

---

text of this document also appears in Allan B. Cole, ed., *Conflict in Indo-China and International Repercussions: A Documentary History, 1945–1955* (Ithaca, N.Y.: Cornell University Press, 1956), pp. 125–130. The Chinese spokesman at Geneva, Huang Hua, denounced this document as "an out and out fabrication" on May 14: New China News Agency, May 14, 1954, in United States, Consulate General in Hong Kong, *Survey of the China Mainland Press*, No. 809 (May 15–17, 1954), p. 17. The Soviet Union denounced the document as a forgery on May 21: *Pravda*, May 21, 1954, p. 3.

[12] Footnote in the original omitted.

[13] Statement made at the President's news conference of March 24, 1954, in United States, Archives, *Public Papers of the Presidents of the United States, Dwight D. Eisenhower, 1954* (Washington: Government Printing Office, 1960), p. 341.

The United States Position

The United States has shown in many ways its sympathy for the gallant struggle being waged in Indochina by French forces and those of the Associated States. Congress has enabled us to provide material aid to the established governments and their peoples. Also, our diplomacy has sought to deter Communist China from open aggression in that area.

President Eisenhower, in his address of April 16, 1953,[14] explained that a Korean armistice would be a fraud if it merely released aggressive armies for attack elsewhere. I said last September that if Red China sent its own army into Indochina, that would result in grave consequences which might not be confined to Indochina.[15]

Recent statements have been designed to impress upon potential aggressors that aggression might lead to action at places and by means of free world choosing, so that aggression would cost more than it could gain.[16]

The Chinese Communists have, in fact, avoided the direct use of their own Red armies in open aggression against Indochina. They have, however, largely stepped up their support of the aggression in that area. Indeed, they promote that aggression by all means short of open invasion.

Under all the circumstances it seems desirable to clarify further the United States position.

Under the conditions of today, the imposition on Southeast Asia of the political system of Communist Russia and its Chinese Communist ally, by whatever means, would be a grave threat to the whole free community. The United States feels that that possibility should not be passively accepted, but should be met by united action. This might involve serious risks. But these risks are far less than those that will face us a few years from now, if we dare not be resolute today.

The free nations want peace. However, peace is not had merely by wanting it. Peace has to be worked for and planned for. Sometimes it is necessary to take risks to win peace just as it is necessary in war to

[14] "The Chance for Peace," Address before the American Society of Newspaper Editors, Washington, in United States, Department of State, *American Foreign Policy 1950–1955: Basic Documents* (2 vols., Washington: Government Printing Office, 1957), Vol. I, pp. 65–71.

[15] Document 88.

[16] Footnote in the original: "e.g., Secretary Dulles' address of Jan. 12, 1954: 'The way to deter aggression is for the free community to be willing and able to respond vigorously at places and means of its own choosing.' (*supra*, p. 80)."

take risks to win victory. The chances for peace are usually bettered by letting a potential aggressor know in advance where his aggression could lead him.

I hope that these statements which I make here tonight will serve the cause of peace.

[Part II, *Communist China,* and the concluding section, *The Dangers Ahead,* are omitted.]

104. *President Eisenhower: Statements at a News Conference [Extracts]* *
   April 7, 1954

[The extracts of the news conference printed here are four of the seven questions and answers which dealt most immediately with Indochina.]

Q. Robert Richards, Copley Press: Mr. President, would you mind commenting on the strategic importance of Indochina to the free world? I think there has been, across the country, some lack of understanding on just what it means to us.

THE PRESIDENT: You have, of course, both the specific and the general when you talk about such things.

First of all, you have the specific value of a locality in its production of materials that the world needs.

Then you have the possibility that many human beings pass under a dictatorship that is inimical to the free world.

Finally, you have broader considerations that might follow what you would call the "falling domino" principle. You have a row of dominoes set up, you knock over the first one, and what will happen to the last one is the certainty that it will go over very quickly. So you could have a beginning of a disintegration that would have the most profound influences.

Now, with respect to the first one, two of the items from this particular area that the world uses are tin and tungsten. They are very important. There are others, of course, the rubber plantations and so on.

Then with respect to more people passing under this domination, Asia, after all has already lost some 450 million of its peoples to the Communist dictatorship, and we simply can't afford greater losses.

But when we come to the possible sequence of events, the loss of Indochina, of Burma, of Thailand, of the Peninsula, and Indonesia fol-

* *Source:* United States, Archives, *Public Papers of the Presidents of the United States: Dwight D. Eisenhower, 1954* (Washington: Government Printing Office, 1960), pp. 382–384, 387–388.

lowing, now you begin to talk about areas that not only multiply the disadvantages that you would suffer through loss of materials, sources of materials, but now you are talking really about millions and millions and millions of people.

Finally, the geographical position achieved thereby does many things. It turns the so-called island defensive chain of Japan, Formosa, of the Philippines and to the southward; it moves in to threaten Australia and New Zealand.

It takes away, in its economic aspects, that region that Japan must have as a trading area or Japan, in turn, will have only one place in the world to go—that is, toward the Communist areas in order to live.

So, the possible consequences of the loss are just incalculable to the free world.

. . . . .

Q. Raymond Brandt, St. Louis Post-Dispatch: Mr. President, what response has Secretary Dulles and the administration got to the request for united action in Indochina?

THE PRESIDENT: So far as I know, there are no positive reactions as yet, because the time element would almost forbid.

The suggestions we have, have been communicated; and we will have communications on them in due course, I should say.[17]

Q. Robert G. Spivack, New York Post: Mr. President, do you agree with Senator Kennedy [18] that independence must be guaranteed the people of Indochina in order to justify an all-out effort there?

THE PRESIDENT: Well, I don't know, of course, exactly in what way a Senator was talking about this thing.

I will say this: for many years, in talking to different countries, different governments, I have tried to insist on this principle: no outside

[17] Footnote in the original: "On April 10, 1954, the White House released a statement by the Secretary of State shortly after his talk with the President before leaving for London and Paris. Secretary Dulles stated that he would consult with the British and French governments about the problems involved in creating 'the obviously desirable united front to resist communist aggression in Southeast Asia.' The Secretary continued: 'The communist bloc with its vast resources can win success by overwhelming one by one little bits of freedom. But it is different if we unite. . . . Our purpose is . . . to create the unity of free wills needed to assure a peaceful settlement which will in fact preserve the vital interests of us all.'

"In a statement released by the White House on April 19, following his return to Washington, Secretary Dulles noted that he had found in both capitals recognition of the need for exploring the possibility of establishing a collective defense.

"The full text of both statements by the Secretary of State are published in the Department of State Bulletin (vol. 30, pp. 590, 668)."

[18] John F. Kennedy (D., Mass.). His statement was reported in *The New York Times,* April 7, 1954, p. 1.

country can come in and be really helpful unless it is doing something that the local people want.

Now, let me call your attention to this independence theory. Senator Lodge,[19] on my instructions, stood up in the United Nations and offered one country independence if they would just simply pass a resolution saying they wanted it, or at least said, "I would work for it." They didn't accept it. So I can't say that the associated states want independence in the sense that the United States is independent. I do not know what they want.

I do say this: the aspirations of those people must be met, otherwise there is in the long run no final answer to the problem.

. . . . .

Q. Henri Pierre, Le Monde (Paris): Mr. President, would you say that the last statement of the Secretary of State of last week about Indochina [20] has improved the chance of reaching a negotiated solution at Geneva of the Indochinese controversy?

THE PRESIDENT: Your question is really, do I think there is a good chance of reaching a negotiated solution?

Q. Mr. Pierre: That is right.

THE PRESIDENT: Well, I wouldn't class the chances as good, no, not one that the free world would consider adequate to the situation.

I must say, let me make clear again, I am certain the United States as a whole, its Congress and the executive portions of its Government, are ready to move just as far as prudence will allow in seeking any kind of conciliation or negotiated agreement that will ease any of the problems of this troubled world. But one thing: we are not going to overstep the line of prudence in keeping ourselves secure, knowing that the agreements we made have some means of being enforced. We are not simply going to take words. There must be some way of making these things fact and deed.

105. *Statement Issued by Secretary of State Dulles and Foreign Secretary Eden [Extract]* *
      April 13, 1954

At the conclusion of their meetings in London on April 12 and 13, during which they discussed a number of matters of common concern,

---

* *Source:* United States, Department of State, *American Foreign Policy 1950–1955: Basic Documents* (2 vols., Washington: Government Printing Office, 1957), Vol. I, pp. 1704–1705.

[19] Henry Cabot Lodge, then U.S. Representative to the United Nations.
[20] Document 103.

Mr. John Foster Dulles and Mr. Anthony Eden issued the following statement:

We have had a full exchange of views with reference to Southeast Asia. We deplore the fact that on the eve of the Geneva Conference the Communist forces in Indochina are increasingly developing their activities into a large-scale war against the forces of the French Union. They seek to overthrow the lawful and friendly Government of Viet-Nam which we recognize; and they have invaded Laos and Cambodia. We realize that these activities not only threaten those now directly involved, but also endanger the peace and security of the entire area of Southeast Asia and the Western Pacific, where our two nations and other friendly and allied nations have vital interests.

Accordingly we are ready to take part, with the other countries principally concerned, in an examination of the possibility of establishing a collective defense, within the framework of the Charter of the United Nations, to assure the peace, security and freedom of Southeast Asia and the Western Pacific.[21]

It is our hope that the Geneva Conference will lead to the restoration of peace in Indochina.[22] We believe that the prospect of establishing a unity of defensive purpose throughout Southeast Asia and the Western Pacific will contribute to an honorable peace in Indochina.

[A section dealing with developments in the field of atomic energy is omitted.]

106. *Statement Issued by Secretary of State Dulles and*
Foreign Minister Bidault *
April 14, 1954

Following their conversations in Paris on April 14th, the United States Secretary of State, Mr. John Foster Dulles, and the French Minister of Foreign Affairs, M. Bidault, issued the following statement:

For nearly two centuries it has been the practice for representatives of our two nations to meet together to discuss the grave issues which from time to time have confronted us.

In pursuance of this custom, which we hope to continue to the benefit of ourselves and others, we have had an exchange of views on Indochina and Southeast Asia.

* *Source:* United States, Department of State, *American Foreign Policy 1950–1955: Basic Documents* (2 vols., Washington: Government Printing Office, 1957), Vol. II, p. 2381.
[21] Footnote in the original omitted.   [22] *Ibid.*

Mr. Dulles expressed admiration for the gallant fight of the French Union forces, who continue with unshakeable courage and determination to repel Communist aggression.

We deplore the fact that on the eve of the Geneva Conference this aggression has reached a new climax in Viet-Nam particularly at Dien-Bien-Phu and has been renewed in Laos and extended to Cambodia.

The independence of the three Associated States within the French Union, which new agreements are to complete, is at stake in these battles.

We recognize that the prolongation of the war in Indochina, which endangers the security of the countries immediately affected, also threatens the entire area of Southeast Asia and of the Western Pacific. In close association with other interested nations, we will examine the possibility of establishing, within the framework of the United Nations Charter, a collective defense to assure the peace, security and freedom of this area.

We recognize that our basic objective at the Geneva Conference will be to seek the re-establishment of a peace in Indochina which will safeguard the freedom of its people and the independence of the Associated States. We are convinced that the possibility of obtaining this objective depends upon our solidarity.

107. *Indochina: Paper Prepared by Foreign Secretary Eden on the Attitude of Her Majesty's Government* *
    April 25, 1954

1. We do not regard the London Communiqué [23] as committing us to join in immediate discussions on the possibility of Allied intervention in the Indo-China war.

2. We are not prepared to give any undertakings now, in advance of Geneva, concerning United Kingdom military action in Indo-China.

3. But we shall give all possible diplomatic support to the French Delegation at Geneva in efforts to reach an honourable settlement.

* *Source:* Great Britain, Parliament, Papers by Command, *Documents Relating to British Involvement in the Indo-China Conflict 1945–1965* (London: Her Majesty's Stationery Office, Cmnd. 2834, 1965), p. 67. According to Eden (*Full Circle* [Boston: Houghton Mifflin Company, 1960], pp. 117–118), this paper was prepared in response to American advocacy of armed intervention in Indochina as the basis for discussion of the Indochina situation at an emergency cabinet meeting on April 25. It was approved by Prime Minister Churchill and unanimously endorsed by the Cabinet.
23 Document 105.

4. We can give an assurance now that if a settlement is reached at Geneva we shall join in guaranteeing that settlement and in setting up a collective defence in South-East Asia, as foreshadowed in the London Communiqué, to make that joint guarantee effective.

5. We hope that any Geneva settlement will make it possible for the joint guarantee to apply to at least the greater part of Indo-China.

6. If no such settlement is reached we shall be prepared at that time to consider with our Allies the action to be taken jointly in the situation then existing.

7. But we cannot give any assurance now about possible action on the part of the United Kingdom in the event of failure to reach agreement at Geneva for a cessation of hostilities in Indo-China.

8. We shall be ready to join with the United States Government now in studying measures to ensure the defence of Siam and the rest of South-East Asia, including Malaya, in the event of all or part of Indo-China being lost.

108. *Communiqué Issued by the Cabinet of H.M. Bao Dai* *
    April 25, 1954

At the moment when the first phase of the Franco-Vietnamese negotiations, which have now been going on for nearly two months, are coming to an end, and the International Conference at Geneva is beginning, the Cabinet of His Majesty Bao Dai, Chief of State of Viet Nam,[24] finds it necessary to make known clearly its position in regard to problems which concern Viet Nam and France, as well as the rest of the world.

The first thought of Viet Nam in the present circumstances goes out to the heroic defenders of Dien Bien Phu. If it is true that French arms have covered themselves with fresh glory in this unequal and difficult combat, it cannot be forgotten that Vietnamese soldiers furnish an ex-

---

* *Source:* Embassy of the State of Viet-Nam (Washington), Press and Information Service, *Vital: Unity and Independence* (Washington: 1954?), pp. 1, 4. Subheadings omitted. The French text of the Declaration is in State of Viet-Nam, High Commission in Paris, *Vietnam*, No. 74 (May 3, 1954), pp. 4–5. The French reply, a communiqué issued on April 25 by the Secretariat of State for Relations with the Associated States and expressing "astonishment" at the Vietnamese communiqué, is in France, Direction de la Documentation, *Chroniques d'Outre-Mer: Etudes et Informations,* No. 5 (May 1954), p. 81.

[24] The Cabinet (or personal staff) of Bao Dai was a separate entity from the Government of the State of Viet-Nam under Premier Buu Loc. There were, at times, reports of disagreements between the Government and Bao Dai.

tremely important proportion of the forces whose valiant resistance will henceforth live in history. As they are associated in the glory and the anguish of the battle, so Viet Nam and France should feel themselves linked together in their political action.

Nevertheless, the Franco-Vietnamese negotiations brought about by the French declaration of last July 3rd [25] and entered into March 8th have still been unable to be concluded by the signing of the treaties which would consecrate the independence of Viet Nam and, subsequently, define the conditions of an equal and voluntary collaboration with France. There were no subjects which offered serious disagreement.

France has proclaimed on several occasions that she recognized Viet Nam's independence. Viet Nam has shown unequivocally its desire to remain associated with France in the framework of a freely-constituted union of sovereign states. These two great principles once admitted on one side and the other, no difficulty should then remain. Viet Nam is aware of having done nothing which would have retarded a solution which seemed imperative before the Geneva Conference.

The Vietnamese Government has finally consented not to conclude this phase of the negotiations by the signing of the two treaties of independence and association on which the agreement has been realized.[26] Actually, in certain respects, Viet Nam does not have all the concrete assurances that its unity and its independence as a freely associated partner are completely guaranteed under conditions which answer to the proclaimed principles.

In connection with its unity, it is known that divers plans have been set forth which envisage a partition of Viet Nam. These solutions may appear to offer certain advantages, diplomatically speaking, but they pose difficulties and extremely grave dangers for the future. They would be in defiance to Vietnamese national sentiment which has affirmed with so much force its desire for unity and independence for the country. Neither the Chief of State nor the National Government of Viet Nam acknowledge that rightfully or legally the unity of the country can be destroyed. If they are not completely enslaved, the partisans of Ho Chi Minh, who have been dragged into a nefarious combat, in the name of unity and independence for their country, ought to be as revolted as we ourselves are before the possibility of a partition of

[25] Document 85.

[26] The two treaties, which were subsequently initialed by both parties, are Documents 118 and 119.

Viet Nam proposed by foreign powers. Without doubt they take the measure of their error in this moment and perceive how their patriotism, often beyond dispute, has been used to further imperialistic designs and how their efforts have been turned against their own goals.

Concerning its independence and its equality in the association with France, Viet Nam would hope that the principles of a general policy worked out in common would be completely respected in subsequent acts. Before the gravity of present circumstances the association of France and Viet Nam ought not to be translated by words or even by legal formulas, but in concrete reality, by a complete unity of views and action.

Viet Nam could not tolerate the prospect of negotiations through which France, contrary to the principle of the French Union which she herself proclaimed, would treat with the rebels of the Vietnamese nation or with powers hostile to it, discarding or even sacrificing her associates.

Certainly, in the course of the meeting of the Permanent Committee of the High Council [27] held February 23, 1954, the French Minister of Foreign Affairs [28] declared that no position would be settled by his government on questions involving Indo-China without the formal agreement of the Associated States. Viet Nam does not wish to doubt that this promise will be loyally kept by the French Government but it feels that in reaffirming this bond and in developing the unity of views between Viet Nam and France through the detailed study of the questions posed by the Geneva Conference, the two states will not only strengthen their position with respect to one another but also that of the free world as a whole. (However, it must be acknowledged that a meeting held Saturday evening [April 24] at the Quai d'Orsay gave the French Minister of Foreign Affairs an opportunity to acquaint the representatives of the Associated States with the projects of the French delegation.)

Neither the Chief of State nor the Government of Viet Nam will consider itself bound by decisions which run counter to the independence and unity of their country at the same time that they violate a people's rights and offer to reward aggression, contrary to the principles of the United Nations Charter and to democratic ideals.

[27] I.e., the High Council of the French Union.   [28] Georges Bidault.

109. *Prime Minister Churchill: Statement in the House of Commons* *
    April 27, 1954

MR. ATTLEE [29] (*by Private Notice*) asked the Prime Minister
whether he has any statement to make with regard to the meeting of
the Foreign Ministers in Paris.

THE PRIME MINISTER: The meeting of the Foreign Ministers in
Paris marked the fifth anniversary of the signing of the North Atlantic
Treaty and reviewed in its military aspects the international situation.
No doubt hon. Members will have read the communiqué issued after
the meeting, which, for convenience, I am circulating in the OFFICIAL
REPORT.[30]

While in Paris there were naturally conversations between the Foreign Ministers especially about the grave local situation in French Indo-
China. No decisions were taken in advance of the Conference at Geneva. All the Powers concerned are now in session there. The preliminary stage of procedure which has so often absorbed much time and
energy has been settled, with the full agreement of the Four Powers
who initiated the Conference, with a smoothness and celerity which is
at least a good augury for the spirit which should animate the proceedings. The House will, I am sure, be anxious that nothing should be
said here today which would render more difficult the momentous discussions and vital contacts which are now in progress.

The episode of the siege of the French fortress of Dien Bien Phu,
the fate of which now hangs in the balance, creates a violent tension
in many minds at a time when calm judgment is most needed. The
timing of the climax of this assault with the opening of the Geneva
Conference is not without significance but it must not be allowed to
prejudice the sense of world proportion which should inspire the Conference and be a guide to those who are watching its progress.

Three of the Commonwealth countries are represented by high authorities at the Conference, and the closest intimacy and sense of unity
prevails between them and us. My right hon. Friend the Foreign Sec-

---

* *Source:* Great Britain, *Parliamentary Debates* (*Hansard*), Fifth Series, House
of Commons, Vol. 526 (April 27, 1954), cols. 1455–1456.

[29] Right Hon. Clement Attlee, Leader of the Opposition.

[30] Communiqué of the NATO Council issued on April 23; text in United States,
Department of State, *American Foreign Policy 1950–1955: Basic Documents* (2
vols., Washington: Government Printing Office, 1957), Vol. I, p. 1637.

retary [31] is also in constant touch with the other members of the Commonwealth. In order that his Cabinet colleagues and he should be in full agreement, he returned to this country last Saturday, and we had lengthy meetings on Sunday at which all the questions pending were considered,[32] and we had the advantage of the professional advice of the Chiefs of Staff. As a result we have the fullest confidence in the wisdom of the course which we have agreed my right hon. Friend should follow in circumstances so largely governed by the unknown.

Her Majesty's Government are not prepared to give any undertakings about United Kingdom military action in Indo-China in advance of the results of Geneva. We have not entered into any new political or military commitments. My right hon. Friend has, of course, made it clear to his colleagues at Geneva that if settlements are reached there Her Majesty's Government will be ready to play their full part in supporting them in order to promote a stable peace in the Far East.

[Supplementary questions are omitted.]

110. *Joint Declaration Issued by France and the State of Viet-Nam* *
      April 28, 1954

France, faithful to the declaration of July 3, 1953,[33] designed to perfect the independence of Vietnam, and to grant it full sovereignty,

Vietnam, resolved to maintain and consolidate the traditional friendship which binds it to the French people,

Affirm their agreement to regulate their mutual relations on the basis of two fundamental treaties.

The first of these treaties recognizes the total independence of Vietnam and its full and complete sovereignty.[34] The second establishes a Franco-Vietnamese association within the French Union, an association founded on equality and destined to develop cooperation between the two countries.[35]

Solemnly affirming their determination to implement these two treaties in a parallel manner, the Government of the French Republic and the Government of Vietnam pledge themselves simultaneously to submit the two treaties to the procedure of ratification provided for by their respective national regulations.

---

* *Source:* France, Direction de la Documentation, *Articles et Documents,* No. 050 (April 29, 1954), "Textes du Jour," p. 1. Translation by the editor.

[31] Anthony Eden.   [32] See Document 107.   [33] Document 85.
[34] Document 118.   [35] Document 119.

111. *President Eisenhower: Statement Read at a News Conference*
   [Extracts] *
   May 5, 1954

[Reading] With the return of the Secretary of State from Geneva, there will of course be a series of conferences on foreign affairs, both within the executive department and between the Secretary of State and bipartisan groups of the Congress. Because of these forthcoming conferences and the probability that the Secretary of State will himself have something to say,[36] and because also of the delicate nature of the issues now pending before the Geneva conference, I shall limit my comments on the Indochina situation to this written statement.

[Six paragraphs on American support for collective defense organizations, the general nature of the Geneva Conference, and the Korean phase of the Geneva Conference are omitted.]

The Indochina phase of the conference is in process of being organized and the issues have not yet been clarified. In this matter a large measure of initiative rests with the governments of France, Viet-Nam, Laos, and Cambodia, which are the countries most directly concerned.

Meanwhile, plans are proceeding for the realization of a Southeast Asia security arrangement. This was publicly suggested by Secretary Dulles in his address of March 29.[37] Of course, our principal allies were advised in advance. This proposal of the Secretary of State was not a new one; it was merely reaffirmation of the principles that have consistently guided our post-war foreign policy and a reminder to interested Asian friends that the United States was prepared to join with others in the application of these principles to the threatened area. Most of the free nations of the area and others directly concerned have shown affirmative interest, and the conversations are actively proceeding.

Obviously, it was never expected that this collective security arrangement would spring into existence overnight. There are too many important problems to be resolved. But there is a general sense of urgency. The fact that such an organization is in the process of formation could have an important bearing upon what happens at Geneva during the Indochina phase of the conference.

* *Source:* United States, Archives, *Public Papers of the Presidents of the United States: Dwight D. Eisenhower, 1954* (Washington: Government Printing Office, 1960), pp. 450–452.

[36] See Document 112.   [37] Document 103.

The countries of the area are now thinking in constructive terms, which include the indispensable concept of collective security. Progress in this matter has been considerable, and I am convinced that further progress will continue to be made. [*Ends reading*]

CHAPTER IX

The Geneva Conference
May-July 1954

Introduction

Although the Korean phase of the Geneva Conference began on April 26, procedural problems delayed the opening of talks on Indochina. Negotiations finally began on May 8, the day after the fall of Dien Bien Phu, and were to continue for more than two months. In reality, progress was rapid, for many of the major participants seemed to have come to the conference table with the conviction that a settlement must be reached. The period during which the talks were held saw a virtual withdrawal by the United States from a leading role in the negotiations, as well as the rise of a new government in France; both events helped to make the final agreements possible.

The major problem delaying the Indochina phase of the Conference was one of participation. The Great Powers finally decided that both the State of Viet-Nam and the Democratic Republic of Viet-Nam (DRV) would be invited, as well as the Associated States of Cambodia and Laos but not the "Resistance Governments" of "Khmer" (Cambodia) and "Pathet Lao" (Laos). With agreement that Foreign Minister Molotov and Foreign Secretary Eden would alternate as Chairman, the opening of the Indochinese discussions was set for May 8.

Dien Bien Phu fell on May 7, striking a blow from which French morale was unable to recover. In announcing the defeat to the National Assembly, Premier Laniel emphasized French determination to continue the fight while working for an armistice at Geneva.[1] Orders were issued to General Navarre, the French commander in Indochina, which emphasized the necessity of preserving French forces even at the cost

---

[1] The text of Laniel's statement to the National Assembly is in France, *Journal Officiel de la République Française Débats Parlementaires, Assemblée Nationale*, Session of May 7, 1954, p. 2223.

of evacuation of most of northern Indochina.[2] Also on May 7, Secretary of State Dulles reported on American policy toward Indochina following his return from Geneva (Document 112).

At the first session of the Indochina phase of the Geneva Conference on May 8,[3] French and Viet Minh negotiators sat at the same table for the first time since the Fontainebleau Conference in 1946. And there were striking similarities to the earlier Conference: the French delegation was headed by Foreign Minister Georges Bidault, who had been Premier of the Provisional French Government in the summer of 1946. The DRV delegation was led by Pham Van Dong, who had been the chief negotiator at Fontainebleau.[4] The chief representative of the State of Viet-Nam, Foreign Minister Nguyen Quoc Dinh, had been a legal adviser to the DRV delegation at Fontainebleau.

At the May 8 session Bidault submitted French proposals for a cease-fire in Indochina (Document 113). Pham Van Dong in turn only demanded that representatives of "Khmer" and "Pathet Lao" be included in the Conference, but at the second plenary session, on May 10, he outlined DRV proposals for a settlement (Document 114). The State of Viet-Nam submitted its proposals at the third plenary session

[2] Extracts from the orders are in Joseph Laniel, *Le Drame Indochinois: de Dien-Bien-Phu au Parie de Genève* (Paris: Libraire Plon, 1957), pp. 106–107.

[3] Extensive documentation on the Conference is in Great Britain, Parliament, Papers by Command, *Documents Relating to the Discussion of Korea and Indo-China at the Geneva Conference, April 27–June 15, 1954* (London: Her Majesty's Stationery Office, Cmd. 9186, 1954); and in France, Ministère des Affaires Etrangères, *Conférence de Genève sur l'Indochine (8 Mai–21 Juillet 1954), Procès-verbaux des Séances–Propositions–Documents Finaux* (Paris: Imprimerie Nationale, 1955) which includes not only all the speeches at plenary sessions and the final documents of the Conference but also summary transcripts of proceedings at the restricted sessions. A second volume on the Conference, dealing with meetings between the Foreign Ministers outside the formal Conference framework, remains classified by the French Government. The best secondary accounts of the Conference are in Jean Lacouture and Philippe Devillers, *End of a War: Indochina, 1954,* Alexander Lieven and Adam Roberts, trans. (New York: Frederick A. Praeger, 1969); and Robert F. Randle, *Geneva 1954: The Settlement of the Indochinese War* (Princeton, N.J.: Princeton University Press, 1969).

[4] Pham Van Dong, one of Ho Chi Minh's most trusted colleagues and a member of the Politburo of the VWP, replaced the non-Communist Hoang Minh Giam as Foreign Minister on May 1 owing to the latter's reported "illness." Pham was accompanied by Phan Anh, Minister of Economy, and Ta Quang Buu, Vice Minister of National Defense, both of whom had been present at Fontainebleau. The fourth DRV delegate was Hoang Van Hoan, Ambassador to Peking, member of the VWP Politburo, and reportedly a specialist in foreign affairs.

on May 12 (Document 115). Later in that session Foreign Secretary Eden stressed the necessity for a halt in fighting as a first step and summarized areas of agreement.[5]

Negotiations soon began to make progress, in large part because Foreign Minister Molotov and Foreign Secretary Eden were, each for his own reasons, committed to ending the Indochina war and each was receptive to doing so through some form of partition. At the May 14 plenary session Molotov proposed a neutral international supervisory commission to watch over the cease-fire,[6] although the makeup of that Commission would not be agreed upon for two months. At the restricted session on May 25 Pham Van Dong proposed the regroupment of contending forces into only two zones in each Indochinese state, each zone with the implied capability for independent existence (Document 116). By May 29 the Conference had agreed on the basic principles of a cease-fire in Viet-Nam, although the specifics of regroupment zones and international control remained to be resolved, as did the thorny question of an eventual political settlement. The Conference issued a communiqué (Document 117) calling for meetings between the two commands at Geneva to study the mechanics of the cease-fire. Progress on Laos and Cambodia, however, remained difficult because of DRV and Chinese insistence on recognition of the "Resistance Governments."

At the beginning of June, General Paul Ely was appointed Commissioner General and Commander-in-Chief in Indochina. On June 4 the long Franco-Vietnamese negotiations, which had begun in March, culminated with the initialing in Paris of the "Treaty of Independence of the State of Viet-Nam" (Document 118) and the "Treaty of Association between France and Viet-Nam" (Document 119).

At a plenary session of the Conference on June 8, Molotov suddenly launched a violent attack on the French Government. The following day there was a major debate on Indochina policy in the French National Assembly, many of whose members apparently felt that the Laniel Government would be unable to bring peace. On June 12 the Government failed to defeat a motion of no-confidence and was forced to resign.

The United States was increasingly unhappy with the proceedings at Geneva, since it was becoming clear that the outcome would be some

[5] The text of Eden's statement is in Great Britain, Parliament, Papers by Command, *Documents Relating to the Discussion of Korea and Indo-China at the Geneva Conference, April 27–June 15, 1954* (London: Her Majesty's Stationery Office, Cmd. 9186, 1954), pp. 126–127.

[6] Extracts from the text of Molotov's statement are in *ibid.*, pp. 127–131.

form of temporary division involving the abandonment of at least part of Viet-Nam to the Communists. On June 8 Secretary Dulles accused the Communists of dragging out the Geneva negotiations and disassociated the United States from the Conference decisions by describing the American role as "that of a friend which gives advice when it is asked for" (Document 120). Dulles elaborated the American position in a June 11 speech, including the conditions under which the United States might intervene in Indochina (Document 121).

On June 18 Pierre Mendès-France was invested as the new French Premier, also assuming the portfolio of Minister of Foreign Affairs. A major point in his program was his promise to obtain an end to the war by July 20 or resign (Document 122). The same day President Eisenhower sent a letter to President Coty of France (Document 123) which reaffirmed American support but which was seen by many as an attempt to force Paris to accede to American wishes on Indochina and the controversial European Defense Community treaty. And, on June 17, Bao Dai accepted the resignation of Prince Buu Loc as Premier of the State of Viet-Nam and appointed Ngo Dinh Diem to form a government.

The investiture of new governments in France and Viet-Nam was accompanied by a major breakthrough at Geneva despite the collapse of the Korean phase of the Conference on June 15. On June 16 Chou En-lai in effect abandoned the Viet Minh claims for separate recognition of the "Resistance Governments" of "Khmer" and "Pathet Lao," clearing the way for talks between the Viet Minh and French high commands for a cessation of hostilities in Laos and Cambodia. The Foreign Ministers then left the Conference while talks between the high commands continued.

During their absence the Foreign Ministers were active in other areas. Eden delivered a report to the House of Commons on June 23 which explained British policy (Document 124). On June 24 Prime Minister Churchill and Eden flew to Washington for talks with President Eisenhower and Secretary of State Dulles. The communiqué issued on June 28 (Document 125) reaffirmed support for France and for eventual formation of a "collective defense" system in Southeast Asia. During talks on June 29 Dulles and Eden agreed on a communication informing the new French Government of the minimum terms for an Indochina settlement which the United States and the United Kingdom felt they could accept (Document 126).

Foreign Minister Chou En-lai visited India, where on June 28 he and Prime Minister Nehru issued a communiqué stressing their friendly relations and including agreement on the "five principles of peaceful coexistence." [7] From July 3 to 5 Chou met with Ho Chi Minh on the border between Viet-Nam and China, presumably to obtain the latter's acquiescence to the settlement taking shape at Geneva. The communiqué issued at the conclusion of the conversations (Document 127) was short and curt, indicating perhaps that there had been disagreement.

During the first week in July France ordered the evacuation of the southwestern part of the Red River delta in Tonkin, including the city of Nam Dinh and the Catholic bishoprics of Phat Diem and Bui Chu. The State of Viet-Nam protested, and a spokesman for the Department of State said that the United States had not been informed of the French move in advance. [8]

On July 12 the Foreign Ministers began to reassemble at Geneva for the final phase of the Indochina talks. On July 8 Secretary of State Dulles had announced that neither he nor Under Secretary Smith would return to Geneva. [9] Eden and Mendès-France agreed to invite Dulles to talk things over. In Paris they convinced Dulles that the United States should keep representation at Geneva on the ministerial level, as was indicated by the communiqué issued on July 14 (Document 128).

Negotiations in Geneva were moving through informal but hard bargaining to a final conclusion. Chou En-lai suggested the compromise on the makeup of the international supervisory commission to include India, Canada, and Poland. Molotov was instrumental in arranging compromise on the 17th parallel as the division line between the two regrouping zones and in bringing agreement on a two-year delay before the holding of general elections in Viet-Nam. Chou En-lai, after a meeting with Mendès-France, also agreed to abandon Viet Minh demands for an autonomous Pathet Lao regime in northern Laos.

The party most unhappy with the negotiations was the State of Viet-Nam, represented by Ngo Dinh Diem's new Foreign Minister, Tran Van Do. His concern was to avoid a partition of Viet-Nam. At a restricted session of the Conference on July 18 he protested both the draft final declaration and the cease-fire agreement itself (Document 129) although the final details of both documents had not yet been determined. The State of Viet-Nam submitted new proposals for a cease-fire "with-

[7] Text in India, Lok Sabha Secretariat, *Foreign Policy of India: Texts of Documents 1947–1959* (2nd ed., New Delhi: 1959), pp. 113–114.

[8] Statement by Henry Suydam, the Department's press officer, quoted in a news story in *The New York Times,* July 2, 1954, p. 2.

[9] Reported in *The New York Times,* July 9, 1954, p. 2.

out partition" on July 19, but they were not considered by the Conference.[10] Under the threat of Mendès-France's July 20 deadline, the Great Powers were more concerned with bringing an end to hostilities than with insuring that the settlement was acceptable to the State of Viet-Nam.

112. *Secretary of State Dulles: Statement on the Geneva Conference* [Extracts] *
   May 7, 1954

[Two introductory paragraphs are omitted.]

This week I returned from the Geneva Conference. My return was not connected with any developments at the Conference. As long ago as last February when the Conference was called, I said I would attend only the opening sessions, and then have my place taken by the Under Secretary of State, General Bedell Smith. He is highly qualified to head our delegation at Geneva.

[The section on Korea and 6 paragraphs on the importance of Indochina and the history of the struggle there are omitted.]

I recall in December 1952 when General Eisenhower, as President-elect, was returning from his Korean trip on the cruiser *Helena,* we discussed gravely the problem of Indochina.

We realized that if Viet-Nam fell into hostile hands, and if the neighboring countries remained weak and divided, then the Communists could move on into all of Southeast Asia. For these reasons, the Eisenhower administration from the outset gave particular attention to the problem of Southeast Asia.

Our efforts took two complementary lines. We sought to strengthen the resistance to communism in Indochina. We sought also to build in Southeast Asia a broader community of defense.

---

* *Source:* United States, Department of State, *American Foreign Policy 1950–1955: Basic Documents* (2 vols., Washington: Government Printing Office, 1957), Vol. II, pp. 2383, 2386–2390.

10 See the Communiqué issued by the Delegation of the State of Viet-Nam to the Conference on July 18, and the proposals of July 19, in State of Viet-Nam, High Commission in Paris, *Vietnam,* No. 80 (August 1, 1954), pp. 4–5 [in French].

INDOCHINA MEASURES

In Indochina itself, the following steps seemed to us important:

1. The French should give greater reality to their intention to grant full independence to Viet-Nam, Laos, and Cambodia. This would take away from the Communists their false claim to be leading the fight for independence.

2. There should be greater reliance upon the national armies who would be fighting in their own homeland. This, we believed, could be done if the peoples felt that they had a good cause for which to fight and if better facilities for training and equipment were provided for them.

3. There should be greater free-world assistance. France was carrying on a struggle which was overburdening her economic resources.

[Twelve paragraphs are omitted. They deal with progress in achieving the steps listed above, the Berlin Conference, the battle of Dien Bien Phu, Chinese Communist assistance to the Viet Minh, and the background to collective defense efforts in Southeast Asia.]

On March 29, 1954, after consultations with Congressional leaders of both parties, and after having advised our principal allies, I stated: "The imposition on Southeast Asia of the political system of Communist Russia and its Chinese Communist ally, by whatever means, would be a grave threat to the whole free community. The United States feels that that possibility should not be passively accepted but should be met by united action." [1]

This declaration was nothing new, although the circumstances of the moment gave the words a new significance.

President Eisenhower speaking almost a year earlier, in his address of April 16, 1953, had said that "aggression in Korea and in Southeast Asia are threats to the whole free community to be met by united action." [2]

After having explained our purposes to the American people, we promptly conferred with the representatives of nine free nations having immediate interest in the area, namely, Viet-Nam, Laos, Cambodia, Thailand, the Philippines, Australia and New Zealand, France, and the

[1] Document 103.

[2] "The Chance for Peace," Address before the American Society of Newspaper Editors, Washington, in United States, Department of State, *American Foreign Policy 1950–1955: Basic Documents* (2 vols., Washington: Government Printing Office, 1957), Vol. I, pp. 65–71.

United Kingdom. We informed others whose interests could be affected.

The Governments of the United Kingdom and of France asked me to visit their capitals to develop further our concept. After conferences at London on April 12 and 13 with Sir Winston Churchill and Mr. Eden, we issued a joint U.S.–U.K. communiqué [3] which, after reciting the danger to the entire area of Southeast Asia and the Western Pacific caused by Communist warfare in Indochina, concluded: "Accordingly we are ready to take part, with the other countries principally concerned, in an examination of the possibility of establishing a collective defense, within the framework of the Charter of the United Nations, to assure the peace, security and freedom of Southeast Asia and the Western Pacific."

A similar agreement was reached in Paris with Prime Minister Laniel and Foreign Minister Bidault.[4]

The progress thus made was that which the United States had sought. We had never sought any sudden spectacular act such as an ultimatum to Red China. Our goal was to develop a basic unity of constructive purpose. We advanced toward that goal. I feel confident that unity of purpose persists, and that such a tragic event as the fall of Dien-Bien-Phu will harden, not weaken, our purpose to stay united.

The United States and other countries immediately concerned are giving careful consideration to the establishment of a collective defense. Conversations are taking place among them. We must agree as to who will take part in the united defense effort, and what their commitments will be.

It must be recognized that difficulties have been encountered, but this was expected. The complexity of the problem is great. As I have pointed out, the complications were such that it was not possible even to get started until recent months. Under all the circumstances, I believe that good progress is being made. I feel confident that the outcome will be such that Communist aggression will not be able to gain in Southeast Asia the results it seeks.

This may involve serious commitments by us all. But free peoples will never remain free unless they are willing to fight for their vital interests. Furthermore, vital interests can no longer be protected merely by local defense. The key to successful defense and to the deterring of attack is association for mutual defense. That is what the United States seeks in Southeast Asia.

[3] Document 105.   [4] Document 106.

CURRENT HOSTILITIES IN VIET-NAM

The question remains as to what we should do about the current hostilities in Viet-Nam.

In Korea we showed that we were prepared under proper conditions to resort to military action, if necessary, to protect our vital interests and the principles upon which stable peace must rest.

In Korea, we, along with others, joined in the defense of an independent government, which was already resisting an armed assault. We did so at the request of the Republic of Korea and under a United Nations mandate. The Korean people were inspired by a deep sense of patriotism and eager to develop a power of their own. The issues were clarified before the world by decisions of the United Nations. Under these circumstances, we and our allies fought until the enemy sued for an armistice.

In Indochina, the situation is far more complex. The present conditions there do not provide a suitable basis for the United States to participate with its armed forces.

The situation may perhaps be clarified as a result of the Geneva Conference. The French have stated their desire for an armistice on honorable terms and under proper safeguards.[5] If they can conclude a settlement on terms which do not endanger the freedom of the peoples of Viet-Nam, this would be a real contribution to the cause of peace in Southeast Asia. But we would be gravely concerned if an armistice or cease-fire were reached at Geneva which would provide a road to a Communist takeover and further aggression. If this occurs, or if hostilities continue, then the need will be even more urgent to create the conditions for united action in defense of the area.

In making commitments which might involve the use of armed force, the Congress is a full partner. Only the Congress can declare war. President Eisenhower has repeatedly emphasized that he would not take military action in Indochina without the support of Congress.[6] Furthermore, he has made clear that he would not seek that unless, in his opinion, there would be an adequate collective effort based on genuine mutuality of purpose in defending vital interests.

[The concluding 8 paragraphs, defending collective defense and emphasizing the anticolonial policy of the United States, are omitted.]

[5] See Documents 92 and 97.   [6] See Document 101.

113. *French Proposals for a Settlement in Indochina: Statement by Foreign Minister Bidault at the First Plenary Session on Indochina [Extracts]* *
May 8, 1954

[Introductory comments are omitted.]

The outcome of the battle of Dien Bien Phu was announced yesterday by the Commander-in-Chief in these words, to which there is nothing to add: "The garrison of Dien Bien Phu fulfilled the mission which had been assigned to it by the command."

The French Delegation cannot conceal here its deep emotion and its pride in the face of the heroism of the fighting men of France, of Viet-Nam, of the whole French Union who resisted beyond human endurance. Such events dictate imperatively its course in the negotiations which are opening; these negotiations are conditioned by two terms of equal firmness: to assure the re-establishment in Indochina of a just and durable peace, and, by accompanying that peace with the necessary guarantees, to prevent whatever possibility there may be of a new threat.

[Fifteen paragraphs, dealing with the background of the war, its conduct, and French actions to grant independence to the Indochinese states and to seek a peaceful solution to the conflict, are omitted.]

The French Government therefore is aware of having neglected nothing in order to put an end to the conflict. Not only has it removed all reason for its existence by recognizing fully and without reservations the independence of Viet-Nam, Laos, and Cambodia; but it also has shown for a long time its disposition and its desire to achieve a reasonable settlement permitting the end of hostilities. Such is, it must be

* *Source:* France, Ministère des Affaires Etrangères, *Conférence de Genève sur l'Indochine (8 Mai–21 Juillet 1954): Procès-verbaux des Séances—Propositions —Documents Finaux* (Paris: Imprimerie Nationale, 1955), pp. 14, 17–19, 395. Translation by the editor. The complete text of Bidault's speech is on pp. 14–19; the text of the proposals was printed separately as an appendix, on p. 395. A complete English translation of the speech and proposals appears in Great Britain, Parliament, Papers by Command, *Documents Relating to the Discussion of Korea and Indo-China at the Geneva Conference, April 27–June 15, 1954* (London: Her Majesty's Stationery Office, Cmd. 9186, 1954), pp. 107–111. The translation is, however, of inferior quality and contains numerous errors.

added, the prime task which has been fixed for this Geneva Conference. As for the political problems, the Governments of the three States competent in this regard [7] will have to say how they envisage they may be resolved, where they arise, once the war ends.

In order to get out of the present war situation, the French delegation, sure of responding to the deep feelings of populations cruelly tried and of all the peace-loving countries, believes it necessary to suggest the following method which appears to it the most appropriate for rapidly arriving at the desired agreement.

We propose that the Conference declare first of all that it adopts the principle of a general cessation of hostilities in Indochina, based on the essential guarantees of security, these terms of principle thus enunciated being inseparable in our mind and our resolution. The necessary guarantees are intended to preserve the security of the forces of the parties involved and to protect the civilian populations from an abusive exploitation of the cessation of hostilities. The arrangements for application are to be established once the principle is adopted.

We can see immediately that the situation does not present itself in the same way for the interested States and it would be wise to take these differences into account.

In two of these States, Laos and Cambodia, the problem is clear. There it is not at all a question of civil war but an invasion, without motive or declaration of war, an invasion which, in addition, menaces neighboring nations. The solution consists, therefore, of agreeing on the withdrawal of the invaders and the re-establishment of the integrity of the territory.

So that the execution of this agreement may be uncontested, and so that its implementation may be carried on without obstacle, a system of international control is essential. On such bases, the Conference can, in a very short time, assure the re-establishment of peace in Laos and Cambodia in conditions conforming with fairness.

In Viet-Nam, the situation has a different and more complex character. In reality we find ourselves faced with a civil war. For France, there exists a Vietnamese State whose unity, territorial integrity, and independence must be respected. If the presence at this Conference of a party—who, in order to fight against this State, has organized armed forces—has been admitted as a necessity for an agreement on the cessation of hostilities, this presence should not be interpreted as implying

[7] I.e., the Associated States of Viet-Nam, Cambodia, and Laos.

a recognition of any kind whatsoever on our part. The situation thus defined compels the provision of a transitory phase in the course of which, hostilities having ceased, the political problems may progressively be resolved. The elements of this solution depend above all, in our eyes, on the opinion which will be expressed by the Government of Viet-Nam. I confine myself here to indicating that the most just solution of the political problem may be found and definitively assured only when the population is in a position to make known in complete independence its sovereign will by the means of free elections. I reiterate, the problem which is before us is that of the cessation of hostilities and its guarantees. These guarantees, in our opinion, should be of two kinds: on the one hand, while the other forces may be disarmed, the regular units of the two parties will be regrouped in clearly defined regrouping zones; on the other hand, the execution of the agreement should be placed under the control of international commissions. As early as last March 5, the head of the French Government had, indeed, made known his views regarding the means of implementing such a decision.[8] These points, and many others as well, will, of course, rest with us to specify. The essential thing is to know if these principles are recognized by all the participants as those which must govern the settlement which the Geneva Conference has the mission to establish. It is desirable and clearly natural that the agreement which we have the mission to reach here, as much for the solution in Laos and Cambodia as for that which will concern Viet-Nam, be guaranteed in appropriate terms by the States participating in this Conference.

Such is, in its general lines, the method which the delegation of the French Government proposes. It was conceived with the hope of arriving at a settlement which will be sure to last. The experience of the past teaches us that without solid guarantees agreements of this kind are fundamentally fragile. Instead of consolidating peace, they represent only brief interludes or ill-respected truces. In the case with which we are concerned, the consequences of a rupture would be unforeseeable; we do not have the right to run such a risk.

I have thus just defined the conception which the French Government has developed for the cessation of hostilities. Its imperative duty of attending to the security of the forces which are in Indochina under French command will remain always in our mind during the negotiation. But the French delegation will be equally guided, with the neces-

[8] See Note 6, p. 219.

sary attention to all legitimate interests, by the desire to put an end as rapidly as possible to the sufferings and the sacrifices, and to stop a conflict whose length and expansion are a danger for the peace of the world.

It is in this spirit that the French delegation has the honor to place before the Conference proposals inspired by the considerations which I have just stated.

FRENCH PROPOSAL

I. Viet-Nam

1. Regroupment of regular units in regrouping zones to be determined by the Conference on proposal of the High Commands.

2. Disarmament of elements which belong neither to the army nor to the police forces.

3. Immediate liberation of prisoners of war and civil internees.

4. Control of the execution of these clauses by international commissions.

5. Cessation of hostilities upon signature of the agreement.

The regroupment of forces and the disarmaments provided above will commence no later than X days after the signing of the agreement.

II. Cambodia and Laos

1. Evacuation of all regular and irregular Viet Minh forces which have invaded the country.

2. Disarmament of all elements which belong neither to the army nor to the police forces.

3. Immediate liberation of prisoners of war and civil internees.

4. Control of the execution of these clauses by international commissions.

III.

The guarantee of the agreements is assured by the member States of the Geneva Conference. Any violation will entail an immediate consultation between these States in order to take the appropriate measures individually or collectively.

114. *Proposals by the Democratic Republic of Viet-Nam for a Settlement in Indochina: Statement by Foreign Minister Pham Van Dong at the Second Plenary Session [Extract]* *

May 10, 1954

[A long introductory statement, in which Pham Van Dong summarized the history of the DRV and the Indochina War, and excoriated France and the United States, is omitted.]

In conformity with the foregoing, the Delegation of the Democratic Republic of Viet-Nam presents to the Conference proposals for the reestablishment of peace in Indochina:

PROPOSALS OF THE VIET MINH DELEGATION

1. Recognition by France of the sovereignty and independence of Viet-Nam over the whole of the territory of Viet-Nam, as well as the sovereignty and independence of Khmer and of Pathet Lao.[9]

2. Conclusion of an agreement on the withdrawal of all foreign troops from the territories of Viet-Nam, Khmer, and Pathet Lao within a time period which must be fixed by concert among the belligerent parties. Before the withdrawal of troops, it is necessary to agree on the

---

* *Source:* France, Ministère des Affaires Etrangères, *Conférence de Genève sur l'Indochine (8 Mai–21 Juillet 1954): Procès verbaux des Séances—Propositions—Documents Finaux* (Paris: Imprimerie Nationale, 1955), pp. 46–47, 397–398. Translation by the editor. The complete text of Pham Van Dong's speech is on pp. 32–48; the text of the proposals was printed separately as an appendix, on pp. 397–398. An English translation of the proposals and Pham Van Dong's concluding remarks appears in Great Britain, Parliament, Papers by Command, *Documents Relating to the Discussion of Korea and Indo-China at the Geneva Conference, April 27–June 15, 1954* (London: Her Majesty's Stationery Office, Cmd. 9186, 1954), pp. 118–121. The translation is, however, of inferior quality and contains numerous errors. A complete English text of the speech appears in *New Times* (Moscow), (May 15, 1954), Supplement, pp. 2–13; *New Times* printed complete English translations of the speeches by Communist delegates in the plenary sessions throughout the Conference. For United States reaction to the DRV and French proposals, see Secretary of State Dulles' news conference statement of May 11, in United States, Department of State, *Bulletin,* XXX (May 24, 1954), pp. 781–782.

9 "Khmer" and "Pathet Lao" were the names applied to Cambodia and Laos by Viet Minh propaganda organs. The purpose of the terminology was to emphasize the status of the "Resistance Governments" formed under Viet Minh auspices in opposition to the French-supported Royalist regimes. The terminology was adopted by the Soviet Union and China in their propaganda coverage of the struggle in Indochina, most of which was taken directly from Viet Minh sources. Both terms were abandoned as descriptions of political entities after the Geneva Conference.

subject of stationing French troops in Viet-Nam, with particular attention to limiting the number of their stationing points as much as possible. It is clearly understood that the French troops are to refrain from interfering in the affairs of the local administration in the areas of their stationing.

3. Organization of free, general elections in Viet-Nam, in Khmer and Pathet Lao in order to form a single Government in each country. Convening of consultative conferences composed of representatives of the Governments of the two parties respectively in Viet-Nam, in Khmer and in Pathet Lao in order to prepare and organize the free general elections. These consultative conferences will take all measures to guarantee the free activity of patriotic parties, groups, and social organizations. No foreign intervention will be allowed. Local commissions will be formed to control the preparation and the organization of elections.

Pending the formation of single governments in each of the Indochinese countries and after an agreement is reached conforming to the agreement on the cessation of hostilities, the Governments of the two parties will administer respectively the regions which are under their control.

4. Declaration by the delegation of the Democratic Republic of Viet-Nam of the intention of the Government of the Democratic Republic of Viet-Nam to examine the question relative to the association of the Democratic Republic of Viet-Nam to the French Union, on the basis of free will, as well as the conditions of such an association. Similar declarations will be made respectively by the Governments of Khmer and of Pathet Lao.

5. Recognition by the Democratic Republic of Viet-Nam as well as by Pathet Lao and Khmer of the fact that France has economic and cultural interests in these States.

After the formation of single Governments in Viet-Nam, in Khmer, and in Pathet Lao, the economic and cultural relations of these States with France should be resolved in conformity with the principles of equality and of reciprocal interests. Pending the formation of single Governments in the three States, the economic and cultural relations between Indochina and France will remain provisionally, without modification, as they presently exist. However, in the regions where communications and commercial exchanges are disrupted, these communications and commercial exchanges may be re-established by mutual agreement between the two parties.

The nationals of each party will enjoy a privileged status, to be determined subsequently, with regard to domicile, movement, and economic activity on the territory of the other party.

6. Pledge by the belligerent parties to refrain from all prosecution of those persons who have collaborated with the opposite party during the war.

7. Exchange of prisoners of war.

8. The implementation of the measures indicated in paragraphs 1 to 7 must be preceded by the cessation of hostilities in Indochina and by the conclusion for that purpose of agreements between France and each of the three countries respectively. Each of these agreements must provide:

a. A complete and simultaneous cease-fire over all the territory of Indochina by all the armed forces—land, sea, and air—of the belligerent parties. In order to consolidate the armistice in each of the three countries of Indochina, the two parties in each case will proceed to a readjustment of the zones which they occupy; in order to assure the aforesaid readjustment, it is equally provided that neither of the two parties will pose an obstacle to the passage across its own territory of the troops of the other party in order to rejoin the zone occupied by the latter;

b. The complete cessation of all introduction into Indochina of new military units, of ground, sea, and air personnel, of all kinds of arms and munitions;

c. The establishment of a control to assure the execution of the provisions of the agreement on the cessation of hostilities, and the formation to that end of mixed commissions composed of representatives of the belligerent parties in each of the three countries.

The delegation of the Democratic Republic of Viet-Nam is convinced that its proposals will be supported by the Resistance Governments and the peoples of Khmer and of Pathet Lao.

It is common knowledge that in order to re-establish peace in Indochina, it is necessary to put an end to the provision by the United States of arms and munitions to Indochina, to recall the American missions, advisors, and military instructors, and to cease all intervention by the United States, in whatever form, in the affairs of Indochina.

In the proposals of the delegation of the Democratic Republic of Viet-Nam, there is the question of the establishment of economic and cultural relations between France and the Democratic Republic of

Viet-Nam. That means that the Democratic Republic of Viet-Nam is ready to establish close economic relations with France, to develop commercial exchanges with France, to utilize the French merchant marine as needed, and to maintain under certain conditions French cultural institutions in Viet-Nam.

Our above-mentioned proposals seek a triple aim:

1. To end the war, to re-establish peace;

2. To assure the re-establishment of peace on the basis of the recognition of the national rights of the peoples of Indochina;

3. To establish friendly relations between the countries of Indochina and France.

It is appropriate to emphasize that the fundamental point of this proposal is the settlement of the question of the re-establishment of peace on the basis of the recognition of the national rights of the peoples of Viet-Nam, Khmer, and Pathet Lao.

The solution of this fundamental question at the same time as the solution of the question of the relations between the peoples of Indochina and France will assure the establishment of a stable and durable peace according to justice and honor.

One other point which it is necessary to emphasize is that our proposal aims at the re-establishment of peace throughout Indochina. The experience of history shows that war as well as peace are indivisible on the whole of the Indochinese territory. From this it follows that the cessation of hostilities and the re-establishment of peace in Indochina must be accomplished simultaneously in the three countries—Viet-Nam, Khmer, and Lao—according to common principles, methods, and procedures, while fully respecting the principle of national sovereignty and the particular conditions of each country. Thus, the settlement of all the questions relative to the re-establishment of peace in Indochina requires the participation of all the interested parties without exception.

[The concluding thirteen paragraphs, including comments on the French proposals of May 8 (Document 113), are omitted. Pham Van Dong observed that "Because this (French) proposal does not take facts into account, including the military facts in the countries of Indochina, it cannot furnish a serious basis for a satisfactory solution to the problem of the cessation of hostilities and of the re-establishment of peace in Indochina as a whole. . . ."]

115. *Proposals by the State of Viet-Nam for a Settlement in Viet-Nam: Submitted at the Third Plenary Session* *
May 12, 1954

The Berlin Conference recommended the re-establishment of peace in Indochina. This re-establishment implies:
—a military settlement, to put an end to hostilities, and
—a political settlement, to establish peace on real and lasting foundations.

A. MILITARY SETTLEMENT

1. The delegation of the State of Viet-Nam declares itself ready to examine any working document submitted to the Conference for this purpose.
These documents must present a serious, positive effort, capable of leading in good faith to a satisfactory military settlement.
2. They must include sufficient guarantees to assure a real and lasting peace, preventing any possibility of new aggression.
3. They must not lead to a direct or indirect partition, final or provisional, in fact or in law, of the national territory.
4. They must provide for an international control of the execution of the conditions of the cessation of hostilities.

B. POLITICAL SETTLEMENT

With regard to the relations between the State of Viet-Nam and France:
These relations will be settled on the basis of the Joint Franco-Vietnamese Declaration of April 28, 1954,[10] which provides for the signature of two fundamental treaties: the first of these treaties recognizes the total independence of the State of Viet-Nam and its full and complete sovereignty; the second establishes a Franco-Vietnamese association in the French Union based on equality.[11]

* *Source:* France, Ministère des Affaires Etrangères, *Conférence de Genève sur l'Indochine (8 Mai–21 Juillet 1954): Procès-verbaux des Séances—Propositions—Documents Finaux* (Paris: Imprimerie Nationale, 1955), pp. 400–401. Translation by the editor. M. Nguyen Quoc Dinh's speech introducing the proposals is in *ibid.*, pp. 59–64.

[10] Document 110.

[11] Documents 118 and 119 respectively. Their texts were first made public when M. Nguyen Quoc Dinh, the Foreign Minister of the State of Viet-Nam, read them during his speech presenting the proposals printed here.

With regard to the internal political settlement in Viet-Nam:

1. By reason of the territorial and political unity of Viet-Nam, recognition of the principle that the only State legally qualified to represent Viet-Nam is the State embodied by His Majesty Bao Dai, Chief of State. This State alone is invested with the powers deriving from the internal and external sovereignty of Viet-Nam.

2. Recognition of the principle of a single army for the whole territory. This army is the national army placed under the control and the responsibility of the State of Viet-Nam.

Settlement of the status of the Viet Minh soldiers within the framework of the legal army of the State of Viet-Nam, in conformity with the principle referred to above and in accordance with methods to be determined.

International control of the implementation of the aforesaid settlement.

3. Within the framework and under the jurisdiction of the State of Viet-Nam, free elections throughout the territory as soon as the Security Council [12] verifies that the authority of the State is established over the whole territory and that the conditions of liberty are fulfilled. To assure the freedom and the honesty of these elections, international control functioning under the auspices of the United Nations.

4. Representative government formed under the aegis of His Majesty Bao Dai, Chief of State of Viet-Nam, after the elections and in accordance with their results.

5. Pledge by the State of Viet-Nam to refrain from all prosecution of those persons having collaborated with the Viet Minh during the hostilities.

6. International guarantee of the political and territorial integrity of the State of Viet-Nam.

7. Assistance by the friendly nations in order to develop the national wealth and to raise the standard of living of the country.

[12] Of the United Nations.

116. *Foreign Minister Pham Van Dong: Statement on the Regroupment of Armed Forces, Made at the Tenth (Restricted) Session [Extract]* *
May 25, 1954

[The first part of M. Dong's statement, dealing with the necessity for a complete, simultaneous, and quick cessation of hostilities throughout Indochina, is omitted. It included a demand for "the guarantees provided by international law" for "our air space and our territorial waters."]

The central question on this point is that of the readjustment of zones, of which mention was made in our proposal set forth to the Conference at the session of May 10, in point 8 *a*.[13]

Here is our point of view on this question.

I. Principles according to which the readjustment should be made.

This readjustment takes place within the framework of each State— Vietnamese, Khmer and Pathet Lao—for each theater of operations of whatever extent.

It is done on the basis of an exchange of territories, taking account of the following elements—area, population, political interests, and economic interests—in such a way that it gives to each party a zone all in one block, relatively extensive, offering facilities for economic activity and administrative control in each zone respectively. The line of demarcation of these zones must, as much as possible, follow geographical features or other landmarks easy to recognize on the ground, and its course must avoid as much as possible the creation of difficulties for transportation and communication within the respective zones.

M. Bidault has spoken of a demilitarized zone. This is an idea which invites us to concern ourselves with the real situation in the theater of war in order to try to produce a solution.

[The balance of Pham Van Dong's statement, dealing with the mechanics of the transfer of the armed forces and the civil administration of territories transferred, is omitted. He also proposed a conference of the high commands on the spot to study the specifics of the cease-fire.]

* *Source:* France, Ministère des Affaires Etrangères, *Conférence de Genève sur l'Indochine (8 Mai–21 Juillet 1954): Procès-verbaux des Séances—Propositions—Documents Finaux* (Paris: Imprimerie Nationale, 1955), p. 146. The complete statement is on pp. 145–147. Translation by the editor. Pham Van Dong's statement is considered by most authorities as reflecting DRV acceptance of a partition solution in Viet-Nam by its implication of two regrouping zones in each state rather than several zones as had been proposed theretofore.

[13] Document 114.

117. *Communiqué Issued by the Geneva Conference* *
May 29, 1954

In order to facilitate the early and simultaneous cessation of hostilities it is proposed that:

(*a*) Represenatives of the two commands [14] should meet immediately in Geneva and contacts should also be established on the spot.

(*b*) They should study the dispositions of forces to be made upon the cessation of hostilities, beginning with the question of regrouping areas in Viet Nam.

(*c*) They should report their findings and recommendations to the Conference as soon as possible.

118. *Treaty of Independence of the State of Viet-Nam* †
June 4, 1954

Article 1

France recognizes Vietnam as a fully independent and sovereign State invested with the jurisdiction recognized by internationl law.

Article 2

Vietnam shall take over from France all the rights and obligations resulting from international treaties or conventions contracted by

* *Source:* Great Britain, Parliament, Papers by Command, *Documents Relating to the Discussion of Korea and Indo-China at the Geneva Conference, April 27–June 15, 1954* (London: Her Majesty's Stationery Office, Cmd. 9186, 1954), pp. 136–137. The communiqué was submitted in draft by Foreign Secretary Eden and adopted by the Conference at its Twelfth Session (Restricted) on May 29. For the discussion, see France, Ministère des Affaires Etrangères, *Conférence de Genève sur l'Indochine (8 Mai–21 Juillet 1954): Procès-verbaux des Séances—Propositions—Documents Finaux* (Paris: Imprimerie Nationale, 1955), pp. 159–167.

† *Source:* France, Direction de la Documentation, *Articles et Documents,* No. 067 (June 15, 1954), "Textes du Jour," p. 1. Translation by the editor. The Treaty was only initialed, not signed, and was never ratified by either France or the State of Viet-Nam.

[14] The French and Viet Minh commands. The talks called for by this communiqué applied only to Viet-Nam. A similar communiqué was issued on June 19, 1954, for discussions between the High Commands for a cessation of hostilities in Cambodia and Laos: text in State of Viet-Nam, High Commission in Paris, *Vietnam,* No. 78 (July 1, 1954), p. 13 [in French].

France on behalf or in the name of the State of Vietnam or all other treaties and conventions concluded by France in the name of French Indochina, insofar as these affect Vietnam.

Article 3

France undertakes to transfer to the Vietnamese Government all jurisdictions and public services still held by her on Vietnamese territory.

Article 4

The present treaty, which shall come into force on the date of its signature, abrogates all earlier and contrary acts and dispositions. The instruments of ratification of the present treaty shall be exchanged immediately following approval by the qualified institutions of France and Vietnam.

Done at Paris, June 4, 1954

JOSEPH LANIEL   BUU LOC

119. *Treaty of Association between France and Viet-Nam* *
June 4, 1954

France and Vietnam,

Resolved to maintain in friendship and confidence the ties which unite them, and affirming their common will to develop their co-operation for the good of their respective peoples,

Have agreed on the following:

Article 1

Vietnam and France affirm their will to associate freely within the French Union, and decide by mutual agreement to proceed to the establishment of conventions, which shall be annexed to the present treaty and which alone shall henceforth fix all conditions for the organization and functioning of this association.

---

* *Source:* France, Direction de la Documentation, *Articles et Documents,* No. 067 (June 15, 1954), "Textes du Jour," p. 2. Translation by the editor. The Treaty was only initialed, not signed, and was never ratified by either France or the State of Viet-Nam.

Article 2

The President of the French Republic, who is President of the Union, incarnates in this title and position the idea of a lasting and friendly association between France and Vietnam, sovereign States, equal in rights and duties.

Article 3

France and Vietnam undertake to develop their free cooperation in the High Council, under the chairmanship of the President of the Union.

They shall therein jointly assure, with respect for the principle of the soverign equality of States, the coordination of their efforts and the harmonization of their respective policies in matters of common interest.

Article 4

Sessions of the High Council shall be held twice a year and, in addition, at any time the member States shall deem it necessary.

The agenda of each session shall be drawn up by mutual agreement.

The resolutions of the Governments attending the sessions of the High Council shall be passed by mutual agreement. Their coming into force shall be assured, in each State, by the interested Government in conformity with its national procedure.

Article 5

The High Council shall have a permanent general Secretariat whose rules of procedure shall be laid down by mutual agreement at the first session to be held after the present treaty has gone into effect. These rules shall take into account the interstate character of the general Secretariat.

Article 6

Legal disputes arising from the application or interpretation of the present treaty and of the conventions to be annexed to it shall be taken before a Court of Arbitration composed of an equal number of French and Vietnamese arbitrators.

This Court shall rule by majority decision. In case of equal votes, the Court shall be enlarged by the admission of foreign arbitrators.

The rules relative to the composition, functioning and procedure of the Court shall be fixed by mutual agreement between the two High Contracting Parties in a convention annexed to this treaty.

Article 7

The present treaty, which shall come into force on the date of its signature, abrogates all earlier contrary acts and dispositions. The instruments of ratification of the present treaty shall be exchanged as soon as it is approved by the qualified institutions of France and Viet-nam.

Done at Paris, June 4, 1954

Joseph Laniel   Buu Loc

120. *Secretary of State Dulles: Statements at a News Conference [Extracts]* June 8, 1954*

[A question and answer on the Korean Phase of the Geneva Conference are omitted.]

In reply to a question of his assessment of the Geneva talks concerning Indochina to date, Mr. Dulles said:

The primary responsibility in those negotiations is being carried, of course, by the French delegation in association with the delegations of the three Associated States of Indochina, Viet-Nam, Laos, and Cambodia.

The United States is playing primarily the role of a friend which gives advice when it is asked for, and of course we have a very deep hope that the result will be one which will maintain the genuine independence of the entire area and bring about a cessation of the fighting.

Whether that result is obtainable or not is of course problematic. It seems that the Communist forces in Indochina are intensifying their activities. They have done so ever since the proposal for peace in Indochina, which was taken at the Berlin Conference. There has been, I think, a deliberate dragging out of the negotiations at Geneva while the Communist military effort has been stepped up in Indochina itself. The fact that under these circumstances the Communists are dragging their feet on peace and intensifying their efforts for war is a commentary upon the general attitude of the Communists and gives a lie, I think, to their greatly professed love for peace.

* *Source:* United States, Department of State, *Bulletin*, XXX (June 21, 1954), pp. 947–948.

[A question and answer in which Secretary Dulles reaffirmed the practicability of "united action" as a response to Communist activity at Geneva and in Indochina is omitted.]

Asked whether the alternative, should the plan for united action not become practical, might imply the United States' dealing with this situation singlehandedly or unilaterally, Mr. Dulles replied:

No. The United States has no intention of dealing with the Indochina situation unilaterally, certainly not unless the whole nature of the aggression should change.

"What change?" Mr. Dulles was asked. He replied:

Well, if there should be a resumption by Communist China of open armed aggression in that area or in any other area of the Far East that might create a new situation.

Asked how long he felt the United States and other free nations should continue to sit at Geneva in a sincere effort to negotiate while the Communists dragged their feet at Geneva and intensified the war in Indochina, Mr. Dulles said:

As I pointed out earlier, the primary responsibility in that respect has to be assumed by the countries that are carrying the principal burden of the fighting in the area, which on our side are France and Viet-Nam. They are recognized by us as having a primacy in this matter. It would be their decision in this respect which would be controlling. I would not want to attempt to establish what I thought should be their policy in this matter.

Mr. Dulles was asked what the objectives of united action would be —would it mean intervention, the holding of a special line in Indochina, or some other objective? The Secretary replied:

It would obviously have an objective. The objective would be to retain in friendly hands as much as possible of the Southeast Asian peninsular and island area. Now the practicability varies from time to time. What was practical a year ago is less practical today. The situation has, I am afraid, been deteriorating.

[Questions and answers on progress of the "united action" idea, military staff talks with Asian and Western countries, and possible Congressional action are omitted.]

121. *Secretary of State Dulles: Address before the Los Angeles World Affairs Council [Extract]* *
June 11, 1954

[Sections on general Pacific policy and Japan, and introductory comments on Indochina are omitted.]

But last winter the fighting was intensified and the long strain began to tell in terms of the attitude of the French people toward a war then in its eighth year. Last March, after the siege of Dien-Bien-Phu had begun, I renewed President Eisenhower's proposal that we seek conditions which would permit a united defense for the area.[15] I went to Europe on this mission, and it seemed that there was agreement on our proposal. But when we moved to translate that proposal into reality, some of the parties held back because they had concluded that any steps to create a united defense should await the results of the Geneva Conference.

Meanwhile, the burdens of a collective defense in Indochina have mounted. The Communists have practiced dilatory negotiating at Geneva, while intensifying their fighting in Indochina. The French and national forces feel the strain of mounting enemy power on their front and of political uncertainty at their rear. I told the Senate Foreign Relations Committee last week that the situation is grave but by no means hopeless.[16] The future depends largely on decisions awaited at Paris, London, and Geneva.

The situation in Indochina is not that of open military aggression by the Chinese Communist regime. Thus, in Indochina, the problem is one of restoring tranquillity in an area where disturbances are fomented from Communist China, but where there is no open invasion by Communist China. This task of pacification, in our opinion, cannot be successfully met merely by unilateral armed intervention. Some other conditions need to be established. Throughout these Indochina developments, the United States has held to a stable and consistent course and has made clear the conditions which, in its opinion, might justify intervention. These conditions were and are (1) an invitation from the

* *Source:* United States, Department of State, *Bulletin*, XXX (June 28, 1954), pp. 972–973.

[15] Document 103.

[16] Text in United States, Department of State, *Bulletin*, XXX (June 14, 1954), p. 921.

present lawful authorities; (2) clear assurance of complete independence to Laos, Cambodia, and Viet-Nam; (3) evidence of concern by
the United Nations; (4) a joining in the collective effort of some of the
other nations of the area; and (5) assurance that France will not itself
withdraw from the battle until it is won.[17]

Only if these conditions were realized could the President and the
Congress be justified in asking the American people to make the
sacrifices incident to committing our Nation, with others, to using
force to help restore peace in the area.

Another problem might, however, arise. If the Chinese Communist
regime were to show in Indochina or elsewhere that it is determined
to pursue the path of overt military aggression, then the situation would
be different and another issue would emerge. That contingency has
already been referred to publicly by the President and myself. The
President, in his April 16, 1953, address,[18] and I myself, in an address
of September 2, 1953,[19] made clear that the United States would take
a grave view of any future overt military Chinese Communist aggression in relation to the Pacific or Southeast Asia area. Such an
aggression would threaten island and peninsular positions which secure
the United States and its allies.

If such overt military aggression occurred, that would be a deliberate threat to the United States itself. The United States would of
course invoke the processes of the United Nations and consult with
its allies. But we could not escape ultimate responsibility for decisions
closely touching our own security and self-defense.

[The concluding 4 paragraphs, emphasizing the American desire for peace,
are omitted.]

---

[17] United States conditions under which military intervention in Indochina
could be "contemplated" should the Geneva Conference fail were communicated
to France on May 15, 1954, in response to a French request of May 13.
Texts of the relevant correspondence remain classified and unavailable to the
editor. See Philippe Devillers and Jean Lacouture, *End of a War: Indochina,
1954,* Alexander Lieven and Adam Roberts, trans. (New York: Frederick A.
Praeger, 1969), pp. 192–195.

[18] See Note 2, p. 254.   [19] Document 88.

122. *Premier Pierre Mendès-France: Policy Statement before the French National Assembly [Extract]* *
June 17, 1954

I come before you, entrusted by the President of the Republic with the same mission as a year ago, almost to the day.[20]

At that time I proposed a policy of recovery and national renovation, and I told you that this policy constituted a single unit of which you could not accept a part and reject the rest without making the entire program ineffective. Three hundred and one among you approved the program as a whole, but 205 abstained, thus indicating, I think, that although they agreed with me on a great many points, they could not, however, give me their wholehearted support on others.

If I did not get their votes, it was not because of the strictness of my economic program, which set great goals for the nation to attain without concealing the difficulties that stood in their way; it was not because they were reluctant to choose a difficult course, but rather because we were then divided on one problem: the problem of Indochina.

I speak to those who abstained a year ago. The events that have occurred since then must have brought our views closer together. And we can now be united, it seems to me, by a common desire for peace, which corresponds to the aspiration of the entire country.

We are also engaged together in negotiations now under way. It is my duty to tell you in what state of mind I shall tackle these negotiations, if you entrust me with that task.

For some years now I have felt that a peace through compromise, a peace negotiated with the enemy, was warranted by the facts, and that on such a peace depended the rehabilitation of our finances, and the recovery and expansion of our economy, for that war laid upon our country a burden too heavy for it to bear.

And now a new and fearful danger has emerged: if the conflict in Indochina is not settled—and settled very soon—it is the risk of

* *Source:* French Press and Information Service (New York), *French Affairs,* No. 10 (June 21, 1954), pp. 1–3. Subheadings omitted. The French text of the speech is in France, *Journal Officiel de la République Française, Débats Parlementaires, Assemblée Nationale,* Session of June 17, 1954, pp. 2992–2994. Mendès-France officially became Premier on June 18.

[20] Mendès-France unsuccessfully attempted to form a Government on June 3, 1953, during the prolonged governmental crisis in May and June.

war, of an international and perhaps atomic war, that we must face.

It is because I wanted a better peace that I wanted it sooner, when we held more trump cards in our hand, but there are concessions and sacrifices which even the present situation does not call for. France need not accept, and will not accept, a settlement under conditions which would be incompatible with her most vital interests. France will maintain her presence in the Far East. Neither our Allies nor our enemies should harbor the slightest doubt as to the significance of our determination.

We have entered into negotiations at Geneva in liaison with our Allies and with the Associated States. The Government I shall form, if you so decide, will pursue these negotiations, prompted by a constant will to peace, but equally resolved—in order to safeguard our interests and reach an honorable settlement—to play for all they are worth the trump cards still held by France: the concentration of our material and spiritual forces in wide areas; the interest and support of our Allies; and, last, the valor and heroism of our soldiers—the essential factor on which France relies above all else. I say this emphatically and pay them a solemn homage, by recalling the painful glory of Dienbienphu and so many sacrifices made in unknown as well as famous battles.

That is why the security of the Expeditionary Corps and the maintenance of its strength are imperative duties in which neither the Government nor the Parliament will falter.

That is why no measure will be neglected that might prove necessary for this purpose.

And that is why, finally, he who stands before you—and whose feelings on the Indochinese problem have never changed—now makes his appeal for support to a majority made up of men who have never, directly or indirectly, espoused the cause of those who are fighting against us, men, therefore, who can demand the confidence of our soldiers and negotiate in complete independence with the enemy.

I have studied the record closely and at length. I have consulted with the most qualified military and diplomatic experts. They have confirmed my conviction that a peaceful settlement of the conflict is possible.

We must, therefore, have a rapid cease-fire. The Government I shall form will give itself—and our adversaries—a period of four weeks to bring it about. Today is June 17. I shall come before you before July 20 and report on the results. If no satisfactory solution can be reached by that date, you will be released from the contract which binds us and my Government will hand its resignation to the President of the Republic.

It goes without saying that, in the meantime—I mean beginning tomorrow—all the necessary military measures will be taken to fulfill the most immediate needs as well as to put the Government that would succeed mine in a position to continue the fight, if it should unfortunately have to do so. If certain of these measures require a parliamentary decision, they will be proposed to you.[21]

My objective is peace.

On the international level, France will seek peace with complete openness.

And I ask your confidence for this single purpose, to fulfill a sacred mission that is dictated to us by the ardent wish of the entire nation.

[The balance of the speech, dealing with matters other than Indochina, is omitted.]

123. *Letter from President Eisenhower to President René Coty of France** *June 18, 1954*

MY DEAR PRESIDENT COTY:

I write to assure you that in these troubled days my country remains warm in its sympathy and staunch in its friendship for your country.

It is of the utmost concern to my country, and indeed to peoples everywhere, that France should continue to play her historic role as the champion of liberty, equality, and fraternity, and as a master craftsman of new and better human relationships.

The United States hopes to see realized, while the opportunity still exists, the imaginative and epochal French concept for blending

* *Source:* United States, Department of State, *American Foreign Policy 1950–1955: Basic Documents* (2 vols., Washington: Government Printing Office, 1957), Vol. I, pp. 1675–1676. President Coty's reply, dated June 26, is in United States, Department of State, *Bulletin*, XXXI (July 5, 1954), pp. 13–14.

[21] This statement implied the threat which made the July 20 deadline meaningful in a military sense: the sending of conscripts to Indochina for the first time, a measure which would enable France to increase significantly her military strength there. Mendès-France reported to the National Assembly on July 7 on military preparations to be taken in case the Geneva negotiations failed; if the war continued, he said, it would be necessary to send conscripts to Indochina. See France, *Journal Officiel de la République Française, Débats Parlementaires, Assemblée Nationale*, Session of July 7, 1954, pp. 3265–3267.

national military forces on the continent of Europe so that they will perform a single service of peace and security.[22] I want to assure you that the pledge of support embodied in my message of April 16 [23] to Monsieur Laniel [24] still stands, and will continue available to his successor.

In Indochina our nation has long shown its deep concern by heavy financial and material aid which continues. The proposals for a united defense which we submitted to Monsieur Laniel represented on our part a momentous and grave decision. Nothing has happened here to change the attitude thus expressed, even though the lapse of time and the events which have come to pass have, of course, created a new situation. But I assure you that we shall be ready in the same spirit to open new discussions as the forthcoming French Government [25] may deem it opportune.

I have mentioned two aspects of our relations which imperatively demand high governmental attention. You can be sure that they will be dealt with upon the foundation of the respect and affection for France which is felt by many millions of individual American citizens. Our past associations have brought sorrows and joys which have indelibly pressed their image upon the very heart of our nations and this is, on our side, a guarantee of our future attitude.

I shall be talking informally with Sir Winston Churchill and Mr. Eden next week [26] and I look forward to resuming with the Government of France such intimate conversations as I have had in the past both as President and previously when I served in Europe in our common cause first of liberation from one tyranny and then of defense against another tyranny.

I extend to you, my dear Mr. President, my respectful greetings.

DWIGHT D. EISENHOWER

[22] I.e., the European Defense Community Treaty, not yet considered by the French parliament.

[23] The message from President Eisenhower to the heads of government of the EDC countries, in United States, Department of State, *American Foreign Policy 1950–1955: Basic Documents* (2 vols., Washington: Government Printing Office, 1957), Vol. I, pp. 1198–1200.

[24] Footnote in the original: "M. Joseph Laniel, Premier from June 28, 1953, to June 12, 1954."

[25] Footnote in the original: "The 'forthcoming French Government' was the Cabinet headed by M. Pierre Mendès-France, appointed June 18, 1954."

[26] See Document 125.

124. *Foreign Secretary Eden: Report to the House of Commons on the Geneva Conference [Extracts]* *
    June 23, 1954

[The introductory paragraph is omitted.]

The House will recall that the [Geneva] Conference was convened by the Governments of France, the United States, Soviet Russia and ourselves in accordance with a resolution which was adopted in Berlin on 18th February last.[27] Its purpose, in the words of the communiqué, was to be that of reaching a peaceful settlement of the Korean question and to discuss the problem of restoring peace in Indo-China. This political Conference on Korea followed many months of patient work at the United Nations in which my right hon. and learned Friend the Minister of State [28] played a conspicuous part. So far as Indo-China is concerned, the main credit for the Conference being arranged at all belongs to M. Bidault, then Minister of Foreign Affairs of France.

Of the two tasks entrusted to the Geneva Conference, that concerning Indo-China has been the more urgent, if only because war is being waged in that country, with all its attendant perils. The interest of the French in a peaceful settlement in Indo-China is direct and obvious. They are themselves involved in war. But our concern is also pertinent. We have both responsibilities and friends in South-East Asia, and I have seldom known a situation in which the risks of a wider conflagration should be more apparent to all. We have, therefore, very good reasons for wishing this Conference to succeed.

This was the responsibility which the Berlin agreement, to which I have already referred, laid directly upon us. We have, in fact, done everything in our power to get agreement. This has involved quite a lot of work and patience, both before and outside the Conference.

[The section on the Korean phase of the Conference, an introductory paragraph on Indochina, and a paragraph on the role of Asian Commonwealth nations in any Indochina settlement are omitted.]

I must now ask the Committee [29] to allow me to give a brief

* *Source:* Great Britain, *Parliamentary Debates (Hansard)*, Fifth Series, House of Commons, Vol. 529, Session of June 23, 1954, cols. 428–429, 432–433, and 434–435.

[27] Document 99.   [28] Mr. Selwyn Lloyd.

[29] Mr. Eden's statement was made during discussion of budget estimates—"Supply"—for which the House of Commons sits as a Committee of the Whole.

account of these discussions—if only to enable me to correct one or two misconceptions which have established themselves in certain places. I have seen it suggested that the possibility of creating a united front of anti-Communist Powers in South-East Asia has been in some way prejudiced or delayed by the attitude of Her Majesty's Government. The facts are these.

There is no dispute that on 13th April Her Majesty's Government stated that they were ready to take part with the other countries principally concerned in an examination of the possibility of establishing a collective defence in South-East Asia and the Western Pacific.[30] The House was so informed. But the membership and the method were also important, and neither was then decided. Nor do I see how they could have been, since the French Government—whose views on the matter were clearly of importance—had still to be consulted. It was agreed in London that if a question were asked about the membership I should reply that this was a matter for further consideration. In the event, I was not asked. However, in a reply to a supplementary question in the House on the same day,[31] I said that the effective outcome of this examination of the possibility of establishing a collective defence would be greatly influenced by what happened at Geneva. Neither then nor later was any criticism made to me about this reply.

When, therefore, I learned that an initial gathering of a number of Powers was to be held in Washington on 20th April, it seemed to me that this fact must inevitably prejudice the question of membership at the outset, and I thought it important not to do this. I said so, and the meeting was accordingly transformed into one of the Powers concerned with the Korean Conference.[32] I think that I should add that at no time in these proceedings did this much over-publicised misunderstanding extend to our relations with the French Government who were, of course, deeply concerned and who have shown, in their public as well as in their private declarations, a full understanding of our position.

I hope that we shall be able to agree to an international guarantee of any settlement that may emerge at Geneva. I also hope that it will be possible to agree on some system of South-East Asian defence to guard against aggression. In other words, we could have a reciprocal

[30] In the joint U.S.–U.K. Communiqué, Document 105.

[31] Great Britain, *Parliamentary Debates (Hansard)*, Fifth Series, House of Commons, Vol. 526, Session of April 13, 1954, col. 972.

[32] See Anthony Eden, *Full Circle* (Boston: Houghton Mifflin Company, 1960), pp. 109–111.

arrangement in which both sides take part, such as Locarno.[33] We could also have a defensive alliance such as N.A.T.O. is in Europe, and, let me add, such as the existing Chinese-Soviet Treaty provides for the Far East so far as the Communist Powers are concerned

[Three paragraphs on the background for a collective defense system in Southeast Asia, a question dealing with part of Mr. Eden's earlier statement, and three paragraphs on five-power staff talks under way in Washington on the Southeast Asian situation are omitted.]

Her Majesty's Government have also been reproached in some unofficial quarters for their failure to support armed intervention to try to save Dien Bien Phu. It is quite true that we were at no time willing to support such action, for three reasons which seemed to us to be good, and still do. First, we were advised that air action alone could not have been effective. Secondly, any such military intervention could have destroyed the chances of a settlement at Geneva. And thirdly, it might well have led to a general war in Asia. I should add that we have at no time been reproached by our French allies for our decision, in spite of the fact that the burden of it fell upon them.

[The balance of Mr. Eden's statement is omitted. It dealt with the progress of the Conference to date.]

125. *Joint Statement Issued in Washington by President Eisenhower and Prime Minister Churchill* [*Extracts*] *
June 28, 1954

At the end of their meetings today, the President and the Prime Minister issued the following statement:

In these few days of friendly and fruitful conversations, we have considered various subjects of mutual and world interest.

* *Source:* United States, Department of State, *American Foreign Policy 1950–1955: Basic Documents* (2 vols., Washington: Government Printing Office, 1957), Vol. I, pp. 1705–1706. The following day the President and the Prime Minister issued a statement on principles of Anglo-American policy, in *ibid.*, p. 1707, which included this statement: "In the case of nations now divided against their will, we shall continue to seek to achieve unity through free elections supervised by the United Nations to insure they are conducted fairly."

[33] A series of agreements and notes of October 16, 1925, which had the object of establishing reciprocal guarantees of the frontiers of Germany on the one hand and France, Belgium, Czechoslovakia, and Poland on the other. The agreements subsequently acquired a bad name, and Eden's reference to them here produced considerable negative reaction, particularly in the United States.

[A section on Western Europe is omitted.]

II. *Southeast Asia*

We discussed Southeast Asia and, in particular, examined the situation which would arise from the conclusion of an agreement on Indochina. We also considered the situation which would follow from failure to reach such an agreement.

We will press forward with plans for collective defense to meet either eventuality.

We are both convinced that if at Geneva the French Government is confronted with demands which prevent an acceptable agreement regarding Indochina, the international situation will be seriously aggravated.[34]

[A section on atomic matters and a discussion of basic principles underlying policy are omitted.]

126. *Joint American-British Note to the French Government* [*Extract*] * *June 29, 1954*

Following are points which U.S. and U.K. have informed French we believe should be included in any agreement reached re Indochina:

1. preserves the integrity and independence of Laos and Cambodia and assures the withdrawal of Vietminh forces therefrom;

2. preserves at least the southern half of Vietnam, and if possible an enclave in the Delta; in this connection we would be unwilling to see the line of division of responsibility drawn further south than a line running generally west from Dong Hoi;

3. does not impose on Laos, Cambodia or retained Vietnam any restrictions materially impairing their capacity to maintain stable non-Communist regimes; and especially restrictions impairing their right

---

* *Source:* Telegram from the Department of State to the American Embassy, Canberra, dated July 2, 1954, declassified and released to the editor in January 1969. The text has been reworded from the telegraphic form. The basic text of the note also appears in Anthony Eden, *Full Circle* (Boston: Houghton Mifflin Company, 1960), p. 149. The full content of the note in which the French were informed of the seven points is unknown.

[34] For further amplification of this point from the British point of view, see Prime Minister Churchill's statement to the House of Commons on July 12, in Great Britain, *Parliamentary Debates* (*Hansard*), Fifth Series, House of Commons, Vol. 530, Session of July 12, 1954, cols. 43–45.

to maintain adequate forces for internal security, to import arms and to employ foreign advisers;

4. does not contain political provisions which would risk loss of the retained area to Communist control;

5. does not exclude the possibility of the ultimate unification of the Vietnam by peaceful means;

6. provides for the peaceful and humane transfer, under international supervision, of those people desiring to be moved from one zone to another of Vietnam; and

7. provides effective machinery for international supervision of the agreement.

127. *Communiqué on Talks between Ho Chi Minh and Chou En-lai* * *July 5, 1954*

Chou En-lai, Premier of the People's Republic of China, and Ho Chi Minh, President of the Democratic Republic of Viet-Nam, held talks on the Chinese-Viet-Namese border from July 3rd to 5th, 1954. Premier Chou En-lai and President Ho Chi Minh had a full exchange of views on the Geneva Conference with respect to the question of the restoration of peace in Indo-China and related questions. Present at the talks were Hoang Van Hoan, Ambassador of the Democratic Republic of Viet-Nam to the Chinese People's Republic,[35] and Chiao Kuan-hua, adviser of the delegation of the Chinese People's Republic to the Geneva Conference.

128. *Communiqué Issued by Secretary of State Dulles, Foreign Secretary Eden, and Premier Mendès-France, Paris* † *July 14, 1954*

We have had intimate and frank discussions. These have resulted in a clear understanding of our respective positions in relation to Indo-China. The United States Secretary of State, Mr. Foster Dulles, explained fully the attitude of his Government towards the Indo-China phase of the Geneva Conference and the limitations which that Govern-

* *Source:* New China News Agency, July 7, 1954, in United States, Consulate General in Hong Kong, *Survey of the China Mainland Press*, No. 843 (July 8, 1954), p. 1.

† *Source:* Great Britain, *Parliamentary Debates (Hansard)*, Fifth Series, House of Commons, Vol. 530, Session of July 14, 1954, col. 503.

[35] Hoang Van Hoan was also a member of the DRV delegation at Geneva.

ment desired to observe as not itself having primary responsibility for the Indo-Chinese war.

The French Premier and Foreign Minister, Mr. Mendès-France, expressed the view, with which Mr. Eden, the Secretary of State for Foreign Affairs for the United Kingdom, associated himself, that it would nevertheless serve the interests of France and of the Associated States, and of the peace and freedom of the area, if the United States, without departing from the principles that Mr. Dulles expressed, were once again to be represented at Geneva at the ministerial level.

Accordingly, President Eisenhower and Mr. Dulles are requesting the United States Under-Secretary of State, General Bedell Smith, to return to Geneva at an early date.

129. *Foreign Minister Tran Van Do of the State of Viet-Nam: Statement at the Thirtieth (Restricted) Session [Official Summary]* *
    July 18, 1954

M. TRAN VAN DO declares that if the objective of the session, as he was informed of it at the end of the morning, is to examine the text of the Final Declaration, his delegation must point out that there can be no question of Viet-Nam's associating itself with it [*s'y associer*], for two reasons: the delegation of Viet-Nam is not in agreement with the principles which seem to inspire the cessation of hostilities; and it has not yet presented, in the name of the new Government,[36] the solution which seems to it the most responsive to the three following criteria: Peace, Independence, and Unity.

With regard to the first reason, the delegation of Viet-Nam notes that the French draft of July 16 speaks of "zones," in particular in articles 6 and 7. It also notes that the Soviet draft of July 15 does the same, particularly in articles 8 and 10. These texts [37] indicate that Viet-

* * *

* *Source:* France, Ministère des Affaires Etrangères, *Conférence de Genève sur l'Indochine (8 Mai–21 Juillet 1954): Procès-verbaux des Séances—Propositions— Documents Finaux* (Paris: Imprimerie Nationale, 1955), p. 377. Translation by the editor. The State of Viet-Nam's proposals of July 19, which are not included in the official records of the Conference and which therefore apparently received little or no acknowledgment, appear in State of Viet-Nam, High Commission in Paris, *Vietnam,* No. 80 (August 1, 1954), p. 5 [in French]. They protested against partition which "could not fail to produce in Viet-Nam the same effects as in Germany, Austria and Korea," and called for United Nations control of a cease-fire and, eventually, of general elections.

36 Of Ngo Dinh Diem.

37 Texts of the draft documents are not available.

Nam will be divided into zones, which the Soviet document calls North and South. Moreover, for several days everybody has been talking about a "partition" and even "parallels." The delegation of Viet-Nam can do nothing other than solemnly protest against the idea of partition. It therefore rejects both drafts.[38]

With regard to the second reason, the delegation of Viet-Nam reserves the right to present a proposal on the whole of the problem and to amplify it at a plenary session, which it earnestly requests the Conference to organize for that purpose. In addition, the delegation of Viet-Nam takes note of the fact, fundamental in its opinion, that neither the French draft nor the Soviet draft mentions the State of Viet-Nam. It cannot, therefore, accept a declaration nor, *a fortiori,* an agreement where there is no mention of the State of Viet-Nam, which as such was invited to the Conference.

[38] Later on in the same session, Under Secretary of State Smith informed the Conference that the United States would not be a formal party to the agreements reached by the Conference but would undertake not to upset them by force. This foreshadowed the unilateral United States declaration found in Document 134. It should be noted that this American position was stated *before* the final details of the Geneva Agreements (notably the location of the military demarcation line at the 17th parallel and the two-year delay before the holding of elections in Viet-Nam) had been agreed upon.

CHAPTER X

The Geneva Agreements

July 20-July 21, 1954

Introduction

The Geneva Conference concluded its work on July 20 and 21 with the elaboration of a series of documents concerned primarily with ending the hostilities in Indochina and only secondarily with providing a political settlement to prevent their resumption.[1] The "Geneva Agreements" consisted of three bilateral cease-fire agreements, a number of unilateral declarations, and the unsigned Final Declaration of the Conference.[2] This last took note of the other documents and ostensibly expressed the views of the Conference as a whole despite the fact that not all the participants agreed to it. Most important for Viet-Nam were the Agreement on the Cessation of Hostilities in Viet-Nam (Document 130), the Declarations by the Government of the French Republic with reference to Articles 10 and 11 of the Final Declaration (Documents 132 and 133), and the Final Declaration (Document 131),

[1] Complete texts of the formal Geneva Agreements may be found in the following sources: Great Britain, Parliament, Papers by Command, *Further Documents Relating to the Discussion of Indo-China at the Geneva Conference June 16–July 21, 1954* (London: Her Majesty's Stationery Office, Cmd. 9239, 1954, reprinted 1965), pp. 5–42; France, Ministère des Affaires Etrangères, *Conférence de Genève sur l'Indochine (8 Mai–21 Juillet 1954): Procès-verbaux des Séances—Propositions—Documents Finaux* (Paris: Imprimerie Nationale, 1955), pp. 427–470; and France, Direction de la Documentation, *Notes et Etudes Documentaires,* No. 1901 (July 30, 1954), pp. 3–12, and No. 1909 (August 18, 1954), pp. 2–16.

[2] The "Geneva Agreements" might also be said to include the July 21 exchange of letters between Mendès-France and Pham Van Dong on the protection of French economic and cultural interests in Viet-Nam. These letters were, however, entirely *pro forma* and had little subsequent effect. The text of the exchange is in France, Direction de la Documentation, *Notes et Etudes Documentaires,* No. 1901 (July 30, 1954), p. 12. In addition, a confidential agreement was concluded between France and the State of Viet-Nam. The editor has been unable to obtain a text for inclusion in this collection.

particularly the provisions for nationwide general elections in July 1956. In addition, the proceedings of the final Conference session (Document 134) contained several statements which, although not considered formal parts of the Agreements, are relevant to their interpretation and to an understanding of the policies of the various participants. Of these, the most important were the protests by the State of Viet-Nam, the adoption of the Final Declaration, and the Declaration by the United States.

It would be futile to attempt an analysis of the Geneva Agreements here, for they are exceedingly complex and there has been wide disagreement over how they should be interpreted. As indicated by many of the documents in subsequent sections, the following questions were among the major ones which arose from the Geneva Agreements:

1. Were the provisions of the Agreement on the Cessation of Hostilities in Viet-Nam, concluded between the High Commands of the French Union and the Democratic Republic of Viet-Nam (DRV), binding on the State of Viet-Nam or any other third powers (i.e., the United States)?

2. What was the status of the Agreement on the Cessation of Hostilities in Viet-Nam after withdrawal of French forces and dissolution of the French High Command in 1956?

3. What was the legal status of the Final Declaration? As an unsigned document, was it binding on some or all of the participants in the Conference? [3] Were the participants bound to ensure elections in Viet-Nam in 1956 as provided by the Final Declaration? Was it France or the State of Viet-Nam which was supposed to undertake consultations with the DRV for the holding of the elections? What form were the consultations and the elections to take?

4. Who was responsible for seeing that the Geneva Agreements, both the cease-fire and the provisions of the Final Declaration, were

---

[3] In this connection, an official British source later observed that the Final Declaration "appears to have the character properly of a statement of intention or policy on the part of those member States of the Conference who approved it" (Great Britain, Parliament, Papers by Command, *Documents Relating to British Involvement in the Indo-China Conflict 1945–1955* [London: Her Majesty's Stationery Office, Cmnd. 2834, 1965], p. 16). It is certainly difficult, under accepted rules and practices of international law, to understand how the Final Declaration could be legally binding on any of the participants, much less those who failed positively to indicate their assent to its provisions at the final session of the Conference. It is worth noting that only four (Great Britain, China, the Soviet Union, and France) of the nine participants positively endorsed the Declaration. See Document 134.

[handwritten: What about the DRV? See Dong's statement.]

implemented? Were any of the powers participating in the Conference bound to take action to enforce the Agreements should they not be followed? If so, which powers, and by what means?

The Geneva Agreements were a success in making possible a cessation of the eight-year war in Indochina, and in enabling France to extricate herself from Viet-Nam and Indochina. As indicated by the questions just cited, however, they were by no means completely clear, and they failed to produce a solution for the political problems in Viet-Nam. Of those political problems, perhaps the most basic was implicit recognition, or at least acceptance, by the Conference of *two* Vietnamese governments—the State of Viet-Nam and the DRV—both exerting claim to what the Conference recognized as only *one* national territory.

Because of the ambiguous nature of the Agreements and the failure to provide adequate sanctions for their enforcement, they could be effective only so long as all the parties concerned cooperated to ensure their full implementation. Unfortunately that cooperation was lacking from the outset, notably because of the total hostility between the two Vietnamese states and the failure of the Conference to produce agreements acceptable to the United States and the State of Viet-Nam. French withdrawal from Viet-Nam in 1956 was to render the continued effectiveness of the Agreements virtually impossible and, sooner or later, to make renewed conflict in some form all but inevitable.

130. *Agreement on the Cessation of Hostilities in Viet-Nam* *
     July 20, 1954

CHAPTER I

PROVISIONAL MILITARY DEMARCATION LINE AND DEMILITARISED ZONE

Article 1

A provisional military demarcation line shall be fixed, on either side of which the forces of the two parties shall be regrouped after their withdrawal, the forces of the People's Army of Viet Nam to the north of the line and the forces of the French Union to the south.

* *Source:* Great Britain, Parliament, Papers by Command, *Further Documents Relating to the Discussion of Indo-China at the Geneva Conference June 16–July 21, 1954* (London: Her Majesty's Stationery Office. Cmd. 9239, 1954, reprinted 1965), pp. 27–38.

The provisional military demarcation line is fixed as shown on the map attached (see Map No. 1).[1]

It is also agreed that a demilitarised zone shall be established on either side of the demarcation line, to a width of not more than 5 kms. from it, to act as a buffer zone and avoid any incidents which might result in the resumption of hostilities.

Article 2

The period within which the movement of all forces of either party into its regrouping zone on either side of the provisional military demarcation line shall be completed shall not exceed three hundred (300) days from the date of the present Agreement's entry into force.

Article 3

When the provisional military demarcation line coincides with a waterway, the waters of such waterway shall be open to civil navigation by both parties wherever one bank is controlled by one party and the other bank by the other party. The Joint Commission shall establish rules of navigation for the stretch of waterway in question. The merchant shipping and other civilian craft of each party shall have unrestricted access to the land under its military control.

Article 4

The provisional military demarcation line between the two final regrouping zones is extended into the territorial waters by a line perpendicular to the general line of the coast.

All coastal islands north of this boundary shall be evacuated by the armed forces of the French Union, and all islands south of it shall be evacuated by the forces of the People's Army of Viet Nam.

Article 5

To avoid any incidents which might result in the resumption of hostilities, all military forces, supplies and equipment shall be withdrawn from the demilitarised zone within twenty-five (25) days of the present Agreement's entry into force.

---

[1] Footnote in the original: "Map not printed—See Annex for details." The Annex is not printed in this collection; it may be found in Great Britain, Parliament, Papers by Command, *Further Documents Relating to the Discussion of Indo-China at the Geneva Conference June 16–July 21, 1954* (London: Her Majesty's Stationery Office, Cmd. 9239, 1954, reprinted 1965), pp. 39–40.

Article 6

No person, military or civilian, shall be permitted to cross the provisional military demarcation line unless specifically authorised to do so by the Joint Commission.

Article 7

No person, military or civilian, shall be permitted to enter the demilitarised zone except persons concerned with the conduct of civil administration and relief and persons specifically authorised to enter by the Joint Commission.

Article 8

Civil administration and relief in the demilitarised zone on either side of the provisional military demarcation line shall be the responsibility of the Commanders-in-Chief of the two parties in their respective zones. The number of persons, military or civilian, from each side who are permitted to enter the demilitarised zone for the conduct of civil administration and relief shall be determined by the respective Commanders, but in no case shall the total number authorised by either side exceed at any one time a figure to be determined by the Trung Gia Military Commission [2] or by the Joint Commission. The number of civil police and the arms to be carried by them shall be determined by the Joint Commission. No one else shall carry arms unless specifically authorised to do so by the Joint Commission.

Article 9

Nothing contained in this chapter shall be construed as limiting the complete freedom of movement, into, out of or within the demilitarised zone, of the Joint Commission, its joint groups, the International Commission to be set up as indicated below, its inspection teams and any other persons, supplies or equipment specifically authorised to enter the demilitarised zone by the Joint Commission. Freedom of movement shall be permitted across the territory under the military control of either side over any road or waterway which has to be taken between

---

[2] The Trung Gia Military Commission was the form agreed upon by the Geneva Conference to handle the "on the ground" details of conclusion and implementation of the cease-fire in Viet-Nam. Meeting at Trung Gia in Tonkin, it consisted of representatives of the French and Viet Minh high commands; representatives of the State of Viet-Nam were present only as observers.

points within the demilitarised zone when such points are not connected by roads or waterways lying completely within the demilitarised zone.

CHAPTER II

PRINCIPLES AND PROCEDURE GOVERNING IMPLEMENTATION
OF THE PRESENT AGREEMENT

Article 10

The Commanders of the Forces on each side, on the one side the Commander-in-Chief of the French Union forces in Indo-China and on the other side the Commander-in-Chief of the People's Army of Viet Nam, shall order and enforce the complete cessation of all hostilities in Viet Nam by all armed forces under their control, including all units and personnel of the ground, naval and air forces.

Article 11

In accordance with the principle of a simultaneous cease-fire throughout Indo-China, the cessation of hostilities shall be simultaneous throughout all parts of Viet Nam, in all areas of hostilities and for all the forces of the two parties.

Taking into account the time effectively required to transmit the ceasc-fire order down to the lowest échelons of the combatant forces on both sides, the two parties are agreed that the cease-fire shall take effect completely and simultaneously for the different sectors of the country as follows:

Northern Viet Nam at 8:00 A.M. (local time) on July 27, 1954.
Central Viet Nam at 8:00 A.M. (local time) on August 1, 1954.
Southern Viet Nam at 8:00 A.M. (local time) on August 11, 1954.
It is agreed that Peking mean time shall be taken as local time.

From such time as the cease-fire becomes effective in Northern Viet Nam, both parties undertake not to engage in any large-scale offensive action in any part of the Indo-Chinese theatre of operations and not to commit the air forces based on Northern Viet Nam outside that sector. The two parties also undertake to inform each other of their plans for movement from one regrouping zone to another within twenty-five (25) days of the present Agreement's entry into force.

Article 12

All the operations and movements entailed in the cessation of hostilities and regrouping must proceed in a safe and orderly fashion:

(*a*) Within a certain number of days after the cease-fire Agreement shall have become effective, the number to be determined on the spot by the Trung Gia Military Commission, each party shall be responsible for removing and neutralising mines (including river- and sea-mines), booby traps, explosives and any other dangerous substances placed by it. In the event of its being impossible to complete the work of removal and neutralisation in time, the party concerned shall mark the spot by placing visible signs there. All demolitions, mine fields, wire entanglements and other hazards to the free movement of the personnel of the Joint Commission and its joint groups, known to be present after the withdrawal of the military forces, shall be reported to the Joint Commission by the Commanders of the opposing forces;

(*b*) From the time of the cease-fire until regrouping is completed on either side of the demarcation line:

(1) The forces of either party shall be provisionally withdrawn from the provisional assembly areas assigned to the other party.

(2) When one party's forces withdraw by a route (road, rail, waterway, sea route) which passes through the territory of the other party (see Article 24), the latter party's forces must provisionally withdraw three kilometres on each side of such route, but in such a manner as to avoid interfering with the movements of the civil population.

Article 13

From the time of the cease-fire until the completion of the movements from one regrouping zone into the other, civil and military transport aircraft shall follow air-corridors between the provisional assembly areas assigned to the French Union forces north of the demarcation line on the one hand and the Laotian frontier and the regrouping zone assigned to the French Union forces on the other hand.

The position of the air-corridors, their width, the safety route for single-engined military aircraft transferred to the south and the search and rescue procedure for aircraft in distress shall be determined on the spot by the Trung Gia Military Commission.

Article 14

Political and administrative measures in the two regrouping zones, on either side of the provisional military demarcation line:

(*a*) Pending the general elections which will bring about the unification of Viet Nam, the conduct of civil administration in each re-grouping zone shall be in the hands of the party whose forces are to be regrouped there in virtue of the present Agreement.

(*b*) Any territory controlled by one party which is transferred to the other party by the regrouping plan shall continue to be adminis-tered by the former party until such date as all the troops who are to be transferred have completely left that territory so as to free the zone assigned to the party in question. From then on, such territory shall be regarded as transferred to the other party, who shall assume respon-sibility for it.

Steps shall be taken to ensure that there is no break in the transfer of responsibilities. For this purpose, adequate notice shall be given by the withdrawing party to the other party, which shall make the neces-sary arrangements, in particular by sending administrative and police detachments to prepare for the assumption of administrative respon-sibility. The length of such notice shall be determined by the Trung Gia Military Commission. The transfer shall be effected in successive stages for the various territorial sectors.

The transfer of the civil administration of Hanoi and Haiphong to the authorities of the Democratic Republic of Viet Nam shall be completed within the respective time-limits laid down in Article 15 for military movements.

(*c*) Each party undertakes to refrain from any reprisals or discrim-ination against persons or organisations on account of their activities during the hostilities and to guarantee their democratic liberties.

(*d*) From the date of entry into force of the present Agreement until the movement of troops is completed, any civilians residing in a district controlled by one party who wish to go and live in the zone as-signed to the other party shall be permitted and helped to do so by the authorities in that district.

Article 15

The disengagement of the combatants, and the withdrawals and transfers of military forces, equipment and supplies shall take place in accordance with the following principles:

(*a*) The withdrawals and transfers of the military forces, equipment and supplies of the two parties shall be completed within three hundred (300) days, as laid down in Article 2 of the present Agreement;

(*b*) Within either territory successive withdrawals shall be made by sectors, portions of sectors or provinces. Transfers from one regrouping zone to another shall be made in successive monthly instalments proportionate to the number of troops to be transferred;

(*c*) The two parties shall undertake to carry out all troop withdrawals and transfers in accordance with the aims of the present Agreement, shall permit no hostile act and shall take no step whatsoever which might hamper such withdrawals and transfers. They shall assist one another as far as this is possible;

Lansdale violated

(*d*) The two parties shall permit no destruction or sabotage of any public property and no injury to the life and property of the civil population. They shall permit no interference in local civil administration;

(*e*) The Joint Commission and the International Commission shall ensure that steps are taken to safeguard the forces in the course of withdrawal and transfer;

(*f*) The Trung Gia Military Commission, and later the Joint Commission, shall determine by common agreement the exact procedure for the disengagement of the combatants and for troop withdrawals and transfers, on the basis of the principles mentioned above and within the framework laid down below:

1. The disengagement of the combatants, including the concentration of the armed forces of all kinds and also each party's movements into the provisional assembly areas assigned to it and the other party's provisional withdrawal from it, shall be completed within a period not exceeding fifteen (15) days after the date when the cease-fire becomes effective.

The general delineation of the provisional assembly areas is set out in the maps [3] annexed to the present Agreement.

In order to avoid any incidents, no troops shall be stationed less than 1,500 metres from the lines delimiting the provisional assembly areas.

During the period until the transfers are concluded, all the coastal islands west of the following lines shall be included in the Haiphong perimeter: meridian of the southern point of Kebao Island, northern coast of Ile Rousse (excluding the island), extended as far as the meridian of Campha-Mines, meridian of Campha-Mines.

2. The withdrawals and transfers shall be effected in the following order and within the following periods (from the date of the entry into force of the present Agreement):

---

[3] Footnote in the original: "Map not printed—See Annex for details." See Note 1, p. 289.

Forces of the French Union

Hanoi perimeter	80 days
Haiduong perimeter	100 days
Haiphong perimeter	300 days

Forces of the People's Army of Viet Nam

Ham Tan and Xuyenmoc provisional assembly area	80 days
Central Viet Nam provisional assembly area—first instalment	80 days
Plaine des Joncs provisional assembly area	100 days
Central Viet Nam provisional assembly area—second instalment	100 days
Pointe Camau provisional assembly area	200 days
Central Viet Nam provisional assembly area—last instalment	300 days

CHAPTER III

BAN ON THE INTRODUCTION OF FRESH TROOPS, MILITARY PERSONNEL, ARMS AND MUNITIONS. MILITARY BASES

Article 16

With effect from the date of entry into force of the present Agreement, the introduction into Viet Nam of any troop reinforcements and additional military personnel is prohibited.

It is understood, however, that the rotation of units and groups of personnel, the arrival in Viet Nam of individual personnel on a temporary duty basis and the return to Viet Nam of the individual personnel after short periods of leave or temporary duty outside Viet Nam shall be permitted under the conditions laid down below:

(*a*) Rotation of units (defined in paragraph (*c*) of this Article) and groups of personnel shall not be permitted for French Union troops stationed north of the provisional military demarcation line laid down in Article 1 of the present Agreement during the withdrawal period provided for in Article 2.

However, under the heading of individual personnel not more than fifty (50) men, including officers, shall during any one month be permitted to enter that part of the country north of the provisional military demarcation line on a temporary duty basis or to return there after short periods of leave or temporary duty outside Viet Nam.

(*b*) "Rotation" is defined as the replacement of units or groups of personnel by other units of the same échelon or by personnel who are arriving in Viet Nam territory to do their overseas service there;

(*c*) The units rotated shall never be larger than a battalion—or the corresponding échelon for air and naval forces;

(*d*) Rotation shall be conducted on a man-for-man basis, provided, however, that in any one quarter neither party shall introduce more than fifteen thousand five hundred (15,500) members of its armed forces into Viet Nam under the rotation policy.

(*e*) Rotation units (defined in paragraph (*c*) of this Article) and groups of personnel, and the individual personnel mentioned in this Article, shall enter and leave Viet Nam only through the entry points enumerated in Article 20 below;

(*f*) Each party shall notify the Joint Commission and the International Commission at least two days in advance of any arrivals or departures of units, groups of personnel and individual personnel in or from Viet Nam. Reports on the arrivals or departures of units, groups of personnel and individual personnel in or from Viet Nam shall be submitted daily to the Joint Commission and the International Commission.

All the above-mentioned notifications and reports shall indicate the places and dates of arrival or departure and the number of persons arriving or departing;

(*g*) The International Commission, through its Inspection Teams, shall supervise and inspect the rotation of units and groups of personnel and the arrival and departure of individual personnel as authorised above, at the points of entry enumerated in Article 20 below.

Article 17

(*a*) With effect from the date of entry into force of the present Agreement, the introduction into Viet Nam of any reinforcements in the form of all types of arms, munitions and other war material, such as combat aircraft, naval craft, pieces of ordnance, jet engines and jet weapons and armoured vehicles, is prohibited.

(*b*) It is understood, however, that war material, arms and munitions which have been destroyed, damaged, worn out or used up after the cessation of hostilities may be replaced on the basis of piece-for-piece of the same type and with similar characteristics. Such replacements of war material, arms and ammunitions shall not be permitted for French Union troops stationed north of the provisional military demarcation line laid down in Article 1 of the present Agreement, during the withdrawal period provided for in Article 2.

Naval craft may perform transport operations between the regrouping zones.

(*c*) The war material, arms and munitions for replacement purposes provided for in paragraph (*b*) of this Article, shall be introduced into Viet Nam only through the points of entry enumerated in Article 20 below. War material, arms and munitions to be replaced shall be shipped from Viet Nam only through the points of entry enumerated in Article 20 below.

(*d*) Apart from the replacements permitted within the limits laid down in paragraph (*b*) of this Article, the introduction of war material, arms and munitions of all types in the form of unassembled parts for subsequent assembly is prohibited.

(*e*) Each party shall notify the Joint Commission and the International Commission at least two days in advance of any arrivals or departures which may take place of war material, arms and munitions of all types.

In order to justify the requests for the introduction into Viet Nam of arms, munitions and other war material (as defined in paragraph (*a*) of this Article) for replacement purposes, a report concerning each incoming shipment shall be submitted to the Joint Commission and the International Commission. Such reports shall indicate the use made of the items so replaced.

(*f*) The International Commission, through its Inspection Teams, shall supervise and inspect the replacements permitted in the circumstances laid down in this Article, at the points of entry enumerated in Article 20 below.

Article 18

With effect from the date of entry into force of the present Agreement, the establishment of new military bases is prohibited throughout Viet Nam territory.

Article 19

With effect from the date of entry into force of the present Agreement, no military base under the control of a foreign State may be established in the regrouping zone of either party; the two parties shall ensure that the zones assigned to them do not adhere to any military alliance and are not used for the resumption of hostilities or to further an aggressive policy.

Article 20

The points of entry into Viet Nam for rotation personnel and replacements of material are fixed as follows:

Zone to the north of the provisional military demarcation line: Laokay, Langson, Tien-Yen, Haiphong, Vinh, Dong-Hoi, Muong-Sen;

Zone to the south of the provisional military demarcation line: Tourane, Quinhon, Nhatrang, Bangoi, Saigon, Cap St. Jacques, Tanchau.

CHAPTER IV

PRISONERS OF WAR AND CIVILIAN INTERNEES

Article 21

The liberation and repatriation of all prisoners of war and civilian internees detained by each of the two parties at the coming into force of the present Agreement shall be carried out under the following conditions:

(*a*) All prisoners of war and civilian internees of Viet Nam, French and other nationalities captured since the beginning of hostilities in Viet Nam during military operations or in any other circumstances of war and in any part of the territory of Viet Nam shall be liberated within a period of thirty (30) days after the date when the cease-fire becomes effective in each theatre.

(*b*) The term "civilian internees" is understood to mean all persons who, having in any way contributed to the political and armed struggle between the two parties, have been arrested for that reason and have been kept in detention by either party during the period of hostilities.

(*c*) All prisoners of war and civilian internees held by either party shall be surrendered to the appropriate authorities of the other party, who shall give them all possible assistance in proceeding to their country of origin, place of habitual residence or the zone of their choice.

CHAPTER V

MISCELLANEOUS

Article 22

The Commanders of the Forces of the two parties shall ensure that persons under their respective commands who violate any of the provisions of the present Agreement are suitably punished.

Article 23

In cases in which the place of burial is known and the existence of graves has been established, the Commander of the Forces of either party shall, within a specific period after the entry into force of the Armistice Agreement, permit the graves service personnel of the other party to enter the part of Viet Nam territory under their military control for the purpose of finding and removing the bodies of deceased military personnel of that party, including the bodies of deceased prisoners of war. The Joint Commission shall determine the procedures and the time limit for the performance of this task. The Commanders of the Forces of the two parties shall communicate to each other all information in their possession as to the place of burial of military personnel of the other party.

Article 24

The present Agreement shall apply to all the armed forces of either party. The armed forces of each party shall respect the demilitarised zone and the territory under the military control of the other party, and shall commit no act and undertake no operation against the other party and shall not engage in blockade of any kind in Viet Nam.

For the purposes of the present Article, the word "territory" includes territorial waters and air space.

Article 25

The Commanders of the Forces of the two parties shall afford full protection and all possible assistance and co-operation to the Joint Commission and its joint groups and to the International Commission and its inspection teams in the performance of the functions and tasks assigned to them by the present Agreement.

Article 26

The costs involved in the operations of the Joint Commission and joint groups and of the International Commission and its Inspection Teams shall be shared equally between the two parties.

Article 27

The signatories of the present Agreement and their successors in their functions shall be responsible for ensuring the observance and enforcement of the terms and provisions thereof. The Commanders of the Forces of the two parties shall, within their respective commands, take all steps and make all arrangements necessary to ensure full compliance with all the provisions of the present Agreement by all elements and military personnel under their command.

The procedures laid down in the present Agreement shall, whenever necessary, be studied by the Commanders of the two parties and, if necessary, defined more specifically by the Joint Commission.

CHAPTER VI

JOINT COMMISSION AND INTERNATIONAL COMMISSION
FOR SUPERVISION AND CONTROL IN VIET NAM

Article 28

Responsibility for the execution of the agreement on the cessation of hostilities shall rest with the parties.

Article 29

An International Commission shall ensure the control and supervision of this execution.

Article 30

In order to facilitate, under the conditions shown below, the execution of provisions concerning joint actions by the two parties, a Joint Commission shall be set up in Viet Nam.

Article 31

The Joint Commission shall be composed of an equal number of representatives of the Commanders of the two parties.

Article 32

The Presidents of the delegations to the Joint Commission shall hold the rank of General.

The Joint Commission shall set up joint groups, the number of which shall be determined by mutual agreement between the parties. The joint groups shall be composed of an equal number of officers from both parties. Their location on the demarcation line between the regrouping zones shall be determined by the parties whilst taking into account the powers of the Joint Commission.

Article 33

The Joint Commission shall ensure the execution of the following provisions of the Agreement on the cessation of hostilities:

(*a*) A simultaneous and general cease-fire in Viet Nam for all regular and irregular armed forces of the two parties.

(*b*) A regroupment of the armed forces of the two parties.

(*c*) Observance of the demarcation lines between the regrouping zones and of the demilitarised sectors.

Within the limits of its competence it shall help the parties to execute the said provisions, shall ensure liaison between them for the purpose of preparing and carrying out plans for the application of these provisions, and shall endeavour to solve such disputed questions as may arise between the parties in the course of executing these provisions.

Article 34

An International Commission shall be set up for the control and supervision over the application of the provisions of the agreement on the cessation of hostilities in Viet Nam. It shall be composed of representatives of the following States: Canada, India and Poland.

It shall be presided over by the Representative of India.

Article 35

The International Commission shall set up fixed and mobile inspection teams, composed of an equal number of officers appointed by each of the above-mentioned States. The mixed [*fixed*] teams shall be located at the following points: Laokay, Langson, Tien-Yen, Haiphong, Vinh, Dong-Hoi, Muong-Sen, Tourane, Quinhon, Nhatrang, Bangoi, Saigon, Cap St. Jacques, Tranchau. These points of location may, at a later date, be altered at the request of the Joint Commission, or of one of the parties, or of the International Commission itself, by agreement between the International Commission and the command of the party concerned. The zones of action of the mobile teams shall be the regions bordering the land and sea frontiers of Viet Nam, the demarcation lines between the regrouping zones and the demilitarised zones. Within the limits of these zones they shall have the right to move freely and shall receive from the local civil and military authorities all facilities they may require for the fulfilment of their tasks (provision of personnel, placing at their disposal documents needed for supervision, summoning witnesses necessary for holding enquiries, ensuring the security and freedom of movement of the inspection teams, &c. . . .). They shall have at their disposal such modern means of transport, observation and communication as they may require. Beyond the zones of action as defined above, the mobile teams may, by agreement with the command

of the party concerned, carry out other movements within the limits of
the tasks given them by the present agreement.

Article 36

The International Commission shall be responsible for supervising
the proper execution by the parties of the provisions of the agreement.
For this purpose it shall fulfil the tasks of control, observation, inspection and investigation connected with the application of the provisions
of the agreement on the cessation of hostilities, and it shall in particular:

(*a*) Control the movement of the armed forces of the two parties,
effected within the framework of the regroupment plan.

(*b*) Supervise the demarcation lines between the regrouping areas,
and also the demilitarised zones.

(*c*) Control the operations of releasing prisoners of war and civilian
internees.

(*d*) Supervise at ports and airfields as well as along all frontiers of
Viet Nam the execution of the provisions of the agreement on the cessation of hostilities, regulating the introduction into the country of
armed forces, military personnel and of all kinds of arms, munitions
and war material.

Article 37

The International Commission shall, through the medium of the inspection teams mentioned above, and as soon as possible either on its
own initiative, or at the request of the Joint Commission, or of one of
the parties, undertake the necessary investigations both documentary
and on the ground.

Article 38

The inspection teams shall submit to the International Commission
the results of their supervision, their investigation and their observations, furthermore they shall draw up such special reports as they may
consider necessary or as may be requested from them by the Commission. In the case of a disagreement within the teams, the conclusions
of each member shall be submitted to the Commission.

Article 39

If any one inspection team is unable to settle an incident or considers that there is a violation or a threat of a serious violation, the
International Commission shall be informed; the latter shall study the

reports and the conclusions of the inspection teams and shall inform the parties of the measures which should be taken for the settlement of the incident, ending of the violation or removal of the threat of violation.

Article 40

When the Joint Commission is unable to reach an agreement on the interpretation to be given to some provision or on the appraisal of a fact, the International Commission shall be informed of the disputed question. Its recommendations shall be sent directly to the parties and shall be notified to the Joint Commission.

Article 41

The recommendations of the International Commission shall be adopted by majority vote, subject to the provisions contained in Article 42. If the votes are divided, the chairman's vote shall be decisive.

The International Commission may formulate recommendations concerning amendments and additions which should be made to the provisions of the agreement on the cessation of hostilities in Viet Nam, in order to ensure a more effective execution of that agreement. These recommendations shall be adopted unanimously.

Article 42

When dealing with questions concerning violations, or threats of violations, which might lead to a resumption of hostilities, namely: (*a*) Refusal by the armed forces of one party to effect the movements provided for in the regroupment plan; (*b*) Violation by the armed forces of one of the parties of the regrouping zones, territorial waters, or air space of the other party; the decisions of the International Commission must be unanimous.

Article 43

If one of the parties refuses to put into effect a recommendation of the International Commission, the parties concerned or the Commission itself shall inform the members of the Geneva Conference.

If the International Commission does not reach unanimity in the cases provided for in Article 42, it shall submit a majority report and one or more minority reports to the members of the Conference.

The International Commission shall inform the members of the Conference in all cases where its activity is being hindered.

Article 44

The International Commission shall be set up at the time of the cessation of hostilities in Indo-China in order that it should be able to fulfil the tasks provided for in Article 36.

Article 45

The International Commission for Supervision and Control in Viet Nam shall act in close co-operation with the International Commissions for Supervision and Control in Cambodia and Laos.

The Secretaries-General of these three Commissions shall be responsible for co-ordinating their work and for relations between them.

Article 46

The International Commission for Supervision and Control in Viet Nam may, after consultation with the International Commissions for Supervision and Control in Cambodia and Laos, and having regard to the development of the situation in Cambodia and Laos, progressively reduce its activities. Such a decision must be adopted unanimously.

Article 47

All the provisions of the present Agreement, save the second sub-paragraph of Article 11, shall enter into force at 2400 hours (Geneva time) on July 22, 1954.

Done in Geneva at 2400 hours on the 20th of July, 1954, in French and in Vietnamese, both texts being equally authentic.

For the Commander-in-Chief of the French Union Forces in Indo-China:

DELTIEL
Brigadier-General

For the Commander-in-Chief of the People's Army of Viet Nam
TA-QUANG-BUU
Vice-Minister of National Defence of
the Democratic Republic of Viet Nam

[The Annex, specifically delineating the provisional military demarcation line and demilitarised zone and the provisional assembly areas, is omitted.]

131. *Final Declaration of the Geneva Conference* *
July 21, 1954

FINAL DECLARATION OF THE GENEVA CONFERENCE ON THE PROB-
LEM OF RESTORING PEACE IN INDO-CHINA, IN WHICH THE REPRESEN-
TATIVES OF CAMBODIA, THE DEMOCRATIC REPUBLIC OF VIET NAM,
FRANCE, LAOS, THE PEOPLE'S REPUBLIC OF CHINA, THE STATE OF
VIET NAM, THE UNION OF SOVIET SOCIALIST REPUBLICS, THE UNITED
KINGDOM AND THE UNITED STATES OF AMERICA TOOK PART

1. The Conference takes note of the agreements ending hostilities
in Cambodia, Laos, and Viet Nam [4] and organising international control and the supervision of the execution of the provisions of these
agreements.

2. The Conference expresses satisfaction at the ending of hostilities
in Cambodia, Laos and Viet Nam; the Conference expresses its conviction that the execution of the provisions set out in the present declaration and in the agreements on the cessation of hostilities will permit Cambodia, Laos and Viet Nam henceforth to play their part, in full
independence and sovereignty, in the peaceful community of nations.

3. The Conference takes note of the declarations made by the Governments of Cambodia and of Laos [5] of their intention to adopt measures permitting all citizens to take their place in the national community, in particular by participating in the next general elections,
which, in conformity with the constitution of each of these countries,
shall take place in the course of the year 1955, by secret ballot and
in conditions of respect for fundamental freedoms.

4. The Conference takes note of the clauses in the agreement on the
cessation of hostilities in Viet Nam prohibiting the introduction into
Viet Nam of foreign troops and military personnel as well as of all
kinds of arms and munitions. The Conference also takes note of the

---

* *Source:* Great Britain, Parliament, Papers by Command, *Further Documents
Relating to the Discussion of Indo-China at the Geneva Conference June 16–
July 21, 1954* (London: Her Majesty's Stationery Office, Cmd. 9239, 1954, reprinted 1965), pp. 9–11. The Final Declaration was *not* signed by any of the
participants, nor was it voted upon by the Conference. For the method of
adoption, see Document 134.

[4] For Viet-Nam, Document 130.

[5] Texts in Great Britain, Parliament, Papers by Command, *Further Documents Relating to the Discussion of Indo-China at the Geneva Conference June
16–July 21, 1954* (London: Her Majesty's Stationery Office, Cmd. 9239, 1954,
reprinted 1965), pp. 40–42.

declarations made by the Governments of Cambodia and Laos [6] of their resolution not to request foreign aid, whether in war material, in personnel or in instructors except for the purpose of the effective defence of their territory and, in the case of Laos, to the extent defined by the agreements on the cessation of hostilities in Laos.

5. The Conference takes note of the clauses in the agreement on the cessation of hostilities in Viet Nam to the effect that no military base under the control of a foreign State may be established in the re-grouping zones of the two parties, the latter having the obligation to see that the zones allotted to them shall not constitute part of any military alliance and shall not be utilised for the resumption of hostilities or in the service of an aggressive policy. The Conference also takes note of the declarations of the Governments of Cambodia and Laos [7] to the effect that they will not join in any agreement with other States if this agreement includes the obligation to participate in a military alliance not in conformity with the principles of the Charter of the United Nations or, in the case of Laos, with the principles of the agreement on the cessation of hostilities in Laos or, so long as their security is not threatened, the obligation to establish bases on Cambodian or Laotian territory [8] for the military forces of foreign Powers.

6. The Conference recognises that the essential purpose of the agreement relating to Viet Nam is to settle military questions with a view to ending hostilities and that the military demarcation line is provisional and should not in any way be interpreted as constituting a political or territorial boundary. The Conference expresses its conviction that the execution of the provisions set out in the present declaration and in the agreement on the cessation of hostilities creates the necessary basis for the achievement in the near future of a political settlement in Viet Nam.

7. The Conference declares that, so far as Viet Nam is concerned, the settlement of political problems, effected on the basis of respect for the principles of independence, unity and territorial integrity, shall permit the Vietnamese people to enjoy the fundamental freedoms, guaranteed by democratic institutions established as a result of free general elections by secret ballot. In order to ensure that sufficient progress in the restoration of peace has been made, and that all necessary conditions obtain for free expression of the national will, general elections shall be held in July 1956, under the supervision of an international

----

[6] *Ibid.*   [7] *Ibid.*

[8] France, however, was allowed to retain two bases in Laos, at Seno and at or near Vientiane, with effectives not to exceed a total of 3,500 men.

commission composed of representatives of the Member States of the
International Supervisory Commission, referred to in the agreement on
the cessation of hostilities. Consultations will be held on this subject
between the competent representative authorities of the two zones from
July 20, 1955, onwards.

8. The provisions of the agreements on the cessation of hostilities
intended to ensure the protection of individuals and of property must
be most strictly applied and must, in particular, allow everyone in Viet
Nam to decide freely in which zone he wishes to live.

9. The competent representative authorities of the Northern and
Southern zones of Viet Nam, as well as the authorities of Laos and
Cambodia, must not permit any individual or collective reprisals against
persons who have collaborated in any way with one of the parties during the war, or against members of such persons' families.

10. The Conference takes note of the declaration of the Government of the French Republic to the effect that it is ready to withdraw
its troops from the territory of Cambodia, Laos and Viet Nam, at the
request of the Governments concerned and within periods which shall
be fixed by agreement between the parties except in the cases where,
by agreement between the two parties, a certain number of French
troops shall remain at specified points and for a specified time.[9]

11. The Conference takes note of the declaration of the French
Government to the effect that for the settlement of all the problems
connected with the re-establishment and consolidation of peace in Cambodia, Laos and Viet Nam, the French Government will proceed from
the principle of respect for the independence and sovereignty, unity and
territorial integrity of Cambodia, Laos and Viet Nam.[10]

12. In their relations with Cambodia, Laos and Viet Nam, each
member of the Geneva Conference undertakes to respect the sovereignty, the independence, the unity and the territorial integrity of the
above-mentioned States, and to refrain from any interference in their
internal affairs.

13. The members of the Conference agree to consult one another
on any question which may be referred to them by the International
Supervisory Commission, in order to study such measures as may prove
necessary to ensure that the agreements on the cessation of hostilities
in Cambodia, Laos and Viet Nam are respected.

[9] Document 132.   [10] Document 133.

132. *Declaration by the Government of the French Republic*
     [Reference: Article 10 of the Final Declaration] *
     July 21, 1954

The Government of the French Republic declares that it is ready to withdraw its troops from the territory of Cambodia, Laos and Viet Nam, at the request of the Governments concerned and within a period which shall be fixed by agreement between the parties, except in the cases where, by agreement between the two parties, a certain number of French troops shall remain at specified points and for a specified time.

133. *Declaration by the Government of the French Republic*
     [Reference: Article II of the Final Declaration] †
     July 21, 1954

For the settlement of all the problems connected with the re-establishment and consolidation of peace in Cambodia, Laos and Viet Nam, the French Government will proceed from the principle of respect for the independence and sovereignty, the unity and territorial integrity of Cambodia, Laos and Viet Nam.

134. *The Verbatim Record of the Eighth Plenary Session*
     on Indochina [Extracts]
     July 21, 1954

[The substantial extracts given here are taken from two different sources as indicated.] ‡

M. EDEN: Before commencing the official proceedings, I would like to give the floor to the representative of the State of Viet-Nam.

* *Source:* Great Britain, Parliament, Papers by Command, *Further Documents Relating to the Discussion of Indo-China at the Geneva Conference June 16–July 21, 1954* (London: Her Majesty's Stationery Office, Cmd. 9239, 1954, reprinted 1965), p. 42

† *Source:* Great Britain, Parliament, Papers by Command, *Further Documents Relating to the Discussion of Indo-China at the Geneva Conference June 16–July 21, 1954* (London: Her Majesty's Stationery Office, Cmd. 9239, 1954, reprinted 1965), p. 42.

‡ *Source:* France, Ministère des Affaires Etrangères, *Conférence de Genève sur l'Indochine (8 Mai–21 Juillet 1954): Procès-verbaux des Séances—Propositions—Documents Finaux* (Paris: Imprimerie Nationale, 1955), pp. 378–379. Translation by the editor.

M. Tran Van Do: The delegation of the State of Viet-Nam has presented its proposal [11] designed to obtain an armistice without partition, even provisional, of Viet-Nam, by the disarmament of all the belligerent forces after their withdrawal into the smallest possible stationing zones, and by the establishment of provisional control by the United Nations organization over the entire territory until such time as the re-establishment of peace and order allows the Vietnamese people to decide their own destiny through free elections.

The delegation of Viet-Nam protests against the rejection, without examination, of that proposal which, alone, respects the aspirations of the Vietnamese people. It earnestly requests that at least the demilitarization and neutralization of the bishoprics of the delta of northern Viet-Nam be accepted by the Conference.[12] It solemnly protests against the hasty conclusion of an armistice agreement by the French and Viet Minh High Commands alone, when the French High Command commands the Vietnamese forces only by a delegation of powers from the Chief of State of Viet-Nam and especially when several clauses of that agreement are of a nature seriously to compromise the political future of the Vietnamese people.

It solemnly protests against the fact that the armistice agreement abandons to the Viet Minh territories some of which are still occupied by Vietnamese forces and which are, moreover, essential to the defense of Viet-Nam against further Communist expansion, and against the fact that it results in practice in depriving the State of Viet-Nam of its imprescriptible right to organize its defense other than by the maintenance of a foreign army on its territory.

It solemnly protests against the fact that the French High Command has arrogated to itself the right, without prior agreement with the delegation of the State of Viet-Nam, to fix the date of future elections when this is an arrangement of an eminently political character.

In consequence, the Government of the State of Viet-Nam asks that it be officially noted that it solemnly protests against the manner in which the armistice has been concluded and against the conditions of that armistice, which do not take into consideration the profound aspirations of the Vietnamese people, and that it reserves for itself com-

[11] See Source Note to Document 129.
[12] I.e., the bishoprics of Bui Chu and Phat Diem, evacuated by the French High Command at the beginning of July.

plete liberty of action in order to safeguard the sacred right of the Viet-namese people to territorial unity, national independence and liberty.

M. MENDÈS-FRANCE: At the point we have now reached, the French delegation has no intention of going over again the various points to which the head of the delegation of the State of Viet-Nam has just referred. The French delegation has confidence that the French High Command has acted within the framework of its competence and its powers in the decisions and responsibilities which belong to it. The French delegation prefers, rather, to dwell on one point which has a particular importance and which is a subject on which it understands and shares the concern which has just been expressed by the delegate of the State of Viet-Nam. It concerns the future of certain communities in Viet-Nam.

The French authorities have always been bound to respect the beliefs of the populations living in the region of the bishoprics of Phat Diem and Bui Chu and to favor the free expression of their will. They have never deviated from that attitude, even in the course of years of combat. Following decisions of a military nature, these communities are today subject to a different authority than that which they have known heretofore. We have the firm hope that the promises given on the guarantee of essential liberties—and I refer here to the recent declaration [13] of President Ho Chi Minh on the respect for freedom of conscience—we have, I say, the firm hope that these promises will be kept, thus permitting the people peaceably to continue their existence within respect for their traditional beliefs.

M. EDEN: The Conference will want without doubt to take note of the declarations of the representative of Viet-Nam as well as those of the delegate of France.

---

[13] See the "Declaration of Governmental Policy in Relation to Religion," of October 4, 1953, in O. A. Arturov, ed., *Demokraticheskaya Respublika Vietnam: Konstitutsia, Zakonodatelnia Akti, Dokumenti* (Moscow: Izdatelstvo Innostrannoi Literaturi, 1955), pp. 133–137 [in Russian]; see also Ho Chi Minh, "Message to Compatriots, Soldiers and Civil Servants in Newly Liberated Areas in North Viet Nam Delta," dated July 3, 1954, in Ho Chi Minh, *Selected Works* (4 vols., Hanoi: Foreign Languages Publishing House, 1961–1962), Vol. III, pp. 442–443: "As regards Catholic people in the newly liberated zones, apart from fulfilling these above-mentioned tasks, you must show your confidence in the Government's policy on freedom of worship, not let the enemy misuse you, and don't let yourselves be misled by their allegations."

[Further extract from the verbatim record. * This extract begins immediately following the extract above with no omission.]

THE CHAIRMAN (Mr. Eden): As I think my colleagues are aware, agreement has now been reached on certain documents. It is proposed that this Conference should take note of these agreements. I accordingly propose to begin by reading out a list of the subjects covered by the documents, which I understand every delegation has in front of them.

First, agreement on the cessation of hostilities in Viet Nam; [14] second, agreement on the cessation of hostilities in Laos; [15] third, agreement on the cessation of hostilities in Cambodia.[16] I would draw particular attention to the fact that these three agreements now incorporate the texts which were negotiated separately concerning the supervision of the Armistice in the three countries by the International Commission and the joint committees.

I should also like to draw the attention of all delegations to a point of some importance in connexion with the Armistice Agreements and the related maps and documents on supervision. It has been agreed among the parties to each of these Agreements that none of them shall be made public for the present, pending further agreement among the parties. The reason for this, I must explain to my colleagues, is that these Armistice terms come into force at different dates.[17] And it is

* *Source:* Great Britain, Parliament, Papers by Command, *Further Documents Relating to the Discussion of Indo-China at the Geneva Conference June 16–July 21, 1954* (London: Her Majesty's Stationery Office, Cmd. 9239, 1954, reprinted 1965), pp. 5–9. As indicated at various spots in the text, there are differences between the British and French minutes of the proceedings of the Session. Most importantly, neither the opening statements by Tran Van Do and Mendès-France nor the concluding statements by the six Foreign Ministers who chose to make them appear in the British version. The British version, however, is headed as "Extracts from the Verbatim Record" although what was omitted is not indicated.

[14] Document 130.

[15] Text in Great Britain, Parliament, Papers by Command, *Further Documents Relating to the Discussion of Indo-China at the Geneva Conference June 16–July 21, 1954* (London: Her Majesty's Stationery Office, Cmd. 9239, 1954, reprinted 1965), pp. 18–26.

[16] *Ibid.,* pp. 11–18.

[17] The Cambodian agreement entered into force at 0000 hours, July 23, 1954; the Lao agreement at 2400 hours, July 22; and the Viet-Nam agreement at 2400 hours, July 22. However, the cease-fire in Viet-Nam was to take effect at different times in different parts of the country: see Document 130, Chapter II, Article 11.

desired that they should not be made public until they have come into force.

The further documents to which I must draw attention, which are in your possession, are: fourth, declaration by the Government of Laos on elections;[18] fifth, declaration by the Government of Cambodia on elections and integration of all citizens into the national community;[19] sixth, declaration by the Government of Laos on the military status of the country;[20] seventh, declaration by the Government of Cambodia on the military status of the country;[21] eighth, [declaration by the Government of the French Republic on the respect for the independence of the three Indochinese countries;[22] ninth], declaration by the Government of the French Republic on the withdrawal of troops from the three countries of Indochina.[23]

Finally, gentlemen, there is the Draft Declaration by the Conference, which takes note of all these documents. I think all my colleagues have copies of this Draft Declaration [24] before them. I will ask my colleagues in turn to express themselves upon this Declaration.

The Representative of France.

M. MENDÈS-FRANCE (France): Mr. Chairman, the French Delegation approves the terms of this Declaration.

THE CHAIRMAN: The Representative of Laos.

MR. PHOUI SANANIKONE (Laos): The Delegation of Laos has no observations to make on this text.

THE CHAIRMAN: The Representative of the People's Republic of China.

MR. CHOU EN-LAI (People's Republic of China): We agree.

THE CHAIRMAN: On behalf of Her Majesty's Government in the United Kingdom, I associate myself with the final Declaration of this Conference.

The Union of Soviet Socialist Republics.

M. MOLOTOV (U.S.S.R.): The Soviet Delegation agrees.

THE CHAIRMAN: The Representative of Cambodia.

[18] Text in Great Britain, Parliament, Papers by Command, *Further Documents Relating to the Discussion of Indo-China at the Geneva Conference June 16– July 21, 1954* (London: Her Majesty's Stationery Office, Cmd. 9239, 1954, reprinted 1965), p. 41.

[19] *Ibid.*, p. 40.   [20] *Ibid.*, p. 41.   [21] *Ibid.*

[22] Document 133; for reasons which are unclear, this item was omitted from the enumeration of documents in the British source used for this part of the proceedings of the final session. The appropriate phrase has therefore been inserted from the French minutes and the numbering rectified.

[23] Document 132.   [24] Document 131.

MR. TEP PHAN (Cambodia): The Delegation of Cambodia wishes to state that, among the documents just listed, one is missing. This is a Cambodian Declaration which we have already circulated to all delegations. Its purport is as follows: Paragraphs 7, 11 and 12 of the final Declaration stipulate respect for the territorial integrity of Viet Nam. The Cambodian Delegation asks the Conference to consider that this provision does not imply the abandonment of such legitimate rights and interests as Cambodia might assert with regard to certain regions of South Viet Nam, about which Cambodia has made express reservations, in particular at the time of the signature of the Franco-Khmer Treaty of November 8, 1949,[25] on relations between Cambodia and France and at the time the French law which linked Cochinchina to Viet Nam [26] was passed. Faithful to the ideal of peace, and to the international principle of non-interference, Cambodia has no intention of interfering in the internal affairs of the State of Viet Nam and associates herself fully with the principle of respect for its integrity, provided certain adjustments and regularisations be arrived at with regard to the borders between this State and Cambodia, borders which so far have been fixed by a mere unilateral act of France.

In support of this Declaration, the Cambodian Delegation communicates to all members of this Conference a note on Cambodian lands in South Viet Nam.[27]

THE CHAIRMAN: If this Declaration was not inscribed on the agenda on the list of documents I have read out, it is because it has only at this instant reached me. I do not think it is any part of the task of this Conference to deal with any past controversies in respect of the frontiers between Cambodia and Viet Nam.

The Representative of the Democratic Republic of Viet Nam.

MR. PHAM VAN DONG (Democratic Republic of Viet Nam): Mr. Chairman, I agree completely with the words pronounced by you. In the name of the Government of the Democratic Republic of Viet Nam

[25] Text of the Franco-Cambodian Treaty in France, *Journal Officiel de la République Française, Lois et Décrets,* March 14, 1953, pp. 2404–2407.
[26] Document 56.
[27] *Memorandum by Cambodia on Her Territories in South Viet-Nam (Cochinchina)* (Geneva: Imprimerie Gloor, 1954). The memorandum is dated April 24, 1954. The Cambodian claims, which remain unresolved as of the summer of 1970, stem from the early stages of French expansion in Indochina when Cochin China was constituted as a French colony, since some of the territories included were then still considered by Cambodia as part of her territory. The Cambodian claims also apply to a number of offshore islands in the Gulf of Siam.

we make the most express reservations regarding the statement made by the Delegation of Cambodia just now. I do this in the interests of good relations and understanding between our two countries.

THE CHAIRMAN: I think the Conference can take note of the statements of the Delegation of Cambodia just circulated and of the statement of the Representative of the Democratic Republic of Viet Nam.

I will continue calling upon countries to speak on the subject of the Declaration. I call upon the United States of America.

MR. BEDELL SMITH (United States): Mr. Chairman, Fellow Delegates, as I stated to my colleagues during our meeting on July 18,[28] my Government is not prepared to join in a Declaration by the Conference such as is submitted. However, the United States makes this unilateral declaration of its position in these matters:

DECLARATION

The Government of the United States being resolved to devote its efforts to the strengthening of peace in accordance with the principles and purposes of the United Nations

Takes Note of the Agreements concluded at Geneva on July 20 and 21, 1954, between (*a*) the Franco-Laotian Command and the Command of the People's Army of Viet Nam; (*b*) the Royal Khmer Army Command and the Command of the People's Army of Viet Nam; (*c*) Franco-Vietnamese Command and the Command of the People's Army of Viet Nam, and of paragraphs 1 to 12 [29] of the Declaration presented to the Geneva Conference on July 21, 1954.

The Government of the United States of America

Declares with regard to the aforesaid Agreements and paragraphs that (i) it will refrain from the threat or the use of force to disturb them, in accordance with Article 2 (Section 4) of the Charter of the United Nations [30] dealing with the obligation of Members to refrain in their international relations from the threat or use of force; and (ii) it would view any renewal of the aggression in violation of the aforesaid Agreements with grave concern and as seriously threatening international peace and security.

In connexion with the statement in the Declaration concerning free elections in Viet Nam, my Government wishes to make clear its posi-

28 See Note 38, p. 285.

29 Thus excluding paragraph 13, which provided for consultations among the members of the Geneva Conference on measures to ensure respect for the agreements on cessation of hostilities. See Document 131.

30 Footnote in the original: " 'Treaty Series No. 67 (1946),' Cmd. 7015."

tion which it has expressed in a Declaration made in Washington on June 29, 1954,[31] as follows:

> "In the case of nations now divided against their will, we shall continue to seek to achieve unity through free elections, supervised by the United Nations to ensure that they are conducted fairly."

With respect to the statement made by the Representative of the State of Viet Nam, the United States reiterates its traditional position that peoples are entitled to determine their own future and that it will not join in an arrangement which would hinder this. Nothing in its declaration just made is intended to or does indicate any departure from this traditional position.

We share the hope that the agreement will permit Cambodia, Laos and Viet Nam to play their part in full independence and sovereignty, in the peaceful community of nations, and will enable the peoples of that area to determine their own future.

Thank you, Mr. Chairman.

THE CHAIRMAN: The Conference will, I think, wish to take note of the statement of the Representative of the United States of America.

I call on the Representative of the State of Viet Nam.

MR. TRAN VAN DO (State of Viet Nam): Mr. Chairman, as regards the final Declaration of the Conference, the Vietnamese Delegation requests the Conference to incorporate in this Declaration after Article 10, the following text:

> "The Conference takes note of the Declaration of the Government of the State of Viet Nam undertaking: to make and support every effort to re-establish a real and lasting peace in Viet Nam; not to use force to resist the procedures for carrying the cease-fire into effect, in spite of the objections and reservations that the State of Viet Nam has expressed, especially in its final statement."

THE CHAIRMAN: I shall be glad to hear any views that my colleagues may wish to express. But, as I understand the position, the final Declaration has already been drafted and this additional paragraph has only just now been received; indeed, it has been amended since I received the text a few minutes ago. In all the circumstances, I suggest that the best course we can take is that the Conference should take note of the Declaration of the State of Viet Nam in this respect. If any of my colleagues has a contrary view, perhaps they would be good enough to say so. (None.) If none of my colleagues wishes to make any other

[31] See Source Note to Document 125.

observations, may I pass to certain other points which have to be settled before this Conference can conclude its labours?

The first is that, if it is agreeable to our colleagues, it is suggested that the two Chairmen should at the conclusion of this meeting address telegrams to the Governments of India, Poland and Canada to ask them if they will undertake the duties of supervision which the Conference has invited them to discharge. Is that agreeable? (Agreed.) Thank you.

The last is perhaps the least agreeable chapter of all our work. Certain costs arise from the decisions which the Conference has taken. It is suggested that it should be left here to your Chairmen as their parting gift to try to put before you some proposal in respect of those costs. I only wish to add in that connexion that, as this Conference is peculiar in not having any Secretariat in the usual sense of the term, the two Chairmen with considerable reluctance are prepared to undertake this highly invidious task. The costs to which I refer are not our own but those of the International Commission.[32]

Does any delegate wish to make any further observation? (None).

Gentlemen, perhaps I may say a final word as your Chairman for this day. We have now come to the end of our work. For a number of reasons it has been prolonged and intricate. The co-operation which all delegates have given to your two Chairmen has enabled us to overcome many procedural difficulties. Without that co-operation, we could not have succeeded in our task. The Agreements concluded to-day could not, in the nature of things, give complete satisfaction to everyone. But they have made it possible to stop a war which has lasted for eight years and brought suffering and hardship to millions of people. They have also, we hope, reduced international tension at a point of instant danger to world peace. These results are surely worth our many weeks of toil. In order to bring about a cease-fire, we have drawn up a series of agreements. They are the best that our hands could devise. All will now depend upon the spirit in which those agreements are observed and carried out.

Gentlemen, before we leave this hospitable town of Geneva I'm sure you would wish your Chairmen to give a message of gratitude to the United Nations and its able staff who have housed and helped us in our work.

---

[32] The French text of this portion of Mr. Eden's remarks reads: "I want to remind you that these expenses are not only our own but also those of the International Commission" (France, Ministère des Affaires Etrangères, *Conférence de Genève sur l'Indochine* [*8 Mai–21 Juillet 1954*]: *Procès-verbaux des Séances—Propositions—Documents Finaux* [Paris: Imprimerie Nationale, 1955], pp. 383–384).

And lastly let me express our cordial thanks to the Swiss Government and to the people and authorities of Geneva who have done so much to make our stay here pleasant as well as of service to the cause of peace.

The Representative of the United States of America.

MR. BEDELL SMITH (U.S.A.): If I presume to speak for my fellow delegates, it is because I know that they all feel as I do. I hope that they join me in expressing our thanks to the two Chairmen of this Conference. Their patience, their tireless efforts, and their goodwill have done a great deal to make this settlement possible. We owe them our sincere thanks.

THE CHAIRMAN: The Representative of the Union of Soviet Socialist Republics.

M. MOLOTOV (U.S.S.R.): Mr. Chairman, as one of the Chairmen at the Geneva Conference, I would like to reply to the remarks just made by Mr. Bedell Smith, who spoke highly of the work done by the Chairmen. Naturally I must stress the outstanding services and the outstanding role played by our Chairman of to-day, Mr. Eden, whose rôle in the Geneva Conference cannot be exaggerated. And I would also like to reply and thank Mr. Bedell Smith for his warm words of to-day.

THE CHAIRMAN: Has any other delegate anything else they want to say?

The Representative of Viet Nam.

MR. TRAN VAN DO (State of Viet Nam): Mr. Chairman, I expressed the view of the Delegation of the State of Viet Nam in my statement and I would have this Conference take note of it in its final act.

THE CHAIRMAN: As I think I explained, we cannot now amend our final act, which is the statement of the Conference as a whole, but the Declaration of the Representative of the State of Viet Nam will be taken note of.[33]

Any other observations? (None.) [34]

I would like to be allowed to add my thanks for what General Bedell Smith has said and also to thank M. Molotov for his words. Both were

[33] The French text of this portion of the meeting reads: "I think I explained that it was not possible for us to modify the final act, but the declarations of the representative of the State of Viet-Nam will be recorded in the minutes of the meeting" (France, Ministère des Affaires Etrangères, *Conférence de Genève sur l'Indochine* [8 Mai–21 Juillet 1954]: *Procès-verbaux des Séances—Propositions—Documents Finaux* [Paris: Imprimerie Nationale, 1955], p. 385).

[34] This sentence does not appear in the French minutes (*ibid.*).

undeserved, but even if things are not true, if they are nice things it's pleasant to hear them said.

But I do want to close this Conference with this one sentence: I'm quite sure that each one of us here hopes that the work which we have done will help to strengthen the forces working for peace.[35]

[The concluding statements by Foreign Minister Molotov, Foreign Minister Pham Van Dong, Foreign Minister Chou En-lai, Foreign Minister Phoui Sananikone, Foreign Minister Tep Phann, and Premier Mendès-France are omitted. They do not appear in the British version of the proceedings of the session.]

[35] This sentence does not appear in the French minutes (*ibid.*).

CHAPTER XI

Reactions to the Geneva Agreements

July 21-July 23, 1954

Introduction

The initial world reaction to the conclusion of the Geneva Agreements was one of relief at the ending of hostilities in Indochina. There was little concern with the specifics of the Agreements or with the difficulties which might accompany their implementation.

The first American reaction from President Eisenhower on July 21 (Document 135) reflected pleasure at the ending of hostilities. He held some reservations, however, on parts of the Agreements and emphasized that the United States had not been a formal party to them. Secretary of State Dulles was less enthusiastic (Document 138).

The Democratic Republic of Viet-Nam (DRV) interpreted the Geneva Agreements as a victory even though they awarded the Viet Minh less than they had desired, particularly in relation to Cambodia and Laos. Ho Chi Minh's appeal of July 22 (Document 136) justified the Agreements and called for a continued struggle to win national unity. Pham Van Dong, in an interview with a correspondent of the Polish Press Agency, noted the responsibility of France to see the Agreements correctly implemented:

To assure the correct execution of the agreements by all the countries concerned, principally by the Government of the Democratic Republic of Viet-Nam and the Government of the French Republic [is the most important step to ensure peace in Southeast Asia]. It is necessary to work actively for the solution of military and political problems which exist between the two countries, in particular the organization of free and democratic general elections to realize the unity of Viet-Nam. For that, it is essential to under-

take and develop direct, close and cordial relations between the two governments.[1]

By contrast, the reaction of the State of Viet-Nam to the Geneva
Agreements was almost wholly negative, as was indicated by Ngo Dinh
Diem's statement of July 22 (Document 137). Flags were flown at
half-mast and the anniversary of the signing was declared a "day of
shame."

China and the Soviet Union characterized the Geneva Agreements as
a victory for the forces of peace while minimizing those aspects which
looked toward a final political settlement. Both these characteristics
were apparent in the official Soviet Government statement on the
Geneva Conference (Document 139). Mao Tse-tung sent a telegram
of congratulations to Ho Chi Minh (Document 140).

It was naturally in France that the Geneva Agreements received
their warmest reception, yet the conditions were less than the best
France could have wanted. In the statement he broadcast to the French
people from Geneva on July 21, Premier Mendès-France said that
some aspects of the Agreements "are cruel," but "I solemnly and
sincerely believe that these conditions are the best we could have
hoped for in the present state of affairs." [2] On July 22 he appeared before the National Assembly to justify the Agreements and ask approval
for them.[3] A general debate took place on the following day, and
the National Assembly adopted an Order of the Day endorsing the
Government's policy (Document 141). British reaction to the Geneva
Agreements was expressed by Foreign Secretary Eden:

I think everyone will agree that the proceedings of this Conference have
been of unparalleled complexity. I am myself convinced that the arrangements now arrived at are the best that could have been contrived in the
circumstances of each individual case.[4]

[1] Text in Polish Institute of International Affairs (Warsaw), *Zbiór Dokumentów*, No. 7–8, 1954, pp. 1830–1837 [in Polish and French].

[2] Text in French Press and Information Service (New York), *Speeches and
Press Conferences*, No. 28 (July 21, 1954), p. 1.

[3] The text of Mendès-France's statement is in France, *Journal Officiel de la
République Française, Débats Parlementaires, Assemblée Nationale*, Session of
July 22, 1954, pp. 3533–3537. An English translation is in French Press and
Information Service (New York), *Indochinese Affairs*, No. 6 (August 1954),
pp. 1–11.

[4] The text of Eden's statement to the House of Commons is in Great Britain,
Parliamentary Debates (Hansard), Fifth Series, House of Commons, Vol. 530,
Session of July 22, 1954, cols. 1570–1574.

135. *President Eisenhower: Statement at a News Conference* *
    July 21, 1954

I am glad, of course, that agreement has been reached at Geneva to stop the bloodshed in Indochina.[1]

The United States has not been a belligerent in the war. The primary responsibility for the settlement in Indochina rested with those nations which participated in the fighting. Our role at Geneva has been at all times to try to be helpful where desired and to aid France and Cambodia, Laos, and Viet-Nam to obtain a just and honorable settlement which will take into account the needs of the interested people. Accordingly, the United States has not itself been party to or bound by the decisions taken by the Conference, but it is our hope that it will lead to the establishment of peace consistent with the rights and the needs of the countries concerned. The agreement contains features which we do not like, but a great deal depends on how they work in practice.

The United States is issuing at Geneva a statement to the effect that it is not prepared to join in the Conference declaration, but, as loyal members of the United Nations, we also say that, in compliance with the obligations and principles contained in article 2 of the United Nations Charter, the United States will not use force to disturb the settlement.[2] We also say that any renewal of Communist aggression would be viewed by us as a matter of grave concern.

As evidence of our resolve to assist Cambodia and Laos to play their part, in full independence and sovereignty, in the peaceful community of free nations, we are requesting the agreement of the Governments of Cambodia and Laos to our appointment of an Ambassador or Minister to be resident at their respective capitals (Phnom Penh and Vientiane). We already have a Chief of Mission at Saigon, the capital of Viet-Nam, and this Embassy will, of course, be maintained.

The United States is actively pursuing discussions with other free nations with a view to the rapid organization of a collective defense in Southeast Asia in order to prevent further direct or indirect Communist aggression in that general area.

* *Source:* United States, Department of State, *American Foreign Policy 1950–1955: Basic Documents* (2 vols., Washington: Government Printing Office, 1957), Vol. II, pp. 2397–2398.

[1] Cross-reference footnote in the original omitted.

[2] See the Declaration made by the United States, in Document 134.

136. *Ho Chi Minh: Appeal Made after the Successful Conclusion of the Geneva Agreements* *
July 22, 1954

To all compatriots,

To all armymen and cadres,

The Geneva Conference has been concluded. We have scored a great victory in [the] diplomatic field.

On behalf of the Government, I cordially address the following appeal to all compatriots, armymen and cadres.

1. It is for the sake of peace, unity, independence and democracy of the fatherland that during the past eight, nine years, our people, army, cadres and Government, closely united, have been undergoing sufferings, overcoming all difficulties, resolutely fighting and have scored brilliant victories. On this occasion, I convey, on behalf of the Government, my cordial congratulations to all compatriots, fighters and cadres from the North to the South. I respectfully bow before the memory of the fighters and compatriots who have heroically sacrificed their lives for the fatherland, and convey my condolences to wounded or sick armymen.

Our great victories are also due to the fact that our fight for the just cause has enjoyed support from peoples in friendly countries, the people of France and peace-loving peoples in the world.

It is thanks to these victories and to the efforts of the delegate of the U.S.S.R. at the Berlin Conference that negotiations have been opened between our Government and the French Government at the Geneva Conference. At the Geneva Conference, thanks to the struggle of our delegation and to the assistance of the two delegations of the U.S.S.R. and the People's Republic of China, we have scored a great victory: the French Government has recognized the independence, sovereignty,

---

* *Source:* New China News Agency, July 24, 1954, citing Viet-Nam News Agency, in United States, Consulate General in Hong Kong, *Survey of the China Mainland Press*, No. 856 (July 27, 1954), pp. 7–9. A number of grammatical mistakes in the original have been corrected. The Appeal also appears in English in Communist Information Bureau, *For a Lasting Peace, For a People's Democracy*, July 30, 1954, p. 3; and in Ho Chi Minh, *Selected Works* (4 vols., Hanoi: Foreign Languages Publishing House, 1961–1962), Vol. IV, pp. 17–20. There are some variations between the *Selected Works* version and the version printed here which seem to change the emphasis on the importance of the struggle in the South; for that reason the version published at the time is used despite the generally poorer quality of the translation in grammar and style.

unity and territorial integrity of our country, has accepted to withdraw French armed forces from our land etc.

Henceforward, we must endeavor to fight to consolidate peace, materialize unity and achieve independence and democracy throughout the country.

2. To materialize peace, the first step to be taken is that the armed forces of the two sides should cease fire.

To carry out cease-fire, it is necessary to regroup the armed forces of the two sides into two separate zones, that is to say the readjustment of the areas occupied by the armed forces of each side.

The drawing of a military demarcation line is a temporary and transition measure to materialize armistice, restore peace and progress towards national unification by means of general elections. The demarcation line does not mean by any way a political or territorial boundary.

During the period of armistice, our armed forces shall be concentrated in Northern Viet-Nam while the French Union Forces in Southern Viet-Nam, it means there will be an exchange of zones. A number of localities occupied by the French will become liberated areas. On the other hand, a number of our liberated areas will become place[s] where the French forces will temporarily station before returning to France.

This is a necessary measure. But, the Northern, Central and Southern Viet-Nam are integral parts of our territory, our country will surely be unified and our compatriots throughout the country will certainly be emancipated.

Our compatriots in the South were the first to wage the patriotic war and are highly awakened. I am confident that they will place the interests of the whole country above the local interests, the lasting interests above the present ones, and will, hand in hand with the rest of our people, endeavor to fight to consolidate peace, materialize unity and achieve independence and democracy throughout the country. The Viet-Nam Lao Dong Party, the Government and myself have always been following the efforts of our compatriots in the South and are confident that they will win success.

3. The struggle for the consolidation of peace, for the materialization of unity, for the achievement of independence and democracy is also a long and hard struggle. To win victory, the whole people, all armymen and cadres from the North to the South must enhance their solidarity, and must be united in thought and action.

We are determined to carry out faithfully the terms we have signed with the French Government, and at the same time, urge the French Government to implement faithfully the terms it has signed with us.

We must endeavor to consolidate peace and keep high our vigilance over the manoeuvres of the saboteurs of peace.

We must endeavor to fight for the holding of general free elections throughout the country to realize national unification.

We must endeavor to recover and build up, consolidate and develop our forces in all spheres so as to materialize complete independence for the fatherland.

We must endeavor to carry out social reforms to improve the living conditions of our people, and materialize genuine democracy.

We further tighten our brotherhood with the two peoples of Laos and Cambodia.

We consolidate the great friendship between Viet-Nam and the Soviet Union, the People's Republic of China and other friendly countries. We further tighten our solidarity with the French people, the peoples in Asia and the world over to safeguard peace.

4. I cordially call on the whole people, all armymen and cadres correctly to implement the political line and policies of the Party and Government, and to fight to consolidate peace, materialize unity, achieve independence and democracy throughout the country.

I earnestly appeal to all persons who sincerely love the fatherland, without distinction of social classes, religious creeds, political af- filiations, without distinction of their former stand on the side of any parties, to sincerely cooperate with each other and work for the benefit of the nation and the fatherland, fight for the materialization of peace, unity, independence and democracy in our beloved Viet-Nam.

With nationwide unity, with the entire people united like one man, we will certainly win victory.

Long live peace, unity, independence and democracy of Viet-Nam!
July 22nd, 1954

(Signed) HO CHI MINH
President,
Viet-Nam Democratic Republic

137. *Premier Ngo Dinh Diem: Statement Regarding the Geneva Agreements* *
July 22, 1954

Dear Compatriots,

You know the facts: a cease-fire concluded at Geneva without the concurrence of the Vietnamese delegation has surrendered to the Communists all the northern and more than four provinces of the central part of our country.

The national Government, constituted less than two weeks ago, in spite of its profound attachment to peace, has lodged the most solemn protest against that injustice.[3] Our delegation at Geneva has not signed that agreement, for we cannot recognise the seizure by Soviet China [*sic*]—through its satellite the Vietminh—of over half of our national territory. We can neither concur in the enslavement of millions of compatriots faithful to the nationalist ideal, nor to the complete destitution of those who, thanks to our efforts, will have succeeded in joining the zone left to us.

Brutally placed before an accomplished fact, Vietnam cannot resort to violence, for that would be moving toward a catastrophe and destroying all hope [of] remaking one day a free Vietnam from the South to the North.

In spite of our grief, in spite of our indignation, let us keep our self-control and remain united in order to give our brother refugees help and comfort and begin at once the peaceful and difficult struggle which will eventually free our country from all foreign intervention, whatever it may be, and from all oppression.

138. *Secretary of State Dulles: Statement at a News Conference* †
July 23, 1954

The Geneva negotiations reflected the military developments in Indochina. After nearly 8 years of war the forces of the French Union

* *Source:* Republic of Viet-Nam, Ministry of Information, *The Problem of Reunification of Viet-Nam* (Saigon?: 1958), p. 29. Several grammatical mistakes in the original have been corrected. A French text of this statement is in State of Viet-Nam, High Commission in Paris, *Vietnam,* No. 80 (August 1, 1954), p. 8; and in Ngo Dinh Diem, *La Voie de la Juste Cause: Traduction des Principaux Discours et Déclarations du Président Ngo-Dinh-Diem* (Saigon: Service de Presse, Présidence de la République du Viêt-Nam, 1956), pp. 20–21.

† *Source:* United States, Department of State, *Bulletin,* XXXI (August 2, 1954), pp. 163–164.

[3] See Document 129 and the protest by Foreign Minister Tran Van Do in Document 134.

had lost control of nearly one-half of Viet-Nam, their hold on the balance was precarious, and the French people did not desire to prolong the war.

These basic facts inevitably dominated the Indochina phase of the Geneva Conference and led to settlements which, as President Eisenhower said, contain many features which we do not like.[4]

Since this was so, and since the United States itself was neither a belligerent in Indochina nor subject to compulsions which applied to others, we did not become a party to the Conference results. We merely noted them and said that, in accordance with the United Nations Charter, we would not seek by force to overthrow the settlement. We went on to affirm our dedication to the principle of self-determination of peoples and our hope that the agreements would permit Cambodia, Laos, and Viet-Nam to be really sovereign and independent nations.[5]

The important thing from now on is not to mourn the past but to seize the future opportunity to prevent the loss in northern Viet-Nam from leading to the extension of communism throughout Southeast Asia and the Southwest Pacific. In this effort all of the free nations concerned should profit by the lessons of the past.

One lesson is that resistance to communism needs popular support, and this in turn means that the people should feel that they are defending their own national institutions. One of the good aspects of the Geneva Conference is that it advances the truly independent status of Cambodia, Laos, and southern Viet-Nam. Prime Minister Mendès-France said yesterday that instructions had been given to the French representatives in Viet-Nam to complete by July 30 precise projects for the transfers of authority which will give reality to the independence which France had promised.[6] This independence is already a fact in Laos and Cambodia, and it was demonstrated at Geneva, notably by the Government of Cambodia. The evolution from colonialism to national independence is thus about to be completed in Indochina, and the free governments of this area should from now on be able to enlist the loyalty of their people to maintain their independence as against Communist colonialism.

A second lesson which should be learned is that arrangements for collective defense need to be made in advance of aggression, not after it is under way. The United States for over a year advocated united

[4] See Document 135.

[5] See the Declaration made by the United States, in Document 134.

[6] In his statement to the National Assembly reporting on the Geneva Agreements; see Note 3, p. 320.

action in the area, but this proved not to be practical under the conditions which existed. We believe, however, that now it will be practical to bring about collective arrangements to promote the security of the free peoples of Southeast Asia. Prompt steps will be taken in this direction. In this connection we should bear in mind that the problem is not merely one of deterring open armed aggression but of preventing Communist subversion which, taking advantage of economic dislocations and social injustice, might weaken and finally overthrow the non-Communist governments.

If the free nations which have a stake in this area will now work together to avail of present opportunities in the light of past experience, then the loss of the present may lead to a gain for the future.

139. *Soviet Government Statement on the Geneva Conference*
     [Extract] *
     July 23, 1954

The Geneva Conference of Foreign Ministers, summoned in conformity with the decision of the Berlin Conference to examine the Korea and Indo-China questions, completed its work on July 21.

As a result of the Conference, which continued for almost three months, agreements have been signed which put an end to hostilities in Viet Nam, Laos and Cambodia. These agreements are designed to accomplish the important tasks connected with the restoration and consolidation of peace in Viet Nam, Laos and Cambodia on the basis, as stated in the Final Declaration adopted by the participants in the Geneva Conference,[7] of respecting the independence and sovereignty, unity and territorial integrity of the three Indo-China states.

The cease-fire in Indo-China has opened up for the peoples of Viet Nam, Laos and Cambodia opportunities for economic and cultural progress in conditions of peace and at the same time lays the foundation for the development of friendly co-operation between them and France.

The decisions of the Geneva Conference prohibiting establishment of military bases by foreign states on the territory of Viet Nam, Laos and Cambodia and the obligations assumed by these three states not to enter into military alliances and not to allow themselves to be utilised

* *Source:* Communist Information Bureau, *For a Lasting Peace, For a People's Democracy*, July 30, 1954, p. 1. The original Russian text of the Statement is in *Pravda* and *Izvestia*, July 23, 1954, p. 1.
[7] Document 131.

for a resumption of hostilities or for purposes of an aggressive policy are vitally important.

The decision of the Geneva Conference on the holding of free elections in Viet Nam in July 1956 creates conditions for the national unification of Viet Nam in accordance with the national interests and aspirations of the entire Viet Nam people. This decision, adopted as a result of the persistent efforts of the democratic countries, signifies a defeat for those aggressive forces who sought to dismember Viet Nam with the object, thereafter, of converting South Viet Nam into one of the spring-boards of the projected new aggressive bloc in South-East Asia.

The agreement on holding general elections in Cambodia and Laos in the course of 1955, as stated in the Final Declaration, by means of secret ballot and observance of basic rights, is also of great significance.

It should be stated that the adoption of such important decisions was facilitated by the positive attitude of the French Government, dictated by the desire to act in accordance with the national interests of France and by the desire to take into account the interests of the peoples of Indo-China.

Notwithstanding certain reservations in the agreements signed at Geneva their enormous significance should not be underestimated, in particular, in view of the aforementioned circumstances and also because of the fact that the Geneva Conference succeeded in overcoming a number of difficulties which arose as a result of the attitude of the United States representatives who tried to prevent the work of the Conference being crowned with success. The United States showed no desire to participate jointly with France, Britain, the U.S.S.R., the People's Republic of China and other countries in the work of ensuring the restoration of peace in Indo-China. The Geneva agreements signify an important victory for the forces of peace and a serious defeat for the forces of war. At the same time the Geneva agreements constitute international recognition of the national-liberation struggle and of the great heroism displayed by the peoples of Indo-China in this struggle.

The fact of the Geneva Conference ending in agreements between the countries concerned provides further evidence of the fruitfulness of international negotiations, given goodwill by the parties concerned, evidence of the possibility of settling in this way major international issues still outstanding.

The Soviet Government welcomes the success achieved in Geneva in solving the highly important problem of restoring peace in Indo-China. The solving of this problem accords with the interests of the peoples who are upholding their freedom and national independence, and in equal measure, with the interests of all peace-loving peoples.

Along with the vital matter of securing a final peaceful settlement in Indo-China there is the urgent task of a final peaceful settlement in Korea.

[The concluding five paragraphs are omitted. They concern Korea, cite the results at Geneva to prove that "at present there are no outstanding questions in international relations which could not be settled through negotiation," and emphasize the importance of the Chinese role.]

140. *Mao Tse-tung: Message to Ho Chi Minh* *
    July 23, 1954

President of the Government of the Democratic Republic of Viet-Nam,

Comrade Ho Chi Minh:

On the occasion of the reaching of agreement on the armistice question and political question regarding Indo-China, on behalf of the Chinese people and the Government of the People's Republic of China, I send to the fraternal Viet-Namese people, the Government of the Democratic Republic of Viet-Nam and you my heartfelt and warmest congratulations.

At the Geneva Conference, the delegation of the Democratic Republic of Viet-Nam, representing the aspirations for peace of the people of Viet-Nam who have been carrying out their heroic struggle for national independence and freedom and have achieved brilliant victories, made great efforts for the restoration of peace in Indo-China and finally attained agreement. This is another great victory for the people of Viet-Nam. This victory is helpful to the promotion of collective peace and security in Asia and further relaxation of international tension.

All the people of China will strive, together with the people of Viet-Nam, for ensuring the thorough implementation of the agreements and for the preservation and consolidation of peace and security in Asia and the whole world.

MAO TSE-TUNG

* *Source:* New China News Agency, July 23, 1954, in United States, Consulate General in Hong Kong, *Survey of the China Mainland Press,* No. 855 (July 24–26, 1954), p. 21.

141. *Order of the Day Adopted by the French National Assembly* *
    July 23, 1954

The National Assembly,

Addresses a moving and grateful tribute to the heroism of the combatants of the French Union and the Associated States;

Notes with satisfaction the cessation of hostilities in Indochina due, for the most part, to the decisive action of the President of the Council [the Premier];

Noting that cruel sacrifices were inevitable, and in spite of the sorrow it feels because of them [*avec la douleur qu'elle en éprouve*], affirms its will to defend, within the framework of the French Union and agreements which have been concluded, the Frenchmen and the peoples of Indochina friendly to France who intend to remain faithful to the emancipatory work which she has constantly carried on;

Requests the Government to continue, in the necessary agreement with our allies, a policy of peace among all peoples;

Approving the Government's declarations and, rejecting all amendment,

Proceeds with the business of the day.

* *Source:* France, *Journal Officiel de la République Française, Débats Parlementaires, Assemblée Nationale,* Session of July 23, 1954, p. 3588. Translation by the editor. After several ballots, on the order of the day as a whole and then on its component parts, the motion was adopted by a final vote of 462 to 13, thus endorsing the conclusion of the Geneva Agreements; formal ratification was not required since there was no treaty involved.

PART FIVE

Emergence of the Two Viet-Nams
July 1954–November 1955

CHAPTER XII

The American Commitment
to South Viet-Nam

July 1954-May 1955

Introduction

The ten months following the conclusion of the Geneva Agreements were a period of readjustment for all parties involved in the Viet-Nam crisis. In South Viet-Nam, the State of Viet-Nam was plunged into political and administrative chaos, and throughout Viet-Nam there were massive readjustments as military and civilian elements moved in accordance with the decisions reached at Geneva. The most significant characteristic of the period, however, was the development of the United States commitment to the State of Viet-Nam and to the defense of Southeast Asia, as manifested by the conclusion of the SEATO Treaty and the replacement of Paris by Washington as the major support for the Saigon government.

The confused situation in Viet-Nam following Geneva was marked by the exodus of refugees from the zone north of the 17th parallel. The refugee movement was encouraged by the State of Viet-Nam and was carried on with substantial aid from the United States; France had first thought the movement would be limited to a few thousands of people, but it soon took on mammoth proportions. The influx of refugees in the zone south of the 17th parallel contributed to the existing political confusion. The authority of the central government of the State of Viet-Nam included little more than the center of Saigon. The population was badly factionalized by years of war and political turmoil, and the army and the "sects" (Hoa Hao, Cao Dai and Binh Xuyen) virtually constituted states within a state.

In addition to ending the Indochina war, the Geneva Conference effected international acceptance of the independence of the Democratic

Republic of Viet-Nam (DRV) and of the State of Viet-Nam from France, although the question of which (if either) of these two governments could lay legitimate claim to the governing of the whole country was deferred to the elections scheduled for 1956. Acquisition of independence by the State of Viet-Nam was symbolized, on September 7, by the formal transfer of the Norodom Palace in Saigon, formerly the official residence of the French Commissioner General. At the same time the representatives of the Associated States and France met in Paris on August 26 to agree on the abolition of "quadripartism," as manifested in the Pau Agreements of 1950,[1] in favor of complete national independence. The negotiations to define the new status of the Indochinese states were to drag on until December.

The Indian government took the initiative in organizing the International Commission for Supervision and Control (ICSC), which was formally established on August 11, the date of cessation of hostilities in the last part of Indochina—Cochin China.

It had become clear soon after Geneva that the United States would support the State of Viet-Nam in the hope of constructing a bastion against further Commnist expansion. A major instrument of American policy was the long-sought Southeast Asia Collective Defense Treaty (Document 142) and the creation of the Southeast Asia Treaty Organization (SEATO) at the September 6–8 Conference in Manila. The creation of SEATO, American support for the Diem government, and the massive exodus from the North combined to bring about a hardening of the DRV position toward both the French and the State of Viet-Nam. The DRV appeared to feel that the Diem regime had scant chance for survival and that reunification would follow almost automatically after the departure of French troops from the South. By September, official DRV sources were calling for the overthrow of the Diem government:

---

[1] For information on the Pau Agreements see the Introduction to Chapter V. Whereas they had provided for a high degree of interdependence among the Indochinese states and France, the new policy, adopted in August 1954 and and reflected in the agreements concluded in December, was one of almost complete independence for each of the Associated States in economic and financial, as well as political and military, matters. The texts of the quadripartite agreements of December 29 and the Franco-Vietnamese agreements of December 30 are in France, Press and Information Service (New York), *Indochinese Affairs*, No. 8 (April 1955), pp. 1–56. French texts are in France, Direction de la Documentation, *Notes et Etudes Documentaires*, No. 1973 (January 25, 1955), pp. 1–44.

However, the root of this contradiction [between the French and the Americans in South Viet-Nam] is the deep hatred of the various strata of the Vietnamese people against Ngo Dinh Diem, a henchman of the American imperialists, for the latter has forced the population in North Viet-Nam to leave for the south and many a time violated the armistice agreements and sabotaged peace. This hatred on the part of the people has influenced the morale of the troops in the Bao Dai army and the members of the Ngo Dinh Diem Cabinet. The movement to oppose Ngo Dinh Diem has been growing since then with every passing day and the latter is becoming more and more isolated.

For this reason Ngo Dinh Diem ought to be overthrown. The people in South Viet-Nam strongly urge the overthrowing of Ngo Dinh Diem and the formation of a new government from which all the lackeys of the American imperialists and the French warmongers would be eliminated. This government should oppose all plots of war provocation and dissension engineered by the American imperialists, and the French warmongers should sincerely implement the armistice agreement to insure democratic liberties for the people and take all necessary measures to consolidate peace, realize unification, and achieve independence and democracy throughout the country.[2]

DRV optimism about collapse of the Diem government seemed well founded as political chaos continued in the South, manifested in conflict between Diem and General Nguyen Van Hinh, Army Chief of Staff, over the organization of the Vietnamese army. Hinh was finally relieved of his duties in November by Bao Dai, but political troubles continued. The developing American commitment may have been instrumental in Diem's victory over Hinh. At the end of September a French delegation arrived in Washington for talks on Indochina; the communiqué (Document 143) issued at the conclusion of the talks reflected the intention of the United States to give its aid directly to the Associated States. During October Senator Mike Mansfield presented a report to the Senate Foreign Relations Committee in which he strongly advocated American support for Diem.[3]

France formally transferred Hanoi to the DRV on October 9, and on October 14 Prime Minister Nehru of India visited the new capital,

[2] Viet-Nam News Agency (VNA) commentary, broadcast by VNA in English Morse, September 23, 1954, 1200 G.M.T.

[3] United States, Congress, Senate, Committee on Foreign Relations, *Report on Indochina: Report of Senator Mike Mansfield on a Study Mission to Vietnam, Cambodia, Laos* (Washington: Government Printing Office, 1954). Senator Mansfield began his report by asserting that "The foreign policy of the United States has suffered a serious reversal in Indochina."

where he and Ho Chi Minh expressed hope for closer cooperation between their two countries.[4] On October 22 a spokesman for the DRV Foreign Ministry denounced the SEATO Treaty (Document 144).

On October 23 the American Ambassador in Saigon delivered a message from President Eisenhower to Premier Diem (Document 145), and on November 3 the President designated General J. Lawton Collins as "Special United States Representative in Viet-Nam" (Document 146). In a November 8 statement to the House of Commons, British Foreign Secretary Anthony Eden indicated that implementation of the Geneva Agreements had been less than ideal and also discussed the question of guarantees (Document 147).[5] The DRV also had indicated unhappiness with the course of events, particularly developments in the South.

General Collins arrived in Saigon in early November and, on November 17, made clear the firm United States support for Premier Diem:

> I came out to Indochina on account of the gravity of the situation in order to take measures to save this region from Communism. . . .
> I have come to Vietnam to bring every possible aid to the Government of [Ngo Dinh] Diem and to his Government only. It is the legal Government in Vietnam, and the aid which the United States will lend it ought to permit the Government to save the country. . . .[6]

His statement came only a day before the arrival of French Premier Pierre Mendès-France in Washington. According to the communiqué issued at the end of that visit, France and the United States reached agreement on their policies in Indo-China (Document 148).

The International Commission for Supervision and Control in Viet-Nam released its first report, covering the period from August 11 through December 1, 1954, on December 25 (Document 149). The report was optimistic about the implementation of the armistice to date,

[4] The text of the communiqué of October 14 is in India, Lok Sabha Secretariat, *Foreign Policy of India: Texts of Documents 1946–1959* (2nd ed., New Delhi: 1959), p. 131.

[5] On November 9, Secretary of State Dulles indicated that the United States was also dissatisfied with the implementation of the Geneva Agreements, although he was not specific about the substance of any violations: "But I have the feeling that in the areas which were supposed to be evacuated by the Communist forces of Ho Chi-Minh there is considerable evasion of what I think was designed to be the result of the armistice." Text in United States, Department of State, Press Release No. 634, dated November 9, 1954, p. 10.

[6] A complete text of the statement is not available. The extracts given here are from a news story in *The New York Times,* November 18, 1954, p. 3.

although it pointed out violations by both sides. On December 31, in a news conference statement summing up the year 1954, Secretary of State Dulles referred to the Geneva Agreements as a "setback" for the United States, but said that it had been offset by the SEATO Treaty.[7] On the same day the United States announced that as of January 1, 1955, American financial aid would be provided directly to the Associated States (Document 150).[8]

On January 20, 1955, the Vietnamese government submitted a request, accompanied by a tentative plan of organization, for the United States to assume responsibility for organization and training of the Vietnamese army under the overall authority of General Paul Ely, the French Commissioner General (Document 151). At approximately the same time it was made known that the Vietnamese armed forces would be reduced by 100,000. Shortly thereafter General Collins returned to Washington for consultations, which apparently were concerned with the degree to which the United States would undertake to support and train the Vietnamese armed forces.

On February 6, 1955, the DRV took the first in a series of diplomatic steps in support of the unification of Viet-Nam by proposing the restoration of "normal relations" between North and South Viet-Nam (Document 152). Although economic and political considerations made such a move desirable for the North, the proposal was perhaps more directly aimed at preventing the solidification of partition between the two zones. The DRV proposal brought no response from the South, where the Diem government had severed nearly all ties with the North and was engaged in a wave of anti-Communism. At the same time, the domestic political crisis continued. Diem's internal policy was characterized by refusal to compromise the principles of national unity and strong central government, which brought him into direct conflict with the semi-autonomous sects.

United States support for Diem was expressed in a letter sent to Bao Dai by President Eisenhower on February 19 (Document 153). This letter was interpreted in some quarters as an implied warning to the former Emperor to refrain from opposing Diem. By an exchange of notes dated February 21 and March 7, the United States implemented

[7] Text in United States, Department of State, *Bulletin,* XXXII (January 10, 1955), pp. 43–44.

[8] The Associated States formally dissolved their quadripartite arrangements by a series of agreements signed on December 29. Viet-Nam acquired financial independence by agreement with France on December 30, providing for establishment of the National Bank of Viet-Nam. For citation, see Note 1 above.

its decision to provide aid directly to the State of Viet-Nam.[9] The financial strength thus provided gave Diem a clear advantage over his internal competitors.

The SEATO powers activated their organization at a conference held in Bangkok from February 23 to 25. The communiqué issued on February 25 reaffirmed "the determination of the member governments to support these three States [Viet-Nam, Cambodia and Laos] in maintaining their freedom and independence as set forth in the Protocol to the Treaty." [10] Following the SEATO meeting Secretary of State Dulles visited Cambodia, Laos and Viet-Nam, as well as other countries in Southeast Asia. He reported to the American people on his trip on March 8 (Document 154).

On the same day the ICSC in Viet-Nam issued its "Second Interim Report," covering the period from December 11, 1954, to February 10, 1955. The report criticized both France and the DRV for a lack of cooperation with each other and with the Commission, and also indicated that there were problems with the Government of the State of Viet-Nam, "which has not signed the agreement" (Document 155).

The DRV continued to take a hard line toward the South. The apparent expectation that the Diem government could not survive the continuing political crisis was reflected in an editoral in the official Communist Party newspaper, *Nhan Dan* (*The People*), on March 31, calling for Diem's overthrow.[11] In early April Foreign Minister Pham Van Dong visited India, where he conferred with Prime Minister Nehru. The joint communiqué issued on April 10 reaffirmed support for the Geneva Agreements and expressed hope for close relations between the two countries.[12]

Meanwhile, confusion continued in South Viet-Nam as the government, the sects and, in some areas, the Viet Minh vied for control of the countryside.[13] The confrontation between the government and the

[9] Texts in United Nations, *Treaty Series,* Vol. 277 (1957), pp. 286–291.

[10] Text in United States, Department of State, *American Foreign Policy 1950–1955: Basic Documents* (2 vols., Washington: Government Printing Office, 1957), Vol. II, pp. 2334–2337.

[11] Text broadcast by VNA in English Morse, March 31, 1955, 0705 G.M.T.; also in Allan B. Cole, ed., *Conflict in Indo-China and International Repercussions: A Documentary History, 1945–1955* (Ithaca, N.Y.: Cornell University Press, 1956), pp. 203–204.

[12] Text in India, Lok Sabha Secretariat, *Foreign Policy of India: Texts of Documents 1947–1959* (2nd ed., New Delhi: 1959), pp. 169–170.

[13] Since the Agreement on the Cessation of Hostilities in Viet-Nam (Document 130) required only the regroupment of regular armed forces, there was no obligation for the Viet Minh to regroup their political cadres, members of

sects led to hostilities with the Binh Xuyen on March 29. A truce was arranged by the French High Command, but the situation remained tense and confused during April. Diem's position was further bolstered by the conclusion of an agreement with the United States for direct financial support for the Vietnamese armed forces.[14]

The dominant international event during April 1955 was the "Conference of Afro-Asian Countries" held at Bandung from April 18 to 24. Both the DRV and the State of Viet-Nam attended, and both had the opportunity to state their positions.[15] The Conference was also the the occasion for a meeting between Pham Van Dong and Premier Katay D. Sasorith of Laos. DRV support for the Pathet Lao had been a continuing irritant between the two countries, but in the joint communiqué issued at the end of the meeting, the DRV agreed to recognize the status of the Pathet Lao as "a question of internal order" in Laos.[16]

The ICSC issued its "Third Interim Report," covering the period

---

local guerrilla units, families, and sympathizers. Nor was there any requirement that the Viet Minh political organization cease to function in the South; indeed, during the political troubles in Saigon, the Viet Minh remained the only effective government in many parts of the country. Even after the Diem government managed to consolidate its position, there is reliable evidence from pro-DRV sources that the Viet Minh organization continued to function (albeit clandestinely) and to follow the "line" laid down in Hanoi; see Wilfred Burchett, *Vietnam: Inside Story of the Guerilla War* (New York: International Publishers, 1965), pp. 112–114. Complete regroupment of all Viet Minh members to the North would have been almost impossible in any event since many were members of the population who lived, farmed, and fought in their native villages. It was the campaign conducted by the Diem government against Viet Minh members and sympathizers ("The Campaign of Denunciation of Communist Subversive Activities") which led to subsequent alleged violations of Article 14 (c) of the cease-fire agreement and the political oppression which was to alienate so many Vietnamese from the Saigon regime during the 1950's. For documentation on this campaign from the point of view of the Diem government, see Republic of Viet-Nam, The People's Directive Committee for the Campaign of Denunciation of Communist Subversive Activities, *Achievements of the Campaign of Denunciation of Communist Subversive Activities (First Phase)* (Saigon?: May 1956). Other views are provided in numerous DRV documents and in the reports of the International Commission for Supervision and Control.

[14] Exchange of letters of April 22 and 23, 1955; text in United Nations, *Treaty Series*, Vol. 277 (1957), pp. 280–284.

[15] The April 19 statement by the representative of the State of Viet-Nam is in Embassy of the State of Viet-Nam (Washington), *News From Vietnam*, Vol. 1, No. 8 (April 29, 1955), pp. 4–7, and also in Cole, *Conflict in Indo-China*, pp. 218–222. Pham Van Dong's April 20 statement is in United States, Consulate General in Hong Kong, *Survey of the China Mainland Press*, No. 1032 (April 21–22, 1955), pp. 7–11.

[16] Text in *Survey of the China Mainland Press*, No. 1034 (April 26, 1955), p. 46.

from February 11 to April 10, on April 25 (Document 156). It reported difficulties with implementation of the provisions of the cease-fire agreement allowing free movement between the two zones, and the Canadian delegation attached a note calling particular attention to that problem.

The internal crisis in South Viet-Nam reached a climax during the last week in April. Fighting between government forces and the Binh Xuyen broke out in the Saigon-Cholon area on April 28, and to the surprise of most observers the government forces drove the rebels out of the city by May 1. A week of very intricate and not entirely clear political maneuvering resulted in a marked strengthening of the government, capped during May by the rallying of many of the sect forces to the government and the military defeat of the others.

The confused events in Viet-Nam had been paralleled, and perhaps decisively influenced, by international activities. Of these the most important were relations between France and the United States. Washington was strongly committed to Diem, but French policy was confused, tending both to oppose Diem and to reduce involvement in Indochina. American influence became predominant because of the ability of the United States to provide funds for the State of Viet-Nam. The tendency of French policy to reduce involvement was indicated by M. Henri Laforest, Minister of State for Relations with the Associated States, in a statement to the Council of the Republic on March 22. He said that on July 20 the State of Viet-Nam and the DRV should meet to work on the problem of the 1956 elections, and that if they did not agree a new international conference should be called to arbitrate the differences, for it "is not France alone which should take responsibility in this matter. The responsibility belongs to all the signatories of the Geneva Agreements, who should meet if agreement is not reached between the two Vietnamese partners." [17] The other tendency of French policy—opposition to, or at least distrust of, Premier Diem—was demonstrated at the height of the political crisis in South Viet-Nam. On April 29, Premier Edgar Faure in essence disowned the Saigon government: "I willingly pay tribute to the services of the Diem government. But it was clearly apparent several weeks ago that his government is not adapted to the mission with which it has been entrusted." [18] These developments, and those that transpired subsequently, indicated that

[17] France, *Journal Officiel de la République Française, Débats Parlementaires, Conseil de la République,* Session of March 22, 1955, pp. 924–928.
[18] Press Conference statement reported in *Le Monde,* April 30, 1955, p. 1.

French policy was based only partially on the Agreements signed at Geneva. As was to become more clear with the passage of time, French policy was also influenced by separate arrangements made with the United States which in some respects contradicted the obligations theoretically undertaken at Geneva. This was to become obvious in early 1956 (see Documents 157 and 176).

The North Atlantic Council met in Paris on May 9, 10, and 11, 1955. The meeting provided an opportunity for extensive discussions of the Viet-Nam situation by Secretary Dulles, Premier Faure, and British Foreign Secretary Macmillan. Although details of the conversations are not available, Dulles apparently applied pressure on the French to refrain from interference with Diem's policy and to liquidate the remnants of French colonialism in Indochina. In a statement made on May 14, Dulles indicated that American preferences had been endorsed at Paris (Document 157).

The aftermath of the Paris talks saw a further decline in French influence. General Collins was replaced on May 27 as the senior American representative in Saigon. The new American ambassador, G. Frederick Reinhardt, stated, "I came here under instructions to carry out United States policy in support of the legal government of Vietnam under Premier Ngo Dinh Diem." [19] On June 1 it was announced that the French garrison would be withdrawn from the Saigon-Cholon area, and on June 2 General Ely left Viet-Nam, to be replaced not by another Commissioner General but, after considerable wrangling, by a French Ambassador with the title of "High Commissioner."

In the meantime the British had become concerned about the movement of refugees from north to south in Viet-Nam. On May 14, in a note to the Soviet Union, London suggested that the two Co-Chairmen of the Geneva Conference take the initiative in extending the time period allowed for free movement between the two zones. The Soviet response, on May 18, rejected the suggestion on the ground that such an action "would mean interference . . . in the function of the International Supervisory Commission for Viet-Nam," but also indicated that the DRV had agreed to a one month extension of the deadline.[20]

[19] Reported in *The New York Times,* May 29, 1955, p. 2.

[20] The exchange of notes is in Great Britain, Parliament, Papers by Command, *Documents Relating to British Involvement in the Indo-China Conflict 1945– 1965* (London: Her Majesty's Stationery Office, Cmnd. 2834, 1965), pp. 92–93.

142. *The Southeast Asia Collective Defense Treaty with Protocol and Understanding by the United States* *
    September 8, 1954 [1]

The Parties to this Treaty,

Recognizing the sovereign equality of all the Parties,

Reiterating their faith in the purposes and principles set forth in the Charter of the United Nations and their desire to live in peace with all peoples and all governments,

Reaffirming that, in accordance with the Charter of the United Nations, they uphold the principle of equal rights and self-determination of peoples, and declaring that they will earnestly strive by every peaceful means to promote self-government and to secure the independence of all countries whose peoples desire it and are able to undertake its responsibilities,

Desiring to strengthen the fabric of peace and freedom and to uphold the principles of democracy, individual liberty and the rule of law, and to promote the economic well-being and development of all peoples in the treaty area,

Intending to declare publicly and formally their sense of unity, so that any potential aggressor will appreciate that the Parties stand together in the area, and

Desiring further to coordinate their efforts for collective defense for the preservation of peace and security,

Therefore agree as follows:

Article I

The Parties undertake, as set forth in the Charter of the United Nations, to settle any international disputes in which they may be involved by peaceful means in such a manner that international peace

* *Source:* United States, Department of State, *American Foreign Policy 1950–1955: Basic Documents* (2 vols., Washington: Government Printing Office, 1957), Vol. I, pp. 912–916. Ratification was advised by the Senate on February 1, 1955; the Treaty was ratified by the President on February 4, 1955; it entered into force on February 19, 1955. The Conference also adopted a statement of principles known as "The Pacific Charter"; text in *ibid.*, pp. 916–917. For analysis of the Treaty, see Secretary Dulles' November 2 letter transmitting the Treaty to President Eisenhower, in *ibid.*, pp. 923–928; and the January 25, 1955, report of the Senate Committee on Foreign Relations, advising ratification, in *ibid.*, pp. 929–945.

[1] Footnote in the original omitted.

and security and justice are not endangered, and to refrain in their international relations from the threat or use of force in any manner inconsistent with the purposes of the United Nations.

Article II

In order more effectively to achieve the objectives of this Treaty, the Parties, separately and jointly, by means of continuous and effective self-help and mutual aid will maintain and develop their individual and collective capacity to resist armed attack and to prevent and counter subversive activities directed from without against their territorial integrity and political stability.

Article III

The Parties undertake to strengthen their free institutions and to co-operate with one another in the further development of economic measures, including technical assistance, designed both to promote economic progress and social well-being and to further the individual and collective efforts of governments toward these ends.

Article IV

1. Each Party recognizes that aggression by means of armed attack in the treaty area against any of the Parties or against any State or territory which the Parties by unanimous agreement may hereafter designate, would endanger its own peace and safety, and agrees that it will in that event act to meet the common danger in accordance with its constitutional processes. Measures taken under this paragraph shall be immediately reported to the Security Council of the United Nations.

2. If, in the opinion of any of the Parties, the inviolability or the integrity of the territory or the sovereignty or political independence of any Party in the treaty area or of any other State or territory to which the provisions of paragraph 1 of this Article from time to time apply is threatened in any way other than by armed attack or is affected or threatened by any fact or situation which might endanger the peace of the area, the Parties shall consult immediately in order to agree on the measures which should be taken for the common defense.

3. It is understood that no action on the territory of any State designated by unanimous agreement under paragraph 1 of this Article or on any territory so designated shall be taken except at the invitation or with the consent of the government concerned.

Article V

The Parties hereby establish a Council, on which each of them shall be represented, to consider matters concerning the implementation of this Treaty. The Council shall provide for consultation with regard to military and any other planning as the situation obtaining in the treaty area may from time to time require. The Council shall be so organized as to be able to meet at any time.

Article VI

This Treaty does not affect and shall not be interpreted as affecting in any way the rights and obligations of any of the Parties under the Charter of the United Nations or the responsibility of the United Nations for the maintenance of international peace and security. Each Party declares that none of the international engagements now in force between it and any other of the Parties or any third party is in conflict with the provisions of this Treaty, and undertakes not to enter into any international engagement in conflict with this Treaty.

Article VII

Any other State in a position to further the objectives of this Treaty and to contribute to the security of the area may, by unanimous agreement of the Parties, be invited to accede to this Treaty. Any State so invited may become a Party to the Treaty by depositing its instrument of accession with the Government of the Republic of the Philippines. The Government of the Republic of the Philippines shall inform each of the Parties of the deposit of each such instrument of accession.

Article VIII

As used in this Treaty, the "treaty area" is the general area of Southeast Asia, including also the entire territories of the Asian Parties, and the general area of the Southwest Pacific not including the Pacific area north of 21 degrees 30 minutes north latitude. The Parties may, by unanimous agreement, amend this Article to include within the treaty area the territory of any State acceding to this Treaty in accordance with Article VII or otherwise to change the treaty area.

Article IX

1. This Treaty shall be deposited in the archives of the Government of the Republic of the Philippines. Duly certified copies thereof shall be transmitted by that government to the other signatories.

2. The Treaty shall be ratified and its provisions carried out by the Parties in accordance with their respective constitutional processes. The instruments of ratification shall be deposited as soon as possible with the Government of the Republic of the Philippines, which shall notify all of the other signatories of such deposit.[2]

3. The Treaty shall enter into force between the States which have ratified it as soon as the instruments of ratification of a majority of the signatories shall have been deposited, and shall come into effect with respect to each other State on the date of the deposit of its instrument of ratification.

Article X

This Treaty shall remain in force indefinitely, but any Party may cease to be a Party one year after its notice of denunciation has been given to the Government of the Republic of the Philippines, which shall inform the Governments of the other Parties of the deposit of each notice of denunciation.

Article XI

The English text of this Treaty is binding on the Parties, but when the Parties have agreed to the French text thereof and have so notified the Government of the Republic of the Philippines, the French text shall be equally authentic and binding on the Parties.

UNDERSTANDING OF THE UNITED STATES OF AMERICA

The United States of America in executing the present Treaty does so with the understanding that its recognition of the effect of aggression and armed attack and its agreement with reference thereto in Article IV, paragraph 1, apply only to communist aggression but affirms that in the event of other aggression or armed attack it will consult under the provisions of Article IV, paragraph 2.

In witness whereof, the undersigned Plenipotentiaries have signed this Treaty.

Done at Manila, this eighth day of September, 1954.

---

[2] Footnote in the original: "Thailand deposited its instrument of ratification Dec. 2, 1954; the remaining signatories (the United States, Australia, France, New Zealand, Pakistan, the Philippines, and the United Kingdom) deposited their instruments Feb. 19, 1955."

PROTOCOL TO THE TREATY, SEPTEMBER 8, 1954 [3]
*Designation of States and Territory as to which provisions of
Article IV and Article III are to be applicable*

The Parties to the Southeast Asia Collective Defense Treaty unanimously designate for the purposes of Article IV of the Treaty the States of Cambodia and Laos and the free territory under the jurisdiction of the State of Vietnam.

The Parties further agree that the above mentioned states and territory shall be eligible in respect of the economic measures contemplated by Article III.

This Protocol shall enter into force simultaneously with the coming into force of the Treaty.

IN WITNESS WHEREOF, the undersigned Plenipotentiaries have signed this Protocol to the Southeast Asia Collective Defense Treaty.

Done at Manila, this eighth day of September, 1954.

143. *Communiqué Regarding Franco-American Conversations* *
      September 29, 1954 [4]

Representatives of the two Governments have had very frank and useful talks which have shown the community of their views, and are in full agreement on the objectives to be attained.

The conclusion of the Southeast Asia Collective Defense Treaty in Manila on September 8, 1954,[5] has provided a firmer basis than heretofore to assist the free nations of Asia in developing and maintaining their independence and security. The representatives of France and the United States wish to reaffirm the support of their Governments for the principles of self-government, independence, justice and liberty proclaimed by the Pacific Charter in Manila on September 8, 1954.[6]

The representatives of France and the United States reaffirm the intention of their governments to support the complete independence of

* *Source:* United States, Department of State, *American Foreign Policy 1950–1955: Basic Documents* (2 vols., Washington: Government Printing Office, 1957), Vol. II, pp. 2400–2401.

[3] Footnote in the original omitted.

[4] Issued at Washington. The United States was represented by Acting Secretary of State Walter Bedell Smith, and France by Guy LaChambre, Minister of State for Relations with the Associated States, Edgar Faure, Minister of Finance, and General Paul Ely, Commissioner General in Indochina.

[5] Document 142.   [6] See Source Note to Document 142.

Cambodia, Laos, and Viet-Nam. Both France and the United States will continue to assist Cambodia, Laos, and Viet-Nam in their efforts to safeguard their freedom and independence and to advance the welfare of their peoples. In this spirit France and the United States are assisting the Government of Viet-Nam in the resettlement of the Vietnamese who have of their own free will moved to free Viet-Nam and who already number some 300,000.[7]

In order to contribute to the security of the area pending the further development of national forces for this purpose, the representatives of France indicated that France is prepared to retain forces of its Expeditionary Corps, in agreement with the government concerned, within the limits permitted under the Geneva agreements and to an extent to be determined. The United States will consider the question of financial assistance for the Expeditionary Corps in these circumstances in addition to support for the forces of each of the three Associated States. These questions vitally affect each of the three Associated States and are being fully discussed with them.

The channel for French and United States economic aid, budgetary support, and other assistance to each of the Associated States will be direct to that state. The United States representatives will begin discussions soon with the respective governments of the Associated States regarding direct aid. The methods for efficient coordination of French and United States aid programs to each of the three Associated States are under consideration and will be developed in discussions with each of these states.

After the bilateral talks, the chiefs of diplomatic missions in Washington of Cambodia, Laos and Viet Nam were invited to a final meeting to have an exchange of views and information on these matters. The representatives of all five countries are in complete agreement on the objectives of peace and freedom to be achieved in Indochina.

[7] For details on American assistance to the Vietnamese refugees, see United States, Department of State, *American Foreign Policy 1950–1955: Basic Documents* (2 vols., Washington: Government Printing Office, 1957), pp. 2398–2400; and the report "Exodus: Report on a Voluntary Mass Flight to Freedom, Viet-Nam, 1954," in United States, Department of State, *Bulletin,* XXXII (February 7, 1955), pp. 222–229.

144. *Statement by a Spokesman of the Foreign Ministry of the*
     Democratic Republic of Viet-Nam on the Southeast Asia
     Collective Defense Treaty [Extract] *
     October 22, 1954

Prior to, and during, the Geneva Conference, the U.S. interventionist circles wanted to create an aggressive military bloc in South East
Asia aiming at preventing the Conference from reaching an agreement,
and at prolonging and extending the Indo-China war under their direction. But they have failed in their attempt. The Geneva Conference has
brought about agreements aiming at re-establishing peace in Indo-China
on the basis of recognition of the national rights of the Indochinese
peoples.

As they could not sabotage the signing of these Agreements the U.S.
interventionist circles are finding the way to hinder the implementation
of the terms arrived at to create conditions for a deeper American intervention in South East Asia and to turn the countries of this area into
American military bases and colonies. That is the political significance
of the Manila Conference and the so-called South East Asia Defence
Treaty.

Everybody knows it is the U.S.A. that has prepared the Manila Conference and drawn up the draft treaty, whereas the countries of South
East Asia such as India, Indonesia, Burma and Ceylon did not only
refuse to adhere to this treaty but also denounced its aggressive aim.
Paragraph 5 of the Final Declaration of the Geneva Conference [8] stipulates that the two signatory parties in Viet-nam have the obligation to
see that the zones allotted to them shall not constitute part of any military alliance and shall not be utilized for the resumption of hostilities
or in the service of an aggressive policy.

The Governments of Cambodia and Laos have also made similar
declarations.[9] Nevertheless, the Manila Treaty, and in particular the

* *Source:* Democratic Republic of Viet-Nam, Ministry of Foreign Affairs,
Press and Information Department, *Documents Related to the Implementation of
the Geneva Agreements Concerning Viet-nam* (Hanoi: 1956), pp. 70–71. The
statement is as given in the source and is extracted from an interview given by
a spokesman of the DRV Foreign Ministry to a correspondent of the Viet-Nam
News Agency. The complete text of the interview, including questions and
answers on French policy and the Franco-American conversations in Washington
at the end of September, was broadcast by Viet-Nam News Agency in English
Morse, October 22, 1954, 0530 G.M.T.

[8] Document 131.   [9] See Document 131.

additional protocol to this Treaty, have, in a unilateral manner and counter to the Geneva Agreements, placed Laos, Cambodia and South Viet-nam in the sphere of implementation of the so-called South East Asian Defence Treaty.

This is a flagrant violation of the Geneva Agreements, an infringement upon the independence and sovereignty of Viet-nam, Laos and Cambodia, a threat to the security and peace of the peoples of South East Asia.

145. *Message from President Eisenhower to Premier Ngo Dinh Diem* *
    October 23, 1954

DEAR MR. PRESIDENT:

I have been following with great interest the course of developments in Viet-Nam, particularly since the conclusion of the conference at Geneva. The implications of the agreement concerning Viet-Nam have caused grave concern regarding the future of a country temporarily divided by an artificial military grouping, weakened by a long and exhausting war and faced with enemies without and by their subversive collaborators within.

Your recent requests for aid to assist in the formidable project of the movement of several hundred thousand loyal Vietnamese citizens away from areas which are passing under a *de facto* rule and political ideology which they abhor, are being fulfilled.[10] I am glad that the United States is able to assist in this humanitarian effort.

We have been exploring ways and means to permit our aid to Viet-Nam to be more effective and to make a greater contribution to the welfare and stability of the Government of Viet-Nam. I am, accordingly, instructing the American Ambassador to Viet-Nam to examine with you in your capacity as Chief of Government, how an intelligent program of American aid given directly to your Government can serve to assist Viet-Nam in its present hour of trial, provided that your Government is prepared to give assurances as to the standards of performance it would be able to maintain in the event such aid were supplied.

The purpose of this offer is to assist the Government of Viet-Nam in developing and maintaining a strong, viable state, capable of resist-

---

* *Source:* United States, Department of State, *American Foreign Policy 1950–1955: Basic Documents* (2 vols., Washington: Government Printing Office, 1957), Vol. II, pp. 2401–2402. The message was delivered by Ambassador Donald R. Heath on October 23.

10 See Note 7, p. 347.

ing attempted subversion or aggression through military means. The Government of the United States expects that this aid will be met by performance on the part of the Government of Viet-Nam in undertaking needed reforms. It hopes that such aid, combined with your own continuing efforts, will contribute effectively toward an independent Viet-Nam endowed with a strong government. Such a government would, I hope, be so responsive to the nationalist aspirations of its people, so enlightened in purpose and effective in performance, that it will be respected both at home and abroad and discourage any who might wish to impose a foreign ideology on your free people.

146. *Statement Issued by the White House on Coordination of United States Aid Programs in Viet-Nam* * *November 3, 1954*

The President on November 3 designated Gen. J. Lawton Collins as Special United States Representative in Viet-Nam with the personal rank of Ambassador, to undertake a diplomatic mission of limited duration. He will coordinate the operations of all U.S. agencies in that country.

General Collins will proceed immediately to Saigon, where he will confer with Ambassador Donald R. Heath prior to the latter's already scheduled return to the United States for reassignment following 4½ years of distinguished service in Indochina. For the duration of this assignment General Collins will relinquish his other duties, including that of U.S. representative on the Military Committee of the North Atlantic Treaty Organization.

Since the conclusion of hostilities in Indochina, the U.S. Government has been particularly concerned over developments in Viet-Nam, a country ravaged by 8 years of war, artificially divided into armistice zones, and confronted by dangerous forces threatening its independence and security.

The U.S. Government is fully aware of the immense tasks facing the Government of Viet-Nam in its effort to achieve solidarity, internal security, and economic rehabilitation. The United States has already played an important role in the evacuation of hundreds of thousands of refugees from Communist rule in North Viet-Nam.[11]

* *Source:* United States, Department of State, *American Foreign Policy 1950–1955: Basic Documents* (2 vols., Washington: Government Printing Office, 1957), Vol. II, pp. 2402–2403.
[11] See Note 7, p. 347.

Moreover, as the President told Prime Minister Ngo Dinh Diem in his letter of October 23d,[12] U.S. representatives in Viet-Nam have been instructed to consider with the Vietnamese authorities how a program of American aid given directly to Viet-Nam can best assist that country. General Collins will explore this matter with Prime Minister Ngo Dinh Diem and his Government in order to help them resolve their present critical problems and to supplement measures adopted by the Vietnamese themselves.

In executing his temporary mission, General Collins will maintain close liaison with the French Commissioner General, Gen. Paul Ely, for the purpose of exchanging views on how best, under existing circumstances, the freedom and welfare of Viet-Nam can be safeguarded.

147. *Statement by Foreign Secretary Eden in the House of Commons on Implementation of the Geneva Agreements [Extracts]* * *November 8, 1954*

[Foreign Secretary Eden's statement was made in the course of debate on a motion endorsing the policy of the Government as expressed in the Geneva Agreements and the Manila Treaty. The introductory seven paragraphs are omitted.]

The value of the settlement which was achieved at Geneva depends, however—as I said at the time of its conclusion—on the spirit in which the agreements are carried out by the parties to them.[13] So far they have displayed in general a willingness to adhere to the terms agreed. There have been a few incidents, but both in Viet Nam and in Cambodia the withdrawal of controls, the transfer of administration and the movements of population—sometimes on a considerable scale—have proceeded remarkably smoothly.

The House should recall that in Viet Nam not only had arrangements to be made to move tens of thousands of the population from the region of Hanoi to the south, but also a considerable transfer had to be arranged from the south to the North; the Vietminh having in fact had control for several years of considerable territories in the south which under the armistice they are now giving up. This is not always remembered.

* *Source:* Great Britain, *Parliamentary Debates (Hansard)*, Fifth Series, House of Commons, Vol. 532, Session of November 8, 1954, cols. 926–930.

12 Document 145.

13 See Eden's concluding comments at the final session of the Geneva Conference, in Document 134.

[Five paragraphs on the implementation of the agreements in Cambodia and Laos are omitted.]

So much for the execution of the agreements up to date. But that is not the only factor this House has to consider. When we survey the position in South-East Asia, we must remember that the agreements reached in Geneva have in no way diminished the formidable military power of Vietminh, to say nothing of that of their Chinese allies. On the contrary, since the Geneva settlement there has been considerable reorganisation and rapid expansion of the Vietminh regular army. By the end of this year this will probably mean that the Vietminh will have twice as many regular field formations as at the time of the Geneva settlements.

From the relatively small population which they control—some 14 million in all—the Vietminh have already raised more regular troops than either Pakistan or Indonesia, each with a population of over 70 million. I suggest to the House that these figures give emphasis to the comments I made on 23rd June last about the need to provide some kind of guarantee of these Geneva settlements.[14]

I come to the point raised by the hon. Member for Broxtowe (Mr. Warbey) at Question time. At that time we envisaged a dual arrangement in respect of these guarantees, a reciprocal international gu[a]rantee that would cover the settlement itself, and then a South-East Asian collective defence treaty to balance the existing Sino-Soviet Treaty and the close relationship which, as we know, exists between Vietminh, China, and the Soviet Union.

I hope that nobody is going to say to me "You ought not to organise yourselves in like manner to China and Soviet Russia because everybody knows their treaty is directed only against Japan." I hope that nobody is going to use that argument. In case they should be moved to use it I should like to answer in advance. This is the same problem the previous Government had to face in respect of N.A.T.O.— a Russian alliance with all its satellites, directed against Germany, did not diminish the need for setting up the N.A.T.O. organisation. If that is a good argument in Europe, it is a perfectly good argument, to me, in Asia.

Unfortunately, it proved impossible to obtain the kind of reciprocal guarantees which we had in mind. This was due to the insistence at Geneva of the Soviet, Chinese and Vietminh delegations that any guarantee given to these agreements must be what they called "collective"

14 See Document 124.

and by this, of course, they meant that the guarantee could only work if there were unanimous agreement that it should be put into force—a not very probable contingency. In other words, this introduced the principle of the veto once again and any such arrangement was completely unacceptable to us.

That is why that form of guarantee lapsed and instead of a reciprocal guarantee we now have the final Declaration of the Geneva Conference. In this each member undertakes to respect the sovereignty, independence, unity and territorial integrity of these countries, that is Laos, Cambodia and Viet Nam, and to refrain from any interference in their internal affairs.

At the same time, the United States, in another declaration [15] gave a like undertaking to refrain from the threat of force to disturb the Geneva settlement. Shortly afterwards, statements of approval and support of the settlement were made by Australia and New Zealand and by all the Colombo Powers. We attach great importance to this. I think it is fair to say we worked quite hard to try to bring it about.

[The balance of the debate on the Geneva Agreements and on the SEATO Treaty is omitted.]

148. *Joint Franco-American Communiqué, Washington [Extracts]* *
    November 20, 1954

1. Following his talk with the President of the United States,[16] the Prime Minister of France [17] met with the Secretary of State on Thursday, November 18, Friday, November 19, and Saturday, November 20. Officials of the two Governments were present. The conversations took place in a spirit of cooperation and mutual confidence and have brought out once again the fundamental unity of outlook of the two countries, and their unshakeable faith and determination in the cause of peace and freedom, which are shared by other like-minded governments and by all the peoples of the world.

[Two paragraphs on European matters are omitted.]

* *Source:* United States, Department of State, *American Foreign Policy 1950–1955: Basic Documents* (2 vols., Washington: Government Printing Office, 1957), Vol. I, pp. 1676–1677.
[15] The United States unilateral declaration at the final session of the Geneva Conference, in Document 134.
[16] On November 18.   [17] Pierre Mendès-France.

4. The understandings reached with regard to Cambodia, Laos and Viet-Nam in the talks of September 27–29 between representatives of the Governments of France and the United States in Washington were reaffirmed.[18] Agreement was reached on coordinated procedures and periodic reviews required to carry out the policies of France and the United States in that area designed to assist the Associated States to maintain their freedom and independence.

The Chiefs of the diplomatic missions of Cambodia, Laos and Viet-Nam in Washington have been informed of the exchange of views relating to their countries.

[The final paragraph, which concerns North African problems, is omitted.]

149. *First Interim Report of the International Commission for Supervision and Control in Viet-Nam* [Conclusion] * *December 25, 1954*

[The "First Interim Report" covered the period from August 11, 1954, to December 10, 1954.]

118. Despite difficulties of communication, frayed tempers due to eight years of strife and differences in the degrees of effectiveness of administration in various parts of Vietnam, the provisions of the Agreement which are of a military or semi-military nature have on the whole been carried out according to the time-schedules and directions given in the Agreement.[19] These are detailed in Chapters II and III. As regards prisoners of war and civilian internees dealt with under Chapter IV, by and large, the parties have and are carrying out the directions under Article 21, and the bulk of the exchanges have been completed, though the time schedule has not been maintained mainly due to administrative difficulties.

119. The two parties in the Joint Commission[20] have on occasions been unable to arrive at mutually satisfactory arrangements to execute the Agreement. On such occasions, the International Commission has been approached for intervention. The International Commission has consistently appealed to the parties to approach problems arising out of

* *Source:* Great Britain, Parliament, Papers by Command, *First and Second Interim Reports of the International Commission for Supervision and Control in Vietnam* (London: Her Majesty's Stationery Office, Cmd. 9461, 1955), pp. 29–30.

18 Document 143.
19 Agreement on the Cessation of Hostilities in Viet-Nam, Document 130.
20 France and the DRV.

the Agreement in a practical spirit and not in a narrow formalistic manner. The Commission feels that a practical approach would be in the long run the most effective way of ensuring that the provisions of the Agreement are properly carried out and it is only in this spirit that the two parties can jointly fulfil the obligations which they have accepted at Geneva.

120. It is obvious from the review [contained in the body of the report] that there is room for improvement in the implementation by both parties of the Articles of the Agreement dealing with democratic freedoms—Chapters V and VII of the Report. The Commission realises that in a climate of suspicion and fear engendered by eight years of strife and with administrative difficulties of some magnitude which the parties have had to face, effective implementation of the provisions of the Agreement dealing with democratic freedoms is bound to be a difficult matter, but the Commission feels that, while difficulties exist, both sides have been sadly lacking in a sense of purpose and urgency in dealing with these matters.

121. The failure of the French High Command to ensure that effective and civil military administration was established in areas taken over by them in Central and South Vietnam and the practical denial of democratic freedoms involved in the number of incidents resulting in injury to life and property of the civil population which have occurred and still continue to occur show that not enough has been accomplished as yet to establish a stable administration which alone can guarantee effectively the exercise of democratic freedoms under Article 14(*c*).

122. Similarly, the High Command of the People's Army of Vietnam, while they did co-operate with the Commission and took measures to secure freedom of movement in the case of about 8,000 Phat Diem [21] refugees, have so far done little to develop adequate administrative arrangements, with the result that complaints continue to pour in. Restrictions on internal movements from province to province and a cumbersome system of permits can hardly assist in the effective exercise of the right of freedom of movement under Article 14(*d*).

123. Apart from informal recommendations and suggestions made already from time to time in the past, the Commission is keeping both these questions under constant review to assist the parties in the effective implementation of the Agreement.

124. Both sides have been generous in their assistance as regards

[21] One of the two Catholic bishoprics in the southwestern part of the Red River Delta, evacuated by the French forces at the beginning of July 1954, from which came many of the refugees who were to move to the South.

logistic support to the Commission and its Fixed and Mobile Teams, concerning matters dealt with under Chapter VI. However, both sides have preferred narrow legalistic interpretation of the Articles of the Agreement regarding the tasks and the spheres of movement of the Commission's teams. The Commission is taking up the matter with both sides on the basis of experience of the last few months, but it must be stated that our Fixed and Mobile Teams have displayed considerable patience and perseverance in the face of restrictions and obstacles they have met in the form of inefficiency of local administration, the narrowness of local officials or general misunderstanding regarding their tasks.

125. In the control of import of war materials and rotation of personnel, the Commission has, as stated in Chapter VI, placed its Inspection Teams at fixed points laid down in the Agreement. Difficulties encountered have been discussed with the parties concerned and spot checks of the entry of equipment and material are from time to time carried out at these points even though no notifications have so far been received under Article 17(*e*). The frequency of control at these fixed points and the adequacy of these for purposes of carrying out the Commission's responsibility for supervision under Article 36 are being kept under review in the light of experience.

126. The Commission is satisfied that, on the whole, the specific points noted in the Final Declaration of the Geneva Powers dated the 21st of July, 1954,[22] have been borne in mind by both sides and that they have made and continue to make efforts to implement the Agreement on the Cessation of Hostilities in Vietnam signed on the 20th of July, 1954.

150. *Statement by the Department of State on Direct Aid*
     to Viet-Nam, Cambodia, and Laos *
     December 31, 1954

Arrangements have been completed so that on January 1, 1955, the United States can begin supplying financial aid directly to the Governments of Viet-Nam, Cambodia, and Laos for the purpose of strengthening their defense against the threat of Communist subversion and aggression. This direct aid reaffirms the independent status these Governments now possess, and is in addition to the economic aid that has

* *Source:* United States, Department of State, *American Foreign Policy 1950–1955: Basic Documents* (2 vols., Washington: Government Printing Office, 1957), Vol. II, p. 2403.
22 Document 131.

been given directly to these three states by the United States since 1950. The aid will be given pursuant to section 121 of the Mutual Security Act of 1954, which provides for "the furnishing, as far as possible, of direct assistance to the Associated States of Cambodia, Laos and Viet-nam. . . ."[23] The provision of U.S. aid directly to these Governments was confirmed by the communiqué issued at Washington on September 29 of this year,[24] following talks between representatives of the United States, France, and the Chiefs of Mission of the three Associated States and by letters from President Eisenhower to the King of Cambodia[25] and to President Diem of Viet-Nam.[26]

151. *Communiqué Issued by the Government of the State of Viet-Nam* *
January 21, 1955

Yesterday the Premier sent to Ambassador Lawton Collins a letter[27] asking the United States to assume entire responsibility for aiding the Vietnamese Government to organize and train its armed forces under the overall authority of General Ely, presently Commander-in-Chief, and in cooperation with the French military aid mission.

At the same time the Premier handed to Ambassador Lawton Collins a summary[28] of the program of organization and composition of the Vietnamese armed forces which the Government of Viet-Nam desires to maintain. This program was drawn up by the Minister of National Defense, M. Ho Thong Minh. The Premier asked Ambassador Lawton Collins to accept this program as a basis for definitive negotiations with the Government of the United States on the subject of the financial aid which the United States may be able to furnish for the implementation of this program.

The Premier has discussed this subject with General Paul Ely, who is entirely in agreement provided that such aid be furnished in accordance with existing agreements.

* *Source:* State of Viet-Nam, High Commission in France, *Bulletin du Viet Nam,* No. 91 (January 29, 1955), p. 18. Translation by the editor.

[23] Text in United States, Department of State, *American Foreign Policy 1950–1955: Basic Documents* (2 vols., Washington: Government Printing Office, 1957), Vol. II, pp. 3105–3140, particularly pp. 3111–3112.

[24] Document 143.

[25] Dated October 2, 1954; text in United States, Department of State, *American Foreign Policy 1950–1955: Basic Documents* (2 vols., Washington: Government Printing Office, 1957), Vol. II, p. 2401.

[26] Document 145.   [27] Text not available.   [28] *Ibid.*

The Premier has received from Ambassador Lawton Collins a letter [29] declaring that he is happy to accept the program proposed by the Minister of Defense for the organization of the armed forces as the basis for definitive negotiations to determine the financial and technical aid that the United States may be able to grant for this program.

152. *Declaration of the Government of the Democratic Republic of Viet-Nam on Readiness to Re-establish Normal Relations between Northern and Southern Viet-Nam* * *February 4, 1955*

Following the appeal made by President Ho-Chi-Minh on New Year's Day,[30] the Council of Ministers of the Democratic Republic of Viet-nam has, in its session early in February 1955, considered the question of restoring normal relations between North and South Vietnam on either side of the provisional military demarcation line. The Council holds that:

1. Viet-nam is a unified country from the North to the South. The political, economic, cultural, social and sentimental relations and the solidarity of the Vietnamese people are indivisible. During the eight to nine years of the patriotic war, the Vietnamese people from the North to the South have heroically fought to restore peace and struggled together to build up the Fatherland. That is why, after the implementation of the armistice and pending the general elections to bring about

* *Source:* Democratic Republic of Viet-Nam, Ministry of Foreign Affairs, Press and Information Department, *Documents Related to the Implementation of the Geneva Agreements Concerning Viet-nam* (Hanoi: 1956), pp. 33–35 (italics in the original). The statement was distributed at a press conference on February 5, 1955, by Pham Van Bach, Vice Minister of Home Affairs. It was also broadcast by Viet-Nam News Agency in English Morse, February 6, 1955, 0530 G.M.T.

[29] Text not available.

[30] "Speech Greeting the New Year and Welcoming the Viet Nam Workers' Party Central Committee and the Government on Their Return to the Capital," in Ho Chi Minh, *Selected Works* (4 vols., Hanoi: Foreign Languages Publishing House, 1961–1962), Vol. IV, pp. 52–55, notably the following from p. 54:

"North and South belong to the same family. They are blood brothers and therefore, can in no way be split up. We must establish close relations between the North and the South.

"We shall unite closely and broadly from North to South and support our southern compatriots in their struggle for freedom and democracy in conformity with the Geneva Agreement. We wish to make economic and cultural relations and travelling between North and South free and easy.

"All this work must be done to prepare the ground for free general elections for national reunification."

the reunification of the country, the re-establishment of normal relations between the Northern and Southern zones fully conforms to the earnest aspiration of the various strata of the population in the two zones and is indispensable for the restoration of a normal and prosperous life of the Vietnamese people throughout the country;

2. The restoration of normal relations between the two zones is in complete conformity with the spirit of the Geneva Armistice Agreement.

The first sentence of the Agreement on the cessation of hostilities in Viet-nam [31] stipulates that the demarcation line, on either side of which the forces of the two parties shall be regrouped after their withdrawal, is only provisional.

The Final Declaration of the Geneva Conference [32] clearly mentioned that: *"The military demarcation line should not in any way be interpreted as constituting a political or territorial boundary."*

The restoration of relations between the two zones does not infringe upon the administrative control of each side. On the contrary, it will provide the authorities of both sides with good opportunity for mutual understanding, thereby creating *"the necessary basis for the achievement of a political settlement in Viet-nam,"* as stipulated in the Final Declaration of the Geneva Conference.

Due to the above-mentioned reasons, the Government of the Democratic Republic of Viet-nam declares that:

1. Responding to the earnest desire of the Vietnamese people and in conformity with the spirit of the Geneva Armistice Agreement, the Government of the Democratic Republic of Viet-nam is disposed to grant all facilities to the people in the Northern and Southern zones on either side of the provisional military demarcation line in sending mail, moving, carrying out business or enterprises from one zone to the other, and in exchanging cultural, artistic, scientific, technical, sporting and other activities. The Government of the Democratic Republic of Viet-nam fully encourages and helps the population in the two zones in all economic, cultural and social exchanges advantageous for the restoration of normal life of the people;

2. The Government of the Democratic Republic of Viet-nam hopes that the authorities in South Viet-nam will agree to the restoration of normal relations between the Northern and Southern zones with a view to bringing about solutions favourable for the entire people.

[31] Document 130.　　　　　[32] Document 131.

153. *Letter from President Eisenhower to H.M. Bao Dai, Chief of State of Viet-Nam* *
February 19, 1955

YOUR MAJESTY:

It might be of interest to you to learn firsthand of General Collins' report to me and of our present views and policies concerning Viet-Nam. General Collins has just left to return to Saigon after a short period of consultations in Washington.[33] I have discussed developments in Viet-Nam with him at some length. He has also talked with the Secretary of State and with our Congressional leaders.

It is gratifying to learn from him of the distinct progress that is being made in Viet-Nam by Prime Minister Diem and the Government of Viet-Nam. General Collins believes that there is a good chance that Viet-Nam can remain free if there is continued effective action on the Government's programs. The Prime Minister's announced programs of land reform [34] and reorganization of the Armed Forces [35] should, when fully carried out, further increase the stability and unity of the Government.

The Government of the United States is vigorously opposed to the forces of world Communism. We continue to support those aspirations of the people of Asia for independence, peace and prosperity. Accordingly, I have concurred in General Collins' recommendation to continue and expand support for Free Viet-Nam.

It is encouraging to me to know that Prime Minister Diem is making substantial progress. The United States Government intends to continue its support of his Government.

Sincerely,
DWIGHT D. EISENHOWER

His Majesty
BAO DAI
Chief of State of Viet-Nam
Cannes, France

* *Source:* United States, Department of State, *Bulletin,* XXXII (March 14, 1955), p. 423. The letter was released to the press by the White House on March 3, 1955, *after* its contents had been made public by Bao Dai.

[33] Footnote in the original omitted.

[34] A summary of the land reform program adopted in January 1955 is in Embassy of Viet-Nam (Washington), *News From Vietnam,* I, No. 3 (April 1, 1955), p. 2; texts of this and subsequent land reform decrees are in United States Operations Mission in Viet-Nam, "English Translations of Basic Vietnamese Land Tenure Legislation" (Saigon: United States Operations Mission, 1957).

[35] See Document 151.

154. *Secretary of State Dulles: Address on Conditions in Asia and the SEATO Ministerial Meeting* [Extracts] *
March 8, 1955

I return from 2 weeks in Southeast Asia and the West Pacific. I visited the forward positions against which the waves of communism are beating and where the issues of war and peace, of freedom and captivity, hang in precarious balance. There a gallant band of independent and freedom-loving nations stand between 600 million Communist-dominated Chinese and the broad reaches of the Pacific Ocean.

[Sections of the speech dealing with the SEATO Treaty, the SEATO Ministerial Conference in Bangkok, and Burma, Laos, and Cambodia are omitted.]

The greatest problems confront the Free Government of Viet-Nam. It has the task of developing an efficient government of its own in substitution for French rule. This task, difficult enough under any conditions, is now complicated by three abnormal problems.

There is the problem of absorbing and resettling the refugees from the north. As always, when international communism moves in, those who love liberty move out, if they can. So far, about 600,000 persons have fled from northern Viet-Nam, and, before the exodus is over, the number of refugees will probably approach 1 million. It is not easy for southern Viet-Nam to absorb these new peoples. They are destitute and penniless persons with only such possessions as they could carry on their backs. They need help.[36]

On dramatic response is Operation Brotherhood. That is privately sponsored by the Philippine Junior Chamber of Commerce. It provides Philippine doctors and nurses who work on a 24-hour-a-day basis at the refugee centers. It is inspiring to see the Philippine people, who only lately achieved their own independence, now turning to help the most recent addition to the ranks of free nations.

A second problem faced by the Free Government of Viet-Nam is created by the fact that various religious groups, known as the "sects," [37] have heretofore had virtual autonomy, maintaining their

---

* *Source:* United States, Department of State, *Bulletin,* XXXII (March 21, 1955), pp. 459, 461–462. The speech was delivered to the nation over radio and television on March 8.

[36] Footnote in the original omitted; see Note 7, p. 347.

[37] The Hoa Hao, the Cao Dai, and the Binh Xuyen.

own police forces, collecting their own taxes, and acting largely independently of a central government.

If Viet-Nam is to maintain its independence and the religious freedom desired by all, including the sects, there needs to be increasing allegiance to the central government. Reports indicate this allegiance is still not being granted by the sects to the Free Government of Viet-Nam. I hope that motives of patriotism will inspire all groups in Free Viet-Nam to join together. Only as a united people will they be able to meet the threat of communism.

The third and greatest problem is, of course, that presented by the Communists in the north. Under the armistice they should have removed their forces from the south.[38] Instead, many of their soldiers there merely put on civilian clothes and faded into the local community as a source of future trouble. Communist propaganda is rife, and, in addition, the free people of the south are subjected to the terrorizing threat of armed aggression from the north. As against this, local forces are being trained. But the principal reliance is the Manila Pact and its deterrent power.

In July of this year, conversations are scheduled to begin between south and north looking toward elections in 1956 to unify Viet-Nam. Under the terms of the armistice, these elections are to be held under conditions of freedom. There can be little doubt but what most of the people of Viet-Nam will want to unite under a genuinely independent and democratic government. In the north there is great discontent with Communist despotism. For each one of the many who have actually fled south to find freedom, there are many more who want freedom. Also, economic conditions in the north are deplorable and in many localities there is near starvation.

It will, however, be hard to create in the north conditions which allow genuine freedom of choice. In northern Korea and in eastern Germany the Communists stubbornly refuse to permit the free elections which would bring unification. We hope this pattern will not be repeated by the Communist Viet Minh.

I was much impressed by Prime Minister Diem. He is a true patriot, dedicated to independence and to the enjoyment by his people of political and religious freedoms. He now has a program for agricultural reform.[39] If it is effectively executed, it will both assist in the resettlement of the refugees and provide his country with a sounder agricultural system. I am convinced that his Government deserves the support

[38] See Note 13, p. 338. See also Note 5, p. 336.   [39] See Note 34, p. 360.

which the United States is giving to help to create an efficient, loyal military force and sounder economic conditions.

[Discussion of the Chiefs of Mission meeting in Manila, the defense of Formosa, and the United States position in Asia is omitted.]

155. *Second Interim Report of the International Commission for Supervision and Control in Viet-Nam* [*Conclusion*] *
March 8, 1955

[The "Second Interim Report" covered the period from December 11, 1954, to February 10, 1955.]

21. By its very structure, the Agreement,[40] which is a balanced document, attempts to reconcile the interests and the sovereignty of the authorities in control of the two zones and, while it puts on the two parties the responsibility for the execution of the Agreement (Article 28), it gives the Commission the task of supervision over the proper execution by the parties of the provisions of the Agreement. Effective implementation of the Agreement requires close co-operation between the parties to the Agreement and this has, in various ways, been lacking during the period under report. Each party is more keen to get the Commission to denounce the other than to take reasonable measures to get the Agreement implemented. The Commission's findings, as in the Ba Lang case,[41] show how, in many cases, the narrow or hostile attitude of local authorities of both parties is responsible for delay or difficulties in the effective implementation of the Agreement.

22. The Commission has been insisting on the co-operation of the two High Commands promised under Article 25 and taking every possible occasion to correct the atmosphere of suspicion and distrust. While the French High Command has been trying hard to carry out its obligations under the Agreement, there have been cases, as in the case of the civilian internees at Poulo Condore, where they have not been able to implement the Commission's decision in view of the independent attitude taken by the Government of South Vietnam, which has not signed

* *Source:* Great Britain, Parliament, Papers by Command, *First and Second Interim Reports of the International Commission for Supervision and Control in Vietnam* (London: Her Majesty's Stationery Office, Cmd. 9461, 1955), pp. 49–50.

[40] Agreement on the Cessation of Hostilities in Viet-Nam, Document 130.

[41] An "incident" in January 1955, in which the State of Viet-Nam alleged that the DRV had used force against Catholics attempting to flee from North to South.

the Agreement. There has, however, been no case so far where either of the High Commands has refused to put into effect a recommendation made by the Commission.

23. There have been cases of intransigence on the part of local civil or military authorities and the Commission's teams have, on occasions, not got the facilities they are entitled to receive in the fulfilment of their task under Article 35. The Commission has informed both the High Commands that they will, in future, ask for specific action under Article 22 against local civil or military authorities who do not give the necessary facilities to the Commission's teams or in any way obstruct the teams in the fulfilment of their task.

156. *Third Interim Report of the International Commission for Supervision and Control in Viet-Nam* [Conclusion] *
April 25, 1955

[The "Third Interim Report" covered the period from February 11, 1955, to April 10, 1955.]

16. Reference was made in paragraphs 21 to 23 of the Second Interim Report [42] to the want of co-operation between the parties to the Agreement,[43] to the failure by the parties to carry out their obligations under the Agreement due to intransigence of local civil or/and military authorities and the general warning given by the Commission to both High Commands regarding need for specific action under Article 22 where required. During the period under report, the Commission has had several occasions to recommend to the High Commands that specific action be taken by them under Article 22 against particular local authorities concerned for violation of the provisions of Article 35 regarding grant of all facilities required by the team from local civil and military authorities. Four cases of this type in the Vinh region have

* Source: Great Britain, Parliament, Papers by Command, *Third Interim Report of the International Commission for Supervision and Control in Vietnam* (London: Her Majesty's Stationery Office, Cmd. 9499, 1955), pp. 10–11. The Report was accompanied by a "Note by the Canadian Delegation" drawing the attention of the Co-Chairmen of the Geneva Conference (Great Britain and the Soviet Union) to paragraphs 11 and 19 dealing with the implementation of Article 14(*d*) in the zone under the control of the P.A.V.N. High Command, and requesting that the matter be referred to the members of the Geneva Conference. See *ibid.*, p. 4.
42 Document 155.
43 Agreement on the Cessation of Hostilities in Viet-Nam, Document 130.

been referred to the High Command of the P.A.V.N.[44] and two in the Nha Trang region to the High Command of the French Union Forces during the period under report.

17. While the Commission has, in view of the complicated administrative and other problems which the parties have had to face, shown a great deal of patience, the action of some local civil authorities in the North in dealing with matters relating to implementation of Article 14(*d*) and some in the South in dealing with matters relating to Article 14(*c*) have retarded the implementation of the democratic freedoms under these Articles in various areas. It must be added that there are substantial areas in Vietnam where there have been no investigations by the Commission's teams and the extent of implementation of these articles in those areas can only be inferred from the extent of implementation ascertained in specific areas which were the subject of investigation by the Commission's teams.

18. The provisions of Article 35 which require the concurrence of the High Command for Mobile Team investigations except along the frontiers and the dependence of the Commission's teams on local civil and military authorities for logistic and security arrangements have led to delays and even obstruction in some cases which have retarded the implementation of various Articles of the Agreement. The Commission has, in addition to bringing specific cases of delays or obstruction by the local authorities to the notice of the High Command, told both High Commands that they must assume responsibility for the actions of subordinate officials.

19. The delay in the implementation of Article 14(*d*), which has a specific time-limit within which the implementation must be completed,[45] has been a matter of serious concern to the Commission so far as the zone under the control of the P.A.V.N. High Command is concerned (*vide* paragraph 11).[46] In addition, there have been, in recent investigations, cases where one group of people demonstrated against another group

---

[44] Peoples' Army of Viet-Nam.   [45] 300 days from July 20, 1954.

[46] Paragraph 11 of this report stated that "the recommendations of the Commission were not being implemented fully" by local DRV officials and that "The preliminary reports of these teams [which made a detailed survey of the provinces of Nam Dinh, Ninh Binh, Thai Binh, Than Hoa, Nghe An, and Ha Tinh] have shown that progress in the implementation of Article 14(*d*) will continue to be unsatisfactory unless administrative arrangements and the provision of transport facilities are urgently improved." It also stated that "in light of the progress made in the implementation of this Article so far, it is not possible to state at this stage that Article 14(*d*) will be implemented in full within the time-limit laid down."

and, though non-violent in its attitude to the Commission's team, caused obstruction to the team's investigation. The implementation of Article 21 and the delays in investigation in this connexion in the zone of the French High Command have been the cause of some anxiety to the Commission, particularly as the reasons therefor mentioned in paragraph 22 of the Second Interim Report [47] still continue despite the provisions of Article 27. There has, in addition, been another undesirable development, viz., demonstrations involving violence, against the Commission's teams and the personnel working with them as referred to in paragraph 16.

20. The Commission hopes that the High Commands of both parties will take all measures necessary to ensure full co-operation and assistance both from the High Commands as stipulated in Article 25 and from the local civil and military authorities as stipulated in Article 35 and secure effective implementation of all provisions of the Agreement throughout Vietnam.

157. *Secretary of State Dulles: Statement on Discussions on Indochina with Premier Edgar Faure of France and Foreign Secretary Harold Macmillan of Great Britain [Extract]* *
    May 17, 1955

[The statement is extracted from the report made over national television on May 17, 1955, on the Secretary's visit to Europe, and in which President Eisenhower also participated.]

[MR. DULLES]: Now I was in Europe and we dealt mostly with European problems, but I never forget the fact that we have got Asian problems as well as European problems, and I took advantage of this NATO Council to talk a bit to them about our Asian problems, because there is a considerable failure to understand the motivation of our Asian policies. And I said to these Ministers there: If you like the United States as you see it manifested in Europe, you should understand what we are doing in Asia because we are doing precisely the same thing in Asia that we want to do here. What are we doing? We are defending free-

* *Source:* United States, Department of State, *Bulletin,* XXXII (May 30, 1955), pp. 872–873. Extracts from Premier Edgar Faure's comments on the Paris conversations, made at a press conference on May 13, are in France, Direction de la Documentation, *Chroniques d'Outre-Mer: Etudes et Informations,* No. 16 (June 1955), pp. 79–80.

[47] Document 155.

dom where there are free men who want to defend their own freedom. We believe in collective security to help them do that. We believe in being loyal to our friends and allies. And, I said, you seem to like those policies when you find them in Europe, and you ought also to recognize that those are the same policies motivating us in Asia, because, I said, we don't have a double personality; we are just one Nation. And the reason we are acting this way in Europe is because we really believe in these things, and if we believe in them we are going to act the same way in Asia.

THE PRESIDENT: That is a wonderful way to tell them.

MR. DULLES: I think they began to understand, perhaps for the first time, what was back of our Asian policies. And then I took the opportunity to talk a good deal with the French Prime Minister, Edgar Faure, and the Foreign Minister, M. [Antoine] Pinay, about the situation in Indochina. And the British Foreign Minister, Harold Macmillan, sat in on some of our talks. It was hard to get them in. Our days were busy. We mostly met at night. We had three or four meetings at night that lasted until 1 o'clock or more in the morning.

The main point I made there was that we had to accept the fact that Viet-Nam is now a free nation—at least the southern half of it is—and it has not got a puppet government, it has not got a government that we can give orders to and tell what we want it to do or we want it to refrain from doing. If it was that kind of government, we wouldn't be justified in supporting it because that kind of government is not going to last there. One can only hold free Viet-Nam with a government that is nationalistic and has a purpose of its own and is responsive to the will of its own people, and doesn't take orders from anybody outside, whether it be from Paris—or Cannes, for that matter [48]—or from Washington. And we have got to coordinate our policies to the acceptance of the fact that it is really a free and independent country.

We talked that over in its various implications and ramifications, hour after hour, during almost every day for the 4 days I was in Paris. And I think we came to a better understanding and that there is more chance of coordination of French policies with ours along sound lines than has been the case heretofore. The government of Diem, which seemed to be almost on the ropes a few weeks ago, I think is reestablished with strength. It has been through a hard experience and I think it is going to have more support, within and without, than it has had

[48] The reference is to Bao Dai. See Document 153.

before. And I look to that situation with more hope than we have had
before. That is a byproduct of this trip, which was designed primarily
for European matters. We did, I think, make a considerable accomplishment both in relation to our China policy and in relation to Viet-Nam.[49]

[49] On May 13, 1955, the London *Times* reported (page 9) on the substance of
an agreement reached on May 11 between Mr. Dulles, M. Faure, and Mr. Macmillan, which was followed by an implementing agreement between the French
and American governments, of which the British were informed. According to *The
Times:*

"That [new] policy represents a compromise between the American belief that
M. Ngo Dinh Diem is the only man capable of preparing south Viet-Nam to meet
the Communist challenge, and the French contention that M. Diem exerts at the
moment little authority and is in danger of being engulfed by the extremist elements surrounding him.

"The main points in the Franco-American compromise are: (1) M. Diem shall
be advised and persuaded to broaden his Government and therefore increase his
authority by including in it men who are more representative of different interests
and tendencies; (2) M. Diem shall be advised and persuaded to desist from his
anti-French attitude and propaganda; (3) The representatives of the Powers in
Saigon shall help to devise some form of popular consultation in south Viet Nam,
in order that the Government and regime shall be based to the greatest practicable
degree upon popular consent; (4) The French will not withdraw the expeditionary
corps at a rate faster than it can be replaced by the Viet Nam Army, *i.e.* no
vacuum will be created by a rapid reduction or withdrawal of French forces;
(5) The Emperor Bao Dai's position as legal head of the State will remain un-
altered.

"There is nothing, it is understood, in the instructions being sent to Saigon about
a time limit for these arrangements, that is, a date after which M. Diem might, if
things are still going badly, cease to enjoy the Franco-American support now being
promised to him. French accounts of last night's meeting between M. Faure and
Mr. Dulles suggest that there is to be such a limit, and that the present agreement
is to run for only two months, until the time forseen by the Geneva agreements for
the first consultations between northern and southern Viet Nam about preparing
the general elections for the whole country in 1956."

There is no official documentation available about these developments and agreements, although the Franco-American agreements may well be those later referred
to by French Foreign Minister Christian Pineau in early 1956 (see Document 176).
On May 10, however, a White House Press Release indicated that General J. Lawton Collins "had assisted the Vietnamese Government in the preparation and implementation of its economic, military, and social programs" and that "General
Collins had successfully concluded arrangements under which the United States,
at the request of the Government of Viet-Nam and with the agreement of the
Government of France, had undertaken responsibility for the training of Viet-Nam
national armed forces." (United States, Archives, *Public Papers of the Presidents
of the United States, Dwight D. Eisenhower, 1955* [Washington: Government
Printing Office, 1959], p. 316). See also *ibid.*, pp. 436–437, and Document 151.

CHAPTER XIII

The Question of Consultations

June-November 1955

Introduction

From June to November 1955 the situation in Viet-Nam changed as the Saigon Government took action to depose former Emperor Bao Dai as Chief of State and to organize a Republic with Ngo Dinh Diem as President. During the same period the Democratic Republic of Viet-Nam (DRV) tightened its relations with the Soviet Union and China. Those two developments served to divide further the two Vietnamese states; the rift was emphasized by the refusal of the Saigon regime to consult with the North for the holding of general elections throughout Viet-Nam in 1956. It thus appeared that the elections in 1956 would not take place, and the DRV introduced a new tactic to bring about reunification under its aegis with the formation of the Viet-Nam Fatherland Front (VFF) in September.

With the completion of the military regroupment provisions of the cease-fire agreements during May 1955, concern shifted to the political provisions of the Final Declaration of the Geneva Conference. On June 6 DRV Foreign Minister Pham Van Dong read a statement expressing the readiness of his government "to hold the consultative conference with the competent representative authorities in South Viet-Nam" in order to prepare for the elections scheduled for July 1956 (Document 158).[1] The statement did not specify whether the DRV expected the "consultative

---

[1] The editor has been unable to determine the origins of the idea of a "consultative conference" as the means for implementation of the "consultations" provided for in paragraph 7 of the Final Declaration, although the term was apparently first used in this connection by the DRV. Pham Van Dong called for "consultative conferences" in presenting the initial DRV proposals at the Geneva Conference: see Document 114, paragraph 3 of the proposals. The distinction between the two terms was not a minor one, as there could be considerable difference between the informality implied by "consultations" and the structured formality implied by "consultative conference."

conference" to be with France or the State of Viet-Nam.[2] But on June 14 the Indian Government endorsed the idea of a "consultative conference" and indicated its view that the State of Viet-Nam was the proper authority to undertake consultations for the South (Document 159). British policy was outlined on June 15 by Anthony Nutting, Minister of State for Foreign Affairs (Document 160). While stating that Britain thought the State of Viet-Nam should undertake consultations, Mr. Nutting emphasized, "We cannot order the Government of South Vietnam about." Secretary of State Dulles, on June 28, refrained from comment on the question of consultations but indicated that the United States had no fear of elections in Viet-Nam provided they were "held under conditions of genuine freedom" (Document 161).

At the end of June, Ho Chi Minh, accompanied by VWP General Secretary Truong Chinh and a number of government officials, set out to visit China and the Soviet Union. The trip was described as *governmental* with no mention of *party* relations. After talks in Peking from June 25 to July 7, the DRV and Chinese governments issued a Joint Communiqué (Document 162). The DRV delegation then went on to Moscow, where the two Governments issued a Joint Communiqué on July 18 (Document 164). Although both China and the USSR expressed support for the DRV position on reunification and offered to provide economic aid, Ho Chi Minh later stressed: "But our people and cadres must not entirely depend on this substantial aid. On the contrary we must learn from the people of the brother countries the spirit of self-reliance, of enthusiastic competition to increase production and thrift." [3]

While Ho Chi Minh was talking with the Communist powers, the State of Viet-Nam was negotiating with France to further confirm its independence. Talks in Paris during July agreed on abolishing the post of Commissioner General in Viet-Nam and replacing it with normal

---

[2] The Final Declaration was unclear as to who the "competent representative authorities" in South Viet-Nam were to be. The relevant portions of the Agreement on the Cessation of Hostilities in Viet-Nam (Document 130, Articles 8 and 14) seem to indicate that at the time the Conference expected that France was to be the responsible party. Pham Van Dong seemed to accept this interpretation in statements immediately following the Conference; see the Introduction to Chapter XI. France, however, helped confuse the issue by taking the position that all civil authority in the South had been transferred to the Saigon government.

[3] Ho Chi Minh's report on the trip to China and the Soviet Union, in Ho Chi Minh, *Selected Works* (4 vols., Hanoi: Foreign Languages Publishing House, 1961–1962), Vol. IV, pp. 95–99.

diplomatic representation in the form of an exchange of High Commissioners between the two states. France also agreed in principle to the withdrawal of her Expeditionary Corps, and in August abolished the Ministry of State for Relations with the Associated States, transferring its functions to the Foreign Ministry. On July 7 Diem announced a referendum to be held in October to decide whether Bao Dai should be deposed as Head of State and Viet-Nam made a Republic. In a July 16 statement the Premier also gave the South Vietnamese position on the Geneva Agreements, emphasizing that his government was not bound by them and would reject "any proposal by the Viet Minh, unless proof is given us that they place the high interests of the national community above those of Communism" (Document 163). On July 18 the DRV made its first formal approach to the State of Viet-Nam for the opening of the "consultative conference," in a letter to Diem and Bao Dai (Document 165).

Viet-Nam was discussed informally by the "Big Four" during the Geneva Summit meeting in July. After demonstrations in Saigon on the July 20 anniversary of the Geneva Agreements (marked in South Viet-Nam as a "day of shame") developed into attacks on the two hotels which housed the members of the International Commission for Supervision and Control (ICSC), the three Western powers agreed on a joint note to the Saigon Government, delivered on July 26.[4] Reportedly this note urged the State of Viet-Nam to open consultations with the North. In an official declaration issued on August 9, however, the State of Viet-Nam reaffirmed the principles expressed in Diem's July 16 statement (Document 166). As a result, the DRV on August 17 requested the Co-Chairmen of the Geneva Conference to take action "to ensure the respect for the Geneva Agreements, the settlement of the political problem in Viet-nam, the immediate convening of the consultative conference." [5]

A different aspect of DRV policy on reunification was reflected at a Congress of the National United Front (the Lien Viet) held in Hanoi in early September. The Congress created yet another "united front," this time known as the "Viet-Nam Fatherland Front" (VFF), with the Lien Viet as a constituent part. The Congress was addressed by VWP

---

[4] The text of this note remains classified by all the governments concerned.

[5] Note from Foreign Minister Pham Van Dong to the Co-Chairmen; text in Democratic Republic of Viet-Nam, Ministry of Foreign Affairs, Press and Information Department, *Documents Related to the Implementation of the Geneva Agreements Concerning Viet-nam* (Hanoi: 1956), pp. 45–50.

General Secretary Truong Chinh (Document 167), and on September 10 adopted the VFF Program (Document 168).

On October 1 the ICSC submitted its "Fourth Interim Report" (Document 169). The report indicated differences between the Indian and Polish delegations on one hand and the Canadian delegation on the other over the position taken by the State of Viet-Nam and over the implementation by the DRV of some provisions of the Agreement on the Cessation of Hostilities. On October 7 Foreign Minister Vu Van Mau explained the position of the State of Viet-Nam in a letter to the British Foreign Secretary.[6]

The referendum on the establishment of a Republic in South Viet-Nam was held on October 23 and produced an overwhelming mandate for the deposition of Bao Dai, following an election campaign and voting procedure which many viewed as less than objective and fair.[7] On October 26 the Republic of Viet-Nam was formally established with Ngo Dinh Diem as President (Document 170); it was recognized by the United States the same day (Document 171).

On October 31, CPR Foreign Minister Chou En-lai, in a letter to the Co-Chairmen of the Geneva Conference, supported the DRV position on reunification and called for action to enforce the holding of the "consultative conference."[8] The British and Soviet Foreign Ministers met in Geneva on November 14 to consider the Viet-Nam situation; the results of their discussions were to be made known in December.[9] The Co-Chairmen also had to consider the situation in Laos, where implementation of the Geneva Agreements was unsatisfactory as the DRV conducted an active propaganda campaign in support of the Pathet Lao and sporadic fighting took place between Pathet Lao and Government forces.

Foreign Minister Pham Van Dong, in a November 25 letter to Foreign Minister Molotov of the Soviet Union, argued that the Republic of Viet-Nam was bound by the Geneva Agreements and labeled the creation of the Republic and the forthcoming election of a National Assembly in the South as "flagrant violations" of the Geneva Agree-

[6] A text of the letter, which is probably accurate, appears in *ibid.,* pp. 100–102.

[7] According to the official results, 98.2 per cent of the votes cast were in favor of the establishment of a Republic with Diem as President, while only 1.1 per cent favored the retention of Bao Dai as Head of State.

[8] Text in Great Britain, Parliament, Papers by Command, *Documents Relating to British Involvement in the Indo-China Conflict 1945–1965* (London: Her Majesty's Stationery Office, Cmnd. 2834, 1965), pp. 113–114.

[9] See Document 173.

ments.[10] He also argued that "the fact that the South Viet-nam authorities have taken in charge large areas in South Viet-nam evacuated by the Vietnamese People's Army implies that they have recognized the Geneva Agreements" and that "the Government of France and the South Viet-nam Administration are jointly responsible for the execution of the Geneva Agreements."

158. *Declaration by Foreign Minister Pham Van Dong of the Democratic Republic of Viet-Nam on the Readiness of His Government to Hold a Consultative Conference on the General Elections Scheduled for July 1956 [Extracts]* *
June 6, 1955

After 300 days of implementing the Agreement on the cessation of hostilities,[1] the withdrawals and transfers of the military forces have been completed, the whole territory of North Viet-nam has entirely been liberated.

[Four paragraphs summarizing the provisions of the Geneva Agreements relevant to the conduct of the elections are omitted.]

Up to now, in the withdrawals and transfers of the military forces, as well as in other questions, the Government of the Democratic Republic of Viet-nam has loyally implemented the Geneva Agreements. From now on, in the organization of the consultative conference [2] and the free general elections in order to achieve the unity of Viet-nam, as well as in other questions, the Government of the Democratic Republic of Viet-nam is resolved to continue to implement loyally the Geneva Agreements.

The Government of the Democratic Republic of Viet-nam declares its readiness to hold the consultative conference with the competent representative authorities in South Viet-nam from July 20, 1955 onwards in order to discuss the organization of free general elections throughout the country in July 1956.

* *Source:* Democratic Republic of Viet-Nam, Ministry of Foreign Affairs, Press and Information Department, *Documents Related to the Implementation of the Geneva Agreements Concerning Viet-nam* (Hanoi: 1956), pp. 37–40. The Declaration was read by Pham Van Dong at a press conference. It was broadcast by Viet-Nam News Agency in English Morse, June 6, 1955, 0600 G.M.T., with only minor textual variations from the official version given here.

[10] Text in *Documents Related to the Implementation of the Geneva Agreements Concerning Viet-nam,* pp. 57–61.

[1] Document 130.   [2] See Note 1, p. 369.

The French Government has manifested its desire to implement the Geneva Agreements. On May 17 of this year, on the occasion of the completion of the withdrawals and transfers of military forces, the representative of the High Command of the French Union Forces, and the representative of the High Command of the Vietnamese People's Army solemnly issued the following joint statement:

Resolved to continue to assume their responsibility in the full implementation of the provisions of the Geneva Agreements and of the Final Declaration of the Nine Powers, both parties affirm once again their determination to respect and to implement scrupulously the clauses and provisions of these conventions, in order to consolidate peace and to achieve the unity of Viet-nam by means of general elections.

The Government of the Democratic Republic of Viet-nam welcomes and takes note of this statement.

[Three paragraphs justifying the unity of Viet-Nam are omitted.]

Viet-nam is one. The Vietnamese nation is one. No force can divide it. Whoever tries to partition Viet-nam is the enemy of the Vietnamese people and will surely be defeated. All the Vietnamese who stand for peace, unity, independence, democracy, regardless of class, political affiliations or religious belief, should unite in the fight for a common aim, they will surely be victorious.

In their struggle for reunification, the Vietnamese people maintain constant vigilance and are on their guard against any manoeuvres of the American imperialists aiming at partitioning Viet-nam. They are ready to unite and to fight against such manoeuvres and to frustrate them.

With the warm sympathy and support of the peoples throughout the world, the Vietnamese people, in their monolithic unity and with their determination to fight, will certainly ensure the strict implementation of the Geneva Agreements and the realization of the unity of Viet-nam by means of free general elections.

159. *Aide-Mémoire to the Co-Chairmen of the Geneva Conference from the Government of India* *
June 14, 1955

The military phase of the implementation of the Geneva Agreement on the Cessation of Hostilities in Viet-Nam having been concluded, it

* *Source:* Great Britain, Parliament, Papers by Command, *Documents Relating to British Involvement in the Indo-China Conflict 1945–1965* (London: Her Majesty's Stationery Office, Cmnd. 2834, 1965), pp. 103–105.

remains now to give attention to the question of general elections which will bring about the unification of Viet-Nam.

2. Paragraph 7 of the Final Declaration of the Geneva Conference [3] mentions that "so far as Viet-Nam is concerned, the settlement of political problems, effected on the basis of respect for the principles of independence, unity and territorial integrity shall permit the Viet-Namese people to enjoy the fundamental freedoms, guaranteed by democratic institutions established as a result of free general elections by secret ballot." According to the time schedule fixed in this paragraph consultations are to be held from July, 1955, onwards between the competent representative authorities of the two zones on the subject of holding general elections in July, 1956.

3. Under Article 14(*a*) of the Geneva Agreement on the Cessation of Hostilities in Viet-Nam,[4] "pending the general elections which will bring about the unification of Viet-Nam, the conduct of civil administration in each regrouping zone shall be in the hands of the party whose forces are to be regrouped there in virtue of the present Agreement." Accordingly, the civil administration in North Viet-Nam was, pending the general elections, to be with the Democratic Republic of Viet-Nam and in South Viet-Nam with the French Union. Subsequently, however, the French Union transferred their sovereign authority in the southern zone to the State of Viet-Nam.[5] The representative authorities of the two zones between whom consultations are to be held are, therefore, the Democratic Republic of Viet-Nam which is responsible for civil administration in North Viet-Nam and, in virtue of Article 27, the State of Viet-Nam which has taken over the civil administration in South Viet-Nam from the French authorities.

4. The date on which these consultations are to commence (20th July, 1955) is not far off, and if paragraph 7 of the Final Declaration of the Geneva Powers is to be implemented, expeditious steps have to be taken to ensure that such consultations do take place on and from the appointed date. The implementation of paragraph 7 of the Declaration must be a matter of vital interest to those who subscribed to the Final Declaration at Geneva. It is also of interest to Canada, Poland and India who as supervisory countries on the International Com-

---

[3] Document 131.   [4] Document 130.

[5] This point indicates one problem with interpretation and application of the Geneva Agreements. It is difficult, under international law, to determine a specific point where legal sovereignty was "transferred" to the State of Viet-Nam, particularly since increasing independence was acquired over a period of years and through a series of agreements. A case can be made that the State of Viet-Nam was "sovereign" at the time of the Geneva Conference.

mission are associated with the implementation of the Geneva Agreement, particularly as non-implementation of paragraph 7 of the Geneva Declaration involves the risk of reversion to a state of war between the parties through breakdown of the main structure of the Geneva settlement.

5. Having regard to the relations between the parties and the circumstances prevailing in Viet-Nam, it appears to the Government of India that consultations may not take place without some initiative being taken by the two Co-Chairmen. The Government of India, therefore, feel that the Co-Chairmen should request the authorities in charge of the Democratic Republic of Viet-Nam and the State of Viet-Nam to start consultations. To facilitate such consultations they may further offer the parties the services of the three Delegates on the International Supervisory Commission in Viet-Nam. The Delegates will act not as members of the Commission but as individuals representing their respective Governments and their task will be to assist the parties: (i) to convene a conference of competent representative authorities of the two sides for inter-zonal consultations and to assist in the preparation and approval of the agenda; and (ii) to elect a Chairman either from among themselves or from outside to preside over the deliberations of the consultative conference. The Delegates from the Supervisory Commission will withdraw from the conference after the agenda has been settled and a Chairman has been chosen to preside over the deliberations.

6. The Chairman agreed upon by the parties will act both as a conciliator and as a technical expert on the essentials of a free general election by secret ballot and will assist the parties to come to agreed conclusions as regards the principles and procedure which would ensure free and fair general elections by secret ballot. The agreed modalities of the elections can thereafter be worked out and adopted by the authorities in each of the two zones as the law in force for the time being to regulate the elections. Thereafter, the Electoral Commission, envisaged in paragraph 7 of the Geneva Declaration, will be set up to supervise the elections in accordance with the agreed principles and procedure.

7. The Government of India would request the two Co-Chairmen to address the authorities in charge of the Democratic Republic of Viet-Nam and the State of Viet-Nam on the lines indicated in paragraphs 5 and 6 above. They are informing the Governments of Canada and Poland that they are making this request with an expression of their

hope that the Governments of Canada and Poland would agree with the procedure outlined herein.

160. *Anthony Nutting: Statement in the House of Commons* [*Extract*] * *June 15, 1955*

[An earlier statement in the same session by Harold Macmillan, Secretary of State for Foreign Affairs, is omitted, as are the first five paragraphs of Mr. Nutting's comments on Indochina.]

[MR. NUTTING, Minister of State for Foreign Affairs]: I now come to the question of elections in Vietnam about which the hon. Gentleman [6] had some comments to make. The final declaration of the Geneva Conference on Indo-China [7] provides that the general elections to be held in Vietnam in July, 1956, shall be supervised by an international commission composed of representatives of the member States of the present International Supervisory Commission in Vietnam, namely, India, Canada and Poland. This electoral supervisory commission has not yet been set up, and agreement has still to be reached on its functions and terms of reference. However, in reply to the direct question put to me by the hon. Gentleman, we are proceeding on the assumption that elections will take place as laid down in the Geneva Agreement in July, 1956.

As the House knows, our policy is to do all we can to uphold the authority and prestige of the international supervisory commissions in Indo-China and to support them in their efforts to make the Geneva Agreements work. They can do no more. Their task in doing that has been by no means an easy one, nor for that matter has ours; but, by and large, I hope the House will agree, and give them credit for it, that they have done all and more than they could be expected to do in seeing that the Geneva settlement is carried out. But what they cannot do, and are not called upon to do, under the Geneva Agreement is to intervene in the internal situation and internal affairs of the State of Indo-China. All they can do is to ensure that elections take place. The International Supervisory Commission should not and cannot

* *Source:* Great Britain, *Parliamentary Debates* (*Hansard*), Fifth Series, House of Commons, Vol. 542, session of June 15, 1955, cols. 715–717.

[6] Mr. Christopher Mayhew; the text of his remarks on Viet-Nam is in Great Britain, *Parliamentary Debates* (*Hansard*), Fifth Series, House of Commons, Vol. 542, Session of June 15, 1955, cols. 705–710.

[7] Document 131.

try to win the elections for whichever side we should like to win.

MR. MAYHEW: What steps are the Government taking, first, to get the supervisory commission set up immediately, and, second, and most important, to ensure that there is a real will on the southern side to reach agreement on the electoral law for elections next year?

MR. NUTTING: We cannot order the Government of South Vietnam about. With regard to getting the supervisory commission going, the hon. Gentleman will know that under the Geneva Agreements the two parties in Vietnam, the Vietminh and the Government of South Vietnam, must agree on the powers and functions of the supervisory commission which is to supervise the elections. It is upon that that we are stuck at the moment, but we shall certainly do all we can to lever that along and get agreement so that the supervisory commission can take up its duties.

MR. MAYHEW: The right hon. Gentleman says that he has no power to order the South Vietnam Government about. That is the crux of the problem. The French signed the agreement before the South Vietnam Government became independent.[8] Now that Government is independent. If the Western Powers seek refuge in saying that it is independent and cannot be influenced, the Geneva Agreements will fall.

MR. NUTTING: I am not saying that we cannot influence it; I am saying that we cannot order it about. We shall use all our influence to get the South Vietnam Government to agree upon the early establishment of the supervisory commission, but, as I say, to be fair, it does not rest with them alone. The Vietminh will have to be brought to agree to the authority as well.

161. *Secretary of State Dulles: Statement at a News Conference* *
    June 28, 1955

At his news conference on June 28, Secretary Dulles was asked the position of the United States with respect to elections in Viet-Nam. The Secretary replied:

Neither the United States Government nor the Government of Viet-Nam is, of course, a party to the Geneva armistice agreements.[9] We

* *Source:* United States, Department of State, *American Foreign Policy 1950–1955: Basic Documents* (2 vols., Washington: Government Printing Office, 1957), Vol. II, p. 2404.

8 See Note 5, p. 375.

9 The reference appears to be primarily to the Agreement on the Cessation of Hostilities in Viet-Nam, Document 130, signed by the Viet Minh and French

did not sign them, and the Government of Viet-Nam did not sign them and, indeed, protested against them. On the other hand, the United States believes, broadly speaking, in the unification of countries which have a historic unity, where the people are akin. We also believe that, if there are conditions of really free elections, there is no serious risk that the Communists would win.

The Communists have never yet won any free election. I don't think they ever will. Therefore, we are not afraid at all of elections, provided they are held under conditions of genuine freedom which the Geneva armistice agreement calls for. If those conditions can be provided we would be in favor of elections, because we believe that they would bring about the unification of the country under free government auspices.

162. *Joint Communiqué of the Government of the People's Republic of China and the Government of the Democratic Republic of Viet-Nam, Peking [Extracts]* *
    July 7, 1955

During the visit to China of the Delegation of the Government of the Democratic Republic of Viet-Nam headed by President Ho Chi Minh, talks were held in Peking from June 27 to July 7 between a delegation of the Government of the People's Republic of China and the Delegation of the Government of the Democratic Republic of Viet-Nam on the basis of principles laid down in the course of consultation by Chairman Mao Tse-tung of the People's Republic of China and President Ho Chi Minh of the Democratic Republic of Viet-Nam.

[Two paragraphs listing the members of the delegations are omitted. The Chinese delegation was headed by Chou En-lai and included Vice Premiers Chen Yun and Teng Hsiao-ping. The DRV delegation included Truong Chinh, Le Van Hien, Phan Anh, Nguyen Van Huyen, Nghiem Xuan Yem, Ung Van Khiem, Nguyen Duy Trinh, Pham Ngoc Thach, and Hoang Van Hoan.]

In the course of the talks, the two parties discussed matters of common interest to the People's Republic of China and the Democratic Republic of Viet-Nam and questions of major significance in the present international situation.

---

* *Source: People's China*, No. 15 (August 1, 1955), Supplement, pp. 2–4.

Union High Commands, although the negative attitude taken by both the United States and the State of Viet-Nam to the Final Declaration (Document 131), is implied as well.

The two parties note with satisfaction that the regrouping and transfer of military forces as provided for in the Geneva agreements have been completed, and that the International Commissions for supervision and control in the three Indo-China states, composed of representatives of India, Poland and Canada and with the Indian representatives as chairmen, have made important contributions in supervising and controlling the implementation of the Geneva agreements. The two parties express the hope that the International Commissions for supervision and control will continue to play an active role in ensuring the thorough implementation of the Geneva agreements.

However, the two parties are aware that the implementation of the Geneva agreements has been obstructed and sabotaged and is threatened with new sabotage. Shortly after the Geneva Conference, the United States Government violated the Geneva agreements by including South Viet-Nam, Cambodia and Laos in the so-called designated area "protected" by the Manila Treaty [10] and by stepping up the equipping and training of troops in South Viet-Nam in order to convert the southern part of Viet-Nam into a colony and war base of the United States. At present, the United States is actively obstructing the holding of consultations for the general elections in Viet-Nam in an attempt to sabotage the cause of consolidating the peace and achieving the unification of Viet-Nam. The United States, again in violation of the Geneva agreements, signed a Military Assistance Agreement with Cambodia [11] and is further attempting to conclude a similar agreement with Laos so as to destroy the neutrality of Cambodia and Laos and jeopardize peace in Indo-China. The two parties to the talks are in agreement that these and similar violations of the Geneva agreements must be stopped and that the Geneva agreements must be carried through.

In accordance with the agreement reached in Geneva on the peaceful unification of Viet-Nam through general elections, consultations shall be held on the subject of general elections between the competent authorities of the two zones in Viet-Nam from July 20, 1955 so that free general elections may be held in July 1956 under the supervision of the International Commission composed of the representatives of India, Poland and Canada to bring about the unification of Viet-Nam. The Government of the Democratic Republic of Viet-Nam is determined to continue to carry out the Geneva agreements faithfully and

[10] The SEATO Treaty, Document 142.
[11] Concluded on May 16, 1955; text in United Nations, *Treaty Series,* Vol. 263 (1967), pp. 274–278.

has already declared its readiness to hold consultations with the competent authorities of South Viet-Nam on matters concerning the general elections. The two parties to the talks are of the common opinion that the countries which participated in the Geneva Conference have the responsibility for guaranteeing the implementation of the Geneva agreements. The two parties fully endorse the appeal and exhortation made by the Chairman of the Council of Ministers of the Soviet Union and the Prime Minister of India in their Joint Declaration on June 22, 1955,[12] namely, that all governments concerned with the carrying out of the Geneva agreements should do their utmost to discharge their obligations so that the purposes of the agreements may be completely achieved; and that where elections are to be held as a preliminary to a political settlement, the efforts of the governments concerned should be directed to the full implementation of the provisions of the agreements. The two parties are deeply convinced that the efforts of the Vietnamese people to achieve the unification of their country through consultations between the northern and the southern zones and through free general elections will certainly enjoy the full support of all countries and peoples who love peace and uphold the Geneva agreements.

The historic Asian-African Conference [13] has set an example of working in harmony by countries with different social systems. The two parties to the talks are pleased to note that the influence of the Asian-African Conference is daily increasing. They warmly support the series of important steps taken recently by the Soviet Union, India and other peace-loving countries, which help to advance the cause of peace. As a result of the efforts of the peace-loving countries and peoples, there have appeared signs of the easing of international tension. But the threat of a new war has not been eliminated, the international situation has not yet been fundamentally improved, and the rulers of certain important countries are still flaunting their so-called "policy of strength." The two parties consider that the "policy of strength" based on the organization of military blocs, establishment of military bases, expanding of armaments and conduct of war propaganda goes entirely against the common desire of the people of the world to maintain international peace and collective security.

The two parties to the talks are pleased to note that the five principles

[12] "Joint Statement Issued by Prime Minister Nehru of India and Premier N. A. Bulganin of the Soviet Union," issued in Moscow: text in Communist Information Bureau, *For a Lasting Peace, For a People's Democracy,* June 24, 1955, p. 1.
[13] The Bandung Conference, held in April 1955.

of peaceful co-existence are being recognized and accepted by more and more countries. They consider that the establishment of mutual confidence between nations, the elimination of international tension and the development of friendly co-operation between various countries depend on the universal and extensive acceptance of these principles by all countries of the world as the principles guiding their relations with one another. The two parties reiterate that the People's Republic of China and the Democratic Republic of Viet-Nam are ready, on the basis of the five principles of peaceful co-existence, to establish normal and cordial relations with all countries, and particularly to establish friendly and good neighbourly relations with the countries around them.

The Chinese and the Viet-Namese peoples have always given each other deep sympathy and support in their respective national liberation movements. At present, the Chinese people are engaged in a struggle to safeguard the sovereignty and territorial integrity of their fatherland and to liberate their territory of Taiwan. The Viet-Namese people are engaged in a struggle to unify their country through consultations between the northern and the southern zones and through the holding of free general elections so as to build a peaceful, united, independent, democratic, prosperous and strong new Viet-Nam. The two parties to the talks express full sympathy and support for the just struggles of the Chinese and Viet-Namese peoples and are deeply convinced that their struggles will certainly triumph.

The two parties to the talks are of the opinion that the economic and technical co-operation between the People's Republic of China and the Democratic Republic of Viet-Nam will be helpful to the efforts of the two peoples in peaceful construction. In order to assist the Viet-Namese people to heal the wounds left by a protracted war and rehabilitate and develop their national economy, the Government of the People's Republic of China decides to present without compensation to the Government of the Democratic Republic of Viet-Nam 800 million Chinese yuan. The Government of the People's Republic of China will use the above sum to help Viet-Nam rebuild railways, river docks, highways and bridges, restore and construct textile mills, tanneries, medical equipment factories, electrical equipment factories, agricultural implement factories, paper mills, etc. The two parties also agree to co-operate fully with each other on the technical side. China will help to design and construct the factories, railways, highways, bridges, etc. which Viet-Nam considers it necessary to repair or build, and will also dispatch technical personnel to Viet-Nam. At the same time, Viet-Nam will dispatch workers as apprentices to certain enterprises in China.

In order to promote the economic development of the two countries and to improve the livelihood of their peoples, the two parties further agree to expand step by step their mutual trade on the basis of equality and mutual benefit.

The Chinese and the Viet-Namese peoples have long and traditional cultural ties in history. In order further to extend their co-operation, exchange experience and study from each other in the fields of culture, education and health, the two parties agree to exchange cultural visits, and exchange students and books and literature. The People's Republic of China will dispatch technical personnel to Viet-Nam and present it as gifts material and apparatus for cultural, educational and health work so as to assist the work of the Viet-Namese people in these fields. The two parties are of the common view that the strengthening of the cultural interflow between the two peoples will further consolidate and develop their close friendship.

The two parties are deeply convinced that their talks held in an atmosphere of sincerity and harmony are not only in the interest of strengthening the unity and friendship of the two peoples and of their just struggles, but are certainly also in the interest of the common cause of safeguarding the peace of the peoples of the world.

163. *Premier Ngo Dinh Diem: Broadcast Declaration on the Geneva Agreements and Free Elections* *
    July 16, 1955

Fellow-countrymen,

The national government has on many occasions stressed the value it attaches to the defence of the Unity of our country and of true democracy.

We did not sign the Geneva agreements.

We are in no way bound by these agreements, which were concluded against the will of the Vietnamese people.

Our policy is one of peace. No stratagems, from wherever they may come, will divert us from our goal: the Unity of our land, but Unity

* *Source:* République du Viet-Nam, Secretariat d'Etat aux Affaires Etrangères, *Le Viet-Nam et Ses Relations Internationales* [published in French and English], I, No. 1–2 (June 1956), p. 105. The statement was originally broadcast over Saigon radio. English translations from Vietnamese and other sources show considerable variation in wording.

in freedom not in slavery. In service to the national cause we are striving more than ever for territorial unification.

We do not reject the principle of elections as a peaceful and democratic means of realising this unity. Still, though elections may form one of the pillars of true democracy, they are senseless if they are not absolutely free.

When we see the system of oppression practised by the Viet-Minh, we cannot but be sceptical as to the possibility of obtaining conditions for a free vote in the North.

We shall miss no opportunity for achieving the unification of our territory in freedom. But there is no question of considering any proposal by the Viet-Minh, unless proof is given us that they place the high interests of the national community above those of communism, unless they renounce terror and totalitarian methods, unless they cease to violate their engagements as they have done in preventing our fellow-countrymen from the North proceeding to the South, or in attacking, as on a recent further occasion in concert with the communist Pathet Lao, the friendly state of Laos.

It is to us, nationalists that falls the mission to re-make the unity of our country in conditions which are at once democratic and sufficiently effective to assure independence.

The free world is with us, we are sure of it.

I am confident that I am the faithful interpreter of the thought of all of you when I solemnly declare our resolve to resist Communism.

To those living beyond the 17th parallel I would say: Do not lose faith. With the support and agreement of the free world, the national government will bring you independence in freedom.

164. *Joint Communiqué Issued by the Soviet Government and the Government of the Democratic Republic of Viet-Nam, Moscow [Extracts]* *
July 18, 1955

At the invitation of the Soviet Government, the Government Delegation of the Democratic Republic of Viet Nam, headed by Comrade Ho Chi Minh, President and Prime Minister, visited the Soviet Union from July 12 to 18. During this period talks were held between the Government of the Soviet Union and the Government Delegation of the Democratic Republic of Viet Nam.

* *Source:* Communist Information Bureau, *For a Lasting Peace, For a People's Democracy,* July 22, 1955, p. 5.

[Two paragraphs listing the members of the delegations are omitted. The DRV delegation was the same as earlier visited Peking (see Document 162) except for the inclusion of Nguyen Long Bang, Ambassador to the U.S.S.R., instead of Hoang Van Hoan. The Soviet delegation included K. E. Voroshilov, N. A. Bulganin, N. S. Khrushchev, L. M. Kaganovich, A. I. Mikoyan, V. M. Molotov, and M. G. Pervukhin.]

The talks took place in an atmosphere of sincere cordiality and friendship.

In the course of the talks the parties discussed the further strengthening and development of friendly relations between the Soviet Union and the Democratic Republic of Viet Nam and international problems which are of concern to both countries. The talks revealed the complete community of views of the two Governments as regards both the international situation and the further development of political, economic and cultural co-operation between the USSR and the Democratic Republic of Viet Nam.

Both Governments, in full agreement, confirmed their readiness unwaveringly to strive for the strict implementation of the Geneva Agreements on Indo-China. They attach special importance to carrying out the clauses of the Geneva Agreements in regard to Viet Nam, bearing in mind the fact that peace in Indo-China can be consolidated only after the unification of Viet Nam on the basis of respect for its sovereignty, independence, unity and territorial integrity, as is stipulated in the Geneva Agreements.

The two Governments noted with satisfaction the successful completion of the regrouping of troops provided for in the Geneva Agreements and the carrying out of other military provisions in the Agreements relating to Viet Nam, achieved as the result of the collective efforts of the states concerned. They agreed that progress in implementing the Geneva Agreements represents a considerable contribution to the cause of strengthening peace and security in Indo-China and the world over. Both sides noted the fruitful work carried out by the International Commissions for Supervision and Control in Viet Nam, Laos and Cambodia, consisting of representatives from India, Poland and Canada and headed by the Indian representatives, and expressed the hope that these Commissions would successfully fulfil their mission in also achieving a political settlement in conformity with the Geneva Agreements.

Both Governments, in complete agreement, stressed the importance of holding consultations between the competent representatives of the Democratic Republic of Viet Nam and of South Viet Nam on questions connected with preparations for the general elections in July 1956 with a view to unifying Viet Nam, within the time limits laid down by the Geneva Agreements.

The Governments of the Soviet Union and the Democratic Republic of Viet Nam consider that the states which signed the Geneva Agreements and all states which are concerned with their implementation must take the necessary measures to carry them out.

Both Governments noted with satisfaction the great positive significance of the decisions of the Asian-African Conference at Bandung, in which the Chinese People's Republic and the Republic of India played particularly fruitful roles. This Conference was a vivid example of successful co-operation in the interests of peace among countries with different political and socio-economic systems.

In the course of the discussions it was stated that in their relations the two Governments are guided by principles of mutual respect for sovereignty and territorial integrity, non-aggression and non-interference in each other's internal affairs, equality and mutual benefit, and peaceful coexistence. It was noted with satisfaction that these principles are being recognised and accepted on an ever-wider scale by various states as the basis of large-scale and fruitful international co-operation.

Both Governments consider that friendly relations between the Democratic Republic of Viet Nam and other Asian countries, based on these principles, will help to establish and expand the zone of peace in South-East Asia, and thus to consolidate world peace.

The Governments of the USSR and the Democratic Republic of Viet Nam categorically condemn the attempts to include South Viet Nam, Laos and Cambodia in the zone of operation of the aggressive military bloc in South-East Asia (SEATO), which run counter to the Geneva Agreements. They also noted the fact that the attempts of certain foreign powers to interfere in the internal affairs of South Viet Nam, Cambodia and Laos and to impose agreements of a military nature on these countries are incompatible with the Geneva Agreements.

Both Governments believe that at present the settlement of international political problems depends completely on the readiness of the states concerned to reach agreement on the basis of respect for the legitimate interests of every country.

The Governments of the Soviet Union and the Democratic Republic of Viet Nam noted with gratification the increasing activity of the peoples aimed at ensuring peace, and that this has already resulted in a certain lessening of tension in international relations.

This finds its reflection particularly in the convening of the Four-Power Conference.[14] Both Governments expressed the hope that the Great Powers would continue their efforts to settle outstanding issues by negotiation, which would undoubtedly help to bring about an atmosphere of mutual trust and strengthen universal peace.

Both Governments noted with satisfaction that the friendly relations and the growing economic and cultural co-operation between the Chinese People's Republic and the Democratic Republic of Viet Nam correspond to the interests of the Chinese and Viet Nam peoples, and represent an important factor in maintaining and consolidating peace in the Far East.

The Governments of the USSR and the Democratic Republic of Viet Nam noted with great satisfaction that the mutual feelings of friendship and solidarity binding the Soviet and Viet Nam peoples constitute the basis of the relations which have been established between the USSR and the Democratic Republic of Viet Nam.

The two Governments are at one in their desire to develop and strengthen political, economic and cultural co-operation between the two countries.

In the course of the discussions both sides examined the question of economic co-operation between the USSR and the Democratic Republic of Vict Nam, whose national economy suffered serious material damage during the many years of war.

In this connection the Soviet Government has allocated 400 million roubles, without recompense, to help raise the living standards of the people and rehabilitate the economy of the Democratic Republic of Viet Nam, including the restoration and construction of 25 industrial and communal enterprises.

The Government of the USSR will help the Democratic Republic of Viet Nam in training Vietnamese specialists in higher and secondary technical educational establishments in the USSR and in organising the training of specialists in the educational establishments of Viet Nam; the Soviet Government will also render technical assistance in geological survey work and in carrying through medical preventive measures to combat infectious diseases, etc.

The two Governments were fully agreed as to the necessity of extending trade between their countries and to this end concluded a trade agreement.

Both Governments are firmly confident that the exchange of opinions

[14] The Geneva Summit Conference, held July 18–23, 1955.

will undoubtedly contribute to the further development of friendly relations between the USSR and the Democratic Republic of Viet Nam for the good of the peoples of both countries and will serve the interests of strengthening peace and security throughout the world.

165. *Message of the President and Prime Minister of the Democratic Republic of Viet-Nam* [15] *to the Chief of State* [16] *and Prime Minister* [17] *of the State of Viet-Nam [Extract]* *
July 19, 1955

[The first seven paragraphs, summarizing provisions of the Geneva Agreements and their implementation during regroupment of contending forces, are omitted.]

The Government of the Democratic Republic of Viet-nam will continue to fully implement the Geneva Agreements and is of the opinion that the Governments concerned must make efforts to ensure the respect of the Geneva Agreements, the achievement of the unity of Viet-nam, the consolidation of peace in Indo-China. That is why, on June 6, 1955, the Government of the Democratic Republic of Viet-nam declared its readiness to hold the consultative conference with the competent representative authorities of the South for the preparation for general elections and achievement of the unity of our country.[18] Following this, the Delegation of the Viet-nam People's Army to the Central Joint Commission has raised with the representatives of the French Union Forces the problem of preparing for the meeting of the competent representative authorities of the two zones.

The holding on schedule of the consultative conference by the competent authorities of the North and the South is of great importance, and has a bearing not only on the prospect of the unity of our country but also on the loyal implementation of the Geneva Agreements, and the consolidation of peace in Indo-China and in the world.

Following the June 6, 1955 declaration by the Government of the Democratic Republic of Viet-nam, Sai-gon Radio on July 16, 1955,

* *Source:* Democratic Republic of Viet-Nam, Ministry of Foreign Affairs, Press and Information Department, *Documents Related to the Implementation of the Geneva Agreements Concerning Viet-nam* (Hanoi: 1956), pp. 42–44. The message was broadcast by Viet-Nam News Agency in English Morse, July 20, 1955, 0602 G.M.T. It was signed by Pham Van Dong in the name of Ho Chi Minh.

[15] Ho Chi Minh.   [16] Bao Dai.   [17] Ngo Dinh Diem.
[18] Document 158.

made known the "position of the Government of the State of Viet-nam on the problem of general elections for the unification of the national territory." [19] The statement mentioned general elections and reunification but did not touch upon a very important and most realistic issue, that of the meeting of the competent representative authorities of the two zones, of the holding of the consultative conference on the question of general elections and reunification, as provided for by the Geneva Agreements. Moreover there were in the statement things which are untrue and which would not help to create a favourable climate for the convening of the consultative conference.

Our compatriots from the South to the North, irrespective of classes, creeds and political affiliations, have deeply at heart the reunification of the country, and are looking forward to the early convening of the consultative conference and to its good outcome. All the countries responsible for the guarantee of the implementation of the Geneva Agreements and in general all the peace-loving countries in the world are anxious to see that the consultative conference will be held and yield good results and that the reunification of our country will be achieved.

The Government of the Democratic Republic of Viet-nam proposes that you appoint your representatives and that they and ours hold the consultative conference from July 20, 1955 onwards, as provided for by the Geneva Agreements, at a place agreeable to both sides, on the Vietnamese territory, in order to discuss the problem of reunification of our country by means of free general elections all over Viet-nam.

166. *Declaration by the Government of the State of Viet-Nam on the Question of Territorial Reunification* *
    August 9, 1955

In a statement broadcast on July 16th last,[20] the Government of Viet-Nam clearly defined its position with regard to the problem of territorial reunification.

The Government does not consider itself bound in any way by the Geneva Agreements, of which it was not a signatory. It declares once again that, giving first priority in all circumstances to the interests of

* *Source:* République du Viet-Nam, Secrétariat d'Etat aux Affaires Etrangères, *Le Viet-Nam et Ses Relations Internationales* [published in French and English], I, No. 1–2 (June, 1956), pp. 105–106. The date of this declaration is often erroneously reported as August 19 or August 10.

[19] Document 163.   [20] Document 163.

the Nation, it is determined to attain the clear goal of all its policy: the unity of the country in peace and freedom.

The Viet-Minh authorities sent the Government a letter dated July 19th,[21] in which they ask that a pre-electoral consultative conference should be opened; by this means they seek to give credence for purposes of propaganda, to the false idea, that they are the defenders of our territorial unity.

It will be recalled that last year at Geneva, the Viet-Minh advocated partition of the country and demanded "a zone which was economically viable," whereas the delegation of Viet-Nam proposed an armistice without partition, even temporary, of Viet-Nam, "with a view to safeguarding the sacred right of the Vietnamese people to territorial unity, national independence, and liberty." Through the voice of its delegation, the Government declared that it "intended to realise the aspirations of the Vietnamese people by all the means afforded to it through the independence and sovereignty solemnly recognised by France as belonging to the State of Viet-Nam, which is the only legal State."

The Government's policy remains unchanged.

Faced with partition of the country accomplished against its will, the Government maintains that men throughout the country as a whole should be able to live without fear, completely free from all dictatorship and oppression.

Serving the cause of true democracy, the Government considers the principle of essentially free elections as a peaceful and democratic institution, but holds that conditions for the people to live and vote in freedom must be assured before anything else.

Nothing constructive can be done towards this end, as long as the Communist regime in the North does not permit each Vietnamese citizen to enjoy democratic liberties and fundamental human rights.

167. *Truong Chinh, Secretary General of the Viet-Nam Workers' Party: Speech at the Congress for the Foundation of the Viet-Nam Fatherland Front [Extracts]* *
September 1955

[The speech, "Let's Unite the Whole People and Strive to Implement the Programme of the Front," was made at the Congress held from September

* *Source: Viet-Nam Fatherland Front and the Struggle for National Unity* (Hanoi: Foreign Languages Publishing House, 1956), pp. 49–61. Several typographical errors in the original have been corrected.
[21] Document 165.

5 to 10, 1955, in Hanoi, probably at the closing session on September 10. The introductory section, I, is omitted.]

II. Unity is strength, unity leads to certain victory. Hence ever since the founding of the Communist Party of Indochina, the predecessor of the present Viet-nam Party of Labour,[22] we, the Vietnamese communists desired and worked for the greatest possible unity.

Thus far the Indochina Communist Party conceived and founded:

The National United Front against imperialism 1930–1931
The Democratic Front 1936–1939
The National Liberation Front 1939–1940
The Viet-nam Independence League (Viet-Minh) 1941–1951 [23]
The Viet-nam Association for National Unity (Lien-Viet) 1946–1955.[24]

Today, the Viet-nam Party of Labour once again actively contributes to the formation of a new Front whose name this Congress has proposed to be the "Viet-nam Fatherland Front."

The Front policy is one of our Party's great policies. The summing up of experiences of Viet-nam revolution as well as of the Chinese Revolution is this: For a nation under colonial or semi-colonial regime which wants to liberate itself, three basic factors of victory are required. They are:

1) A pure and strong vanguard Party.

2) A National United Front, broad and stable, the foundation of which is forged by the worker-peasant alliance.

3) A Liberation Army manned by the heroic people, which fights for the people and is supported by the people.

After the August Revolution, we seized power and founded the People's Power. Therefore, we should now add another factor to those three mentioned above, that is a firm People's Power.

Besides, for our struggle to triumph, we must unite with the world's peace-loving peoples including the French people, and stand in the camp of peace and democracy under the leadership of the Soviet Union.

In order to achieve the Viet-nam national democratic and people's

22 The Viet-Nam Lao Dong Party, or Viet-Nam Workers' Party (VWP).

23 In 1951 the Viet Minh Front was incorporated into the Lien Viet Front. See Document 77.

24 The Lien Viet Front, formed in 1946, was enlarged in 1951; the program of the enlarged Front is Document 77. The Lien Viet Front ceased to exist in 1955 with its incorporation into the Fatherland Front at this Congress.

revolution, we maintain that these factors of victory should ceaselessly be fostered.

This Congress the aim of which is to achieve the broadening and consolidation of the National United Front is making an effective contribution to the preparation of the conditions required to achieve a great victory for our Vietnamese nation.

Just as the founding of the Viet-Minh Front was closely connected with the successful August Revolution and the founding of the Lien-Viet was closely connected with the victory of the long armed resistance, the founding of the Fatherland Front this time will greatly influence the struggle to unify the country on the basis of independence and democracy.

[The first five paragraphs of Section III are omitted.]

[III.] The American imperialists and their mercenaries thought they could exploit questions of religion and nationality to divide our country, to stir up disorder and trouble in our rear. They planned to divide North and South, to cling to the South and use it as a military base to prepare an attack against the North. Certain pro-American elements are busying themselves to offer South Viet-nam to their American masters, helping them transform the South into an American colony. If they keep on pursuing this criminal path they will be despised by the entire people and punished.

For the time being they are engaged in the "denouncing Communists" action. Under the guise of "opposing Communism," they are repressing all those who love peace and our country, exerting reprisals against the former Resistance members. But the more frantically they terrorize the Communists in the South, the more the latter are loved by the people because the Communists, like all other truly patriotic people, always devote their body and mind to the service of the people, the cause of the Fatherland. Opposing Communism is tantamount to opposing the nation. Those who oppose Communism reveal themselves to be the enemy of the nation.

Why do they denounce the Communists? Just because the agents of the imperialists fear them, fear those who at all times work for the unity of the people, who with a will resist these agents. Because the Communists are those who have most truly at heart the cause of peace, unity, independence and democracy of the Fatherland and no force whatever can shake their iron patriotism. To repress the Communists, to indulge in reprisals against the former resistance members is to act counter to the people's will and to violate the Geneva agreements, to destroy the peace, unity, independence and democracy of Viet-nam.

[Section IV, stating the support of the Viet-Nam Workers' Party for the Fatherland Front Program, is omitted.]

V. Nevertheless, one thing is certain, that is our struggle for the implementation of the new [VFF] platform [program] will be difficult, hard, and complex. There can be no doubt that the American imperialists will not let us accomplish our task easily. There can be no doubt either that they will resort to every possible means to prevent us from implementing that programme.

Consequently we must on one hand be broadly and closely united from South to North, wage an unremitting, persevering and conscious fight against the American imperialists, the pro-American gang, the gang of partition-mongers, on the other hand we must win the active approval and support of peoples and governments in every part of the world for the new programme; bringing about a powerful pressure to bear on the American imperialists and their hirelings from inside and outside the country. The political struggle of our people will develop until the moment when the balance of forces between the two sides— the one for peace and unification and that of the pro-American partition-mongers—will change in favour of the former. Then additional favourable conditions will be available for the opening of the consultative conference and the holding of nation-wide free general elections to unify our country on the basis of this programme. Then we can advance to the carrying out of the programme in its entirety throughout the country after the elections.

[The final four paragraphs of Section V and the first paragraph of Section VI are omitted.]

[VI] Furthermore every achievement in the consolidation of the North should be considered as affecting the South, as contributing to the struggle for national unification on the basis of independence and democracy. In order to stimulate interest in the new programme, efforts should be made to urge workers in factories, mines and construction sites, people in the countryside and in the cities, workers in government services, school students, and army units to issue mutual patriotic emulation challenges for the implementation of the new programme.

We also expect that our people in the South will see the necessity of coordinating their struggle for the defence of their lives and properties and their struggle against terrorism, with that for the improvement of their living conditions, for the respect of democratic liberties, for the re-establishment of normal relations between the two zones, the opening of the consultative conference by the authorities of the South with the Government of the Democratic Republic of Viet-nam[,] for opposing the continued introduction of arms, ammunition and military personnel into the South by the American imperialists, for opposing their plan of including South Viet-nam into the American sponsored military bloc. It is in the course of that struggle that efforts should be exerted to build up, broaden and consolidate the Front in the South.

[The concluding six paragraphs are omitted.]

168. *The Program of the Viet-Nam Fatherland Front* * *September 10, 1955*

Our Viet-Nam is an independent nation with an age-old history. But since 1862, because of betrayal by the feudal kings and lords, it became a French colony and subsequently was occupied by the Japanese imperialists. For nearly a century, our people were oppressed, enslaved and divided. In order to free themselves from the colonial yoke, in order to regain national independence and freedom, our people united closely together and waged a tenacious and heroic struggle.

In 1945, at the end of the Second World War, our people rose up and carried out the August Revolution, proclaimed independence and founded the Democratic Republic of Viet-Nam. But the French colonialists unleashed a new aggressive war against us; the American imperialists prolonged this war by helping them in their attempt to annex our country once again.

Thanks to the close unity of our people, their iron will to resist and the warm support from peace-loving peoples throughout the world, the nine-power conference in Geneva in 1954 concluded [the] Agreements on the cessation of hostilities in Indo-China, the restoration of peace in Viet-Nam, Cambodia and Laos.[25] The Conference issued a Final

---

* *Source:* All Viet-Nam Congress of the National United Front, *Viet-Nam Fatherland Front: Resolutions, Manifesto, Programme and Statutes* (Rev. ed., Hanoi: Foreign Languages Publishing House, 1956), pp. 17–28. Several typographical errors in the original have been corrected. The Program was also broadcast by Viet-Nam News Agency in English Morse, September 15, 1955, 0552 G.M.T.

[25] The Agreement on the Cessation of Hostilities in Viet-Nam is Document 130.

Declaration [26] recognising Viet-Nam's independence, sovereignty, unity and territorial integrity. It set the date for a consultative conference to discuss arrangements for general elections and [the] date for holding these free, general elections under international supervision to achieve the unity of Viet-Nam. This was a great victory for our people in their struggle for independence.

Now that the armed forces of both sides have regrouped, the next urgent and important task for the Vietnamese people is to continue the strict and complete implementation of the Geneva Agreements to consolidate peace, achieve unity and complete independence and democracy throughout the country.

In every respect, historical, geographical, economic, cultural, social and national, Viet-Nam is a single, indivisible entity, built up by our ancestors in generations of labour and struggle. Certainly, no force can divide it. This is why our entire people from North to South, both men and women, regardless of class or creed should assume the sacred duty of reunifying our country, in a single-hearted and common effort.

And on our free territory in its entirety, our people will work together to repair the ravages of war: to build up a happy and civilised life; to build up a peaceful, united, independent, democratic, prosperous and strong Viet-Nam.

To consolidate peace and achieve unity, we should do our utmost to overcome all internal and external difficulties.

After the Geneva Conference, the American imperialists left no stones unturned to sabotage the Geneva Agreements. They intervened on an ever greater scale in Indo-China's affairs. They placed South Viet-Nam in the "protective area" of their Southeast Asian military bloc. They aim at the permanent partition of Viet-Nam; at transforming South Viet-Nam into an American colony and military base in preparation for the resumption of hostilities in Indo-China; to sabotage peace in Asia and in the world. The criminal schemes of the American imperialists threaten and infringe on the sacred rights of our people. We should realise that the consolidation of peace and national reunification are closely bound together. Only by defeating the American schemes to restart the war can we achieve our national unity; conversely only by achieving national unity can peace in Indo-China and in Asia be consolidated. We must therefore resolutely oppose the schemes of the American imperialists to sabotage peace and our national unity.

[26] Document 131.

Today, there are still a small number of people in our country who do not have the interests of the Fatherland at heart, who wittingly or unwittingly follow on the heels of the American imperialists to sabotage peace and partition our country. "For the glorious future of our nation, they should quickly correct their errors and discharge their duties to the Fatherland. They should make their contribution to the work of national unification. Should they persist in opposing and sabotaging the reunification of the Fatherland, they will be regarded as enemies of the entire people. As such they will be disgraced and punished." [27]

Today, the social and political situations in the North and South are different. To achieve in favourable conditions the peaceful reunification of our Fatherland, we must take into account the real situation in the two zones, the interests and legitimate aspirations of all sections of the population. At the same time, we must conduct negotiations to arrange the holding of free, general elections in order to achieve national unity without either side trying to exert pressure on, or trying to annex the other.

Thus, to the entire nation, to the authorities of both zones, to all political parties, to all the armed forces, to all people's organisations and to personalities of the South and North, we submit the following common programme for the reunification of our country.

We invite representatives of organisations and of the various sections of the population of both zones to hold discussions and consultations as soon as possible and once agreement is reached on the basis of the common programme, to fight for the achievement of national unity.

We invite the governments and people of those countries which took part in the 1954 Geneva Conference; the governments and peoples of those neutral countries entrusted with the task of helping the Vietnamese people in the strict implementation of the Geneva Agreements; and the peace-loving countries and peoples of the world to give their wholehearted support to the Vietnamese people in their task of national reunification. We demand that the French government, one of the two signatories to the Geneva Agreements, honour France's signature of these Agreements and the Final Declaration of the Geneva Conference.

The common programme includes the following points:

1. *Achievement of National Independence*

Viet-Nam's national sovereignty belongs to the entire Vietnamese people without distinction of nationality, class, political or religious

---

[27] The source of this quotation is not indicated in the original.

convictions. Whether in the political, military, economic, cultural, diplomatic or any other field, the Viet-Nam nation has the sacred and inviolable right to self-determination.

The Final Declaration of the Geneva Conference, recognising Viet-Nam's independence, sovereignty, unity and territorial integrity which are Viet-Nam's inviolable rights must be put into effect. All activities and schemes to tear up the Geneva Agreements must be opposed, the heritage of colonialism in Viet-Nam must be eliminated.

2. *To Achieve National Unity*

Hold nation-wide, free, general elections on the scheduled date. The authorities of North and South to convene a consultative conference to work out electoral procedures and to make practical arrangements for nation-wide free general elections.

Representatives of political parties, of the armed forces and people's organisations, of the various sections of the population and personalities in the North and South, to establish contact in order to support and urge the holding of the consultative conference between the two sides so that agreement will quickly be reached for the nation-wide free elections to achieve national unification.

A National Assembly to be elected by free, general elections. A Central Coalition Government to be chosen by the National Assembly. Because of the realities of the present situation in North and South, councils elected by the people and having executive organs with wide powers to be created in each locality.

Equality of the various nationalities in the country to be guaranteed; every attempt to divide the people to be forbidden. Each nationality to have the right to use and develop their spoken and written language, to preserve or to change their customs. In the reunified Viet-Nam, autonomous regions to be established wherever the minorities are in groups of sufficient density.

Normal economic, cultural and social relations to be reestablished and free movement to be respected between North and South Viet-Nam in order to satisfy the pressing needs of the population.

3. *To Build up a Democratic Life*

The Vietnamese people to have the right of freedom of religious beliefs, of speech, press, assembly, organisation, residence, movement, correspondence, etc. . . .

All Vietnamese citizens of both sexes, regardless of nationality, profession, financial situation, social class, religious conviction, cultural level, length of residence to have the right to elect from the age of 18 and to be elected from the age of 21 years.

Electoral procedure to be based on universal suffrage, equal, direct and secret ballot.

The National Assembly elected by the free, general elections to be the supreme law-making body of the State. It will work out a new Constitution for the whole country. Parliamentary privileges of all members of the National Assembly, including the opposition, to be effectively guaranteed.

The Government whose power is to be based on the National Assembly will be the supreme executive power of the State and will be responsible to the National Assembly.

The formation of a coalition government to be aimed at reinforcing the unity between political parties, social classes, the various nationalities and regions in Viet-Nam; also at receiving advice and suggestions from the population.

Taking into account the different situation in the two zones, each region to have the right to enact regional measures in accordance with the characteristics of the region, but not in conflict with the general laws of the country.

As long as the country remains not unified, the responsible authorities in the two zones are to recognise without any discrimination the legal existence of all political parties and groups and all mass organisations which support peace, unity, independence and democracy.

For the free, general elections, political parties to be permitted to present their candidates on common lists or separately.

4. *To Develop the Economy, To Restore Production*

To repair the ravages of war and improve the life of the people, the national economy to be restored according to plan and by stages, in order gradually to raise Viet-Nam from an economically backward country to an advanced industrial country, prosperous and strong.

Efforts to be made to restore and develop agriculture, handicrafts, the fishing industry, salt manufacture, the various means of communications and transport; to restore destroyed industries and raise the production of existing industries, gradually to build factories for production of essential consumer goods.

State industrial and commercial enterprises, consumer and producer cooperatives, to be formed and gradually developed. Private industry and commerce to be protected. Restoration and development of private industrial and commercial enterprises useful to the State economy and the people's livelihood to be encouraged.

A policy which takes into account the interests of employees and employers to be applied.

A strong impetus to be given to trade between urban areas and the countryside. Normal economic relations between North and South to be re-established and developed. Aid to be given for the restoration and exploitation of those which are of use to the Viet-Nam people, privileges which foreign economic enterprises formerly enjoyed to be abolished.

Economic enterprises of foreigners to be protected.

Foreign trade to be developed on the principle of equality and mutual benefit.

The budget to be balanced; a plan to be drafted for the gradual unification of the currency; onerous contributions and taxes to be abolished; taxation to be simplified and rationalised; prices to be stabilised; hoarding and black marketeering to be combated.

5. *Land Reform*

Land reform to be carried out on the principle of "Land to the Tillers."

In the North, land reform to be completed.

In the South rent reduction to be applied; land reform to be carried out, through purchase by the State at a fair and reasonable price, of land belonging to landlords who hold above a certain amount. The amount to be purchased will vary according to the agrarian situation in each locality, and will be distributed to landless peasants or those with insufficient land. Those to whom the land is distributed will pay nothing either to the landlords or the State.

The rights which peasants in the South won during the resistance to be safeguarded.

6. *To Apply a Reasonable Social Policy*

Physical freedom of the workers to be guaranteed by the State, every vestige of feudal exploitation in the factories and workshops to be abolished, the 8 to 10 hours working day to be introduced, minimum wages to be fixed, labour insurance laws gradually to be applied.

Liberty of belief and religion to be guaranteed, protection of churches, pagodas, temples, places and objects of worship and religious seminaries to be guaranteed.

Men and women are equal. In all respects, political, economic, cultural and social, women are to enjoy the same rights as men. Expectant mothers and children are to be helped by the State.

The living standards of all sections of the population gradually to be improved. Social welfare to be applied; all those deprived of the means of existence due to sickness or infirmity, to unemployment or any sort of accident, to be aided. The unemployment problem to be solved, work assured for workers, employees and public servants.

Specially privileged treatment to be accorded to war wounded; particular medical care to be given to war invalids, aid to be given to families of those who died for the Fatherland and those who became incapacitated in serving the common cause.

7. *To Develop Culture and Education*

Culture and education which serve the Fatherland and the people to be developed. Colonialist and all other enslaving cultures to be combated. War propaganda and that aimed at dividing the peoples to be prohibited. An effort to be made to end illiteracy and to raise the cultural level of the population. Compulsory, free, primary education gradually to be introduced; secondary and higher education to be developed.

Science, technique, the arts and literature to be developed; the level of technical cadres in different branches connected with national construction to be improved; cultural exchanges with foreign countries to be developed. Intellectuals to be encouraged and helped to develop their talents and capacities to serve the Fatherland and the people. A nation-wide movement of physical culture to be launched; a strong impetus to be given to the medical and sanitary service to promote public health.

8. *To Strengthen National Defence*

A unified army to be built up for national defence. All the existing armed forces in the North and in the South to be the components of the unified army for national defence. At the beginning of reunification the rules and regulations in force in the armed forces of the two zones will not immediately be unified. Gradual and complete unification of the armed forces to be achieved by negotiation.

The introduction into Viet-Nam of foreign troops, of military personnel, of foreign arms and munitions to be forbidden; the establishment of military bases on the territory of Viet-Nam by any country whatsoever to be absolutely forbidden. American military personnel to be withdrawn immediately from Viet-Nam.

In accordance with the Geneva Agreements, French military personnel to be gradually withdrawn from Viet-Nam.

9. *To Conduct a Foreign Policy of Peace and Independence*

A foreign policy to be pursued which guarantees the national sovereignty, independence, the territorial integrity of our country and the safeguarding of world peace. Diplomatic relations to be established and maintained with any country in the world on the basis of the five following principles: mutual respect for national sovereignty and territorial integrity, non-aggression, non-interference in internal affairs, equality and mutual benefit, peaceful coexistence. Non-adherence to any military bloc. The Geneva Agreements to be correctly implemented.

Viet-Nam to establish good neighborly relations with the Kingdom of Cambodia, the Kingdom of Laos and all Southeast Asian countries.

Economic and cultural relations with France to be developed on the basis of equality and mutual benefit.

Vietnamese nationals residing abroad to be protected.

10. *The Broad Unity of the Vietnamese People*

To accomplish the sacred task of building up a peaceful Viet-Nam, unified, independent, democratic, prosperous and strong, all our compatriots, men and women alike, regardless of nationality, profession, financial situation, social class, religious conviction and irrespective of what side they supported previously, should closely unite to form the All Viet-Nam United National Front. The Front will canalise the powerful action of the workers and peasants, the two most important classes in our country, englobing the overwhelming majority of the Vietnamese people.

. . . . .

Peace, unity, independence, democracy, prosperity and strength, these are the ardent aspirations, the just and sacred cause of the entire Vietnamese people. We are certain that this cause will triumph. Let the entire Vietnamese people on the broadest basis closely unite and resolutely struggle so that the great cause of our Nation will rapidly be crowned with success.

169. *Fourth Interim Report of the International Commission for Supervision and Control in Viet-Nam [Extract]* *
  October 1, 1955

[The "Fourth Interim Report" covered the period from April 11 to August 10, 1955.]

---

* *Source:* Great Britain, Parliament, Papers by Command, *Fourth Interim Report of the International Commission for Supervision and Control in Vietnam, April 11, 1955, to August 10, 1955* (London: Her Majesty's Stationery Office, Cmd. 9654, 1955), pp. 16–18.

Problems of the Future

44. Apart from delays and obstructions due to the intransigence or truculence of the local authorities, the political developments during June and July 1955 and the Commission's experience regarding the working of its investigating teams and the delay in implementing its recommendations have made it clear that the French High Command cannot carry out its obligations under Article 25 [28] in the zone south of the provisional demarcation line in the face of the categorical attitude adopted by the State of Vietnam that they have not signed the Geneva Agreement, that they are not, therefore, bound by its provisions and are opposed both to the Agreement and the Final Declaration.[29] Apart from the demonstrations against the Geneva Agreement on 20th July, 1955, which degenerated into violence against the two hotels, Majestic and Gallieni where [the] Commission's personnel were staying, on which a special report was sent to the Co-Chairmen,[30] the political attitude of the State of Vietnam to the Geneva Accords and its effects on the work of this Commission and the implementation of the Vietnam Agreement require very early consideration by the Co-Chairmen to resolve the uncertainty regarding (1) the sanction for the working of the Commission and (2) the probable duration of its activities:

Sanction for the Working of the Commission in Vietnam

(i) As civil and military administration in the zone south of the provisional demarcation line has been passing into the hands of the Government of the State of Vietnam, which has not signed and is according to its repeated public declarations opposed to both the Geneva Agreement and the Final Declaration, further continuance of the Commission's activities and the effective discharge of its responsibilities are in serious jeopardy as the Commission, established under Article 44 of the Agreement, can only draw its authority from the Agreement itself and has no other sanction. We would like to add in this connexion that during our discussions with the Government of the State of Vietnam, we have been told that it will give full protection and practical co-operation to the Commission as an International Peace Commission but will not make a formal or public declaration to that effect in view of the

[28] Of the Agreement on the Cessation of Hostilities in Viet-Nam, Document 130.

[29] Document 131. Note the ICSC's clear differentiation between the Agreement on the Cessation of Hostilities and the Final Declaration.

[30] Text not available.

position taken up by it with reference to the Geneva Agreement and the Final Declaration. It is obvious that the International Commission which has, in the discharge of its responsibilities under the Agreement, to undertake various tasks which, in effect, result in the curtailment of the sovereignty of both Administrations in the North and in the South, cannot carry on its activities in the face of the declared opposition of the Government of the State of Vietnam to the Geneva Agreement merely on the basis of a personal or practical understanding which can be revoked at any time. In any case, any *ad hoc* arrangement outside the Agreement, however effective, naturally amounts to revocation of the Agreement and the Commission cannot be a party to any such arrangement.

Duration of the Commission

(ii) Another point arising out of the political developments is the uncertainty regarding the duration of the Commission's activities. Article 14(*a*) of the Agreement which specifies political and administrative measures in the two regrouping zones on either side of the provisional military demarcation line refers to the conduct of civil administration in each regrouping zone "pending the general elections which will bring about the unification of Vietnam." The various tasks with which the Commission is entrusted under the Agreement have to be carried on as long as these provisional arrangements for civil administration, north and south of the provisional demarcation line, continue. The Commission can wind up its activities only after political problems arising out of the regrouping, south and north of the provisional demarcation line, are settled. The programme for the settlement of political problems is outlined in the Final Declaration of the Geneva Powers but as this cannot be carried out in view of the categorical opposition of the Government of the State of Vietnam, both to the Agreement and the Final Declaration, the Commission is faced with the prospect of continuing its activities indefinitely and, as pointed out above, so far as the zone under control of the State of Vietnam is concerned, without any sanction for its working.

45. Despite the uncertainty regarding the sanction for the working of the Commission created by the political developments in the last few months and the increasing ineffectiveness due to these developments of the French High Command to carry out their obligations under Article 25 in respect of Commission's activities in the zone south of the provisional demarcation line, the Commission has continued to supervise and control the execution by the parties of the Articles of the Agree-

ment throughout Vietnam under extremely trying conditions. It cannot, however, continue to function with any effectiveness unless the difficulties mentioned in the above paragraph are resolved satisfactorily by the Co-Chairmen and the Geneva Powers at a very early date.

46. The Canadian Delegation accepts the Fourth Interim Report, with the exception of paragraphs 24 to 34 of Chapter V dealing with freedom of movement,[31] and paragraph 21 of Chapter V [32] and the concluding paragraphs 44 and 45 of Chapter VIII dealing with co-operation of the parties to the Agreement and problems of the future. The views of the Canadian Delegation as given to the Commission during the discussions are set out in the following paragraphs [33] in substitution for the paragraphs in question.

170. *Provisional Constitutional Act Establishing the Republic of Viet-Nam* * *October 26, 1955*

The Head of State,[34]

Considering that the results of the referendum of October 23, 1955, have clearly indicated the will of the Vietnamese people to establish a democratic regime;

Considering that, pending the entering into force of a constitution, the public institutions of the State should be regulated by a provisional constitutional act;

Considering that the Republic was solemnly proclaimed; [35]
Proclaims:

Article 1

The State of Viet-Nam is a Republic.

* *Source:* André Siegfried and others, eds., *L'Année Politique 1955* (Paris: Presses Universitaires de France, 1956), p. 673. Translation by the editor.

[31] The purport of these paragraphs is that despite the problems encountered in the matter of freedom of movement, there is little that the Commission can do to ensure that everybody who wants to move can do so, because of the magnitude of the task, "the definite stand taken by the Government of the State of Vietnam against the Geneva Agreement, and the strained relations between the parties."

[32] Dealing with the inability of the French High Command to carry out its responsibilities in its zone.

[33] Not printed. See source, pp. 19–25.   [34] Ngo Dinh Diem.

[35] Text of President Diem's Proclamation in République du Viet-Nam, Secretariat d'Etat aux Affaires Etrangerès, *Le Viet-Nam et Ses Relations Internationales* [published in French and English], I, No. 3–4 (December 1956), pp. 139–140.

Article 2

The Head of State is at the same time Head of the Government, with the title of President of the Republic of Viet-Nam.

Article 3

A committee charged with drawing up a draft constitution for the Republic of Viet-Nam is established.

The draft constitution will be submitted to the examination of the National Assembly, to be elected before the end of the year.

Article 4

Pending the entering into force of the Constitution, existing laws and regulations are provisionally kept in force in so far as they are not contrary to the republican form of the State.

Article 5

The Ministers are charged, each in his own area, with the application of the present provisional constitutional act, which enters into force on the date of its signature.

Saigon, October 26, 1955

Signed:

NGO DINH DIEM

171. *United States Recognition of the New Chief of State of Viet-Nam: Statement by the Department of State * October 26, 1955*

On October 26, the Government of Viet-Nam sent the following communication to the American Embassy at Saigon:

"The Ministry of Foreign Affairs has the honor to inform the United States Embassy that by referendum October 23 the Vietnamese people have pronounced themselves in favor of the deposition of Bao Dai and have recognized President Diem as Chief of State. It is hoped that the Government of the United States will continue as in the past to entertain diplomatic relations with the new Government of the State of Viet-Nam."

* *Source:* United States, Department of State, *American Foreign Policy 1950–1955: Basic Documents* (2 vols., Washington: Government Printing Office, 1957), Vol. II, pp. 2404–2405.

U.S. Ambassador G. Frederick Reinhardt, under instructions, has replied as follows:

"The Government of the United States looks forward to maintaining with the new Government of Viet-Nam the same cordial and friendly relations which have in the past so happily existed between the two governments."

The United States affirms its intention to maintain friendly relations with the Government of Viet-Nam. We are glad to see the evolution of orderly and effective democratic processes in an area of Southeast Asia which has been and continues to be threatened by Communist efforts to impose totalitarian control.

PART SIX

The Collapse of
the Geneva Agreements
December 1955–August 1956

CHAPTER XIV

The French Withdrawal
from Viet-Nam

December 1955-May 1956

Introduction

At the end of 1955 the Co-Chairmen of the Geneva Conference began to show increasing concern with the failure of the two Vietnamese states to fully implement the portions of the Geneva Agreements providing for a political solution in Viet-Nam. Yet as discussion of the problem continued, it became clear that the Great Powers which had participated in the Geneva Conference were unlikely to take action to rectify the situation. A proposal for a new Geneva Conference made little progress. At the same time France continued withdrawal of her military forces from Viet-Nam, a process completed with dissolution of the French High Command at the end of April 1956. With French withdrawal, the situation in Viet-Nam with regard to the Geneva Agreements was thrown into confusion.

In early December 1955 the British Foreign Office published a statement which in effect denied any responsibility by the Co-Chairmen for enforcement of the Geneva Agreements (Document 172). It was also during early December that Premier Bulganin and First Secretary Khrushchev of the Soviet Union made their famous trip to Burma, India, and Afghanistan. It was notable that they did not visit the Democratic Republic of Viet-Nam (DRV). The Joint Statement issued by the Soviet leaders and Prime Minister Nehru on December 13 called for full implementation of the political provisions of the Geneva Agreements and prophetically observed that "The violation of these Agreements would have exceptionally dire consequences both for Indo-China and for the whole world." [1]

[1] Text of the Joint Statement in Communist Information Bureau, *For a Lasting Peace, For a People's Democracy,* December 16, 1955, p. 1.

On December 21, 1955, the Co-Chairmen of the Geneva Conference, the Foreign Ministers of the United Kingdom and the Soviet Union, sent a message to the members of the Conference and the members of the International Commission for Supervision and Control (ICSC). Resulting from the November meeting between Foreign Minister Molotov and Foreign Secretary Macmillan in Geneva,[2] the message (Document 173) asked for suggestions on implementation of the Geneva Agreements. That the situation in Viet-Nam had not improved during the second half of 1955 was indicated by the ICSC in its "Fifth Interim Report," submitted on January 8, 1956 (Document 174).

The Government of the Chinese People's Republic responded on January 25, 1956, by condemning the Republic of Viet-Nam and calling for the convening of "another Geneva Conference on Indo-China" (Document 175). The Chinese proposal was supported by DRV Foreign Minister Pham Van Dong in a February 14 letter to the Co-Chairmen.[3] Pham also accused the South Vietnamese of violation of the military clauses of the Geneva Agreements, of "creating a separate state in the Southern part of Viet-nam," and of "instigating their troops to prepare for a 'March to the North.' "

The Government of the Republic of Viet-Nam continued its refusal to be bound by the Geneva Agreements and, on January 19, officially requested that France withdraw her Expeditionary Corps from Viet-Nam.[4] At the end of January British Prime Minister Anthony Eden and Foreign Secretary Selwyn Lloyd visited Washington; the talks with American officials may have dealt in part with Viet-Nam, but the communiqué issued on February 1 limited its statements on Southeast Asia to an endorsement of SEATO and the Colombo Plan.[5]

In February a delegation from the Viet-Nam Workers' Party (VWP) attended the Twentieth Congress of the Communist Party of the Soviet Union (CPSU), which saw First Secretary Khrushchev's now famous denunciation of Stalin. During the Congress, on February 18, the Foreign Ministry of the Soviet Union delivered a note to the British Embassy in Moscow endorsing the Chinese proposal for a new Geneva

[2] On November 14, at the time of the "Big Four" Foreign Ministers' meeting on disarmament.

[3] Text in Democratic Republic of Viet-Nam, Ministry of Foreign Affairs, Press and Information Department, *Documents Related to the Implementation of the Geneva Agreements Concerning Viet-nam* (Hanoi: 1956), pp. 117–121.

[4] Text not available; see Documents 176, 177, and 178.

[5] Text in United States, Department of State, *American Foreign Policy, Current Documents, 1956* (Washington: Government Printing Office, 1959), pp. 447–449.

Conference on Indo-China and enclosing a draft message from the two Co-Chairmen to the members of the Conference and of the ICSC asking their views.[6] On February 23, French Foreign Minister Christian Pineau outlined French policy before the Council of the Republic (Document 176). He indicated doubt that the Republic of Viet-Nam was bound to accept the role of successor to French responsibilities under the Geneva Agreements and was pessimistic about the prospects for a new conference on Indochina.

On March 4 the State of Viet-Nam held elections for a National Assembly, which returned an overwhelming majority of supporters for the Diem government. The elections immediately preceded the meeting of the SEATO powers, held from March 6 to 8 at Karachi. Despite the importance of the Viet-Nam problem, it was accorded little attention in the communiqué issued by the SEATO Council beyond an expression of pleasure at the "steady economic progress" which had been made by the Indochinese states and a reaffirmation of concern about Communist subversion in the Treaty area.[7]

Great Britain responded on March 9 to the Soviet note of February 18, stating that it would be "premature" to propose a new Geneva Conference and suggesting instead that the two Co-Chairmen confer together.[8] On March 23 the Indian Government expressed concern about the future of the Geneva Agreements after dissolution of the French High Command, for the ICSC would then have to "supervise an agreement which will cease to have any legal basis since one party to the agreement—the French High Command—will have disappeared" (Document 177). The Soviet Union replied on March 30 to the British note of March 9, delivering a lengthy denunciation of the policy of the Saigon government but agreeing to consultations between the two Co-Chairmen during April.[9]

On March 30 France and the Republic of Viet-Nam reached agree-

---

[6] Text in Great Britain, Parliament, Papers by Command, *Documents Relating to British Involvement in the Indo-China Conflict 1945–1965* (London: Her Majesty's Stationery Office, Cmnd. 2834, 1965), pp. 118–120.

[7] Text in *American Foreign Policy, Current Documents, 1956*, pp. 775–779.

[8] Text of the British note in *Documents Relating to British Involvement in the Indo-China Conflict 1945–1965*, Cmnd. 2834, p. 120.

[9] Text of the Soviet note in Great Britain, Parliament, Papers by Command, *Vietnam and the Geneva Agreements: Documents Concerning the Discussions between Representatives of Her Majesty's Government and the Government of the Union of Soviet Socialist Republics held in London in April and May 1956, March 30–May 8, 1956* (London: Her Majesty's Stationery Office, Cmd. 9763, 1956, reprinted 1965), pp. 5–7.

ment on the timetable for the withdrawal of French troops, to be completed by the end of April, and on April 3 the French High Commissioner informed the ICSC of the forthcoming withdrawal and dissolution of the French High Command (Document 178). The same day the Republic of Viet-Nam delivered a note to the British Embassy in Saigon outlining Vietnamese policy on the Geneva Agreements after the departure of the French (Document 179). A public declaration of Vietnamese policy, couched in similar terms, was made on April 6.[10]

Anastas Mikoyan, First Vice Chairman of the U.S.S.R. Council of Ministers, arrived in Hanoi on April 2 at the head of a Soviet Government delegation on the first official visit to North Viet-Nam by a ranking Soviet leader. Mikoyan's statements during the visit did not manifest strong Soviet support for the reunification of Viet-Nam and, whether on this issue or others, it was clear that there was disagreement between the two parties. At the end of the visit the customary joint communiqué was not issued.

The British Government on April 5 proposed to the Soviet Union that talks between the two Co-Chairmen of the Geneva Conference begin in London on April 13.[11] On April 9, having been officially informed of the forthcoming dissolution of the French High Command, Pham Van Dong sent a note to the Co-Chairmen emphasizing joint French and South Vietnamese responsibility for enforcement of all provisions of the Geneva Agreements and calling once more for a new Geneva Conference.[12] On the same day the British Government, in a note to the Soviet Union, took issue with Moscow's interpretation of the situation in Viet-Nam, particularly with regard to the policy of the South Vietnamese government.[13] Increasing DRV concern with the French position was also shown by an April 12 note from Pham Van Dong to French Foreign Minister Christian Pineau, calling upon France to fulfill her obligations under the Geneva Agreements despite her withdrawal from Viet-Nam.[14]

Following the Mikoyan visit to North Viet-Nam, the Central Com-

[10] Text in République du Viet-Nam, Secretariat d'Etat aux Affaires Etrangères, *Le Viet-Nam et Ses Relations Internationales* [published in French and English], I, No. 1–2 (June 1956), pp. 106–107.

[11] Text of the British note in *Vietnam and the Geneva Agreements,* Cmd. 9763, pp. 7–8.

[12] Text in *Documents Related to the Implementation of the Geneva Agreements Concerning Viet-nam,* pp. 126–128.

[13] Text in *Vietnam and the Geneva Agreements,* Cmd. 9763, pp. 8–9.

[14] Text in *Documents Related to the Implementation of the Geneva Agreements Concerning Viet-nam,* pp. 134–136.

mittee of the VWP met from April 19 to 24 to consider developments at the Twentieth Congress of the Communist Party of the Soviet Union. The resolution adopted at the conclusion of the meeting (Document 180) endorsed the decisions of the Congress but also showed considerable ingenuity in adapting the new ideological principles to the problems of Viet-Nam.

172. *Statement by the Foreign Office of the United Kingdom on the Responsibility of the Co-Chairmen of the Geneva Conference* * *December 1955*

[The following statement is taken from the foreword to the British publication of the "Fourth Interim Report of the International Commission for Supervision and Control in Vietnam" (Document 241).]

2. The passages in the Commission's Fourth Interim Report, particularly the Canadian Commissioner's amendment to paragraphs 24 to 34 of Chapter V,[1] dealing with the implementation of Articles XIV(*c*) and XIV(*d*) of the Agreement on the Cessation of Hostilities in Vietnam (see "Miscellaneous No. 20 (1954)," Cmd. 9239, page 27 *et seq.*) [2] and the inadequate co-operation received by the Commission from the competent civil and military authorities in both zones of Vietnam, have caused Her Majesty's Government considerable concern. They accordingly proposed to the Soviet Government that Her Majesty's Government and the Soviet Government, as representing the two Co-Chairmen of the Geneva Conference of 1954, should send a message about this Report to members of the Conference and to the three Supervisory Powers.[3]

3. In this connexion, and in view of numerous public references to the role of the two Co-Chairmen of the Geneva Conference, Her Majesty's Government consider it desirable to place on record their view of the position. There is no reference in the Agreements on the Cessation of Hostilities in Cambodia, Laos and Vietnam or in the Final Declaration of the Geneva Conference on July 21, 1954 ("Miscellaneous No. 20 (1954)," Cmd. 9239) [4] to the Co-Chairmen as such or to any

* *Source:* Great Britain, Parliament, Papers by Command, *Fourth Interim Report of the International Commission for Supervision and Control in Vietnam, April 11, 1955, to August 10, 1955* (London: Her Majesty's Stationery Office, Cmd. 9654, 1955), p. 2.

[1] See Document 169.   [2] Document 130.   [3] See Document 173.
[4] Document 131.

special responsibilities devolving upon Her Majesty's Government and the Soviet Government by virtue of the fact that Sir Anthony Eden and M. Molotov had acted as Chairmen at alternate sessions of the Geneva Conference on Indo-China. In the view of Her Majesty's Government their obligations and responsibilities and those of the Soviet Government are neither more nor less than those of the other Powers adhering to the Final Declaration of the Geneva Conference. For reasons of practical convenience, however, it has become customary for Her Majesty's Government and the Soviet Government to act as a channel of communication between the International Supervisory Commissions and the Geneva Powers, to co-ordinate arangements for the distribution and publication of the Commissions' reports and to initiate proposals for financing the work of the Commissions. On occasions, of which this is one, Her Majesty's Government, the Soviet Government or other Powers have also employed this channel as a convenient means of bringing their views on matters concerning the implementation of the Geneva Agreements to the attention of members of the Geneva Conference as a whole. The existence of these informal arrangements does not, of course, in any way affect the position and obligations under the Geneva Agreements of Her Majesty's Government and the Soviet Government or derogate in any way from the responsibilities of members of the Geneva Conference as a whole in regard to the Geneva Agreements, under Article 13 of the Final Declaration of the Conference.

Foreign Office, December 1955

173. *Message from the Co-Chairmen of the Geneva Conference to Members of the Geneva Conference* *
    December 20, 1955

Mr. Molotov and Mr. Macmillan, in their capacity as Co-Chairmen of the Geneva Conference on Indo-China,[5] met in Geneva on 14

* *Source:* Great Britain, Parliament, Papers by Command, *Documents Relating to British Involvement in the Indo-China Conflict 1945–1965* (London: Her Majesty's Stationery Office, Cmnd. 2834, 1965), pp. 114–115.

[5] Mr. Macmillan replaced Mr. Eden in this capacity in July, it having been agreed between the United Kingdom and the Soviet Union that the Foreign Ministers of the two states, rather than Mr. Eden and Mr. Molotov personally, would fulfill the functions of the Co-Chairmanship. See the "Extract from a message from the Prime Minister, Geneva, July 24, 1955," in Great Britain, Parliament, Papers by Command, *Documents Relating to British Involvement in the Indo-*

November, 1955,[6] to discuss the implementation in Viet-Nam of the agreements reached by the Geneva Conference of 1954. They had before them:

(*a*) A communication addressed to the two Co-Chairmen on 17 August by Mr. Pham Van Dong;[7]

(*b*) A communication addressed to Mr. Macmillan on 7 October by Mr. Mau;[8]

(*c*) A communication addressed to the two Co-Chairmen on 31 October by Mr. Chou En-lai;[9]

(*d*) The fourth interim report of the International Supervisory Commission for Viet-Nam;[10]

(*e*) Communications received by the two Co-Chairmen from the Government of India in September.[11]

These documents have already been communicated to members of the Conference.

From these documents and in particular from the fourth interim report of the International Supervisory and Control Commission, the two Co-Chairmen have noted with concern that the implementation in Viet-Nam of certain provisions of the Geneva Agreements is unsatisfactory. The two Co-Chairmen regard the work of the International Supervisory and Control Commission in Viet-Nam as an important contribution to the preservation of peace in South-East Asia and deplore any obstruction of the Commission's activities.

The two Co-Chairmen would be grateful to receive the comments of other members of the Geneva Conference and of the States exercising supervision and control in Indo-China together with any suggestions for improving the implementation in Viet-Nam of the Geneva Agreements.

China Conflict 1945–1965 (London: Her Majesty's Stationery Office, Cmnd. 2834, 1965), p. 90.

[6] At the time of the "Big Four" Foreign Ministers' meeting on the problem of disarmament.

[7] Text in Democratic Republic of Viet-Nam, Ministry of Foreign Affairs, Press and Information Department, *Documents Related to the Implementation of the Geneva Agreements Concerning Viet-nam* (Hanoi: 1956), pp. 45–50.

[8] Vu Van Mau, Foreign Minister of the Republic of Viet-Nam. A text published by the North Vietnamese is in *ibid.*, pp. 100–102.

[9] Text in Great Britain, Parliament, Papers by Command, *Documents Relating to British Involvement in the Indo-China Conflict 1945–1965* (London: Her Majesty's Stationery Office, Cmnd. 2834, 1965), pp. 113–114.

[10] Document 169.   [11] Texts not available.

174. *Fifth Interim Report of the International Commission for Supervision and Control in Viet-Nam [Conclusions]* *
   January 8, 1956

[The "Fifth Interim Report" covered the period from August 11, 1955, to December 10, 1955.]

51. Further political developments involving the transfer of authority in the zone of the French High Command have made it increasingly difficult for it to carry out by itself its obligations under the Agreement [12] in respect of the Commission's activities in that zone. As a result of these developments, the French High Command, which is the signatory of the Agreement, in most cases can only take action to fulfil its obligations with the specific concurrence of the authorities of the Republic of Vietnam, which did not sign the Agreement and do not consider themselves bound by it, and in cases where they decline to act, the French High Command can only transmit their views to the Commission.

52. In paragraphs 44 and 45 of the Fourth Interim Report,[13] the Commission, with the Canadian Delegation submitting a minority report, drew the attention of the co-Chairmen to the transfer of authority by the French High Command to the Republic of Vietnam, which did not subscribe to the Geneva Agreement. This had created uncertainties about the sanction for its operations in the zone south of the demarcation line and had faced the Commission with the prospect of continuing its activities indefinitely. The majority asked the co-Chairmen and the Geneva Powers to resolve these difficulties at an early date.

53. The review of the four months' activities presented in this Report, in the view of the majority of the Commission, shows a further deterioration of the situation in Vietnam, causes serious concern about the implementation of the Geneva Agreement particularly in view of the continued non-acceptance of the Geneva Agreement and the Final Declaration of the Geneva Conference by the Republic of Vietnam, and also confirms the fear expressed by the majority of the Commission in the Fourth Interim Report that the Commission cannot work with any effectiveness unless the difficulties mentioned in these paragraphs are

* *Source:* Great Britain, Parliament, Papers by Command, *Fifth Interim Report of the International Commission for Supervision and Control in Vietnam, August 11, 1955, to December 10, 1955* (London: Her Majesty's Stationery Office, Cmd. 9706, 1956), pp. 15–16.

[12] The Agreement on the Cessation of Hostilities in Viet-Nam, Document 130.
[13] Document 169.

resolved by the co-Chairmen and the Geneva Powers without further delay.

54. The Canadian Delegation considers that the position set forth in the Canadian Minority Note in the Fourth Interim Report has not substantially changed during the period covered by the present Report. Despite certain difficulties, in the view of the Canadian Delegation, there have been indications of an increased measure of practical co-operation with the Commission on the part of the authorities of the Republic of Vietnam, which was not a signatory of the Agreement. At the same time the Canadian Delegation restates its view that the present arrangement is unsatisfactory under which the Commission must in fact depend more and more on the protection, assistance and co-operation of the Government of the Republic of Vietnam, although it can only claim this support through the agency of the French High Command. The Canadian Delegation reaffirms the hope expressed in its minority report that the parties directly concerned would be able to work out a more durable and dependable arrangement which will place the Commission in a more favourable position to carry out its functions, while the Commission continued to supervise and control the execution by the parties of the Agreement throughout Vietnam, to the extent made possible by the co-operation of the French High Command and the Government of the Republic of Vietnam on the one hand and the High Command of the P.A.V.N.[14] on the other.

55. The Commission notes that the views of its members expressed in the Fourth Interim Report are now under consideration by the co-Chairmen in consultation with the members of the Geneva Conference.

56. From this review of the activities presented in this report, it is clear that until these difficulties are settled, the Commission cannot function as satisfactorily as it should in carrying out its tasks in regard to the Agreement for the cessation of hostilities in Vietnam.

175. *Letter from Foreign Minister Chou En-lai of the People's Republic of China to the Foreign Secretary of the United Kingdom* *
   January 25, 1956

The Government of the People's Republic of China has received the letter of 21 [*sic*] December, 1955, from the Co-Chairmen of the Ge-

* *Source:* Great Britain, Parliament, Papers by Command, *Documents Relating to British Involvement in the Indo-China Conflict 1945–1965* (London: Her Majesty's Stationery Office, Cmnd. 2834, 1965), p. 118.

[14] People's Army of Viet-Nam.

neva Conference on Indo-China.[15] The Chinese Government strongly condemn the continued disregard of the Geneva Agreements by the Ngo Dinh Diem Government in South Viet-Nam. The Ngo Dinh Diem Government has, up to now, refused to hold consultations with the Government of the Democratic Republic of Viet-Nam on free general elections for Viet-Nam, and refused to undertake to give the International Commission in Viet-Nam full protection, assistance and co-operation. Although the International Commission in Viet-Nam, under the Chairmanship of the Indian representative, made every effort, no result has been achieved in bringing about consultations between the southern and northern zones of Viet-Nam on elections. Furthermore, the work of the International Commission in Viet-Nam has been subjected to flagrant obstruction and disruption by the Ngo Dinh Diem Government.

In view of the above mentioned serious violations of the Geneva Agreements and of the fact that Geneva Agreements specifically provide for the holding of general elections in Viet-Nam in July, 1956, the Chinese Government deems it necessary that another Geneva Conference on Indo-China be convened by the Co-Chairmen of the Geneva Conference, to discuss the question of implementation of the Geneva Agreements in Viet-Nam. The Chinese Government also holds that the three member countries of the International Commission in Viet-Nam —India, Poland and Canada—should be invited to take part in this conference.

I have sent a letter of the same contents to the other Chairman of the Geneva Conference, the Minister for Foreign Affairs of the Union of Soviet Socialist Republics, Mr. V. M. Molotov.

176. *Foreign Minister Christian Pineau of France: Statement to the Council of the Republic [Extracts]* *
    February 23, 1956

[The extracts of M. Pineau's statement printed here are the sections relevant to French policy in Viet-Nam.]

I come now to the political situation in Viet-Nam. It must be recognized that we are not entirely masters of that political situation. It

* *Source:* France, *Journal Officiel de la République Française, Débats Parlementaires, Conseil de la République,* Session of February 23, 1956, pp. 197–198. Translation by the editor.

[15] Document 173.

results from three principal facts: the Geneva Agreements, the independence we have granted to Viet-Nam, and the agreements we have concluded with the Americans.

After the Geneva Agreements we find ourselves confronted with a problem of which you are all aware, for those agreements were not signed by the Americans or by South Viet-Nam. We are, in consequence, the guarantors in the southern zone of agreements which have not been signed either by those whom we are supposed to protect nor by those who protect them. This is a completely impossible juridical situation.

[Three paragraphs on general French colonial policy since World War II are omitted. M. Pineau prefaced his personal comments in that regard with the statement: "With respect to the independence of Viet-Nam, we have obviously granted it in actual fact without any kind of restriction."]

With regard to the Government of President Diem, it must be recognized that we have concluded agreements with the Americans. I was formerly, in the National Assembly, the Chairman of the sub-committee charged with control of the credits for national defense, in which capacity I presided over various missions to Indochina, and I am in a good position in this House to say that when the government of M. Diem was formed I declared very clearly that it was not, in my opinion, the best formula. You see that, on this point, Monsieur Berlioz, I have not changed my opinion.[16]

I am convinced that if at that time it had been possible to form a government of true national union in South Viet-Nam, that government would have had more authority; it would certainly have been infinitely more conciliatory towards us—for there are still people in South Viet-Nam who are grateful for what France has been able to do for them—and the conditions of future negotiations between the South and the North would probably have been better. But at that time we took an engagement with regard to the Americans and, having done that, we are morally bound to support the government of M. Diem. That engagement, to be very frank, we have kept only with a great deal of reticence so that having undertaken it, perhaps in error, but not respecting it, we have lost on both accounts.

[16] M. Berlioz had, earlier in the session, spoken strongly against the policy of the Government in Viet-Nam. His statement is in *Journal Officiel de la République Française, Débats Parlementaires, Conseil de la République,* Session of February 23, 1956, pp. 190–192.

[An interjected comment and one paragraph on general principles of French foreign policy are omitted.]

Today it is too late—I say this very frankly—to take toward President Diem a position which would not be realistic. He is head of the Government and, after having accepted his accession to power, to play the little game of causing him perpetual difficulties in the exercise of that power would not be worthy of French policy. This present game is not, perhaps, the best that we might have been able to play, but, in any case, it is better to play it honestly.

Presently, therefore, the situation has deteriorated in matters which concern us in South Viet-Nam. Relations are practically broken with North Viet-Nam. Our position is better only with Cambodia and Laos.

Let us examine, if you will, the situation in these different countries. Our relations with South Viet-Nam are considerably damaged. A commercial agreement links us with that country. That agreement expires on February 29 next. We are now discussing, I do not even say its renewal, but the granting to France of a simple most favored nation clause (*Movements in the center*) and that under conditions which are not favorable to us, for what M. Marius Moutet said just a little while ago about the new position of the Government of South Viet-Nam with regard to certain imports is perfectly correct.[17]

On the other hand, the military situation is rather peculiar. Indeed, the Government of South Viet-Nam has officially asked us to withdraw our Expeditionary Corps [18] and we find ourselves in a rather curious juridical position which results from a contradiction in the Geneva Agreements; indeed, in virtue of those Agreements if the Government of South Viet-Nam demands the withdrawal of our Expeditionary Corps we must accept that withdrawal; but, by virtue of the same Agreements, the French Expeditionary Corps is the guarantor of the security in the country and in particular of the protection of the Commissions.[19] As you can see, there is there a contradiction which is particularly difficult to resolve. (*Movements in the center.*)

M. DURAND-RÉVILLE: It is this that they call good agreements!

THE MINISTER: We are extricating ourselves—permit me that ex-

17 M. Moutet's statement is in *Journal Officiel de la République Française, Débats Parlementaires, Conseil de la République,* Session of February 23, 1956, pp. 192–195.

18 On January 19, 1956; text not available.

19 I.e., the International Commission for Supervision and Control, and the Joint Commission.

pression—by the only means we have available, which consists of posing the following question to the Government of South Viet-Nam: since you ask us to withdraw our Expeditionary Corps, we cannot refuse, but we ask you who, in that case, should succeed us in assuring the respect of a certain number of conventions. I do not need to tell you that that question will be raised on the occasion of the Karachi Conference,[20] since it very clearly concerns the status of Southeast Asia.

M. BERLIOZ: May I interrupt you?

THE MINISTER: Please.

THE CHAIRMAN: M. Berlioz has the floor, with the permission of the speaker.

M. BERLIOZ: M. Minister, there is all the same, in the Geneva Agreement,[21] an article, Article 27, worded as follows: "The signatories of the present Agreement and their successors in their functions shall be responsible for ensuring the observance and enforcement of the terms and provisions thereof."

In South Viet-Nam, M. Diem is the successor in their functions of those who signed the treaty.

Several Senators: No! No!

M. BERTHOIN: No! He is not a party to the treaty!

M. BERLIOZ: Who then? Nobody? He is the successor to the guarantors of the treaty!

M. ERNEST PEZET: It is impossible to be the guarantor for oneself! (*Very good!*)

THE CHAIRMAN: There are numerous Ministers of Foreign Affairs here! (*Smiles.*)

THE MINISTER: Permit me to reply to you that it is there, precisely, that the juridical difficulty lies: it is France or her successor, but who may be her successor? Can it possibly be a country which has not signed the Geneva Agreements?

M. BERLIOZ: Yes!

THE MINISTER: Would the other signatories admit that a non-signatory country could be the successor to France?

We are faced, therefore, with a very serious juridical difficulty.

I add, to respond to M. Berlioz who has asked us if we are in favor of a conference of the signatories of the Geneva Agreements, that France is not opposed but that if the Americans and the South Vietnamese are not participants in that conference we do not see what

[20] Of the SEATO Ministerial Council, held March 6 to 8, 1956.
[21] The Agreement on the Cessation of Hostilities in Viet-Nam, Document 130.

good it would bring anew in relation to Geneva, for we would remain trapped in the kind of vicious circle which I described to you only a little while ago. Consequently, the situation could be changed only insofar as South Viet-Nam and the Americans would participate in the conference, which, in the present state of things, does not appear very probable to me.

In any event, the problem will be raised on the occasion of the Karachi meeting. I point out that if it is raised, it is not at all because we think—I want to state our position on this point—that countries such as South Viet-Nam should be integrated into S.E.A.T.O. (Southeast Asia Treaty Organization) but because it is indicated in that pact that the protection of the organization extends to three countries: South Viet-Nam, Laos, and Cambodia. The protection extends over them but that does not mean that for that reason they have the right to be part of the organization.

It is precisely because we have taken, within the framework of the Southeast Asia Treaty Organization, the engagement of protection with regard to these three States that we will be led to pose the question which we have not been able to resolve within the framework of the Geneva Agreements.

[Two paragraphs on attempts to improve economic and cultural relations with North Viet-Nam are omitted.]

Finally, the problem of the reunification of the country and that of the elections may be raised. France, on this point, has a position which she cannot abandon, which is to assure the respect for the Geneva Agreements of which she is the guarantor. But it is evident that she does not have the practical means, especially given her military policy over there, to oblige the parties in question to bring about the elections after the scheduled delay and that, in consequence, she alone is not able to solve this problem.

The question which arises is to find out to what extent the South and the North will be able to reach agreement on fixing a date, which may or may not be that of July 1956. This problem will very likely be studied in the course of the coming weeks, and it appears to me a little premature to give a definite answer to it now.

177. *Note to the Co-Chairmen of the Geneva Conference from the Government of India* *
    March 23, 1956

The Government of India have learnt from the Chairman of the Viet-Nam Commission that an agreement has been reached between the French and the South Viet-Namese authorities on the evacuation of the French Expeditionary Corps from the Viet-Nam territories. Although it is learnt that the French authorities are awaiting the approval of the French Government, the Commission has been informed that there would be no French High Command in the Viet-Nam after the 15th of April.

2. It will be recalled that a representative of the Commander-in-Chief of the French Union Forces signed the agreement pertaining to Viet-Nam [22] and Laos, assumed responsibility for the execution of the agreement and pledged the co-operation of the Franco-Viet-Namese Command with the International Supervisory Commission to help administer it. Neither the French authorities nor the Viet-Nam authorities have made any proposals as to the manner in which the Commission could continue to supervise the Cease-fire Agreement after the withdrawal of the French High Command. Although the South Viet-Namese authorities have promised to give practical co-operation and to take over the responsibility for the security of the Commission from the 1st April onwards, they are not prepared to assume the legal obligations of the French High Command, as successors of the French Power in South Viet-Nam.

3. In the circumstances, the Commission views with serious concern the prospect of having to supervise an agreement which will cease to have any legal basis since one party to the agreement—the French High Command—will have disappeared. It is clear that the Commission will be unable to hold the South Viet-Nam accountable, unless it accepts the full residuary obligations undertaken by the French High Command.

---

* *Source:* Great Britain, Parliament, Papers by Command, *Documents Relating to British Involvement in the Indo-China Conflict 1945–1965* (London: Her Majesty's Stationery Office, Cmnd. 2834, 1965), pp. 93–94. Prior correspondence between the Republic of Viet-Nam, France, and the International Commission on the matter of withdrawal of the French Expeditionary Corps is not available.

[22] The Agreement on the Cessation of Hostilities in Viet-Nam, Document 130.

4. The Commission, therefore, desires that the two Co-Chairmen should consider the situation as early as possible and, in any case, before the 15th of April, 1956, with a view to resolve the legal lacuna and to enable the Commission to discharge the functions entrusted to it by the Geneva Conference on Indo-China.

5. A similar approach is being made to Mr. Molotov the Co-Chairman, through the Indian Embassy in Moscow.

178. *Note from M. Henri Hoppenot, French High Commissioner to the Republic of Viet-Nam, to the Chairman of the International Commission for Supervision and Control in Viet-Nam * April 3, 1956*

I have the honour of informing the I.C.S.C. that the Foreign Secretary of State of the Republic of Viet-nam, on behalf of his Government and by a letter dated the 19th January 1956,[23] has requested the withdrawal of the French Expeditionary Forces.

In conformity with the provisions of Article 10 of the Geneva Conference Final Declaration,[24] the Government of the French Republic has met that request and started working out with the Vietnamese Government the withdrawal schedule of the French Forces.

Following these talks, it looks as if the French Expeditionary Forces will have to leave Viet-nam by 28th April 1956. It is therefore on this date that the dissolution of the Command-in-Chief of the F.U.F.[25] will take place, as the said dissolution is automatically caused by that departure.

However, with a view to saving the I.C. the trouble of any physical difficulty, the French authorities will continue, up to 30th June 1956, to give logistic support to the Commission as previously.

* *Source:* Democratic Republic of Viet-Nam, Ministry of Foreign Affairs, Press and Information Department, *Documents Related to the Implementation of the Geneva Agreements Concerning Viet-nam* (Hanoi: 1956), pp. 123–124. It has not been possible to obtain a copy of this document other than from the North Vietnamese source cited here. The source has generally proven to be reliable, however, and the editor has no reason to question the authenticity of the document despite the very poor quality of the translation.

[23] Text not available.   [24] Document 131.   [25] French Union Forces.

179. *Note Delivered by the Government of the Republic of Viet-Nam*
to the Embassy of the United Kingdom, Saigon *
April 3, 1956

In his letter of December 21 [*sic*], 1955,[26] Her Britannic Majesty's
Ambassador Saigon informed us, in accordance with Your Excellency's
instructions, of the concern you felt on examining the fourth interim
report of the International Control Commission [27] which notes that the
opening clauses of the Geneva Agreements have not been satisfactorily
carried out in Viet-Nam.

We did not deem it appropriate to reply to this letter since, not being a signatory of these Agreements, the Government of Viet-Nam has
declared on several occasions that it does not consider itself as bound
by their provisions.

However, on the eve of the withdrawal of the French expeditionary
corps, we believe it useful to recall the permanent principles of policy
of the Government of the Republic of Viet-Nam.

This policy continues to be based on the defence of full and complete sovereignty of Viet-Nam and on the maintenance of peace to
which the Government and people of Viet-Nam are profoundly attached. It is therefore in the light of this dual principle that problems
concerning Viet-Nam will be resolved.

1. The withdrawal of the French Expeditionary Corps

To protect its sovereignty and in the interests of peace the Republic
of Viet-Nam consider that it cannot accept the presence on its territory
of any foreign troops nor the granting of any military base. It does not,
moreover, see the necessity of joining any military alliance.

By virtue of this principle the Government of Viet-Nam has decided,
in agreement with the French Government, that the French expeditionary corps be withdrawn.

---

* *Source:* Great Britain, Parliament, Papers by Command, *Documents Relating
to British Involvement in the Indo-China Conflict 1945–1965* (London: Her Majesty's Stationery Office, Cmnd. 2834, 1965), pp. 95–96. The Republic of Viet-
Nam on April 6 made a public declaration on the withdrawal of French troops
and Saigon's subsequent attitude toward the Geneva Agreements in terms almost
identical with those in this document. The text of the public declaration is in
République du Viet-Nam, Secrétariat d'Etat aux Affaires Etrangères, *Le Viet-
Nam et Ses Relations Internationales* [published in French and English], I, No.
1–2 (June, 1956), pp. 106–107.
[26] Document 173.   [27] Document 169.

The departure of French troops, which has as an immediate consequence the reduction of the military potential below the 17th parallel,
can only prove in the most striking manner the Viet-Namese Government's desire for peace.

2. The demarcation line

True to this same policy of peace, the Government of Republic of
Viet-Nam will not have recourse to violence to resolve its problems
and will uphold existing conditions of the present state of peace (Main-
tiendra les données de fait de l'état actuel de paix).[28] It will not seek
to violate the demarcation line and the demilitarised zone, as they have
resulted from the situation of facts existing at the present time in Viet-
Nam.

As it has declared on many occasions, the Government of the Republic of Viet-Nam will seek unification of the country on which it
has set its heart by all peaceful means, in particular by means of truly
free and democratic elections when conditions of freedom have been
really established.

3. The International Control Commission

The Government of the Republic of Viet-Nam consider the International Control Commission to be an organisation working for peace.
Because of their common peaceful objectives the Government of Viet-
Nam will continue to extend effective co-operation to the Commission,
will ensure security of its members and will, to the fullest extent possible, facilitate the accomplishment of its mission of peace, although
the Government of Viet-Nam still consider the Geneva Agreements as
res inter alios acta.[29]

I hope that the above statement, in making clear to Your Excellency
the policy which my Government intends to pursue will enable you,
should you deem it appropriate, to give the necessary assurances to
the Powers interested in the situation in Viet-Nam.

[28] In the original.
[29] Lit., "transactions among others." The meaning is that agreements concluded
by two parties (France and the DRV) cannot bind a third party (the Republic of
Viet-Nam).

180. *Resolution Adopted by the Central Committee of the Viet-Nam
     Workers' Party [Extract]* *
     April 24, 1956

[The portion of the Central Committee Resolution printed here is that ap-
plying the decisions of the Twentieth Congress of the Communist Party of
the Soviet Union to the problem of the unification of Viet-Nam. The Viet-
Nam Workers' Party (VWP) delegation to the Congress was headed by
Truong Chinh, General Secretary of the VWP, and included Le Duc Tho,
also a member of the VWP Politburo.]

(Studying?) the 20th Congress of the Communist Party of the Soviet Union,[30] our Party will take into account the new possibilities of
the present revolutionary struggle. While we consider the possibility of
stopping the existing war, we do not forget that imperialism (constitutes?) the economic basis of war. Thus, the peoples of the world must
constantly reinforce their struggle for peace and be always vigilant in
face of the manoeuvres of the warmongers. While we consider that a
certain number of countries have the ability to move toward Socialism
by peaceful means, we must remind ourselves that under conditions
when the bourgeoisie still holds the military and police power and are
determined to . . . (*several words missing*), an armed struggle for
power is inevitable and the work of proletarians must be prepared in
advance.

   In the light of the 20th Congress of the Soviet Communist Party,
our Party reaffirms its confidence in the policy of the consolidation of
the North and of the struggle for the realization of unity on the basis
of independence and democracy and by peaceful means. However, the
presence in half of our country of reactionary forces which are plotting
to provoke a war reminds us of the necessity of increasing our vigilance, reinforcing our national defense and always keeping on the alert
to be ready for all eventualities in the situation.

---

   * *Source:* Broadcast by Hanoi, Voice of Viet-Nam, in French, April 27, 1956,
0530 G.M.T. There are several gaps in the monitored text of the Resolution, as
indicated. The Resolution was adopted by the Ninth Expanded Meeting of the
Central Committee of the VWP, held from April 19 to 24.

   30 The three issues endorsed by the Twentieth CPSU Congress which are here
discussed by the VWP Central Committee are the endorsement of peaceful co-
existence as the "general line" of the international Communist movement;
Khrushchev's condemnation of the "cult of personality," which was an open
attack upon Stalinism; and the principle of "peaceful transition to Socialism."

We warmly approve the successes of the 20th Congress of the Soviet Communist Party whose valuable documents we shall ourselves strive to study. We approve its heroic spirit of criticism and self-criticism with a view of attaining new victories in the consolidation of the North and in the struggle for the unification of the country.

Simultaneously, it is necessary for us to break down all the false propaganda of the enemy about the struggle of the Congress against the cult of individualism. The 20th Congress of the Soviet Communist Party worked and developed to the highest degree the initiating spirit of all militants. This fact has great significance in the establishment and reinforcement of our Party.

[The Resolution continued with interpretation of the decisions of the Twentieth CPSU Congress for internal party problems in the DRV, particularly the relationship between the leadership and the masses, and criticism and self-criticism.]

The Failure
to Hold Elections
May-July 1956

Introduction

The final phase of the post-Geneva attempt to bring a political settlement to Viet-Nam through application of the provisions of the Geneva Agreements began with another attempt by the Co-Chairmen to
promote general elections as well as to ensure continued acceptance
of the cease-fire agreement despite the French withdrawal. But the
State of Viet-Nam still refused to consult with the North and was supported by the United States, while in the South the attempts to suppress
any possible revival of the Viet Minh movement continued unabated.
It became clear that elections would not be held without decisive action by the Great Powers, but these were divided among themselves
and unwilling to act. Consequently the July 1956 target date for the
elections was allowed to pass almost unnoticed, and Viet-Nam entered a
period in which *de facto* partition appeared likely to continue indefinitely.

On May 8, after conversations in London, the Co-Chairmen of the
Geneva Conference sent messages to the Governments of the Democratic Republic of Viet-Nam (DRV) and the Republic of Viet-Nam
(Document 181), to the International Commission for Supervision and
Control (ICSC) (Document 182), and to the French Government
(Document 183). The messages called for continued implementation
of the Geneva cease-fire, continued operation of, and cooperation with,
the ICSC, and efforts to implement the political provisions of the Geneva Agreements. A new Geneva Conference was not proposed.

On May 11 DRV Foreign Minister Pham Van Dong once again
proposed to the Republic of Viet-Nam that the North and South hold

a "consultative conference" (Document 184). On May 14 the French Government replied to the message from the Co-Chairmen, offering its cooperation contingent on the cooperation of the Republic of Viet-Nam but refusing to accept any new responsibilities (Document 185). The Republic of Viet-Nam, on May 22, promised to help maintain peace in Viet-Nam but rejected consultations and elections because of "the absence of all liberty in North Viet-Nam" (Document 186). The May 29 reply to the Co-Chairmen from the ICSC expressed hope that the parties concerned would respond to the appeals in the May 8 messages.[1]

The United States maintained its firm support for the Diem government. That support was particularly apparent at the meeting of the American Friends of Viet-Nam, held in Washington on June 1, 1956; there Walter Robertson, Assistant Secretary of State for Far Eastern Affairs, praised Diem and pledged continued American support for "a friendly non-Communist government in Viet-Nam" (Document 187).[2]

On June 4 Pham Van Dong presented the DRV's reply to the May 8 letter from the Co-Chairmen (Document 188), re-emphasizing the responsibility of both France and the Republic of Viet-Nam for a political settlement and offering to begin consultations for elections in July. Vice President Nixon arrived in Saigon on July 6 for an official visit and delivered a letter of congratulation to President Diem on the occasion of the second anniversary of his accession to power (Document 189).

On July 6 Ho Chi Minh addressed a letter to the Vietnamese people (Document 190). Although Ho reaffirmed DRV determination to "struggle for the execution of the Geneva Agreements," he stressed: "Our line of struggle at present is to achieve the broad and close unity of the entire people from South to North within the Viet-nam Fatherland Front, and to strive to consolidate North Viet-nam into a strong base of the struggle for the reunification of our country." A week later, only a few days before the second anniversary of the Geneva Agreements, Foreign Minister Pham Van Dong sent notes to the French For-

[1] The ICSC reply to the Co-Chairmen is not included in this collection since it was little more than a summary of the three May 8 notes. For source information see the Source Note to Document 182.

[2] For further documentation on the American Friends of Viet-Nam meeting, including a statement by then Senator John F. Kennedy (D., Mass.), see American Friends of Vietnam, *A Symposium on America's Stake in Vietnam* (New York: American Friends of Vietnam, 1956). Senator Kennedy's statement also appears in Wesley R. Fishel, ed., *Vietnam: Anatomy of a Conflict* (Itasca, Illinois: F. E. Peacock Publishers, Inc., 1968), pp. 142–147.

eign Minister [3] and the Co-Chairmen.[4] He called on the Co-Chairmen to take all necessary measures so that a consultative conference between the two Governments of North and South Viet-nam can be held, that free nation-wide elections throughout the country be organized, that the reunification of Viet-nam be achieved, that peace in Viet-nam be consolidated, and that the Geneva Agreements be honoured and fully implemented.

He requested of the French Foreign Minister "that the French Government fulfil the task and responsibility of a signatory to the Geneva Agreements and carry out the Co-Chairmen's recommendations."

It was, however, clear that the elections were not to be held and that the "temporary" partition of Viet-Nam had become more or less permanent. The refusal of the South to consult with the North, American support for the South, the French withdrawal from Viet-Nam, and the failure (or inability) of the Co-Chairmen to take any meaningful action all meant that the division of Viet-Nam would continue, with the North Vietnamese powerless to affect the situation short of resort to armed force. That prospect seemed remote despite repeated statements from Hanoi that peace could be assured only after reunification of Viet-Nam.

On July 21 the Soviet Foreign Ministry proposed to the British that the Co-Chairmen send a further note to the South Vietnamese.[5] The Soviet Union did not, however, suggest reconvening the Geneva Conference and omitted all mention of French responsibility for the elections. Pham Van Dong, on August 10, sent a note to the Co-Chairmen [6] which seemed more a last gasp than an attempt to provoke action despite the warning "Peace in Viet-Nam, in Southeast Asia, can be consolidated only if the reunification of Viet-Nam is realized." This note marked the end of the flurry of diplomatic activity which had surrounded the collapse of the political provisions of the Geneva Agreements. As far as is known the Co-Chairmen took no further action on the matter, and Viet-Nam appeared partitioned in much the same way as Germany and Korea.[7]

[3] Text in Democratic Republic of Viet-Nam, Ministry of Foreign Affairs, Press and Information Department, *Documents Related to the Implementation of the Geneva Agreements Concerning Viet-nam* (Hanoi: 1956), pp. 159–161.

[4] Text in *ibid.*, pp. 155–158.

[5] Text in France, Direction de la Documentation, *Articles et Documents*, No. 386 (July 24, 1956), pp. 3–4.

[6] Text in Polish Institute of International Affairs (Warsaw), *Zbiór Dokumentów*, No. 8, 1956, pp. 1318–1322 (in Polish and French).

[7] The analogy among the three divided countries was not lost on the North Vietnamese. In an interview with Ho Chi Minh on November 8, 1954, Agence

181. *Message from the Two Co-Chairmen of the Geneva Conference
on Indo-China to the Governments of the Democratic Republic
of Viet-Nam and the Republic of Viet-Nam **
May 8, 1956

Acting with the authority of the Governments of the United Kingdom and the Soviet Union, the Minister of State for Foreign Affairs of Great Britain, Lord Reading, and the First Deputy Foreign Minister of the Union of Soviet Socialist Republics, Mr. A. A. Gromyko, have met in London, as representatives of the two Co-Chairmen of the Geneva Conference on Indo-China, and have made a thorough examination of the problems relating to the fulfilment of the Geneva Agreements in Vietnam. They have also exchanged views on the proposal to convene a further conference of Members of the original Geneva Conference and of the Supervisory Powers to discuss these problems.

2. In the course of these talks they expressed their concern about the present situation in relation to the fulfilment of the Geneva Agreements in Vietnam, where the implementation of the political provisions of the Geneva Agreements has not yet begun. In particular, consultations have not taken place about the preparation and holding of free, nation-wide elections in Vietnam under the supervision of an International Commission with a view to the re-establishment of the national unity of Vietnam. There is thus at present a threat to the fulfilment of this important provision of the Geneva Agreements, although both sides in Vietnam have accepted the principle of national reunification by means of free general elections.

3. Pending the holding of free general elections for the reunification of Vietnam, the two Co-Chairmen attach great importance to the maintenance of the cease-fire under the continued supervision of the Inter-

---

* *Source:* Great Britain, Parliament, Papers by Command, *Vietnam and the Geneva Agreements: Documents Concerning the Discussions between Representatives of Her Majesty's Government and the Government of the Union of Soviet Socialist Republics held in London in April and May 1956, March 30–May 8, 1956* (London: Her Majesty's Stationery Office, Cmd. 9763, 1956, reprinted 1965), pp. 10–11.

France Presse Correspondent Bernard Ullman inquired whether Ho felt that the partition of Vietnam could be as lasting as partition in Germany and Korea. Ho replied that "the conditions in Vietnam are different from those in Korea and Germany," a most accurate observation. See Ho Chi Minh, *Statements by President Ho Chi Minh after the Geneva Conference* (Hanoi: Foreign Languages Publishing House, 1955), pp. 27–28.

national Commission for Vietnam. They recognise that the dissolution of the French Union High Command has increased the difficulties of the International Supervisory Commission in Vietnam in carrying out the functions specified in the Geneva Agreements, which are the basis for the Commission's activities, and that these difficulties must be overcome. The Co-Chairmen are confident that the authorities in both parts of Vietnam will show effective co-operation and that these difficulties will in practice be removed.

4. Prompted by their desire to strengthen peace in Indo-China on the basis of the principles and provisions of the Geneva Agreements, the Co-Chairmen strongly urge the authorities of the Democratic Republic of Vietnam and those of the Republic of Vietnam to make every effort to implement the Geneva Agreements on Vietnam, to prevent any future violation of the military provisions of these agreements and also to ensure the implementation of the political provisions and principles embodied in the Final Declaration of the Geneva Conference. To this end the authorities of both parts of Vietnam are invited to transmit to the Co-Chairmen as soon as possible, either jointly or separately, their views about the time required for the opening of consultations on the organisation of nation-wide elections in Vietnam and the time required for the holding of elections as a means of achieving the unification of Vietnam.

5. Having noted with appreciation the valuable work performed by the International Supervisory Commission for Vietnam, the Co-Chairmen strongly urge the authorities in both parts of Vietnam to give the Commission all possible assistance in future in the exercise of their functions as defined by the Geneva Agreements on Vietnam.

6. The Co-Chairmen will continue to consult together about the situation in Vietnam and, if necessary in the light of that situation, they will also discuss the measures which should be taken to ensure the fulfilment of the Geneva Agreements on Vietnam, including the proposal to convene a new conference of the Members of the original Geneva Conference and of the States represented in the International Commissions in Indo-China.

182. *Message from the Two Co-Chairmen of the Geneva Conference on Indo-China to the International Supervisory Commission for Viet-Nam* *
May 8, 1956

Acting with the authority of the Governments of the United Kingdom and the Soviet Union, the Minister of State for Foreign Affairs of Great Britain, Lord Reading, and the First Deputy Foreign Minister of the Union of Soviet Socialist Republics, Mr. A. A. Gromyko, have met in London as representatives of the two Co-Chairmen of the Geneva Conference on Indo-China in order to discuss the present situation in relation to the fulfilment of the Geneva Agreements on Vietnam. They have received the message from the International Supervisory Commission dated May 2 [1] and also the separate note of the same date from the Canadian Member of the Commission.[2]

2. The Co-Chairmen record their appreciation of the valuable contribution made by the International Supervisory Commission for Vietnam towards the fulfilment of the Geneva Agreements in Vietnam. The Co-Chairmen hope that the International Supervisory Commission will persevere in their efforts to maintain and strengthen peace in Vietnam on the basis of the fulfilment of the Geneva Agreements on Vietnam with a view to the reunification of the country through the holding of free nation-wide elections in Vietnam under the supervision of an international commission.

3. Pending the holding of free general elections for the reunification of Vietnam, the two Co-Chairmen attach great importance to the maintenance of the Cease-fire under the continued supervision of the International Commission for Vietnam. They recognise that the dissolution of the French Union High Command has increased the difficulties of the International Supervisory Commission in Vietnam in carrying out

* *Source:* Great Britain, Parliament, Papers by Command, *Vietnam and the Geneva Agreements: Documents Concerning the Discussions between Representatives of Her Majesty's Government and the Government of the Union of Soviet Socialist Republics held in London in April and May 1956, March 30–May 8, 1956* (London: Her Majesty's Stationery Office, Cmd. 9763, 1956, reprinted 1965), p. 11. The reply from the International Commission to the Co-Chairmen, dated May 29, 1956, is not included in this collection: the text may be found in Great Britain, Parliament, Papers by Command, *Documents Relating to British Involvement in the Indo-China Conflict 1945–1965* (London: Her Majesty's Stationery Office, Cmnd. 2834, 1965), pp. 99–101. It consists almost entirely of a summary of, and expression of agreement with, the three May 8 letters from the Co-Chairmen.

[1] Text not available.   [2] *Ibid.*

the functions specified in the Geneva Agreements, which are the basis for the Commission's activities, and that these difficulties must be overcome. The Co-Chairmen are confident that the authorities in both parts of Vietnam will show effective co-operation and that these difficulties will in practice be removed. The Co-Chairmen have strongly urged the authorities in both parts of Vietnam to give the Commission all possible assistance in the exercise of their functions.[3]

4. If, however, the Commission encounter any obstacles or difficulties in their activities that cannot be resolved on the spot, the Co-Chairmen would be grateful to be informed, so that they may consider whether any further measures are required to facilitate the work of the Commission.

5. The Co-Chairmen will inform the remaining members of the Geneva Conference of this appeal to the International Commission.

183. *Message from the Two Co-Chairmen of the Geneva Conference on Indo-China to the French Government* *
    May 8, 1956

The two Co-Chairmen of the Geneva Conference on Indo-China have made a thorough examination of the problems relating to the fulfilment of the Geneva Agreements in Vietnam. They have noted the announcement made by the French Government that the French Union High Command in Vietnam will be dissolved on April 28 as a result of the withdrawal of French armed forces from Vietnam under Article 10 of the Final Declaration.[4]

2. They recognise that the dissolution of the French Union High Command has created problems for the International Supervisory Commission that require serious attention. They are, however, confident that the authorities in both parts of Vietnam will show effective co-operation and that these problems will in practice be resolved. They are sending messages to this effect to the competent authorities in both parts of Vietnam and to the International Commission.[5]

3. The two Co-Chairmen believe, however, that the continued good

* *Source:* Great Britain, Parliament, Papers by Command, *Vietnam and the Geneva Agreements: Documents Concerning the Discussions between Representatives of Her Majesty's Government and the Government of the Union of Soviet Socialist Republics held in London in April and May 1956, March 30–May 8, 1956* (London: Her Majesty's Stationery Office, Cmd. 9763, 1956, reprinted 1965), p. 12.

[3] Document 181.

[4] Document 131. For the French announcement, see Document 178.

[5] Documents 181 and 182 respectively.

offices of the French Government could be very valuable while the practical problems already mentioned are being resolved. The[y] accordingly have the honour to invite the French Government to discuss this question with the authorities of South Vietnam with a view to reaching an arrangement that will facilitate the tasks of the International Supervisory Commission and of the Joint Commission in Vietnam.

4. The two Co-Chairmen also ask that, until the arrangements envisaged above are put into effect, the French Government should preserve the *status quo*.

184. *Foreign Minister Pham Van Dong of the Democratic Republic of Viet-Nam: Note to President Ngo Dinh Diem of the Republic of Viet-Nam [Extracts]* *
    May 11, 1956

[The introductory four paragraphs, summarizing the applicable provisions of the Final Declaration of the Geneva Conference, Document 131, earlier correspondence between the DRV and the Republic of Viet-Nam, and the May 8, 1956, letter from the Co-Chairmen, Document 181, are omitted.]

On the basis of the Geneva Agreements and of the message of the two Co-Chairmen, in full accordance with the keenest aspirations of the whole Vietnamese people, I hereby propose to the Government of the Republic of Viet-nam to hold the consultative conference between representatives of the Governments of the two zones, at a place to be agreed upon by mutual consent on the territory of Viet-nam, to discuss the question of free nation-wide general elections for the reunification of Viet-nam as provided for by the Geneva Agreements.

These general elections will be held simultaneously throughout the country to elect a single National Assembly. This Assembly will appoint one coalition Government for the whole country. The fundamental principles of the general elections are these: free nation-wide general elections by universal, equal, direct and secret ballot. All questions connected with the organization and the supervision of the general elections will be subject to the decision of both sides, on mutual agreement.

The Government of the Republic of Viet-nam has many a time

* *Source:* Democratic Republic of Viet-Nam, Ministry of Foreign Affairs, Press and Information Department, *Documents Related to the Implementation of the Geneva Agreements Concerning Viet-nam* (Hanoi: 1956), pp. 142–145.

stated that it stands for the reunification of the country through peaceful means and through free general elections. Thus, on this fundamental point, we are agreed. That is why, although on other points we may disagree, we may and must strive our hardest, in the supreme interest of our Fatherland, to consult together and discuss with a spirit of understanding and conciliation in order to reach agreement on the steps to be taken to achieve national unity through free nation-wide general elections. Pending the free nation-wide general elections for the reunification of the country, the Governments of both zones should continue to implement the cease-fire provisions of the Geneva Agreements, with a view to the consolidation of peace and to the creating of favourable conditions for general elections.

[Two paragraphs, on the necessity for continued operation of the ICSC and the Joint Commission, are omitted.]

Viet-nam is a united country, the Vietnamese people a united people. The North and the South belong to the same family, they are of the same blood and they are indivisible. Only if Viet-nam is re-unified, can peace be firmly and lastingly consolidated.

Now, our Fatherland finds itself in a situation in which unity is not yet achieved and peace not yet consolidated. The keenest aspiration of all our compatriots from the North to the South, at home and abroad, is the reunification of our Fatherland through free nation-wide elections.

It is beyond doubt that every Vietnamese patriot would approve the position of the Government of the Democratic Republic of Viet-nam which is in keeping with the feelings of our hearts and the requirements of our reason. I hope that the Government of the Republic of Viet-nam will be true to the aspiration of our compatriots and respond to the appeal of the two Co-Chairmen of the Geneva Conference: that is to appoint immediately representatives to hold consultations with the representatives of the Government of the Democratic Republic of Viet-nam and discuss the question of the free nation-wide general elections for the reunification of Viet-nam.

At the same time, in order to create favourable conditions for the achievement of national unity, in accordance with the most eager aspirations of our compatriots in the North and in the South, I reiterate our former proposal [6] as to the necessity to restore and develop normal relations in every respect between the two zones.

[6] Document 152.

I wish to receive an answer from the Government of the Republic of Viet-nam.

185. *Reply from the French Ministry of Foreign Affairs to the Two Co-Chairmen of the Geneva Conference ** *May 14, 1956*

The French Government has the honour to acknowledge receipt of the message which was addressed to it by the co-chairmen of the Geneva Conference on Indo-China on May 9[sic], 1956.[7]

In respect for the obligations undertaken by France in 1954 at Geneva, the French Government carries out the withdrawal of the expeditionary corps in Indo-China on the request of the Vietnamese Government.

This withdrawal which has now been completed involved, ipso facto, dissolution of the High Command of the French Union and a new situation was created.

Since April 28, France has no longer had special responsibilities relative to the application of the 1954 agreements. She nevertheless remains too attached to the preservation of peace in Southeast Asia not to contribute, to the extent of her capabilities, to upholding these agreements. She is therefore ready, as the co-chairmen have requested, to use her good offices and discuss problems that arise with the Government of South Vietnam.

It must be understood that this contribution to the general effort has the following reservations:

1. The French Government cannot accept new responsibilities specially its own.

2. Its good offices are given in the framework of effective cooperation with the Government of South Vietnam. These good offices would stop if such cooperation was absent.

With regard to what concerns the mixed commission,[8] whose task at present is trifling, the French Government will be able to define its position only after the authorities of North Vietnam have clearly made

---

* *Source:* République du Viet-Nam, Secretariat d'Etat aux Affaires Etrangères, *Le Viet-Nam et Ses Relations Internationales* [published in French and English], I, No. 3–4 (December 1956), pp. 179–180. Several typographical errors in the original have been corrected.

[7] Document 183.

[8] I.e., the Joint Commissions provided by the Agreement on the Cessation of Hostilities in Viet-Nam, Document 130.

theirs known. In any case, the French Government could eventually participate in the work only as an intermediary between the interested parties and without her responsibility being committed to any other heading.

At the present and while waiting for the adoption of the arrangement desired by the co-chairmen, the French Government considers maintaining things provisionally as they are actually.

186. *Foreign Minister Vu Van Mau of the Republic of Viet-Nam: Reply to the Two Co-Chairmen of the Geneva Conference* *
   May 22, 1956

I have the honour to acknowledge receipt of the message dated May 9 [*sic*] last addressed to the Government of the Republic of Vietnam [9] at the conclusion of the talks in London between Lord Reading and Mr. Andrei Gromyko, representing the foreign ministers of the governments of the United Kingdom and the U.S.S.R.

The Government of the Republic of Vietnam, faithful to its declarations, in particular that of last April 6,[10] reaffirms its desire to maintain the peace to which it has on many occasions furnished examples of profound attachment. Not bound by the Geneva agreements, it has kept looking for practical solutions to the problems raised by the agreements on Vietnam, to the extent that such solutions are compatible with its policy of peace and the requirements of its sovereignty.

The Government of the Republic of Vietnam will not resort to violent solutions and will not seek to attack the demarcation line and the demilitarized zone which are the result of the actual situation.

A menace against peace therefore will not come from the Republic of Vietnam which, moreover, since July 1954, has considerably reduced its armed forces and brought about the withdrawal of the entire [French] expeditionary corps.

In the framework of the same policy of peace, the Government of the Republic of Vietnam has judged that the contribution of the International Control Commission merits effective cooperation that should be strengthened in future.

* *Source:* République du Viet-Nam, Secretariat d'Etat aux Affaires Etrangères, *Le Viet-Nam et Ses Relations Internationales* [published in French and English], I, No. 3–4 (December 1956), p. 179. The note was sent only to the Foreign Secretary of the United Kingdom, acting in his capacity as a Co-Chairman of the Geneva Conference. Typographical errors in the original have been corrected.

[9] Document 181.

[10] See the Source Note to Document 179.

It considers, on the other hand, that really free general elections are a democratic method to bring about the reunification of the country. But the absence of all liberty in North Vietnam makes the question of electoral and pre-election campaigns practically unattainable for the moment.

The Government of the Republic of Vietnam is following this question with the greatest attention and will not fail to keep the Government of Her Majesty informed of its views.

187. *Walter S. Robertson, Assistant Secretary of State for Far Eastern Affairs: Address to the American Friends of Viet-Nam, Washington [Extracts]* *
June 1, 1956

[The introductory paragraph is omitted.]

Among the factors that explain the remarkable rise of Free Viet-Nam from the shambles created by 8 years of murderous civil and international war, the division of the country at Geneva,[11] and the continuing menace of predatory communism, there is in the first place the dedication, courage, and resourcefulness of President Diem himself.[12] In him, his country has found a truly worthy leader whose integrity and devotion to his country's welfare have become generally recognized among his people. Asia has given us in President Diem another great figure, and the entire free world has become the richer for his example of determination and moral fortitude. There is no more dramatic example of this fortitude than President Diem's decisions during the tense and vital days of the battle against the parasitic politico-religious sects in the city of Saigon in the spring of 1955. These decisions were to resist the multiple pressures to compromise that were building up around him, and to struggle to the victorious end for the sake of a just cause. The free world owes him a debt of gratitude for his determined stand at that fateful hour.

* *Source:* United States, Department of State, *American Foreign Policy, Current Documents, 1956* (Washington: Government Printing Office, 1959), pp. 859–863.

[11] Footnote in the original omitted.

[12] Footnote in the original: "Ngo Dinh Diem, appointed President of the Council of Ministers of the State of Viet-Nam on June 16, 1954, was proclaimed Chief of State (which title was simultaneously changed to President of the Republic) on October 26, 1955. As President, Mr. Diem retained his post as Prime Minister."

[Five paragraphs summarizing the history of Viet-Nam since the Geneva Conference are omitted.]

The United States is proud to be on the side of the effort of the Vietnamese people under President Diem to establish freedom, peace, and the good life. The United States wishes to continue to assist and to be a loyal and trusted friend of Viet-Nam.

Our policies in Viet-Nam may be simply stated as follows:

To support a friendly non-Communist government in Viet-Nam and to help it diminish and eventually eradicate Communist subversion and influence.

To help the Government of Viet-Nam establish the forces necessary for internal security.

To encourage support for Free Viet-Nam by the non-Communist world.

To aid in the rehabilitation and reconstruction of a country and people ravaged by 8 ruinous years of civil and international war.

[Two paragraphs on the specifics of American aid are omitted.]

The Communist conspiracy continues to threaten Free Viet-Nam. With monstrous effrontery, the Communist conspirators at Hanoi accuse Free Viet-Nam and its friends of violating the armistice provisions which the Vietnamese and their friends, including ourselves, have scrupulously respected despite the fact that neither the Vietnamese nor ourselves signed the Geneva Accords while they, the Communists, who have solemnly undertaken to be bound by these provisions, have violated them in the most blatant fashion.

The facts are that while on the one hand the military potential of Free Viet-Nam has been drastically reduced by the withdrawal of nearly 200,000 members of the French Expeditionary Corps and by the reduction of the Vietnamese Army by more than 50,000 from the time of the armistice to the present as well as by the outshipment from Viet-Nam since the cessation of hostilities of over $200 million worth of war equipment, we have on the other hand reports of steady, constant growth of the warmaking potential of the Communists north of the 17th parallel.

Our reports reveal that in complete disregard of its obligations, the Viet Minh have imported voluminous quantities of arms across the Sino-Viet Minh border and have imported a constant stream of Chinese Communist military personnel to work on railroads, to rebuild roads, to establish airports, and to work on other projects contributing to the growth of the military potential of the zone under Communist occupation.

As so eloquently stated by the British Government in a diplomatic note released to the press and sent to Moscow in April of this year, and I quote:

> The Viet Minh army has been so greatly strengthened by the embodiment and re-equipment of irregular forces that instead of the 7 Viet Minh divisions in existence in July 1954 there are now no less than 20. This striking contrast between massive military expansion in the North and the withdrawal and reduction of military forces in the South speaks for itself.[13]

By lies, propaganda, force, and deceit, the Communists in Hanoi would undermine Free Viet-Nam, whose fall they have been unable to secure by their maneuverings on the diplomatic front. These people, whose crimes against suffering humanity are so vividly described in the book by Lt. Dooley [14] who addressed you this morning, have sold their country to Peiping. They have shamelessly followed all the devious zigzags of the Communist-bloc line so that their alliance with Communist China and the Soviet Union is firmly consolidated. These are the people who are now inviting President Diem to join them in a coalition government to be set up through so-called "free elections."

President Diem and the Government of Free Viet-Nam reaffirmed on April 6 of this year [15] and on other occasions their desire to seek the reunification of Viet-Nam by peaceful means. In this goal, we support them fully. We hope and pray that the partition of Viet-Nam, imposed against the will of the Vietnamese people, will speedily come to an end. For our part we believe in free elections, and we support President Diem fully in his position that if elections are to be held, there first must be conditions which preclude intimidation or coercion of the electorate. Unless such conditions exist there can be no free choice.

[The concluding paragraph is omitted.]

[13] Note delivered on April 9 to the Foreign Ministry of the Soviet Union by the Embassy of the United Kingdom, Moscow; text in Great Britain, Parliament, Papers by Command, *Vietnam and the Geneva Agreements: Documents Concerning the Discussions between Representatives of Her Majesty's Government and the Government of the Union of Soviet Socialist Republics held in London in April and May 1956, March 30–May 8, 1956* (London: Her Majesty's Stationery Office, Cmd. 9763, 1956, reprinted 1965), pp. 8–9.

[14] Footnote in the original: "Thomas A. Dooley, *Deliver Us From Evil: The Story of Viet-Nam's Flight to Freedom* (New York: 1956)."

[15] See the Source Note to Document 179.

188. *Foreign Minister Pham Van Dong of the Democratic Republic of Viet-Nam: Reply to the Two Co-Chairmen of the Geneva Conference [Extract]* *
June 4, 1956

[Eight paragraphs summarizing the content of the messages sent by the Co-Chairmen on May 8, Documents 181, 182, and 183, are omitted. Pham Van Dong interpreted the position of the Co-Chairmen as calling on both Viet-Nams to "open a consultative conference to discuss the problem of re-unification of Viet-nam through free general elections as stipulated by the Geneva Agreements."]

The Government of the Democratic Republic of Viet-nam agrees with the two Co-Chairmen on the responsibility of the Governments of the two zones in the continuation of the execution of the Geneva Agreements. The Government of the Democratic Republic of Viet-nam constantly holds that in law, in fact, and in practice, the South Viet-nam authorities are bound by the Geneva Agreements. It is not sufficient that the South Viet-nam authorities merely make vague statements in favour of peace and national unity. The South Viet-nam authorities have the responsibility, together with the Government of the Democratic Republic of Viet-nam, to consolidate peace and bring about Viet-nam's reunification on the basis of the provisions of the Geneva Agreements. The statements of the South Viet-nam authorities in favour of national reunification through general elections are without substance if they refuse to confer with the Government of the Democratic Republic of Viet-nam with a view to discussing free national elections to reunify Viet-nam. Only in a reunited Viet-nam, can peace be consolidated in a stable and lasting manner.

On the recommendations of the two Co-Chairmen of the Geneva Conference, the Government of the Democratic Republic of Viet-nam sent a note to the South Viet-nam authorities on May 11, 1956,[16] proposing the holding of a consultative conference to discuss free nation-wide general elections. That note clearly specifies: "The fundamental principles of these elections are: free nation-wide general elections by universal, equal, direct and secret ballot."

The Government of the Democratic Republic of Viet-nam is ready to transmit, jointly with the South Viet-nam authorities, a common re-

* *Source:* Democratic Republic of Viet-Nam, Ministry of Foreign Affairs, Press and Information Department, *Documents Related to the Implementation of the Geneva Agreements Concerning Viet-nam* (Hanoi: 1956), pp. 146–149.
16 Document 184.

ply to the Co-Chairmen about the dates for the consultative conference and general elections, as was recommended by the two Co-Chairmen. However, so far the Southern authorities have not yet replied to the note of May 11, 1956 of the Government of the Democratic Republic of Viet-nam. For its part, the Government of the Democratic Republic of Viet-nam is prepared to open the consultative conference at a date in the first half of June, 1956, to be chosen by the South Viet-nam authorities.

The date for the holding of free general elections to reunify Viet-nam has been clearly fixed by the Geneva Agreements. At present, the whole Vietnamese people are urging that the South Viet-nam authorities should scrupulously carry out the recommendations of the two Co-Chairmen, that it should, together with the Government of the Democratic Republic of Viet-nam open the consultative conference to discuss free general elections to reunify the country.

In view of this situation, the Government of the Democratic Republic of Viet-nam has the honour to request the two Co-Chairmen to take necessary measures so as to bring about the consultative conference between the representatives of the authorities of the two zones to discuss all problems relating to the consolidation of peace and the reunification of Viet-nam, on the basis of the Geneva Agreements and in accordance with the recommendations of the two Co-Chairmen. If the South Viet-nam authorities continue to reject the holding of consultations and general elections, the Government of the Democratic Republic of Viet-nam will be obliged to request the two Co-Chairmen to reconvene the 1954 Geneva Conference on Indo-China so as to discuss the implementation of the Geneva Agreements in Viet-nam.

189. *Letter from President Eisenhower to President Diem* * [17]
July 6, 1956

DEAR MR. PRESIDENT: At this time I wish to extend to you and to your associates my warmest congratulations. The people of my country and of the entire Free World admire the devotion, the courage and determination which you have shown in surmounting the difficulties which confronted your newly independent country.

* *Source:* United States, Department of State, *Bulletin,* XXXV (July 23, 1956), pp. 150–151.

[17] Footnote in the original: "Delivered at Saigon on July 6. The Republic of Viet-Nam on July 7 marked the second anniversary of President Diem's government." The letter was delivered by Vice President Nixon.

We recall, in particular, your success in inspiring a sense of national unity among your people; the courage of the Vietnamese nation in withstanding the pressures of aggressive Communism; and the notable progress made by your country toward the great goal of constitutional government.

I am proud that the Government and the people of the United States have been able to contribute to your successful efforts to restore stability and security to your country, and to help lay a solid basis for social and economic reconstruction.

I speak for the people of the United States in our well wishes today to you and your countrymen and I look to many years of partnership in the achievement of our common goals.

Sincerely yours,

DWIGHT D. EISENHOWER

190. *Ho Chi Minh: Letter to the Vietnamese People throughout the Country [Extract]* *
July 6, 1956

[The introductory three paragraphs are omitted.]

The Government of the Democratic Republic of Viet-nam, scrupulously implementing the Geneva Agreements, has time and again proposed to the authorities in South Viet-nam the *opening of a consultative conference* [18] to discuss free general elections to reunify the country.

But, the U.S. imperialists and the pro-American Administration in South Viet-nam have been scheming to partition our country per-

* *Source:* Democratic Republic of Viet-Nam, Ministry of Foreign Affairs, Press and Information Department, *Documents Related to the Implementation of the Geneva Agreements Concerning Viet-nam* (Hanoi: 1956), pp. 161–163. As indicated (Footnotes 18 and 19) there are differences between the version of Ho Chi Minh's statement printed here and that contained in the later *Selected Works,* notably in the substitution of the phrase "political consultations" for "consultative conference" in the *Selected Works* version. For comments on the significance of this distinction, see Note 1, p. 369. The emphasis in the text of the statement printed here is as in the original.

[18] Emphasis in the original. In the version of this statement which appears in Ho Chi Minh, *Selected Works* (4 vols., Hanoi: Foreign Languages Publishing House, 1961–1962), Vol. IV, pp. 162–165, this phrase reads "has repeatedly proposed to the South Viet Nam authorities the holding of political consultations to discuss free general elections to reunify the country." For the significance of the distinction between "consultations" and "consultative conference," see Note 1, p. 369.

manently and sabotage the holding of free nation-wide general elections at the time stipulated by the Geneva Agreements. They have acted counter to the interests of our Fatherland, to the aspirations of our people.

In face of this situation, our *sacred* duty is resolutely to continue to struggle for the execution of the Geneva Agreements and for the reunification of the country on the basis of independence and democracy through peaceful means, and to make the glorious cause of national liberation triumph.

OUR LINE OF STRUGGLE at present is to achieve the broad and close unity of the entire people from South to North within the Viet-nam Fatherland Front, and to strive to consolidate North Viet-nam into a strong base of the struggle for the reunification of our country.

[Two paragraphs, calling for national unity and describing the struggle as "long, hard, and intricate, but surely victorious," are omitted.]

In order to meet the most eager demand of the Vietnamese people which is the consolidation of peace and the achievement of unity on the basis of the Geneva Agreements, the Government of the Democratic Republic of Viet-nam stands for these practical steps:

1. NORMAL RELATIONS AND FREEDOM OF TRAVEL between the two zones to be restored; facilities to be provided for contacts between various political, economic, cultural and social organizations of the North and of the South;

2. A CONSULTATIVE CONFERENCE TO BE HELD [19] between representatives of the Administrations of both zones to discuss the issue of free general elections for the reunification of the country, on the basis of the Geneva Agreements.

[The concluding paragraph, calling for national unity on the basis of the program of the Viet-Nam Fatherland Front, Document 168, is omitted.]

[19] In the version of the statement in Ho Chi Minh's *Selected Works,* this point reads: *"To open political consultations* between representatives of the two zones. . . ." See Note 18 above.

Selected Bibliography

Selected Bibliography

This bibliography is a list of secondary sources which may be most usefully consulted for further details on the development of the Viet-Nam crisis through 1956, although several books included here cover events after 1956 as well. With two exceptions, the bibliography is limited to books rather than articles or contributions to collections. The fact that a book appears, or does not appear, in this bibliography should in no way be interpreted as reflecting the editor's approval, or disapproval, of the arguments and judgments contained therein nor of the accuracy of the factual and analytical content thereof.

Bibliographies

By far the most complete bibliography on Viet-Nam, with concentration on its international relations, is Nguyen The-Anh, *Bibliographie Critique sur les Relations entre le Viet-Nam et l'Occident (Ouvrages et Articles en Langues Occidentales)* (Paris: G-P Maisonneuve & Larose, 1967). It lists 1,627 items, mostly in French and English, and is fairly complete through 1963 with some entries for items published after that time. Coverage includes periodical articles and some official government publications (mostly French). There is a useful index by author. Works in Slavic languages are not included.

For Soviet works on Viet-Nam, the reader should consult Peter Berton and Alvin Z. Rubinstein, *Soviet Works on Southeast Asia: A Bibliography of Non-Periodical Literature, 1946–1965* (Los Angeles: University of Southern California Press, 1967); and Akademia Nauk SSSR, Institut Narodov Azii, *Bibliografiia Yugo-Vostochnoi Azii; Dorevoliutsionnaia i Sovetskaia Literatura na Russkom Yazike Originalnaia i Perevodnaia* (Moscow: Izd. vost. lit. ry, 1960).

Very comprehensive and useful bibliographies are contained in some of the secondary works listed below, notably Buttinger, *Vietnam: A Dragon Embattled;* Duncanson, *Government and Revolution in Vietnam;* and Hammer, *The Struggle for Indochina.*

Secondary Works

Azeau, Henri. *Ho Chi Minh, Dernière Chance: La Conférence Franco-Vietnamienne de Fontainebleau, Juillet 1946* (Paris: Flammarion, 1968).

Bain, Chester A. *Vietnam: The Roots of Conflict* (Englewood Cliffs, N.J.: Prentice-Hall, Inc., A Spectrum Book, 1967).

Bator, Victor. *Viet-Nam: A Diplomatic Tragedy* (Dobbs Ferry, N.Y.: Oceana Publications, 1965).

Bodard, Lucien. *The Quicksand War: Prelude to Vietnam*, Patrick O'Brien, trans. (Boston: Little, Brown and Company, 1967).

Brimmell, J. H. *Communism in South East Asia: A Political Analysis* (New York: Oxford University Press, 1959).

Buttinger, Joseph. *The Smaller Dragon: A Political History of Vietnam* (New York: Frederick A. Praeger, 1958).

——. *Vietnam: A Dragon Embattled* (2 vols., New York: Frederick A. Praeger, 1967).

——. *Vietnam: A Political History* (New York: Frederick A. Praeger, 1968).

Cameron, Allan W. "The Soviet Union and Vietnam: The Origins of Involvement," in W. Raymond Duncan, ed., *Soviet Policy in Developing Countries* (Waltham, Mass.: Ginn-Blaisdell, 1970).

Chen, King C. *Vietnam and China, 1938–1954* (Princeton, N.J.: Princeton University Press, 1969).

Cooper, Bert, and others. *Case Studies in Insurgency and Revolutionary Warfare: Vietnam, 1941–1954* (Washington: Special Operations Research Office, American University, 1964).

Cooper, Chester L. *The Lost Crusade: America in Vietnam* (New York: Dodd, Mead & Company, 1970).

Devillers, Philippe. *Histoire du Viêt-Nam de 1940 à 1952* (Paris: Editions du Seuil, 1952). [The Bobbs-Merrill Company plans to publish an English translation.]

Duncanson, Dennis J. *Government and Revolution in Vietnam* (New York: Oxford University Press, 1968).

Fall, Bernard B. *Hell in a Very Small Place: The Siege of Dien Bien Phu* (Philadelphia: J. B. Lippincott Company, 1967).

——. *Street Without Joy: Indochina at War, 1946–1954* (Harrisburg, Pa.: The Stackpole Company, 1961).

——. *The Two Viet-Nams: A Political and Military Analysis* (2nd rev. ed., New York: Frederick A. Praeger, 1967).

Fifield, Russell H. *The Diplomacy of Southeast Asia, 1945–1958* (New York: Harper & Brothers, 1958).

Gurtov, Melvin. *The First Vietnam Crisis: Chinese Communist Strategy and*

United States Involvement, 1953–1954 (New York: Columbia University Press, 1967).

Hammer, Ellen J. *The Struggle for Indochina* (Stanford, Cal.: Stanford University Press, 1954). [Reprinted 1966, with additional chapter covering events through early 1955 but without the bibliography.]

Hinton, Harold C. *Communist China in World Politics* (Boston: Houghton Mifflin Company, 1966). [Particularly Chapters 9 and 13.]

Hoang Van Chi. *From Colonialism to Communism: A Case History of North Vietnam* (New York: Frederick A. Praeger, 1964).

Honey, Patrick J. *Genesis of a Tragedy: The Historical Background to the Vietnam War* (London: Ernest Benn, 1968).

Lacouture, Jean. *Ho Chi Minh: A Political Biography*, Peter Wiles, trans. (New York: Random House, 1968).

——, and Philippe Devillers. *End of a War: Indochina, 1954*, Alexander Lieven and Adam Roberts, trans. (New York: Frederick A. Praeger, 1969).

Lancaster, Donald. *The Emancipation of French Indochina* (New York: Oxford University Press, 1961).

McAlister, John T., Jr. *Viet Nam: The Origins of Revolution* (New York: Alfred A. Knopf, 1969).

——, and Paul Mus. *The Vietnamese and Their Revolution* (New York: Harper & Row, 1970).

McLane, Charles B. *Soviet Strategies in Southeast Asia: An Exploration of Eastern Policy under Lenin and Stalin* (Princeton, N.J.: Princeton University Press, 1966).

Murti, B. S. N. *Vietnam Divided: The Unfinished Struggle* (New York: Asia Publishing House, 1964).

Mus, Paul. *Viet-Nam: Sociologie d'une Guerre* (Paris: Editions du Seuil, 1952).

O'Ballance, Edgar. *The Indo-China War, 1945–54* (London: Faber & Faber, 1964).

O'Neill, Robert J. *General Giap: Politician and Strategist* (New York: Frederick A. Praeger, 1969).

Randle, Robert F. *Geneva 1954: The Settlement of the Indochinese War* (Princeton, N.J.: Princeton University Press, 1969).

Roy, Jules. *The Battle of Dienbienphu*, Robert Baldick, trans. (New York: Harper & Row, 1965).

Sacks, I. Milton. "Marxism in Viet Nam," in Frank N. Traeger, ed., *Marxism in Southeast Asia: A Study of Four Countries* (Stanford, Cal.: Stanford University Press, 1959).

Sainteny, Jean. *Histoire d'une Paix Manquée: Indochine 1945–1947* (Paris: Amiot-Dumont, 1953).

Smith, Ralph. *Viet-Nam and the West* (London: Heinemann, 1968).

Weinstein, Franklin B. *Vietnam's Unheld Elections: The Failure to Carry out the 1956 Reunification Elections and the Effect on Hanoi's Present Outlook* (Ithaca, N.Y.: Cornell University, Southeast Asia Program, Data Paper No. 60, 1966).

Zasloff, J. J. *The Role of the Sanctuary in Insurgency: Communist China's Support to the Vietminh, 1946–1954* (Santa Monica, Cal.: The RAND Corporation, Memorandum RM–1618–PR, 1967).